2 0 0 8
STATE OF THE WORLD
Innovations for a
Sustainable Economy

Other Norton/Worldwatch Books

State of the World 1984 through *2007*
(an annual report on progress toward a sustainable society)

Vital Signs 1992 through *2003* and *2005* through *2007*
(a report on the trends that are shaping our future)

Saving the Planet
  Lester R. Brown
  Christopher Flavin
  Sandra Postel

How Much Is Enough?
  Alan Thein Durning

Last Oasis
  Sandra Postel

Full House
  Lester R. Brown
  Hal Kane

Power Surge
  Christopher Flavin
  Nicholas Lenssen

Who Will Feed China?
  Lester R. Brown

Tough Choices
  Lester R. Brown

Fighting for Survival
  Michael Renner

The Natural Wealth of Nations
  David Malin Roodman

Life Out of Bounds
  Chris Bright

Beyond Malthus
  Lester R. Brown
  Gary Gardner
  Brian Halweil

Pillar of Sand
  Sandra Postel

Vanishing Borders
  Hilary French

Eat Here
  Brian Halweil

Inspiring Progress
  Gary T. Gardner

2008
STATE OF THE WORLD

Innovations for a Sustainable Economy

A Worldwatch Institute Report on
Progress Toward a Sustainable Society

Gary Gardner and Thomas Prugh, *Project Directors*

Erik Assadourian	Brian Halweil
Bill Baue	Tim Jackson
Ricardo Bayon	L. Hunter Lovins
Ger Bergkamp	Lisa Mastny
Jason S. Calder	Danielle Nierenberg
Zoë Chafe	Jonathan Rowe
Christopher Flavin	Claudia Sadoff
Hilary French	John Talberth
Mark Halle	

Linda Starke, *Editor*

W·W·NORTON & COMPANY

NEW YORK   LONDON

The text of this book is composed in Galliard, with the display set in Gill Sans. Book design, cover design, and
composition by Lyle Rosbotham; manufacturing by Victor Graphics.

First Edition
ISBN 978-0-393-33031-1

W.W. Norton & Company, Inc., 500 Fifth Avenue, New York, N.Y. 10110
www.wwnorton.com

W.W. Norton & Company Ltd., Castle House, 75/76 Wells Street, London W1T 3QT

1 2 3 4 5 6 7 8 9 0

Acknowledgments

This twenty-fifth anniversary edition of *State of the World* is the product of a collaborative effort, involving dedicated individuals from dozens of countries. All deserve our sincere thanks for their contributions to the book and to the Institute's work.

We give special thanks to our energetic Board of Directors for their tremendous support and leadership: Chairman Øystein Dahle, Vice Chair and Treasurer Thomas Crain, Secretary Larry Minear, President Christopher Flavin, Adam Albright, Geeta B. Aiyer, Leo Russell Bennett, Cathy Crain, James Dehlsen, Robert Friese, Lynne Gallagher, Ed Groark, Satu Hassi, Jerre Hitz, Nancy Hitz, Akio Morishima, Izaak van Melle, Samuel Myers, Wren Wirth, and Emeritus members Abderrahman Khene and Andrew E. Rice.

This year we recognize in particular our Board Chair, Øystein Dahle, who has served the Institute with wisdom, grace, and humor for nearly two decades. Last summer Øystein was honored for his work in advancing the cause of sustainable economies by the King of Norway, who bestowed on him the Cross of St. Olaf, one of Norway's most prestigious awards. Øystein was nominated by the environmental leaders of every major political party in Norway, a testament to his skill in appealing to a broad range of constituencies on the issue of building sustainable societies. We are proud of our long association with Øystein and congratulate him for this well-deserved honor.

We are especially indebted to the Royal Ministry of Foreign Affairs of the Government of Norway for its third year of strong support of our flagship report. The Royal Ministry has been a leader in its support for sustainable development, and we appreciate its assistance in allowing us to reach key decisionmakers in the developing world. We also thank the V. Kann Rasmussen Foundation, a major supporter of the Institute's Global Economy Project, of which this volume is the primary output to date.

Thank you as well to the many foundations and other institutions whose support over the past year made the Institute's work possible, including the Blue Moon Fund, Ecos Ag–Basel, the Energy Future Coalition and the Better World Fund, the German Government, the Richard and Rhoda Goldman Fund, The Goldman Environmental Prize, Greenpeace, the W. K. Kellogg Foundation, the Steven C. Leuthold Family Foundation, the Marianist Sharing Fund, the Natural Resources Defense Council, the Rockefeller Brothers Fund, the Shared Earth Foundation, the Shenandoah Foundation, the Sierra Club, the Food and Agriculture Organization of the United Nations, the United Nations Population Fund, the United Nations Environment Programme, the Wallace Genetic Foundation, Inc., the Wallace Global Fund, the Johanette Wallerstein Institute, and the Winslow Foundation.

We are also grateful that the Institute's work is supported by more than 3,500 Friends of Worldwatch, who provide nearly one third of the Institute's annual budget. Their faithful support is indispensable to our work.

For our twenty-fifth anniversary edition the Institute drew on the talents of a wide range of skilled authors from a variety of organizations. We are grateful for their commitment to the project amid the many pressures of their own work. John Talberth of Redefining Progress draws on his knowledge of yardsticks for measuring sustainability to produce Chapter 2. Hunter Lovins applies decades of expertise in sustainable production to the analysis of cutting edge manufacturing practices in Chapter 3. Tim Jackson, who has worked at the University of Surrey and as a consultant to the U.K. government, explores the conundrum of consumption in Chapter 4. Ger Bergkamp and Claudia Sadoff, both at IUCN–The World Conservation Union, explore the world of markets and water use in Chapter 8, while Ricardo Bayon of Ecosystem Marketplace examines markets and biodiversity services in Chapter 9. Jonathan Rowe reintroduces us to the important world of the commons in Chapter 10, drawing on his affiliation with the Tomales Bay Institute. Jason Calder identifies new methods of promoting economic development in Chapter 12, while Bill Baue explores the world of finance for sustainability in Chapter 13. Finally, Mark Halle of the International Institute for Sustainable Development explores the challenges for trade regimes in promoting sustainability in Chapter 14. We are also indebted to our colleague Hilary French, whose long experience in sustainability circles helped identify several of these authors.

Many outside specialists provided guidance and key information for the project. The project overall was influenced by insights from Ray Anderson, William Carmichael, Clifford Cobb, Aaron Cosbey, Robert Costanza, Gretchen Daily, Dan Friedlander, Kevin Gallagher, Ian Gary, Joshua Goldstein, Raquel Gomes, John Gowdy, Jonathan Harris, Tom Higley, Daniel Kammen, Stefano Pagiola, Patricia Rosenfield, James Salzman, Astrid Scholz, Juliet Schor, Michael Shepard, Keith Slack, Paul Stern, Sean Sweeney, Daniel Taylor, Tim Wise, and Ted Wolf. Chapter 1 benefited from input from Frank Ackerman, Herman Daly, Josh Farley, and Neva Goodwin; Chapter 2 from Suntara Loba; Chapter 4 from Sharon Afshar, Stephen Hall, and Jonny Tinsdale; Chapter 5 from Jennifer Lacquet, Miyun Park, and William Weida; Chapter 7 from Katherine Hamilton, Kristen Hite, Thomas Marcello, Kyle Meng, Melanie Nakagawa, Annie Petsonk, Mark Trexler, and Tomas Wyns; Chapter 8 from Josh Bishop, Megan Cartin, Charlotte de Fraiture, John Dixon, Lucy Emerton, Mark Giordano, Kirk Hamilton, and Mark Smith; Chapter 11 from Lois Arkin, Montserrat Besnard, Mabel Cañada, Nancy Chege, Diana Leafe Christian, Jonathan Dawson, Scott Denman, Edie Farwell, Kirstin Henninger, Jennifer Henry, Ann Karlen, A. E. Luloff, Christopher Lynch, the Can Masdeu Community, Grady and Tena Meadows O'Rear, Graham Meltzer, Kenneth Mulder, Richard and Cheyenne Olson, Steve Pretl, Meghan Quinn, Angela Williams, and Kierson Wise; Chapter 12 from Tage Kanno, Mike McGahuey, Deepa Narayan, Chris Reij, Tony Rinaudo, Manjunath Shankar, Jed Shilling, George Taylor, Bob Winterbottom, and Michael Woolcock; and Chapter 13 from Michael Liebreich.

We also thank our energetic team of interns for their hard work. We acknowledge with appreciation the work of Morgan Innes on Chapter 1; Jessica Hanson on Chapter 5; Stanford MAP Fellow James Russell on Chapter 6; Zoe Fonseca on Chapter 7; Meghan Bogaerts, Sean Charles, Joy Chen, and Wendy

Wallace on Chapter 11; and Dang Du on Chapter 12. And a special thank you to the Institute's Senior Editor, Lisa Mastny, for her quick and thorough work in compiling the set of significant global events that appear in the book's Year in Review timeline.

State of the World chapters undergo a rigorous review that includes a day of in-house critique and comment. We are grateful to staff from all Institute departments who participated in the 2008 review. In addition, we acknowledge the careful comments provided by reviewers from outside the Institute, whose involvement boosts the quality of our research and writing. In particular we thank Frank Ackerman, Sara Afshar, Philippe Ambrosi, Josh Bishop, Ed Cain, Megan Cartin, Herman Daly, Jonathan Dawson, Charlotte de Fraiture, Alex Dewar, John Dixon, Dang Du, Lucy Emerton, Josh Farley, Zoe Fonseca, Mark Giordano, Neva Goodwin, Stephen Hall, Katherine Hamilton, Kirk Hamilton, Kristen Hite, Tage Kanno, Anja Kollmuss, Michael Kramer, Jennifer Lacquet, Christopher Lynch, Thomas Marcello, Mike McGahuey, Bill McKibben, Ricardo Meléndez-Ortiz, Melanie Nakagawa, Deepa Narayan, Miyun Park, Chris Reij, Tony Rinaudo, Manjunath Shankar, Jed Shilling, Mark Smith, Gordon Streeb, Daniel Taylor, George Taylor, Mark Trexler, William Weida, Bob Winterbottom, Robert Wolfe, Michael Woolcock, and Tomas Wyns.

State of the World has had only one editor over its 25-year history. We are happy again to acknowledge the skill and hard work of Linda Starke, whose knack for turning the language of diverse authors into clear, readable prose makes the book accessible to a broad audience. Linda is also a nimble manager who coordinates the work of dozens of staff and non-staff contributors to meet an unmoving deadline. We are grateful to Linda for her quarter-century service to the book, and for meeting the unique challenges posed by this edition.

Behind the scenes, Art Director Lyle Rosbotham rapidly turned typescript into the beautifully designed book in your hands. We are grateful to Lyle for bringing the volume into the world of two colors. We also thank Kate Mertes, who kindly stepped in on short notice to prepare the index.

Getting the book to press is only the beginning of getting *State of the World* to readers. The Institute's communications department, led by Communications Director Darcey Rakestraw and assisted by Communications Associate Julia Tier, works to ensure that the book's messages reach far beyond our Washington offices. Meanwhile, Director of Publications and Marketing Patricia Shyne coordinates with our global publishing partners and infuses our marketing efforts with energy and creativity. Director of Finance and Administration Barbara Fallin underpins all the Institute efforts through her efficient management of our daily operations. And none of our operations would be possible without our hard-working development staff. Mary Redfern manages our foundation relations effort with consummate thoroughness. On the individual giving side, Courtney Berner and Kimberly Rogovin apply their energy and enthusiasm to deepening our relationships with Institute friends.

W. W. Norton & Company in New York has published *State of the World* in each of its 25 years. We are grateful to Amy Cherry, Leo Wiegman, Nancy Palmquist, and Devon Zahn for their work in producing the book and ensuring that it gets maximum exposure in bookstores and university classrooms across the United States.

State of the World would have a limited international audience were it not for our network of publishing partners, who provide advice, translation, outreach, and distribution assistance. We give special thanks to Eduardo Athayde of the Universidade Mata

Atlântica in Brazil; Soki Oda of Worldwatch Japan; Benoit Lambert in Switzerland, who also connects us to France and French-speaking Canada; Klaus Milke of Germanwatch in Germany; Jin Jiaman from the Global Environment Institute in China; Anna Bruno Ventre and Gianfranco Bologna of WWF Italy, who has spearheaded the publishing of *State of the World* in Italy for the last 20 years; Maria Antonia Garcia for the Castilian version and Anastasia Monjas for the Catalan version in Spain; Yiannis Sakiotis in Greece; Kartikeya Sarabhai and Kiran Chhokar in India; Sangik Kim in South Korea; Hans Lundberg and Ivana Kildsgaard of Worldwatch Norden in Sweden; George Cheng in Taiwan; Yesim Erkan in Turkey; Tuomas Seppa in Finland; Marcin Gerwin in Poland; Anna Ignatieva in Russia; Milan Misic in Serbia, and Jonathan Sinclair Wilson, Michael Fell, Rob West, Gudrun Freese, and Alison Kuznets of Earthscan in the United Kingdom.

Our readers are ably served by the customer service team at Direct Answer, Inc. We are grateful to Katie Rogers, Ginger Franklin, Katie Gilroy, Lolita Harris, Cheryl Marshall, Valerie Proctor, Ronnie Hergett, Marta Augustyn, Heather Cranford, Rosey Heath, Sharon Hackett, and Karen Piontkowski for providing first-rate customer service and fulfilling our customers' orders.

We would also like to acknowledge the valuable service of several staff members who have moved on to new challenges this year. We are especially grateful for Vice President Georgia Sullivan's work to strengthen the Institute's communications, marketing, and fundraising capabilities over the past two years. During the same period, Suzanne Hunt put the Institute on the biofuels research map with her pioneering study of the field. Web Manager Steve Conklin brought the Institute into the virtual world, a boon to dissemination of our research as well as to our business model. And Development Associate Laura Parr ably supported the Institute's fundraising operations and contributed to internal staff development. We will miss each of them and we thank them for their contributions. Meanwhile, we welcome Robert Engelman, our new Vice President for Programs, who leads our research programs and provides strategic leadership on the issues the Institute faces; Development Assistant Kimberly Rogovin, who supports Worldwatch's president and Development Department; Web Manager Andrew Burnette, who is further developing our Web presence and our Internet strategy; and Research Associate Raya Widenoja, the new leader of our biofuels research.

We close by noting with gratitude the tremendous contributions made by Herman Daly over the past half-century in reshaping economic thought to embrace environmental concerns. A pioneer in the field of ecological economics and a former member of the Institute's Board of Directors, Herman's thinking was a major inspiration as we undertook this project on innovations for a sustainable economy. We are grateful for his many decades of intellectual leadership. Our deep hope is that his clear vision—of economies that operate within ecological boundaries to advance genuine human development—will become the dominant path of economic progress in this unfolding century.

Gary Gardner and Thomas Prugh
Project Directors

Worldwatch Institute
1776 Massachusetts Ave., N.W.
Washington, DC 20036
worldwatch@worldwatch.org
www.worldwatch.org

Contents

Acknowledgments   *vii*

List of Boxes, Tables, and Figures   *xii*

Foreword   *xv*
    Dan Esty, Yale University

Preface   *xix*
    Christopher Flavin
    President, Worldwatch Institute

State of the World: *xxiii*
    A Year in Review
    Lisa Mastny

1   Seeding the Sustainable
    Economy   *3*
    Gary Gardner and Thomas Prugh

2   A New Bottom Line for Progress   *18*
    John Talberth

3   Rethinking Production   *32*
    L. Hunter Lovins

4   The Challenge of Sustainable
    Lifestyles   *45*
    Tim Jackson

5   Meat and Seafood: The Global
    Diet's Most Costly Ingredients   *61*
    Brian Halweil and Danielle Nierenberg

6   Building a Low-Carbon
    Economy   *75*
    Christopher Flavin

SPECIAL SECTION: PAYING FOR NATURE'S SERVICES

7   Improving Carbon Markets   *91*
    Zoë Chafe and Hilary French

8   Water in a Sustainable Economy   *107*
    Ger Bergkamp and Claudia W. Sadoff

9   Banking on Biodiversity   *123*
    Ricardo Bayon

10   The Parallel Economy of
    the Commons   *138*
    Jonathan Rowe

11   Engaging Communities for a
    Sustainable World   *151*
    Erik Assadourian

12   Mobilizing Human Energy   *166*
    Jason S. Calder

13   Investing for Sustainability   *180*
    Bill Baue

14   New Approaches to Trade
    Governance   *196*
    Mark Halle

Notes   *211*

Index   *255*

List of Boxes, Tables, and Figures

Boxes

1 Seeding the Sustainable Economy
1–1   Conceptual Reform in Key Sectors   10

2 A New Bottom Line for Progress
2–1   Gross Domestic Product: Blind to Economic, Social, and Environmental Crises   20

3 Rethinking Production
3–1   The Robot Versus the Hair Dryer   37
3–2   Biomimicry and Carpets   41

6 Building a Low-Carbon Economy
6–1   What About Nuclear Power?   81

7 Improving Carbon Markets
7–1   North American Carbon Trading Systems under Development   95
7–2   Who Gets Permission to Emit?   97
7–3   Carbon Neutrality—Not a Neutral Term   103

8 Water in a Sustainable Economy
8–1   Water as Capital   113
8–2   Total Economic Value   114
8–3   The Dublin Principles   115
8–4   Water Pricing and Water Prices   118

9 Banking on Biodiversityxx
9–1   The Escalating Problem of Biodiversity Loss   125
9–2   The Evolution of a Wetland Banker   128
9–3   Perverse Incentives on Endangered Species   131

10 The Parallel Economy of the Commons
10–1 Property: A Social Construct   140
10–2 Trusting Commons   148

11 Engaging Communities for a Sustainable World
11–1 What Is a Community?   152
11–2 Preparing for the Long Emergency   159
11–3 Dockside Green: Developers Taking the Lead   163

12 Mobilizing Human Energy

12–1 Reshaping the Development Agenda in the 1990s   *169*
12–2 Common Critiques of Community-based Development   *170*
12–3 Basic Principles of Seed-Scale   *173*
12–4 Common Ways to Scale Up Successful Programs   *175*

13 Investing for Sustainability

13–1 Definition and Scope of Investing for Sustainability   *181*
13–2 Importing Sustainability to China   *188–89*
13–3 Hedge Funds Marry Ecology with Economics   *189*
13–4 TXU Buyout Is History's Biggest—and Greenest   *190*

14 New Approaches to Trade Governance

14–1 Good Governance   *197*
14–2 Multidimensional Problems   *208*

Tables

1 Seeding the Sustainable Economy

1–1 Net Worth Per Person, by Country Income Group, 2000   *9*

2 A New Bottom Line for Progress

2–1 Sustainable Development Objectives and Macroeconomic Indicators   *23*
2–2 Genuine Progress Indicator Components and Values, United States, 2004   *24*
2–3 Sustainable Development Objectives and Microeconomic Indicators   *28*

4 The Challenge of Sustainable Lifestyles

4–1 Population and Carbon Dioxide Emissions, Selected Countries, 2004   *47*

5 Meat and Seafood: The Global Diet's Most Costly Ingredients

5–1 Meat and Seafood Consumption in Top Five Countries or Regions, 2005, and Increase since 1961   *63*

6 Building a Low-Carbon Economy

6–1 Global Energy Use and Carbon Emissions in 2006 and in 2050 Under Two Scenarios   *77*
6–2 Energy-Related Carbon Emissions, Selected Countries, 2006   *78*
6–3 Estimates of Potential Contribution of Renewable Energy Resources   *83*

7 Improving Carbon Markets

7–1 Carbon Transactions, Selected Markets, 2005 and 2006   *93*
7–2 Selected Clean Development Mechanism and Joint Implementation Projects   *101–02*

8 Water in a Sustainable Economy

8–1 Water Use by Sector   *109*
8–2 Selected Examples of Payments for Watershed Services   *120*

9 Banking on Biodiversity
9–1   Examples of Legal Requirements for Biodiversity Offsets   123

11 Engaging Communities for a Sustainable World
11–1 How Selected Communities Model Sustainability   153

13 Investing for Sustainability
13–1 The World of Sustainability Investments   181
13–2 Socially Responsible Investments, by Region, Mid-2000s   183

Figures

2 A New Bottom Line for Progress
2–1   World Indicator Trends, 1970–2005   19

3 Rethinking Production
3–1   Waves of Innovation   43

4 The Challenge of Sustainable Lifestyles
4–1   Carbon Intensity of GDP, 1990–2004   48
4–2   Subjective Well-being and Per Capita Income, 2000   51
4–3   Domain Satisfaction by Social Group, England   55

5 Meat and Seafood: The Global Diet's Most Costly Ingredients
5–1   World Meat Production and Seafood Harvest, 1950–2006   62

6 Building a Low-Carbon Economy
6–1   Atmospheric Concentration of Carbon Dioxide, 1744–2004   76
6–2   Estimates of Available Energy Resources Using Today's Technology 82
6–3   Global Investment in Renewable Energy, 2000–06   85
6–4   Electricity Use Per Capita, California and Rest of the United States   89

7 Improving Carbon Markets
7–1   Average Price of EU Emissions Contracts, 2005–07   96
7–2   Distribution of CDM Credits Expected 2002–12, for All Projects in Pipeline   99
7–3   Sources of CDM Credits Expected 2002–12, for All Projects   100

8 Water in a Sustainable Economy
8–1   Physical and Economic Water Scarcity   108

12 Mobilizing Human Energy
12–1 Farmer-managed Tree Regeneration in Galma Village, Niger, 1975 and 2003   167

13 Investing for Sustainability
13–1 Venture Capital and Private Equity Investment, 2000–06   191

Units of measure throughout this book are metric unless common usage dictates otherwise.

Foreword

Daniel C. Esty
Hillhouse Professor of Environmental Law & Policy, Yale University
Director of the Center for the Environment and Business at Yale
Director of the Yale Center for Environmental Law and Policy

State of the World 2008 makes it clear that our planet and every individual on it face substantial environmental challenges. From the buildup of greenhouse gas emissions in the atmosphere to significant water shortages and a wide range of pollution and natural resource management issues, the road to a sustainable economy is full of potholes. But there are signs of hope. As documented throughout this volume, the pace and scale of environmental innovation is extraordinary.

Most notably, there has been a sea change in business attitudes toward the environment over the last several years. Companies large and small, in manufacturing and in services, in the old economies of the United States and Europe as well as the emerging economic powerhouses of the developing world, have come to recognize that the environment is more than regulations to follow, costs to bear, and risks to manage. As society steps up to a wide range of pollution control and natural resource management challenges—and commits substantial resources to finding solutions—there will be significant market opportunities for those who can bring solutions to bear.

A number of CEOs are remaking their companies around this emerging "cleantech" opportunity. At General Electric, for example, CEO Jeff Immelt launched an "ecomagination" campaign designed to promote the company's high-efficiency locomotives and jet engines, wind turbines, solar power technologies, water purification systems, and cleaner coal electric generating equipment. This is not because he is a "do gooder" but because he believes that these markets offer the prospect of high growth and high margins.

Similarly, Andrew Liveris, CEO of Dow, a company that I have worked with, wants his top managers to drive innovation and Dow revenues by having the company lead the way toward a world of sustainable chemistry, solutions to climate change, and progress on such environmental problems as water availability.

Action at the business-environmental interface is, of course, not limited to the United States. In Norway, REC has emerged as a leading producer of photovoltaic panels with a market capitalization in excess of $17 billion. Japan-based Toyota has become the fastest-growing and most profitable automaker in the world by putting fuel economy and environmental sensitivity at the heart of its strategy. Grupo Nueva, a Chilean forest products company, is building its business by putting environmental commitment into everything the company does.

In addition, hundreds of small cleantech companies have been launched worldwide in the past several years. From solar power businesses like Ausra and Solarec to geothermal energy producers such as Altarock to cellulosic ethanol technology developers such as Range and Coskata, environmental innovation is being pushed in hundreds of directions. More than $100 billion in venture capital, private equity, corporate research and development funding, and government support for technology development was invested in environmental start-up ventures over the past year.

In parallel with the business world's new environmental focus lies an important policy story centered on innovation as the key to environmental progress and a sustainable economy. A fundamentally changed environmental trajectory requires substantial technological breakthroughs.

How do we promote environment-related innovation? The answer is increasingly apparent: private-sector investment guided by carefully structured market-based incentives.

A technology development process that depends on a few thousand government officials setting standards and defining "best available technologies" cannot possibly explore or even imagine all the ideas that need to be funded and tested. It makes more sense to shift the burden of action to the business community so that companies have an incentive to think broadly about opportunities for progress. And the private sector has a much larger scale of capital available to devote to technology development. The funding required amounts to hundreds of billions of dollars—not the hundreds of millions of dollars that government might spend.

The private sector is also better positioned to take the requisite risks to produce technology breakthroughs. Venture capitalists do not blink at the prospect of only 1 project in 10 paying off. That kind of success ratio in government would be entirely unacceptable. In addition, the business community is in a better position to reward success in a way that will draw the most talented people into the quest for environmental solutions. Entrepreneurs who recognize the opportunity for a big payday put in long hours and motivate a team of people to put in extra effort.

There is still a critical role for government and regulations. But the Environmental Protection Agency and state-level regulators as well as environmental ministries around the world need to shift from doing technology development to establishing incentives in the marketplace that promote innovation and that draw in the private sector. In particular, they need to put a price on causing environmental harms so that those who offer ways to eliminate pollution and cut down on nonrenewable resource use will be rewarded.

Two parallel trends in the environmental arena promise to further an innovation emphasis. First, the move to market-based mechanisms and away from "command and control" regulation dramatically shifts the focus of the private sector. Under the traditional environmental protection model, where government not only sets the standards but also dictates the particular technology that needs to be deployed, companies have little incentive to innovate. They simply follow the guidelines and regulations provided. Under an economic-incentive-based approach, in contrast, as companies (and the individuals who buy their products) find themselves paying a price for every increment of harm caused or natural resource consumed, a strong incentive emerges to figure out ways to reduce these payments. Thus, the shift toward a serious commitment to the Polluter Pays Principle offers the prospect of sharpening the incentive at every level in society for energy conservation, improved resource productivity, and innovation.

The second broad trend that supports a shift toward an innovation-centered environmental policy approach emerges from the opportunities of the Information Age to tailor economic incentives with greater precision. Historically, it has been extremely difficult and expensive to track individual emitters or natural resource consumers. But in our digital era, sensors, data collection technologies, and information management systems are increasingly cheap and easy to deploy. It is possible to keep track of emissions and resource use on a much more refined basis. The acid rain allowance trading program of the Clean Air Act of 1990, for instance, depends on sulfur dioxide emissions monitors being placed in each power plant in the United States. Similar monitoring and measurement technologies are now available to track emissions from every smokestack, factory, and business in the country and from every car's tailpipe as well. Why not send a car pollution bill at the end of each month to every driver? There is no better way to motivate car owners to demand more fuel-efficient and less-polluting cars than to have them pay for the harms that their vehicles individually cause.

Information technologies can also be used to identify and disseminate "best practices" in terms of technologies and policies. Advanced information management systems make it much easier to benchmark performance, track trends, spot problems, and identify which environmental interventions are effective. Governments, companies, communities, and individual families can then focus on replicating successful strategies and not investing in projects or approaches that are not producing good results.

It is easy to be a pessimist in the face of the daunting environmental challenges that every one of us faces. But the prospect of environmental innovation makes me an optimist, at least over the longer term.

Progress, of course, depends on redoubling the business community's focus on the environment. The logic of making the environment a core element of corporate strategy seems straightforward. No company or industry today can afford to ignore energy costs, pollution issues, and other environmental challenges. Those that do risk competitive disadvantage. And CEOs who take these challenges seriously are often finding ways to innovate that translate into reduced costs (eco-efficiency), better managed risks, new lines of revenue, and strengthened brand loyalty.

Continued environmental progress will require smart government policies. Moving companies toward a sustainable trajectory will happen faster with clear economic incentives. But individual consumers must also be made to understand the part they play in polluting and consuming nonrenewable natural resources.

In blazing a path toward a world of sustainable economies, *State of the World 2008* highlights the importance of innovation. This volume shows the next steps that must be taken in the business world, in the policy community, and by every one of us.

Preface

Christopher Flavin
President, Worldwatch Institute

In his groundbreaking study on the economics of climate change, former World Bank chief economist Nicholas Stern describes the changes now under way in Earth's atmosphere as "the greatest and widest-ranging market failure ever seen." It is an economic failure that the global economy is not prepared to cope with and that most of today's economic analysis is not able to understand.

It is ironic that it is the very triumph of market economics that is now challenging the basic tenets that have helped make it so successful. Conventional economics relies on markets—large numbers of buyers and sellers—rather than planners to determine the most efficient allocation of resources. The price mechanism and profit motive have been enormously successful in spurring technological change and meeting human needs, bringing adequate nutrition, clean water, housing, transportation, and myriad other goods and services to billions of people. Market capitalism has, in the words of Daniel Yergin, reached the "commanding heights" of the modern world, leaving communism and other competing theories in the ash heap of history.

Early economic thinkers such as Thomas Malthus had a sense of the biophysical limits in which the economy of their day operated. But the Industrial Revolution at the end of the eighteenth century allowed many of these limits to be overcome—with new materials replacing those that had grown scarce and new technologies allowing unexpected gains in everything from agricultural production to energy use. At the same time, colonial expansion and migration opened up little used resources in the Americas and other parts of the globe. By the twentieth century, economic growth had become the primary goal of most governments and their economic advisors: rising incomes helped bring many people out of poverty, while creating opportunities across the economic spectrum.

That economic model has lasted a long time, but it will not survive the twenty-first century. In a physically constrained world, material growth cannot continue indefinitely, and when that growth is exponential—and involves mega-countries like China and India—the limits are reached more abruptly and catastrophically than even the best scientists are able to predict. From falling water tables to soaring oil prices and collapsing fisheries, the ecological systems that underpin the global economy are under extraordinary stress. Economists who thought they could analyze the economic world as if it were separate from the physical world may have a hard time finding work in the years ahead.

Continued human progress—both material and spiritual—now depends on an economic transformation that is more profound than any seen in the last century. A world of limits will require a shift from the unfettered conventional economics that prevailed then to the emerging field of sustainable economics, which embraces many of the principles of market economics, including its ability to allocate scarce resources, while at the same time explicitly recognizing that the human economy is but a part of the larger global ecosystem that contains it. This new field of sustainable economics goes on to analyze the economic limits imposed by the physical world, and proposes a range of innovative ideas for bringing the economy into balance with the global ecosystem.

The focus of *State of the World 2008* is on the innovations that will be needed to make a sustainable economy possible. To do that, we have recruited an unusually thoughtful group of expert authors who have written on topics ranging from new approaches to industrial production to new measures of economic progress, microfinance, and the development of markets for carbon emissions and protection of biodiversity. The book includes scores of exciting examples of pioneering business ventures in fields like solar energy, venture capitalists who are financing the creation of environmental businesses, and communities that are mobilizing to spur sustainable innovation at the local level. These diverse initiatives create new economic models and business practices that foster economies that meet people's needs while protecting the planet.

We come away from this project with a strong sense that something large, perhaps even revolutionary, is struggling to be born as business leaders, investors, politicians, and the general public create the architecture of sustainable economics. Indeed, it is breathtaking to see how much innovation has been unleashed by the wave of concern about climate change that has broken across the world in the past year, culminating in the awarding of the Nobel Peace Prize to the world's leading climate scientists and their most effective evangelist, Al Gore.

Emblematic of the innovative proposals emerging on an almost daily basis is one announced just as we were going to press: Virginia Tech has teamed up with a private investor, Hannon Armstrong, to put $100 million a year into improving the energy efficiency of Washington area buildings. As with hundreds of similar announcements, this one involves a creative combination of private capital, nonprofit expertise, and supportive government policies.

Innovative ideas and big money are a powerful combination—and the sums now moving in a green direction are eye-popping. Citigroup announced plans in May 2007 to invest $50 billion to address climate change over the next decade. And Goldman Sachs invested $1.5 billion in renewable energy in 2006, exceeding its initial commitment by 50 percent. Global investment in new energy technologies is estimated at $71 billion in 2006, up 43 percent from the previous year. Both in China and the United States, "clean technology" is now the third largest sector for venture capital investment. More momentous still are innovations such as China's new renewable energy law and Europe's carbon emissions trading system, which ensure that these kinds of investments will continue to flow for many years to come.

Shifting from the conventional economic paradigm to one based on ecological or sustainable economics will require years of change on many levels—from classroom theory to business practice and government policy. Pricing goods and services so that environmental costs and benefits are counted is one key measure—easy in principle but often difficult for people or politicians to accept. And creative ways must be found to knock down the barriers to change—for example, changing electric utility regulations so that saving energy is at least as profitable as building new power plants.

Sustainable economics will need to meet human as well as planetary needs if it is to prevail. Proponents of market economics and globalization often point to the 300 million people who have escaped from poverty since 1990—most of them in China and India. This still leaves more than a billion desperately poor people in today's world, and the developing countries that have not yet benefited from the immense growth in the global economy over the past century are determined to close this gap in the decades ahead. It is therefore gratifying to see that the same kinds of innovation—from $100 laptops to drip irrigation—that is going into environmental improvement is also delivering new approaches to agriculture, health care, and education in poor rural communities.

There is a great deal to be admired—and valued—about market economics in today's ever-smaller world. With so much to do in such a short time, efficient allocation of resources and motivating people to action are more important than ever. But twenty-first century economics must be grounded in a more realistic understanding of the physical and biological world on which we depend. As Albert Einstein once said, "We can't solve problems by using the same kind of thinking we used when we created them." This sentence should be posted on the walls of economics classrooms, corporate boardrooms, and the grand halls where the world's legislators make public policy.

Christopher Flavin

State of the World: A Year in Review

Compiled by Lisa Mastny

This timeline covers some significant announcements and reports from October 2006 through September 2007. It is a mix of progress, setbacks, and missed steps around the world that are affecting environmental quality and social welfare.

Timeline events were selected to increase awareness of the connections between people and the environment. An online version of the timeline with links to Internet resources is available at www.worldwatch.org/features/timeline.

MARINE ECOSYSTEMS
UN report says the number of low-oxygen "dead zones" in the world's oceans and seas has increased from 149 to some 200 in the past two years, endangering fish stocks.

BIODIVERSITY
WWF warns that birds are headed toward a major extinction due to climate change, with some populations already showing declines of up to 90 percent.

FORESTS
WWF says two thirds of forests in the Congo River Basin, the second largest tropical forest, could disappear within 50 years if exploitation continues at current rates.

ATMOSPHERE
Scientists say unusually low temperatures have led to record ozone loss over Antarctica, helping to push the "ozone hole" to a near-record 28 million square kilometers.

FORESTS
Brazil says the rate of Amazon deforestation has slowed to about half the level of the previous year—the second lowest rate since recordkeeping began in 1988.

CLIMATE
Australian researchers report that global carbon dioxide emissions have more than doubled since 1990 and the rate of increase is accelerating.

NATURAL DISASTERS
Officials report that the US wildfire season set an all-time record in 2006, with more than 96,000 wildfires burning a total of nearly 4 million hectares.

2006 STATE OF THE WORLD: A YEAR IN REVIEW

OCTOBER · NOVEMBER · DECEMBER

NATURAL DISASTERS
World Bank estimates that the 360 reported disasters in 2005 killed more than 90,000 people, affected more than 150 million, and caused record damages of $159 billion.

MARINE ECOSYSTEMS
Scientists project that at today's rates of withdrawal, all currently fished species of wild seafood could collapse—experiencing 90-percent depletion—by 2050.

BIODIVERSITY
Scientists declare the baiji, a rare Yangtze River dolphin and one of the oldest species, effectively extinct—the first loss of a large aquatic mammal in 50 years.

HEALTH
WHO reports that urban air pollution causes some 2 million premature deaths annually, more than half of which are in developing countries.

CLIMATE
The Stern Review, a detailed report on the economics of climate change, warns unabated global warming could cause damages worth 5 to 20 percent of global GDP.

FORESTS
Brazil creates the world's largest tropical rainforest preserve—a 15-million-hectare area in the state of Pará—to protect the Amazon from logging and agriculture.

CLIMATE
IPCC reports unequivocal proof that Earth is warming and confirms that human activities are behind increased atmospheric greenhouse gas concentrations since 1750.

BIODIVERSITY
Study reports elephant poaching is at its highest level in two decades and illegal ivory trade is flourishing, threatening to undermine global conservation efforts.

ENERGY
The United States and Brazil announce a new partnership to boost research and production of ethanol, paving the way for broader global trade in biofuels.

SECURITY
Scientists move the hand of the "Doomsday Clock," indicating vulnerability to nuclear and other threats, from seven to five minutes to midnight, the first change since 2002.

ENERGY
Report says global wind energy markets exceeded expectations in 2006, with a record 32-percent increase in growth bringing global capacity to 74,223 megawatts.

CLIMATE
Governments of the 27-member European Union approve a new target to cut collective greenhouse gas emissions by 20 percent from the 1990 level by 2020.

WATER
Report says the Yangtze, Mekong, Salween, Ganges, and Indus are among the 10 rivers at greatest risk as a result of climate change, pollution, dams, and other threats.

JANUARY — FEBRUARY — MARCH

2007

4 6 8 10 12 14 16 18 20 22 24 26 28 30 | 2 4 6 8 10 12 14 16 18 20 22 24 26 28 | 2 4 6 8 10 12 14 16 18 20 22 24 26 28 30

FORESTS
UN warns that Indonesia's rainforest is being destroyed up to 30 percent faster than previously thought, and orangutan populations could be extinct within three decades.

ENERGY
In a world first, Australia mandates a nationwide phaseout of incandescent light bulbs by 2010, hoping to reduce greenhouse gas emissions by 4 million tons by 2012.

TOXICS
Melamine-tainted gluten imports from China trigger the deaths of thousands of US dogs and cats, spurring a nationwide pet-food recall.

CLIMATE
An alliance of major US corporations and NGOs issues a landmark call for the federal government to enact strong legislation to reduce greenhouse gas emissions.

TOXICS
Study finds that exposure while in the womb to chemicals in everyday plastics and pesticides may alter human gene functions and increase risk of obesity and disease.

ENERGY
The US government approves the first new site permit for a nuclear power plant in 30 years, a sign of renewed interest in nuclear energy in the country.

SECURITY

The UN Security Council holds its first debate on the impact of climate change on security, triggering questions about the Council's authority in addressing the issue.

CLIMATE

In a landmark recognition of climate change, President George W. Bush directs federal agencies to develop regulations limiting greenhouse gas emissions from vehicles.

BIODIVERSITY

US officials remove the bald eagle from protection under the Endangered Species Act as numbers in the lower 48 states reach some 9,789 pairs, up from only 417 in 1963.

POVERTY

World Bank reports that the number of people living on less than $1 a day fell 18.4 percent between 2000 and 2004, to an estimated 985 million.

HEALTH

Scientists link the rising premature birth rate in the United States with increased use of pesticides and fertilizers containing nitrates, which can contaminate surface water.

ENERGY

UN reports that investments in renewable energy reached a record $100 billion in 2006, spurred by climate change concerns, greater government support, and high oil prices.

2007 STATE OF THE WORLD: A YEAR IN REVIEW

APRIL	MAY	JUNE
2 4 6 8 10 12 14 16 18 20 22 24 26 28 30	2 4 6 8 10 12 14 16 18 20 22 24 26 28 30	2 4 6 8 10 12 14 16 18 20 22 24 26 28

POLLUTION

European officials sign law requiring that all heavy-oil tankers entering European ports be double-hulled, in response to recent disastrous oil spills in the region.

ENERGY

First solar-powered boat to cross the Atlantic arrives in New York after a five-month trip to demonstrate the feasibility of clean energy vessels on the open seas.

BIODIVERSITY

UN panel adds Ecuador's Galapagos Islands to the list of World Heritage sites in danger, as the islands are threatened by invasive species, growing tourism, and immigration.

WATER

Report on China's Yangtze River says that 10 percent of the waterway is in "critical condition" and 30 percent of its major tributaries are "seriously polluted."

MARINE ECOSYSTEMS

More than 20 nations agree to restrict the practice of dragging heavy nets along the seafloor in the South Pacific, an area with a quarter of the world's oceans.

CLIMATE

At the G-8 summit, the world's eight largest industrial nations agree to "substantial" greenhouse gas emissions cuts by 2050, though no mandatory targets are set.

CLIMATE
Researchers say glaciers and ice caps now contribute about 60 percent of the ice melt into the oceans and that the rate has been accelerating over the past decade.

ENERGY
Spanish biofuels developers select Kansas as the site of the first US cellulosic ethanol plant, slated to produce fuel from corn stalks, switchgrass, and other woody biomass.

BIODIVERSITY
US scientists warn that two thirds of polar bears could be extinct in 50 years as Arctic sea ice shrinks, and they consider adding the species to the Endangered Species List.

AGRICULTURE
Study says organic farming can yield up to three times as much food as conventional farming in developing countries, refuting claims that organics cannot feed the world.

BIODIVERSITY
Four slaughtered mountain gorillas are found in the DR of Congo's Virunga National Park, renewing fears about threats to the rare species from poachers and rebel groups.

TOXICS
Toy giant Mattel recalls millions of toys manufactured in China after high levels of lead are found in the items, prompting consumer concern about Chinese-made products.

CLIMATE
Scientists report that Arctic sea ice has thinned by half since 2001, with large areas of ice now only one meter thick as the ocean and atmosphere continue to warm.

JULY   AUGUST   SEPTEMBER

See page 211 for sources.

4 6 8 10 12 14 16 18 20 22 24 26 28 30   2 4 6 8 10 12 14 16 18 20 22 24 26 28 30   2 4 6 8 10 12 14 16 18 20 22 24 26 28

CLIMATE
CEOs of 153 companies commit to greater action on climate change and call on governments to develop measures for the post-2012 Kyoto Protocol period.

NATURAL DISASTERS
China experiences "once-in-a-century" rains and floods as millions of people in the southwest, center, and east are displaced over a period of weeks.

WASTE
Coca-Cola announces goal of recycling or reusing 100 percent of the PET plastic bottles it uses in the United States.

ENERGY
Earthquake in Japan causes leakages at a nuclear power plant, raising alarm about the risks of nuclear power and putting the country's nuclear plans in disarray.

TOXICS
Survey reports that asthma rates among the 25,000 rescue and recovery workers who responded to the 2001 World Trade Center disaster are 12 times the normal adult rate.

BIODIVERSITY
IUCN adds 188 species to its Red List of threatened species, which includes one in four mammals, one in eight birds, a third of amphibians, and 70 percent of assessed plants.

2 0 0 8

STATE OF THE WORLD

...ons for a
...ble Economy

CHAPTER I

Seeding the Sustainable Economy

Gary Gardner and Thomas Prugh

To critique the dominant economic system of the twentieth century would seem a fool's errand, given the unprecedented comfort, convenience, and opportunity delivered by the world economy over the past 100 years. Global economic output surged some 18-fold between 1900 and 2000 (and reached $66 trillion in 2006). Life expectancy leaped ahead—in the United States, from 47 to nearly 76 years—as killer diseases such as pneumonia and tuberculosis were largely tamed. And labor-saving machines from tractors to backhoes virtually eliminated toil in wealthy countries, while cars, aircraft, computers, and cell phones opened up stimulating work and lifestyle options. The wonders of the system appear self-evident.[1]

Yet for all its successes, other signals suggest that the conventional economic system is in serious trouble and in need of transformation. Consider the following side effects of modern economic activity that made headlines in the past 18 months:

- Atmospheric carbon dioxide levels are at their highest level in 650,000 years, the average temperature of Earth is "heading for levels not experienced for millions of years," and the Arctic Ocean could be ice-free during the summer as early as 2020.
- Nearly one in six species of European mammals is threatened with extinction, and all currently fished marine species could collapse by 2050.
- The number of oxygen-depleted dead zones in the world's oceans has increased from 149 to 200 in the past two years, threatening fish stocks.
- Urban air pollution causes 2 million premature deaths each year, mostly in developing countries.
- The decline of bees, bats, and other vital pollinators across North America is jeopardizing agricultural crops and ecosystems.
- The notion of an approaching peak in the world's production of oil, the most important primary source of energy, has gone from an alarming speculation to essentially conventional wisdom; the mainstream World Energy Council recently predicted that the peak would arrive within 15 years.[2]

These and other environmental consequences of the push for economic growth threaten the stability of the global economy. Add to this list the social impacts of modern economic life—2.5 billion people living on $2 a day or less and, among the wealthy, the rapid advance of obesity and related diseases—and the need to rethink the purpose and functioning of modern economies is clear.[3]

Even in business circles the sense that something is wrong with modern economies is palpable. An annual assessment of the most significant risks to the world's economies commissioned by the business-sponsored World Economic Forum found that many of the 23 diverse risks were nonexistent at the global level a quarter-century ago. These include environmental risks such as climate change and the strain on freshwater supplies; social risks, including the spread of new infectious diseases in developing countries and chronic diseases in industrial nations; and risks associated with innovations like nanotechnology. Beyond being new and serious, what is most striking is that half of the 23 are economic in nature or driven by the activities of modern economies. In other words, national economies, and the global economy of which they are a part, are becoming their own worst enemies.[4]

But if economies built according to the conventional model are increasingly self-destructive, a new kind of economy—a sustainable economy—is struggling to be born. Where the conventional economy depends largely on fossil fuels, is built around use-and-dispose materials practices, and tolerates extreme poverty even amid stunning wealth, the evolving sustainable economy seeks to operate within environmental boundaries and serve poor and rich alike.

The emergence of the sustainable economy is visible in a burst of creative experimentation involving design for remanufacture, "zero-waste" cities, environmental taxes, cap-and-trade carbon markets, car-sharing companies, maturing markets for solar and wind power, microfinance, socially responsible investment, land tenure rights for women, product take-back laws, and other innovations discussed in this book. Scaled up and replicated across the world, these and other experiments could form the basis of economies that meet the needs of all people at the least cost to the natural environment.

An Outdated Economic Blueprint

The world is very different, physically and philosophically, from the one that Adam Smith, David Ricardo, and other early economists knew—different in ways that make key features of conventional economics dysfunctional for the twenty-first century. Humanity's relationship to the natural world, the understanding of the sources of wealth and the purpose of economies, and the evolution of markets, governments, and individuals as economic actors—all these dimensions of economic activity have changed so much over the last 200 years that they signal the close of one economic era and the need for a new economic beginning.

In Smith and Ricardo's time, nature was perceived as a huge and seemingly inexhaustible resource: global population was roughly 1 billion—one seventh the size of today's—and extractive and production technologies were far less powerful and environmentally invasive. A society's environmental impact was relatively small and local, and resources like oceans, forests, and the atmosphere appeared to be essentially infinite.[5]

At the same time, humanity's perception of itself was changing, at least in the West. The discoveries of Enlightenment-era scientists suggested that the universe operated according to an unchanging set of physical laws whose unmasking could help humans understand and take control of the physical world. Once the Swiss mathematician Daniel Bernoulli, for example, worked out key ideas of the physics of flight in 1738, it was only a matter of time before humans claimed the air for themselves. After eons of helpless suffering from the effects of plagues, famines, storms, and other wildcards of nature, this growing sense of human prowess—along with a seemingly inexhaustible resource endowment—encouraged the conviction that humanity's story could now be written largely independent of nature.[6]

This radically new worldview became entrenched within economics, and even late in the twentieth century most economic textbooks gave little attention to nature's capacity to absorb wastes or to the valuable economic role of "nature's services"—natural functions from crop pollination to climate regulation. One Nobel economist in the 1970s made the claim (since recanted) that "the world can, in effect, get along without natural resources." Even as growth in population and technological power in the last century raised concerns about resource scarcity, economists predicted confidently that price signals from free markets would prompt more-efficient production and consumption or that human effort would produce or discover substitutes. Nature would not be a roadblock to human progress.[7]

But the assumed independence of economic activity from nature, always illusory, is simply no longer credible. Global population has expanded more than sixfold since 1800 and the gross world product more than 58-fold since 1820 (the first year for which nineteenth-century data are available). As a result, humanity's impact on the planet—its "ecological footprint"—exceeds

Earth's capacity to support the human race sustainably, according to the Global Footprint Network. (See Chapter 2.) For rich countries, the overshoot is especially high. Industrial economies today survive by dipping ever more deeply into reserves of forests, groundwater, atmospheric space, and other natural resources—practices that cannot continue indefinitely.[8]

> The assumed independence of economic activity from nature, always illusory, is simply no longer credible.

These changing circumstances demand the upending of some fundamental economic notions. With the Industrial Revolution, for instance, factories, machines, financing, and other forms of created capital replaced land as the principal drivers of wealth production. Factories and funding remain important today, but resource scarcity has made "natural capital" an increasingly vital consideration in economic advance. Declines in oceanic fish catch, for example, are often caused by the growing scarcity of fish stocks (natural capital) rather than by a lack of fishing boats (created capital). (See Chapter 5.) Modern fishing practices now overpower nature's fish endowment: a 2006 study showed that the populations of 29 percent of oceanic species fished in 2003 had collapsed (meaning that catch had fallen to 10 percent or less of their peak abundance). Similar losses of natural capital are found at the regional level for forests, water, and other key resources.[9]

A second outdated tenet is that growth ought to be the primary goal of an economy. This remains the central operating assumption in finance ministries, stock markets, and shopping malls worldwide despite the clear threat to natural capital, because rapidly growing populations and the creation of consumer-driven economies have made growth seem indispensable. But growth (making an economy bigger) is not always consistent with development (making it better): the nearly fivefold expansion of global economic output per person between 1900 and 2000 caused the greatest environmental degradation in human history and coincided with the stubborn persistence of mass poverty.[10]

Markets do little to provide public goods such as parks and mass transportation.

A third shaky axiom of conventional economic thinking is that markets are always superior to government spending and policies as economic tools. Markets are adept at generating vast quantities of private goods, but some of these—such as the dozens of redundant breakfast cereal choices—are of dubious social value. At the same time, markets do little to provide public goods such as parks and mass transportation. And although they help to allocate scarce resources "efficiently" across different products and modes of production, according to Tufts University economist Neva Goodwin, "the very definition of efficiency contains an acceptance of inequality." In economics, efficiency means allocating every resource to its highest value use, where value is defined mainly by purchasing power, so "a market works efficiently when the rich get a lot of what they want and the poor get just as much as they can pay for." Markets thus do little to ensure a just distribution of goods: those with the greatest wealth get the most, no matter that 40 percent of the global population lives in wrenching poverty.[11]

Finally, humans themselves differ sharply from the model of "economic man" held by early economists. The celebrated insight of Adam Smith was that the "invisible hand" leads self-interested individual actions to positive collective outcomes. This is a powerful idea, but it has overshadowed the equally important communitarian dimension of human societies—a dimension with deep roots in evolutionary history. People are motivated not only by self-interest but also by the desire to participate in a larger community, as with volunteer work or in response to local or national disasters. Recognizing the strong communitarian impulse of human beings, as sustainable economics does, offers a fuller and more realistic understanding of humans as economic actors.

Ballooning Liabilities

Conventional economies in the twentieth century churned out cornucopian prosperity and opportunity for people in dozens of countries. But as the century wore on, troubling numbers began to appear in environmental and societal balance sheets, suggesting that what is called "economic growth" entails significant losses—of species, healthy ecosystems, and a stable climate, for instance. Today, the alarming liabilities of modern economies threaten to undermine economic stability worldwide. Three issues—climate change, ecosystem degradation, and wealth inequality—illustrate the self-subversion of economies and economic activity today.

Climate change. The hidden story behind the headline-grabbing drama of climate change—melting glaciers, rising sea levels, and hundred-year storms—is the costs inflicted by global warming. The Intergovernmental Panel on Climate Change, the international scientific body charged with assessing the issue, reported in 2007 that the cost of curbing climate change through reductions in greenhouse gas emissions would run about 0.1 percent of gross world product annually. An independent review in 2006 conducted by Nicholas Stern, head of the

Government Economic Service in the United Kingdom, came to a more sobering conclusion: the cost of mitigation would be around 1 percent of gross world product. One percent in 2007 would have represented $650 billion, equivalent to the cost of the Viet Nam War (in 2007 dollars). This cost is steep, but it would be spread over many countries each year.[12]

Whatever the cost of action, it is a bargain compared with the cost of doing nothing. The Stern Report concluded that inaction on climate change could dampen global economic output by anywhere from 5 to 20 percent every year over the course of this century, the upper limit likely being closer to the final tally. It noted that heat waves like the one in 2003 in Europe, which killed 35,000 people and caused agricultural losses of $15 billion, will be commonplace in a few decades. And hurricane wind speeds in the United States, which are projected to increase 5–10 percent because of rising sea temperatures, would double annual hurricane damage costs. The report's low estimate reflects estimated market costs, while the 20 percent estimate sums market costs, nonmarket health and environmental costs, and an equity weighting factor that accounts for the fact that poor countries will bear a disproportionate burden of the total.[13]

The Stern Report's findings were largely echoed in a survey of climate research by the Global Development and Environment Institute (GDAE) at Tufts University, which noted that two major modeling efforts estimated annual climate damages by the end of this century at 8 percent or more of world output. Business as usual would lead to declining agricultural yields later in this century, as well as more immediate damage to water supplies, human health, and essential natural ecosystems. The Stern and GDAE assessments suggest that early preventive action is a prudent investment necessary to address what the Stern report calls "the greatest and widest-ranging market failure ever seen."[14]

Ecosystem degradation. In 2005, a comprehensive report entitled the Millennium Ecosystem Assessment documented the extent of global ecosystem destruction in the last half of the twentieth century. It concluded that human activity had changed the world's ecosystems, largely for the worse, more rapidly during those 50 years than during any period in recorded human history. Species extinction rates, on the rise since the Industrial Revolution, increased to at least 50–500 times the natural rate. Some 20 percent of the world's coral reefs were lost and another 20 percent were degraded. And more than half of the increase in atmospheric carbon dioxide levels, which stand some 36 percent above their 1750 levels, has occurred since 1959. The web of life weakened as ecosystems became less resilient and less stable.[15]

The report made an effort to measure the drag that ecosystem destruction has already had on economies. Citing World Bank data, it noted that in 2001 some 39 countries experienced a decline of 5 percent or more in wealth (measured as net savings) once unsustainable forest harvesting, depletion of non-renewable mineral and energy sources, and damage from carbon emissions were taken into account. For 10 countries, the decline ranged from 25 to 60 percent. And these estimates were conservative because they ignored fisheries depletion, atmospheric pollution, degradation of freshwater sources, and loss of noncommercial forests, all of which carry their own economic costs.[16]

Comprehensive data on the economic value of ecosystem services are scarce, but the picture emerging from research over the last decade suggests that these services are of major, though often hidden, economic importance. A 1997 study conservatively estimated the total global value of 17 ecosystem services to be at least as large as the combined annual output of the world's economies. A follow-up 2002 study estimated that current rates of habitat conversion cost the world's economies some $250 billion, year in and year out. And a 2006 set of case studies from Europe documents how biodiversity losses—of assets from crayfish to peatbogs to agricultural land—lead to the loss of ecosystem services, with clear economic costs. Plantation forests in Portugal, for example, have been associated with a fourfold increase in burnt area from forest fires between 1975 and 2003. Those losses totaled some 137 million euros in 2001, roughly 10 percent of the total economic value of the country's forests that year.[17]

Despite early indications of their enormous economic value, ecosystems continue to be lost. A lack of hard data regarding the actual value of the services of particular ecosystems hampers the incorporation of value into business and government decisionmaking. In addition, even when a value can be credibly estimated, it is often an externality—a cost or benefit accruing to society at large, rather than to the individuals or companies responsible—so there is little incentive for those actors to care for the species or ecosystem in question. And finally, the net value of converting an ecosystem may be artificially skewed by subsidies, tax breaks, and other government-sponsored incentives for the conversion. These market failures are common drivers of the huge environmental losses of the past half-century documented by the Millennium Ecosystem Assessment.[18]

Poverty amid affluence. Economic activity in the last century generated enough wealth, in principle, to have made extreme poverty obsolete. Global economic output increased more than 18-fold between 1900 and 2000 and nearly fivefold on a per person

basis, dwarfing the total growth of the previous 19 centuries. Yet extreme deprivation became and remains the norm for a huge share of humanity: even now, as noted earlier, some 40 percent of people worldwide survive on $2 or less per day. One in every eight people in the world was chronically hungry in 2001–03, while one in five lacked access to clean water and two in five lacked adequate sanitation.[19]

Meanwhile, those at or near the economic pinnacle are fabulously wealthy. The gulf between the richest and poorest is now almost incomprehensible: the U.N. Development Programme reported in 2006 that the combined income of the world's 500 richest people was about the same as the income of the world's poorest 416 *million* people—imagine a tiny village somewhere in South America with as much wealth as the rest of the continent. While income inequality worldwide has lessened slightly since the Chinese economic surge began, China's course of development could not spread to Africa, South Asia, and other impoverished regions without catastrophic environmental ramifications.[20]

If inequality is measured in terms of net assets (a fuller measure of wealth than income), the skewing is even greater. (See Table 1–1, which uses household data to derive per capita wealth.) A 2006 United Nations University study found that in 2000 the richest 2 percent of adults globally owned more than half of the world's household assets—that is, financial assets such as investments, plus physical assets such as a home, minus debt—while the poorest 50 percent controlled only about 1 percent. The United States had the highest average net worth per household, at $143,857, while India had the lowest, at $6,500.[21]

Inequity can dampen development prospects. The World Bank's *World Development Report 2006* noted that when some

Table 1–1. Net Worth Per Person, by Country Income Group, 2000			
Country Group	Net Worth per Person	Share of World Net Worth per Person	Share of World Population
	(dollars in purchasing power parity)	(percent)	(percent)
High-income OECD*	113,675	64	15
High-income non-OECD*	91,748	3	1
Upper middle-income	21,442	9	11
Lower middle-income	12,436	16	33
Low-income	5,485	8	40
World	26,421	100	100

*Organisation for Economic Co-operation and Development.
Source: See endnote 21.

people lack access to markets for credit, land, or jobs, resources likely do not flow to where they can do the most good for an economy. A hard-working peasant might generate more wealth for the economy than a less talented shopkeeper, but the shopkeeper, being wealthier and better connected, is more likely to obtain credit or title to land. Multiply the example across many victims of economic discrimination and many input markets, and the losses of wealth to an economy could be sizable. And once these inequities are set, they tend to be reinforced by institutions and social arrangements that favor the interests of the wealthy, which can lock in inequality—and underperforming economies—for generations.[22]

Conceptual Reform in Economics: Seven Big Ideas

As understanding of humanity's interactions with nature evolved and economic liabilities expanded, reformist economists have developed "corrective lenses" to shed light on the blind spots of the conventional economic worldview. At least seven key areas of revisionist thinking—scale, growth versus development, prices, nature's contributions, the precautionary principle, the commons, and women—are influencing economic theory and helping to turn economic activity in more-sustainable directions. (See Box 1–1 on the connections between these ideas and the issues discussed in the rest of *State of the World 2008*.)

Adjust economic scale. The economy's scale is its physical size—the sheer volume of its energy and materials flows—relative to its host, the ecosystem. An analogy might be a baby growing in its mother's womb; it is a subsystem of the mother, totally contained by and dependent upon her. Birth marks the point at which the baby has reached the limit of the mother's ability to host it. Further growth in the womb makes both baby and mother worse off.

Similarly, the global economy depends completely on nature for raw materials, energy stocks, and indispensable services such as water and air purification, soil fertility, and waste absorption. When the economy reaches a certain size, further growth makes both system and subsystem worse off, not better. In the language of economists, growth has become "uneconomic." At the extreme, an economy that tries to grow beyond a size the biosphere can support will simply destroy it. So there must be a limit on the size of the economy; its physical growth cannot go on forever.[23]

Positive signs are beginning to emerge of concrete efforts to restrain the economy's physical size. In February 2007, for instance, the leaders of more than 90 international

Box 1–1. Conceptual Reform in Key Sectors

The conceptual reforms discussed in this chapter are reshaping economics in a variety of ways that are described throughout this book. The key idea of the global economy's scale, for instance, is integral to the new yardsticks used by economists and others to assess human well-being and sustainability (Chapter 2). Economic scale also comes up indirectly when considering how to boost resource efficiency, reform food production, build a low-carbon economy, and reform the global trading system (Chapters 3, 5, 6, 7, and 14). For example, huge livestock-raising and fish farming operations today create environmental and social problems unknown to earlier, small-scale efforts.

The role of prices in telling the ecological truth and nature's contributions to the economy are a key part of discussions on carbon markets, water, and biodiversity (Chapters 7, 8, and 9). The contrast between economic growth and true development is explored in chapters on new economic measures, consumption, and communities designed for sustainability (Chapters 2, 4, and 11). Is it really "progress," for instance, when cities are transformed into sprawling metropolises, family farms are turned into agribusinesses, and rainforests become monoculture tree plantations, as Chapter 2 asks?

The precautionary principle informs much of the discussion of ways to make production safe and sustainable (Chapter 3). And issues of resource ownership and the property rights regimes that are suitable for a sustainable economy are part of any discussion of "the commons" (Chapter 10).

The value of women's contributions to economies is increasingly acknowledged both in community-driven development programs and in the expanding field of microfinance (Chapters 12 and 13). Women-centered grassroots development can improve the health of children and mothers, for instance, and even overturn centuries-old practices like child marriage, in the process releasing untapped skills and energy for economic development.

corporations, including General Electric, Volvo, and Air France, called on governments to set uniform international goals for reductions in emissions of the greenhouse gases that cause climate change. The initiative addresses one key dimension of scale: greenhouse gas emissions, which are too large for the global ecosystem to handle. On the government side, the entry into force of the Kyoto Protocol in 2005 and the launch of the European cap-and-trade system that same year are part of a landmark attempt to commit the world to the goal of slowing the rate of greenhouse gas emissions.[24]

Meanwhile, many businesses are finding ways to "dematerialize" economic activity, which can also reduce an economy's physical size. The movie rental firm Netflix, for example, began to offer its movies online in 2007, reducing the need for packaging, stores, and trips to a rental store. Waste minimization is another strategy to shrink physical flows through an economy. The Interface carpet company in the United States has adopted a "Mission Zero" waste minimization goal, aiming "to eliminate any negative impact our company may have on the environment by the year 2020." The company reports clear progress: manufacturing waste sent to landfills has fallen by 70 percent since the mid-1990s, which the company says has saved some $336 million in disposal costs.[25]

Waste minimization can be promoted through governments as well. In New Zealand, for example, some 70 percent of local councils have declared a zero-waste-to-landfills goal for their communities. The town of Opotiki, the first in the nation to set such a goal, has diverted 90 percent of its waste away from landfills each year since 1999, according to Zero Waste New Zealand. Spurred by national waste minimization legislation and using tools like extended producer responsibility laws—which require companies to take back their worn products or packaging—most communities expect to meet their goals by 2020.[26]

Shift from growth to development. What's an economy for? The conventional answer has long been: to produce ever-greater quantities of goods and services. But as just discussed, this goal is untenable in this "full world," so the growth mandate is giving way in some quarters to a new focus on development. Development is ultimately about improving human well-being—meeting fundamental human needs for food and shelter, security, good health, strong relationships, and the opportunity to achieve individual potential. Much of conventional economic activity is indifferent to this well-being focus: the $1.2 trillion spent on the world's militaries in 2006, plus the billions spent on emergency room visits, police, security systems, hazardous-waste site cleanups, litigation, and other "defensive" measures, are all major contributions to economic growth, even though they may have contributed little or nothing to actually improving people's well-being.[27]

To be sure, improving well-being can involve growth: offering access to food and shelter for all, especially the desperately poor, will require economic expansion in some locales. And whether growth is involved or not, the poor need serious economic attention to advance their well-being. Initiatives from the Millennium Development Goals to grassroots campaigns led by End Poverty Now and other nongovernmental groups suggest a growing global consciousness around the need to help the poorest. And initiatives like microcredit seem to offer significant promise for the poor to increase their claim to a country's economic pie through provision of very small loans to the poor to build microbusinesses. The Microcredit Summit Campaign has involved tens

of millions of families in microfinance and aims to extend its work to 175 million of the world's poorest families by 2015. While comprehensive studies on the impact of microcredit are yet to be done, initial research suggests that something valuable is being produced.[28]

The need to focus on well-being applies to wealthy people as well. A large body of research conducted over the past 30 years suggests that after a certain point, wealth does not generally increase happiness. (See Chapter 4.) Landmark studies done in the 1990s showed, for example, that self-reported levels of happiness in Japan were no greater in 1987 than in 1958, despite a five-fold increase in real income. Even in China, where real incomes grew by 2.5 times between 1994 and 2005, the share of people saying they were satisfied fell about 15 percentage points during this period, and the share saying they were dissatisfied rose by about as much. When economic growth no longer makes people any happier, it is beyond pointless—it is self-destructive.[29]

Efforts to advance human well-being within prosperous populations involve a wide range of initiatives, including campaigns for healthy eating, work leave for new parents, shortened workweeks, and encouragement of exercise. Promotion of cycling, for example, is on the rise, with recent initiatives in Australia, France, Taiwan, the United Kingdom, and the United States. Cycling and walking offer major health and environmental benefits, and they can be cost-effective: as the share of trips made by cycling, walking, and public transport rises, the share of the economy needed for transportation falls. While promoting cycling may seem quixotic, some European cities are inspiring models: in Amsterdam, for instance, some 27 percent of all urban trips are made by bike, compared with less than 1 percent in the United States.[30]

Some businesses are stepping up to the well-being challenge as well, by providing discounted gym memberships or by extending commuter subsidies to employees who bike or walk to work. The Sprint Corporation went a step further, designing exercise into its new headquarters. To encourage walking, its corporate campus was built with parking lots and food courts located far from offices, and with elevators deliberately designed to be slow—in order to encourage the use of stairs.[31]

Interest in ways to promote human well-being is widening among policymakers as well. Well-being is now a national policy goal in Australia, Canada, and the United Kingdom. And for the last 35 years, the Himalayan kingdom of Bhutan has made "gross national happiness," not economic growth per se, its official goal. (See Chapter 2.) Government policies there aim less at boosting raw gross domestic product (GDP) numbers than at raising educational levels and reducing poverty while preserving the country's environment and its cultural traditions.[32]

Make prices tell the ecological truth. Reformist economists have borrowed a principle from their conventional colleagues— "get the prices right"—and applied it to the effort to build sustainable economies. Environmental costs often go unrecognized by markets, as when costs created by carbon emissions are not included in the price of gasoline or electricity. These costs do not disappear, however, but are shouldered by bystanders, such as the poor in developing countries who pay to rebuild homes ruined by the storms or rising seas generated by climate change. Any economist will acknowledge that this sort of classic market failure sends distorted signals about the costs of economic activity and thus makes it difficult or impossible to achieve an efficient marketplace—the Holy Grail of conventional economics.

Governments are finding imaginative ways to include such costs, typically through taxes or fees. Ecotaxes, which in countries that belong to the Organisation for Economic Co-operation and Development provided 6–7 percent of tax revenues between 1994 and 2004, often involve shifting levies away from things valued by society, such as work, to undesirable things like pollution. Germany, for example, increased taxes on energy from 1999 through 2002 and reduced taxes on labor, resulting in lower emissions of carbon and the creation of 250,000 new jobs through 2003. Or consider feebates—a combination of fees and rebates—that subsidize the cleanest products or practices via a tax on the dirtiest ones. Sweden charged power plants a fee in the early 1990s for their emissions of nitrogen oxide—a principal cause of acid rain—and redistributed the revenues to the least polluting plants, providing a strong incentive for plants to reduce emissions. This led to a 34-percent reduction in the offending emissions in 1992 compared with 1990.[33]

Another example of a green tax is "congestion pricing" of automobiles entering urban centers. These charges are meant to raise the cost of driving, especially at peak hours, inducing people to shift to less-polluting public transportation. In Stockholm, a six-month congestion tax trial saw traffic levels fall an average 22 percent, personal injuries drop 5–10 percent, and ridership on public transportation increase some 4.5 percent. The trial was expensive, but the city estimates that if adopted permanently, the charge would produce 1.90 kronor of benefits for every krona invested, largely because of shorter travel times, increased road safety, and health and environmental benefits.[34]

Account for nature's contributions. Nature is a ready storehouse of the raw materials of civilization—food, fiber, fuel, minerals—and the collective annual value of these goods is in the trillions. But the global ecosystem also provides many services that are the indispensable substrate of economies, including air and water purification, mitigation of droughts and floods, soil generation and soil fertility renewal, waste detoxification and breakdown, pollination, seed dispersal, nutrient cycling and movement, pest control, biodiversity maintenance, shoreline erosion protection, protection from solar ultraviolet rays, partial climate stabilization, and moderation of weather extremes.[35]

Far from being free, the value of ecosystem services is sobering. For instance, honeybees' work as pollinators is worth up to $19 billion a year in the United States alone. Farmers around the world spend $30–40 billion annually on pesticides to control crop pests, but the pests' natural enemies eliminate at least as large a share of the pest population—in fact, perhaps far more—and without them, expenditures on chemicals would be far higher.[36]

Fortunately, nature's contributions are increasingly being factored into economic decisionmaking through administrative and market mechanisms. In Costa Rica, landowners receive payments for preserving forests and their biodiversity, with the money coming from fuel taxes and the sale of "environmental credits" to businesses. In Mexico, water users pay into a fund that is used to protect upstream watersheds from exploitation, thereby helping to preserve water quality; nearly 1 million hectares are protected under the program. In the state of Victoria in Australia, landowners can bid competitively for government payments to conserve biodiversity and achieve other environmental benefits. (See Chapter 9.) These programs all assign prices to valuable natural services that have historically been taken as free—and therefore have been widely abused and degraded.[37]

Apply the precautionary principle. The precautionary principle is folk wisdom—Look before you leap, *Más vale prevenir que lamentar* (Better to prevent than lament)—embodied in public policy. It is commonly defined this way: "where an activity raises threats of serious or irreversible harm to the environment or human health, precautionary measures should be taken even if some cause-and-effect relationships are not fully established scientifically." Put more plainly, traditional risk analysts ask, How much environmental harm will be allowed? Precautionists prefer the question, How little harm is possible? If safe alternatives to a product or substance exist, they argue, why use a product with even a small, highly uncertain risk?[38]

> In Mexico, water users pay into a fund that is used to protect upstream watersheds from exploitation.

The principle reflects an understanding that the modern economy is highly complex, globally integrated, and capable of deploying immense technological powers, all of which create an irreducible level of potentially dangerous uncertainty. Critics charge that the precautionary principle will stifle innovation, because unknown dangers by definition cannot be prevented. But precautionists note that a set of clues can help investigators determine if an innovation is likely to pose a danger. If a new product or technology is likely to generate irreversible consequences, harmful persistent wastes, or a large-scale impact, it becomes a candidate for serious investigation regarding its potential for harm.[39]

Today, precaution is increasingly embraced as public policy. The 1991 Maastricht Treaty that created the European Union established this as the guiding principle for environmental policy. In 1998, the Danish Environment Agency banned phthalates, a softener, from plastic toys because of its connection to reproductive abnormalities in animals, even though no danger to humans had been documented. Similarly, in 1999 the Los Angeles School Board chose to ban chemical pesticides in favor of a safer alternative, integrated pest management. And in 2003 San Francisco led U.S. cities in adopting precaution as official policy.[40]

The precautionary principle may evolve further to cover cases where unforeseen problems arise even after new products or processes have been deemed safe. In those cases, another mechanism—the surety bond—could mitigate the damage or compensate victims. A company wishing to introduce a new product would be required to deposit an appropriate sum, keyed to the best estimate of potential future damages, in an interest-bearing escrow account. The money would circulate and support other economic activity, just as other deposited funds do, and would be returned (plus interest) when the firm could show that the damage had not occurred or was less severe than estimated.[41]

Revitalize commons management. Human societies have evolved a wide range of institutions for the long-term management of natural resources, but today it is not unusual to hear it argued—especially in discussions of the so-called tragedy of the commons (see Chapter 10)—that private property is the only workable arrangement or that central government control is necessary. But some resources (such as the atmosphere) arguably ought to belong to everyone or are difficult or impossible to privatize. In any case, privatization is no guarantee against mismanagement or abuse. And government controls, while workable in some instances, have been shown to be inferior to private or user-group-sponsored systems in others.[42]

The most difficult challenge is posed by resources that are accessible to all and whose use by one party reduces the availability to other parties. Global examples include the atmosphere and open-ocean fisheries; regional examples include aquifers and irrigation systems. Unless there are agreed-upon and enforceable rules to control access (property rights systems), such resources are vulnerable to rampant exploitation and overuse. In fact, this is precisely what often happens in open access systems, in which anyone can use the resource with no restrictions—the very scenario that can give rise to the tragedy of the commons. The global atmosphere is only one vivid example of this; anyone can use it as a free dumping place for greenhouse gas emissions.[43]

An often-overlooked alternative to private or government ownership is group property systems, which assign the rights to a group that can deny access to nonmembers. For centuries there has been common management of irrigation works, forests, and pastureland in Spain, Switzerland, Japan, and the Philippines, for instance. (See Chapter 10.) Now the practice is being revitalized in other situations. The European Union cap-and-trade scheme for controlling greenhouse gas emissions, for example, is based on the principles that the atmosphere is commonly held by all and that access to its carbon-absorption capacity should come at a price—ideally and ultimately, a price high enough to hold carbon emissions to sustainable rates. [44]

In *Capitalism 3.0*, Peter Barnes of the Tomales Bay Institute proposes that commons management systems be used as an alternative to government and private ownership of resources such as the atmosphere, the oceans, and great forests. Trusts would govern access to these commons, within sustainable limits, and would charge fees to those granted access. Revenues earned from the fees, in Barnes's vision, would be used to maintain the commons, with surpluses returned as dividends to the commons owners—all citizens. And because people would have a financial stake in a healthy commons, they would follow with interest the trusts' management of them.[45]

Barnes and his colleagues at the Institute monitor commons management on a smaller scale in their "report to owners" entitled *Commons Rising*. For instance, they cite a 40,000-member food cooperative in Washington state that formed a trust to buy critical farmland and thus prevent its "development" as a housing tract. The trust is designed to manage the property as farmland for generations to come. Another example is efforts to resist the increasing "enclosure" of the information commons—attempts to privatize all intellectual property and thereby profit from it; responses such as the Creative Commons licensing scheme have sprung up to allow creative works to be shared and modified freely without charge.[46]

Value women. "Most poor people are women and most women are poor," noted a 1994 U.N. report, yet "almost all low-income women are economically active." This is still true, and it follows that ensuring economic opportunity and equality for women is likely to give economies a major shot in the arm. Gender bias in everything from asset ownership to wage rates to credit access dampens economic activity.[47]

Most fundamentally, women typically are not paid equally for equal work. Women's wages in manufacturing as a percentage of men's wages, for example, are 78 percent in Costa Rica, 66 percent in Egypt, 60 percent in Japan, and 91 percent in Sweden and Myanmar. Many countries have passed some version of an Equal Pay Act, but discrepancies between men and women persist: the United States, for instance, passed its Equal Pay Act in 1963, but women still earn only 77¢ for every dollar earned by men.[48]

Women also often lack access to land and credit. Women are responsible for 60–80 per-

cent of the world's food production today, yet they own less than 15 percent of the land in developing countries. Creative solutions include the Grameen Bank's initiative to set eligibility rules for housing loans that require that titles to land and houses be in the name of wives as well as husbands. Thus in a divorce a wife is legally entitled to her share of the couple's assets.[49]

Beyond issues of formal discrimination, women could be better supported in the often-disproportionate roles they play in child care, elder care, volunteer work, and other unpaid labor, which account for a substantial share of all economic activity. The Canadian government, for example, estimates that unpaid work is worth 31–41 percent of GDP. Some governments in industrial countries—where the single breadwinner is no longer the norm and where paid and unpaid work are often closely intertwined—are examining how to take women's unpaid work into account in policy development. By providing liberal parental leave, giving workplaces incentives to offer day care, changing the tax structure to benefit those caring for aging parents, and other similar benefits, governments are working to support the social and economic value of women's unpaid work.[50]

Innovation Revolutionaries

Some analysts believe the innovations fueling sustainable economies are spawning the sixth major wave of industrial innovation since the start of the Industrial Revolution. (See Chapter 3.) From the steam engine in the first wave to biotechnology and information networks in the fifth, surges of innovation have accelerated the rates at which natural capital could be converted to human-made capital, thereby ushering in new eras of material prosperity throughout the industrial era. The sixth wave, which taps green chemistry, biomimicry, industrial ecology, and other sustainability innovations, offers the promise of breakthroughs in using natural wealth efficiently, wisely, and equitably. And because it takes advantage of social and institutional innovations as well—not just technological ones—this new wave provides leadership roles for consumers and nongovernmental groups, businesses, and governments.[51]

Consider first the role of consumers. Using their market muscle, consumers are already helping to drive interest in green products of all kinds. Sales of Toyota's hybrid vehicles, for example, jumped from 18,000 in 1998 to 312,500 in 2006 and now number more than 1 million worldwide. Sales of compact fluorescent lightbulbs (CFLs) in the United States alone totaled 100 million in 2005. And purchases of organic foods worldwide jumped by 43 percent between 2002 and 2005, to $43 billion. Impressive as the growth in green products has been, sales constitute just a small share of the consumption of each product line—U.S. sales of CFLs accounted for only 5 percent of lightbulb sales in 2007, and organic agriculture is practiced on less than 1 percent of global agricultural land. Given that consumption accounts for a large share of the GDP of most economies—in the United States in 2006 it was 70 percent—consumers are barely tapping their power to swing economies in a sustainable direction. They need help.[52]

Using their market muscle, consumers are already helping to drive interest in green products of all kinds.

Businesses can provide assistance—and increase profitability—by meeting consumer demand for green products. Wal-Mart has taken a leadership role regarding CFLs, for example, setting a sales goal of 100 million bulbs in 2007, which would roughly double U.S. sales of these energy-efficient products. Other firms seem to be trying but are constrained by the pressures of corporate governance. British Petroleum has taken steps to remake itself as an energy company rather than an oil company. Its BP Alternative Energy business is set to invest $8 billion in solar, wind, and hydrogen power over the next decade. But BP cannot abandon its petroleum business wholesale in the near term without sacrificing the high returns that shareholders expect from today's lucrative oil market. Not surprisingly, its planned investment in BP Alternative Energy represents just 5 percent of its average annual capital investments.[53]

A key constituency with the power to reshape economies is investors, because capital invested today shapes industries for years and even decades to come. Socially responsible investments, project financing governed by the Equator Principles, and microfinance can help advance sustainability values. (See Chapter 13.) So can venture capital (VC) investments, the funds that seed many new, innovative businesses built on great ideas that can transform societies.

Venture capital has looked favorably on the "cleantech" sector—those businesses in the fields of energy, agriculture, water, and waste disposal that use innovative technologies or practices to deliver the services people want in a clean way. The field is booming: in 2006, VC cleantech investments in North America jumped 78 percent over 2005 levels to become the third-largest VC investment category, with 11 percent of all venture investments. Cleantech now gets more of these investments than the medical devices, telecommunications, and semiconductor sectors, and trails only software and biotech. Venture capital is growing in other regions as well, especially in China. There, cleantech VC investments increased some 147 percent between 2005 and 2006 and accounted for some 19 percent of all VC investment in the country.[54]

Perhaps the greatest boost to sustainability initiatives can be given by governments, which can shape markets and design nonmarket policies for sustainability. In Sweden, the government is using its regulatory and market-shaping powers to move the country rapidly away from fossil fuels. In 2006 a government commission recommended that by 2020 the use of oil in road transport be cut by 40–50 percent, that industry reduce its consumption of oil by 25–40 percent, and that heating oil use be eliminated entirely. While the commission envisioned many government/private initiatives to achieve these goals, government leadership is critical, through dozens of initiatives ranging from research on energy efficiency to promotion of affordable train service and tax incentives for biofuels production.[55]

At the municipal level, many cities are introducing bus rapid transit (BRT), an innovative system of expedited bus lanes and loading systems pioneered by the government of Curitiba, Brazil. Municipal governments have discovered in BRT a remarkably efficient mass transit option that is far cheaper than underground metro systems. As a result, BRT systems have been built in Quito, Bogotá, Jakarta, Beijing, Mexico City, and Guayaquil and are under development in dozens of other cities.[56]

BRT provides perhaps the best example of how good government is indispensable to achieving sustainability—and indeed ought to be in the forefront of the movement. Governments not only can launch initiatives such as BRT themselves, they can shape the rules for markets to ensure that the energy and creativity of business is harnessed for sustainable ends. And as the embodiment (ideally) of the collective will, values, and priorities of the societies that give them legitimacy, governments must step up and take on those necessary tasks that civil society and the private sector cannot or will not do adequately or competently—to look after the well-being of society as a whole.

With business, civil society, and government all showing serious interest in sustainability in dozens of countries worldwide, the chances of creating sustainable economies appear better than ever. As the vulnerabilities of conventional economies continue to be revealed, and as sustainability innovations proliferate and scale up, the prognosis is hopeful. Societies worldwide stand poised to rewrite the ongoing human drama of economics with a new chapter: the sustainable wealth of nations.

CHAPTER 2

A New Bottom Line for Progress

John Talberth

The way societies have defined and measured progress has had a profound influence on world history. Inspired by the idea of progress, humanity has eradicated infectious diseases, achieved explosive growth in agricultural productivity, more than doubled life expectancy, explored the origins of the universe, and vastly increased the amount and variety of information, goods, and services available for modern life. To be sure, progress has had its darker side. The evolution of weaponry from spears to atom bombs may be considered progress, but only in the most cynical sense. Likewise, transformation of vibrant cities to sprawl, family farms to agribusiness, and rainforest to monoculture tree plantations may only constitute progress for the minute fraction of humanity who have—often brutally—positioned themselves to benefit from mass exploitation of both human and natural capital.[1]

In the West, faith in the linear evolution of history framed how progress was viewed through the ages and remains a fundamental justification for today's progress mantra: economic globalization and consumerism. While this notion of progress is largely inconsistent with religious, moral, and economic frameworks common in Eastern and indigenous cultures, economists Rondo Cameron and Larry Neal point out that "nearly every nation in the world has now accepted the need to adjust its own economic policy and structure to the demands of the emerging global marketplace." Under economic globalization, progress is judged by how well nations implement policies to grow the scale and scope of market economic activity, improve efficiency of factors of production, remove regulatory barriers, and both specialize and integrate with the rest of the world. While gross domestic product (GDP) is the best-recognized measure of overall economic performance, many other metrics related to economic openness, productivity, tariffs, income, and privatization are equally influ-

---

Dr. John Talberth is Director of the Sustainability Indicators Program at Redefining Progress.

ential. This chapter describes the shortcomings of traditional metrics and provides an overview of new indicators designed to capture the environmental and social dimensions of progress.[2]

Economic Globalization and Genuine Progress: A Growing Disparity

Undoubtedly, economic globalization has gone well by many standards. The era of globalization has been accompanied by significant improvements in key indicators such as the human development index, life expectancy, cereal yields, and dissemination of critical information technologies. (See Figure 2–1.) Nonetheless, there is widespread recognition that globalization indicators are increasingly irrelevant and out of touch with the great environmental and humanitarian disasters unfolding on the planet, that they mask gross inequities in the distribution of resources, and that they fail to register over-

all declines in well-being that stem from loss of community, culture, and environment.[3]

It is beyond dispute, for example, that GDP fails as a true measure of societal welfare. While it measures the economic value of consumption, GDP says nothing about overall quality of life. In 1906, economist Irving Fischer coined the term "psychic income" to describe the true benefit of all socioeconomic activity. Goods and services are valued not for themselves, Fischer argued, but in proportion to the psychic enjoyment derived from them. Higher levels of consumption may or may not have anything to do with a higher quality of life if such consumption is detrimental to personal health, to others, or to the environment.[4]

GDP gives no indication of sustainability because it fails to account for depletion of either human or natural capital. It is oblivious to the extinction of local economic systems and knowledge; to disappearing forests, wetlands, or farmland; to the depletion of oil, minerals, or groundwater; to the deaths, displacements, and destruction caused by war and natural disasters. (See Box 2–1.) And it fails to register costs of pollution and the non-market benefits associated with volunteer work, parenting, and ecosystem services provided by nature. GDP is also flawed because it counts war spending as improving welfare even though theoretically, at best, all such spending really does is keep existing welfare from deteriorating.[5]

Per capita income and trade numbers are

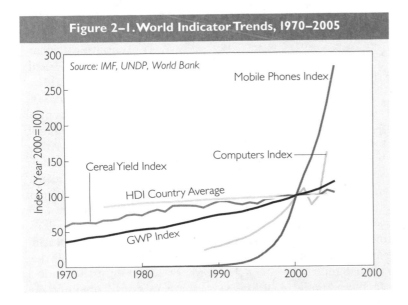

Figure 2–1. World Indicator Trends, 1970–2005

Source: IMF, UNDP, World Bank

Index (Year 2000=100)

Mobile Phones Index

Computers Index

Cereal Yield Index

HDI Country Average

GWP Index

Box 2–1. Gross Domestic Product: Blind to Economic, Social, and Environmental Crises

The most tragic humanitarian and natural disasters of the past five years have been largely unnoticed by GDP accounts. (See figure.) In Sudan, for example, the per capita GDP has risen 23 percent in this decade, yet 600,000 people were acutely at risk of famine from a prolonged drought in 2001. And more than 400,000 people were killed there and some 2.5 million displaced by alleged genocide in Darfur between 2003 and 2007. Similarly, in Sri Lanka the tsunami that killed at least 36,000 people and devastated coastal infrastructure in 2004 did not affect the steady rise in the nation's GDP. In the 2003 to 2005 period, the United States spent over $1.4 trillion on defense ($188 billion on the war in Iraq) and suffered great losses from Hurricane Katrina, yet the GDP there continued to rise. Income inequality in 2005 reached its highest level since 1928, with the top 300,000 Americans earning the same as the bottom 150 million.

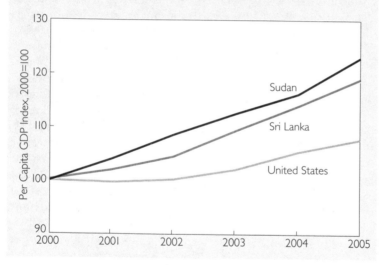

also increasingly suspect macroeconomic indicators. Rising per capita income says nothing about the distribution of that income—it may drop for the majority, rise for a handful at the top, and still show an overall gain. Indeed, while per capita income soared by 9 percent in the United States in 2005, the increase all went to the wealthiest 10 percent of the population. The bottom 90 percent experienced a 0.6-percent decline. Similarly, a nation may have rapidly growing trade volumes but lose countless jobs that are exported to "more efficient" regions, become more vulnerable as its economy becomes more specialized, and lose a large degree of its economic self-determination as ownership and control over economic decisionmaking gets displaced to distant corporate offices.[6]

Traditional microeconomic indicators for businesses and institutions are becoming obsolete as well. A company's stock price might rise on news of successful downsizing, outsourcing, or mergers, but tens of thousands of people could be laid off despite obscene CEO salaries and an ever greater concentration of market power. In agriculture, global conglomerates have become very adept at improving the efficiency of food production when measured by output per dollar. At the same time, the amount of food per hectare has dropped relative to what used to be produced on smaller, supposedly less efficient farms—creating food deserts in some of the world's most productive agricultural regions.

And finally, at the personal level, measuring economic progress by the size of salaries, stock portfolios, or houses or by the number of SUVs, plasma televisions, computers, or clothes someone owns fails to acknowledge the empty side of materialism. A rapidly emerging field called "hedonics" combines economics and psychology in an attempt to better understand what triggers "feelings of pleasure or pain, of interest and boredom, of joy and sorrow, and of satisfaction and dissatisfaction," as the authors of *Well-being: The Foundation of Hedonic Psychology* put it. An increasingly large and robust body of hedonics research confirms what people know intuitively: beyond a certain threshold, more material wealth is a poor substitute for community cohesion, healthy relationships, a sense of purpose, connection with nature, and other dimensions of human happiness. In his recent book *Deep Economy*, Bill McKibben provides an excellent overview of findings from this emerging field. One remarkable finding is that above an income of roughly $10,000 per person, the correlation between happiness and income no longer exists. (See also Chapter 4.)[7]

According to the World Bank, economic indicators serve three basic functions: they provide a measure of wealth, they help shape development policies, and they inform citizens on how their economies are being managed so that they can make appropriate political choices and thereby exert control over their governments. To accomplish all this, clearly some new indicators are needed.[8]

Sustainable Development: The New Bottom Line

In response to the grim realities of climate change, resource depletion, collapsing ecosystems, economic vulnerability, and other converging crises of the twenty-first century, a consensus is emerging among scientists, governments, and civil society about the need for a rapid but manageable transition to an economic system where progress is measured by improvements in well-being rather than by expansion of the scale and scope of market economic activity. We need to measure economic progress by how little we can consume and achieve a high quality of life rather than how fast we can add to the mountains of throwaway artifacts bursting the seams of landfills. We need to measure progress by how quickly we can build a renewable energy platform, meet basic human needs, discourage wasteful consumption, and invest in rather than deplete natural and cultural capital. We need an economic system that replaces brutal and wasteful competition between nations, businesses, and individuals with one that binds us together in cooperative frameworks for solving civilization's most urgent problems. We need an economic system that is firmly ensconced within Earth's ecological limits and guided by our spiritual and ethical traditions. We need an economic system that is diverse, adaptable, and resilient. All these objectives can be grouped under the rubric of sustainable development—the new bottom line for progress in the twenty-first century.

In 1987 the World Commission on Environment and Development defined sustainable development as meeting "the needs of the present without compromising the ability of future generations to meet their own needs." Since then, there has been a proliferation of frameworks giving substance to this basic definition by specifying goals, objectives, standards, and indicators of sustainable development for societies as a whole, for broad economic sectors, and for individual institutions. In *The Sustainability Revolution*, Andres Edwards suggests seven themes or objectives common to all frameworks: stewardship, respect for limits, interdependence, economic restructuring, fair distribution, intergenerational perspective, and nature as a model and teacher.[9]

Each framework is accompanied by a

unique blend of indicators for measuring progress or lack thereof in advancing these objectives. The remainder of this chapter considers a range of these new indicators, which can be subdivided into two broad categories and two broad types. The basic categories are macro-level indicators developed for economies as a whole and micro-level indicators for institutions or businesses. The two major types include aggregates or "headline indicators" (which attempt to combine individual indicators into a single numerical index) and specific, single-issue indicators. Given past misuses of single indices such as GDP, most sustainability practitioners recognize the need for a suite of indicators balanced across economic, environmental, and social domains.

A Macroeconomic View

Table 2–1 provides a sample of important macroeconomic indicators responsive to challenges of sustainable development in the twenty-first century. Each indicator is linked to one of five macroeconomic objectives common to popular sustainable development frameworks:

• promoting genuine progress based on multiple dimensions of human well-being,
• fostering a rapid transition to a renewable energy platform,
• equitable distribution of both resources and opportunity,
• protecting and restoring natural capital, and
• economic localization.

Since the late 1980s, researchers have been working to develop substitutes for GDP that address the costs and benefits of economic activity on environmental and social dimensions of well-being. Collectively, these indicators are known as "green" GDP accounting systems, the most comprehensive

of which is the genuine progress indicator (GPI) and its variants.

The GPI is designed to measure sustainable welfare and thus replace GDP as a nation's most important yardstick of economic progress. It adjusts a nation's personal consumption expenditures upward to account for the benefits of nonmarket activities such as volunteering and parenting and downward to account for costs associated with income inequality, environmental degradation, and international debt. The GPI has been reviewed extensively in the scientific literature and found to offer the greatest potential for measuring national sustainable development performance.[10]

Redefining Progress has done a breakdown of GPI contributions and deductions for the United States in 2004. (See Table 2–2.) These calculations show the GPI at $4.4 trillion, compared with a GDP of nearly $10.8 trillion, implying that well over half of the economic activity in the United States that year was unsustainable and did not contribute to genuine progress.[11]

GPI accounts for the United States and many other countries show the gap between GPI and GDP widening since the mid- to late 1970s. Economists call this divergence the "threshold effect." It implies that after a particular threshold, environmental and social benefits of economic growth are more than offset by rising environmental and social costs. Before that point is reached, genuine progress generally rises with GDP.[12]

Despite its theoretical validity, the GPI and other green accounting systems have yet to be formally adopted by national governments as replacements for GDP—perhaps because the news they communicate is so sobering. In early 2007, the Chinese government abandoned its efforts to develop a green GDP; preliminary results of the project showed pollution-adjusted growth rates to be

Table 2–1. Sustainable Development Objectives and Macroeconomic Indicators

Economic Objective	Sample Indicators and Desired Direction of Effect	Description
Genuine human progress	Genuine progress indicator (+)	Aggregate index of sustainable economic welfare
	Happy planet index (+)	Aggregate index of well-being based on life satisfaction, life expectancy, and ecological footprint
	Well-being index (+)	Aggregate index of well-being based on health, wealth, knowledge, community, and equity
	Human development index (+)	Aggregate index of well-being based on income, life expectancy, and education
Renewable energy platform	Carbon footprint (–)	Provides spatial and intensity measures of life cycle carbon emissions
	Energy return on investment (+)	Ratio between energy a resource provides and the amount of energy required to produce it
	Energy intensity (–)	Energy used per unit of economic output
Social equity	Index of representational equity (–)	Measures consistency between ethnic composition of elected officials and that of the general population; zero indicates "perfect" consistency
	GINI coefficient (–)	Measures extent to which an income distribution deviates from an equitable distribution; zero indicating "perfect" equity
	Legal rights index (+)	Measures degree to which collateral and bankruptcy laws protect rights of borrowers and lenders, scale of 0 to 10.
	Access to improved water and sanitation (+)	Percent of population with access to improved water and sanitation services
Protect and restore natural capital	Ecological footprint (–)	Ecologically productive land and ocean area appropriated by consumption activities
	Genuine savings (+)	Net investment in human-built and natural capital stocks adjusted for environmental quality changes
	Environmental sustainability index (+)	Weighted average of 21 separate environmental sustainability indicators
Economic localization	Local employment and income multiplier effect (+)	Direct, indirect, and induced local economic activity generated by a given expenditure
	Ogive index of economic diversity (–)	Measures how well actual industrial structure matches an ideal structure; zero indicates "perfect" diversity
	Miles to market (–)	Average distance a group of products travels before final sale

nearly zero in some provinces. Nonetheless, there are dozens of encouraging pilot programs implemented by national governments and nongovernmental organizations (NGOs) to apply various green accounting systems.[13]

A recent global assessment found green accounting programs in place in at least 50 countries and identified at least 20 others that were planning to initiate such programs soon. Broader GPI applications that consider factors such as social equity or the value of nonmarket time uses are thus far relegated to academic institutions or NGOs such as Canada's Pembina Institute, which calculates an Alberta GPI and uses it to inform policy debates over economic diversification, trade, transportation, taxes, and many other economic, social, and environmental issues.[14]

Other macroeconomic indicators have been created to supplement GDP with information on overall well-being. One example is the happy planet index (HPI), first published by the New Economics Foundation and Friends of the Earth in 2006. The authors note that the HPI "measures the ecological efficiency with which, country by country, people achieve long and happy lives." The basic formula is to multiply a country's self-reported life satisfaction index (determined through surveys) by its average life expectancy and then divide by its ecological footprint. The

first HPI assessment found Central America to be the region with the highest average score due to its relatively long life expectancy, high satisfaction scores, and an ecological footprint below its globally equitable share.[15]

Table 2–2. Genuine Progress Indicator Components and Values, United States, 2004		
Component		Amount
		(billion dollars)
Contributions		
Weighted personal consumption expenditures (adjusted for inequality)	+	6,318.4
Value of housework and parenting	+	2,542.2
Value of higher education	+	828.0
Value of volunteer work	+	131.3
Services of consumer durables	+	743.7
Services of streets and highways	+	111.6
Net capital investment (positive in 2004, so included in contributions)	+	388.8
Total positive contributions to the GPI		$11,064.0
Deductions		
Cost of crime	–	$34.2
Loss of leisure time	–	401.9
Costs of unemployment and underemployment	–	177.0
Cost of consumer durable purchases	–	1089.9
Cost of commuting	–	522.6
Cost of household pollution abatement	–	21.3
Cost of auto accidents	–	175.2
Cost of water pollution	–	119.7
Cost of air pollution	–	40.0
Cost of noise pollution	–	18.2
Loss of wetlands	–	53.3
Loss of farmland	–	263.9
Loss of primary forest cover	–	50.6
Depletion of nonrenewable resources	–	1,761.3
Carbon emissions damage	–	1,182.8
Cost of ozone depletion	–	478.9
Net foreign borrowing (positive in 2004, so included in deductions)	–	254.0
Total negative deductions to the GPI		$6,644.8
Genuine progress indicator 2004		$4,419.2
Gross domestic product 2004		$10,760.0

Source: See endnote 11.

HPI data provide further corroboration of the threshold effect. Countries classified by the United Nations as medium human development fare better than either low or high development countries. An independent statistical analysis of HPI and per capita income values for 157 countries found the two rising together up to a threshold, then diverging after that. The HPI authors concluded that "well-being does not rely on high levels of consuming."[16]

As with the green GDP, well-being indices have yet to gain official prominence—with one notable exception. Since 1972 the government of Bhutan has been using the concept of gross national happiness (GNH) as a sustainable development framework. According to Prime Minster Lyonpo Jigmi Y Thinley, GHN is "based on the premise that true development of human society takes place when material and spiritual development occur side by side to complement and reinforce each other." The four pillars of GHN are equity, preservation of cultural values, conservation of the natural environment, and establishment of good governance. Recently, a major international conference in Bhutan was held to explore GHN in more depth, including ways to put it into operation as a replacement measure for GDP.[17]

On the second macroeconomic objective, the transition to renewable energy, there are dozens of useful metrics such as energy intensity (which measures conservation) or energy return on investment (which is critical for evaluating the feasibility of renewable energy investments). But the most ubiquitous measure in use is the carbon footprint, which is expressed in three basic ways: emissions in tons of carbon, the area of Earth's surface needed to sequester those emissions, and carbon intensity or emissions per unit of economic output. A zero carbon footprint is an often-stated policy goal. But measuring this is quite complex. For example, communities that want to assess their carbon footprints almost universally fail to consider carbon emissions associated with imports of either intermediate inputs or final consumer goods from other regions or land use activities like logging or urban growth that reduce carbon sequestration capacity.

Nonetheless, carbon footprint analysis is a useful way to monitor progress toward greater use of renewable energy as well as to identify firm policy targets. For example, to stabilize carbon dioxide concentrations in the atmosphere at 450 parts per million, various models suggest that global emissions must be reduced by 50 percent in 2050 and 80 percent by century's end. (See Chapter 6.) Combining this reduction target with various projections of growth in gross world product (GWP) allows calculation of the required carbon footprint of all economic processes needed to achieve this goal. Even under the most pessimistic GWP growth scenario of 1.1 percent a year, the required footprint reduction is on the order of 93 percent—from 2.88 ounces of carbon per dollar today to just 0.16 ounces by 2100.[18]

Social equity, another macroeconomic objective, has two key dimensions: equitable distribution of resources and equitable access to health care, education, economic opportunities, representation, cultural amenities, natural areas, and everything else considered essential to a good quality of life. Quantitative equity measures already inform policy debates over taxes, affordable housing, living wages, diversity, and location of public services, and their use is on the rise. One common way to measure social equity is to compare the distribution of resources or access with some ideal distribution described as fair or equitable. The index of representational equity (IRE) and the GINI coefficient are two permutations. The IRE compares the ethnic or racial composition of elected officials, corporate management, or any other representative body with that of the general population of the relevant jurisdiction. It measures the degree of deviation, so values close to zero indicate more equitable representation if it is assumed that leaders should reflect the diversity of the populations they represent. The GINI coefficient measures the deviation between the actual income distribution of a given nation or community and a "fair" distribution, where different income brackets earn a proportional share of national income.[19]

Concerning the fourth objective, in *A Short History of Progress* Canadian novelist Ronald Wright succinctly notes: "If civilization is to survive, it must live on the interest, not the capital, of nature." Nature's interest is the flow of goods and services received from stocks of natural capital. These stocks include wild areas, healthy soils, genetic diversity, and the various atmospheric, terrestrial, and aquatic sinks for wastes inherited from the last generation. Natural capital yields goods such as foods, medicines, organic fertilizers, and raw materials for countless manufacturing processes as well as ecosystem services such as controlling floods, recycling wastes, building soils, and keeping atmospheric gases in balance free of charge. When natural capital is lost or degraded, the flow of goods and services is compromised or eliminated entirely, just as when decimation of human capital stocks destroys a community's ability to provide shelter, communications, water supply, or energy. As such, nondepletion of natural capital stocks and ecosystem service flows is a prerequisite for sustainability.[20]

The ecological footprint is perhaps the best known measure of natural capital depletion. Ecological footprint analysis (EFA) compares the surface area of Earth needed to sustain current consumption patterns and absorb wastes with what is available on a renewable basis. When the footprint exceeds biological capacity, the world is engaged in unsustainable ecological overshoot and depleting natural capital. The most recent accounts published by the Global Footprint Network find that "our footprint exceeds the world's ability to regenerate by about 25%," implying that we need 1.25 Earths to sustain present patterns of consumption. While there remain some theoretical and computational challenges to resolve, EFA has nonetheless gained status as one of the world's most ubiquitous and widely used sustainability metrics. According to the Secretariat of the U.N. Convention on Biological Diversity, EFA "provides a valuable form of ecological accounting that can be used to assess current ecological demand and supply, set policy targets, and monitor success in achieving them."[21]

Economic localization, the fifth objective, is the process by which a region, county, city, or even neighborhood frees itself from an overdependence on the global economy and invests in its own resources to produce a significant portion of the goods, services, food, and energy it consumes from its local endowment of financial, natural, and human capital. Localization is gaining new traction as a response to the looming crises over peak oil and climate change, since the global distribution system for goods is almost exclusively based on cheap fossil fuels. The World Bank acknowledges that localization "will be one of the most important new trends in the 21st century."[22]

Economic multipliers and measures of economic diversity such as the Ogive index are useful indicators of localization since they show how well a community is rebuilding its manufacturing base and creating linkages between multiple sectors. Another indicator of increasing importance and use is "miles to market," which for an individual good or group of goods measures the distance traveled (including components) from source to market. The most popular variant is food miles—a concept that illustrates the wide-ranging benefits associated with locally grown foods, such as freshness, reduced carbon emissions, higher economic multiplier effects, and the absence of resource-intensive packaging, preservatives, and refrigeration.[23]

Five Microeconomic Objectives

Some of the most innovative sustainability initiatives are being undertaken at the institutional level by businesses, schools, and NGOs. To measure effectiveness, a wide range of micro-level metrics are being deployed and used as benchmarks of organizational success. Table 2–3 provides a small sample of these.

Increasingly, sustainability metrics are being reported side by side with more-traditional financial indicators to satisfy investor and stakeholder demand for accountability with respect to important environmental, social, and economic impacts. Accountability itself is a proven force for change. As Andrew Savitz and Karl Weber note in *The Triple Bottom Line*, such metrics have become a "key driver" of progress toward sustainable business.[24]

Like macro indicators, institutional sustainability metrics can be grouped by objectives common to popular sustainability frameworks:

- certification of products, operations, and supply chains;
- zero waste;
- eco-efficiency;
- workplace well-being; and
- community vitality.

Certification is a response to a pernicious effect of globalization: the disassociation between consumers and producers caused by supply chains that now span the globe. Consumers tend to know very little about the labor or environmental practices of corporations that produce goods they consume. This lack of accountability has contributed to a "race to the bottom" in which corporations choose locations that impose the least regulatory burden on their operations. Forced relocation of entire communities, sweatshops, contamination of water supplies, collapsing fisheries, and tropical deforestation are among the results.

The burgeoning new movement to independently certify goods as humanely and sustainably produced is a direct response to these practices. A key indicator is the degree to which institutions procure goods and services from certified sources. Some well-known companies are using certification to influence practices further down the supply chain. For example, Unilever's policy is to buy 100 percent of its fish from sustainable sources. To achieve this goal, the company helped design and now promotes Marine Stewardship Council certification by its suppliers. (See Chapter 5.)[25]

Other certification or sustainability rating systems evaluate a company's overall operations, not just the products or services they provide. The Global Reporting Initiative (GRI) has become the world's leading benchmark for measuring, monitoring, and reporting corporate sustainability efforts. Currently, the GRI includes 146 indicators drawn from economic, social, and environmental domains and 33 "aspects" within these domains, such as biodiversity, relations between labor and management, and investment and procurement practices.[26]

A conspicuous manifestation of unsustainable operations is a big waste stream in the form of air emissions, water pollutants, and refuse. Thus, a second key sustainability objec-

Economic Objective	Sample Indicators and Desired Direction of Effect	Description
Table 2–3. Sustainable Development Objectives and Microeconomic Indicators		
Sustainability certification	Percent certified (+)	Percent of goods, services, and materials procured from certified sources
	Sustainability reporting compliance (+)	Degree of consistency with Global Reporting Initiative (GRI) or similar standards
	Pacific sustainability index score (+)	PSI score based on environmental, economic, and social criteria for relevant sector
Zero waste	Recycling rate (+)	Percent of waste stream recycled
	Emissions (–)	Air and water emissions including greenhouse gases total and per unit output
	Longevity (+)	Useful product life
Eco-efficiency	Recycled content (+)	Percent of materials used as inputs that are recycled
	Intensity (–)	Energy, water, and materials use per unit output
	Facility rating (+)	Level of LEED certification for buildings and facilities
Workplace well-being	Job satisfaction (+)	Average scores from employee satisfaction surveys
	Turnover rate (–)	Percent of employees voluntarily or involuntarily leaving organization each year by category
	Commuting (–)	Employee vehicle miles traveled
Community vitality	Local procurement (+)	Proportion of spending on goods and services provided by locally owned businesses
	Local economic impact (+)	Direct, indirect, and induced economic impact of local expenditures
	Community support (+)	Value of cash and in-kind goods and services donated for public benefit
	Living wage ratio (+)	Ratio of wage rate paid to living wage for relevant employment categories

tive is "zero waste." Recycling rates and emissions of air and water pollutants, including greenhouse gases (GHGs), are common indicators linked to zero waste strategies. Once adopted, regularly published, and used to set targets, such indicators often drive substantial changes in business practices.

One of the longest running zero waste initiatives is 3M's Pollution Prevention Pays program, based on the notion that waste is a sign of inefficiency and that its elimination should save money. For decades, 3M has monitored all aspects of the waste stream and urged its employees to develop innovative waste reduction programs. The company now reports cumulative reduction of over 2.2 billion pounds of pollutants. Emissions of volatile organic compounds have dropped from over 70,000 tons per year in 1988 to less than 6,000 tons today. 3M estimates it has saved at least $1 billion by reusing the waste stream and avoiding expensive pollution mitigation measures.[27]

Carbon neutrality is another zero waste strategy, and offsets are one tool that companies are using to get there. (See Chapter 7.) For example, Green Mountain Coffee Roasters has monitored both its carbon emissions and the amount of offsets since 2003. In 2005, the company reported 9,823 tons of GHG emissions and an equal amount of offsets in the form of investments in wind and methane capture projects.[28]

Another important indicator related to zero waste is product longevity, often measured by useful product life. Products designed with longevity and upgradability in mind substantially reduce the flow of refuse to landfills. Additional longevity indicators listed in the Electronic Product Environmental Assessment Tool framework include availability of extended warranties, upgradability with common tools, modular design, and availability of replacement parts.[29]

Eco-efficiency, a third microeconomic objective, is about reducing the amount of water, energy, chemicals, and raw materials used per unit output. Eco-efficiency is motivated not only by environmental concerns but by the prospects of significant financial savings in the form of reduced energy and water bills, less money spent on raw materials, and fewer regulatory hurtles. Swiss-based ST Microelectronics cut electricity use by 28 percent and water use by 45 percent in 2003 and reported saving $133 million. DuPont committed to a policy of keeping energy use flat no matter how much production increased, which reportedly saved over $2 billion in the past decade. The company Advanced Micro Devices tracks "kilowatt hours per manufacturing index" and reports a 60-percent reduction from 2.17 in 1999 to 0.86 in 2005. One way to monitor eco-efficiency for facilities as a whole is the Leadership in Energy and Environmental Design's Green Building Rating System, which is used to certify home, schools, or commercial buildings as silver, gold, or platinum based on green design features that conserve electricity, water, and waste throughout the entire life cycle—from construction to demolition.[30]

The World Health Organization identifies meaningful and satisfying work, open decisionmaking, worker health and safety, and just compensation as key aspects of sustainable workplace environments. Workplace satisfaction, turnover rates, and health and safety factors such as commuting distances are common indicators of workplace well-being—another sustainable development objective—and ones that are driving change. The work satisfaction of full-time staff at Finland's Turku Polytechnic has been monitored since 2000. In a Web-based questionnaire, respondents are asked to assess on a scale of one to five their satisfaction with work, features of the job, the working community, their supervisor's performance, recognition of their knowledge and skills, and the organization's operations. The aggregate employee satisfaction score rose steadily from 3.30 to 3.78 between 2000 and 2004. Problem areas uncovered by the surveys included collaboration and communication, which motivated the school to publish a weekly electronic newsletter for personnel.[31]

In 2004 and 2005, Mountain Equipment Co-op (MEC) in Canada undertook comprehensive employee engagement surveys with Hewitt Associates. They asked for responses to such statements as "our people practices create a positive work environment for me" and monitored the percent of employees in agreement. MEC's overall Hewitt engagement score was quite low—48 percent in 2004—and as a result the firm undertook a wide range of improvement measures such as a continuing education assistance, an upgraded maternity leave policy, extension of employee assistance programs, and increased accountability of senior staff. MEC's engagement score rose to 63 percent after the indicator was put in use.[32]

A final sustainability objective to consider is community vitality. Institutions committed to sustainable development universally recognize that they must contribute to the vitality of the communities in which they operate. While in-kind and cash donations are common, fundamental changes to business practices are increasingly important. One example is raising the share of goods and services procured from the local community rather than imported from afar. Local procurement can be a critical tool for regeneration of communities hard hit by globalization. For example, the London-based Overseas Development Institute is working with South African tourism companies and associations to promote local procurement as a way to fight poverty and other social ills plaguing rural villages.[33]

Paying living wages is another fundamental way for institutions to promote community vitality. Living wages take into account the cost of living at the local level and seek to provide a wage that fulfills the basic needs of workers and their families. Monitoring wages paid in relation to a living wage is a way to identify where adjustments need to be made. An exemplary example of this kind of monitoring is the international pharmaceutical corporation Novartis. The company works with local NGOs to identify a "basic needs basket" for a worker and family and to quantify the basket in local currencies. Using a methodology developed by Businesses for Social Responsibility, Novartis then calculates market-specific living wages and compares those with actual wages paid. By early 2006, the company had aligned the pay of all 93,000 employees with living wage levels.[34]

Fostering the New Bottom Line

How does the world move away from traditional measures such as GDP, trade volume, or factor efficiency? Encouraging the wider use of newer macroeconomic measures requires political pressure on international, national, and local governments. While there are many examples of alternative indicators used in research settings, clearly adaptation is slow and civil society leadership is key. As one step in the right direction, in November 2007 the European Commission, the Organisation for Economic Co-operation and Development, and several NGOs held a conference in Brussels entitled "Beyond GDP: Measuring Progress, True Wealth, and the Well-Being of Nations." Key objectives of the meeting included clarifying what indices are most appropriate to measure progress and how these can best be integrated into decisionmaking.[35]

Civil society can also participate in legal and administrative processes to enforce policies already in effect. For example, international finance agencies such as the World Bank are obliged to use benefit-cost analysis (BCA) to evaluate the feasibility of infrastructure development projects such as roads, oil pipelines, ports, and dams. As the Bank acknowledges, BCA "is a technique intended to improve the quality of public policy decisions. It uses as a metric a monetary measure of the aggregate change in individual well-being resulting from a policy decision." Typically, traditional economic measures like GDP are used as a proxy for well-being—a clearly erroneous practice—so there are opportunities to change such practices to be more in line with policy by using substitutes like the genuine progress indicator in these contexts.[36]

Market forces are already fostering greater

use of sustainable development indicators at the micro level. In their recent book *Green to Gold*, Daniel Esty and Andrew Winston of Yale University evaluated the stock performance of "Waveriders," a subset of companies they consider leaders in sustainability reporting and initiatives. They found that Waveriders "significantly outperformed the market" over the past 10 years, and they make a compelling case as to why maintaining credible sustainability metrics is a proven strategy for business success in the new century. Nonetheless, there is still a great deal that governments can do at all levels to tip the scales in favor of responsible Waverider-type companies.[37]

One obvious strategy is sustainable procurement policies. Given the immense resources under their control, governments at all levels can insist that companies they do business with do not just give lip service to sustainable development but demonstrate progress toward it through the GRI and other credible indicator systems. Another emerging strategy is the cultivation of markets for environmental goods and services through payments for ecosystem services and other market-based approaches. (See Chapter 9.) Governments can use their regulatory powers to create markets for flood control, pollination, biodiversity, water purification, and carbon sequestration services of healthy ecosystems by requiring offsets for urban development projects, power plants, or industrialized agriculture or forestry operations. Such markets would stimulate landholders to monitor both the stocks of natural capital under their care and the economic value of the ecosystem services those stocks generate. Taxes and subsidies are other important

tools. For example, a simple carbon tax would automatically stimulate widespread use of carbon footprint analysis.

More direct approaches are legal requirements for simple disclosure. As documented in this chapter, the mere reporting of sustainability metrics like recycling rates, energy and water intensity, and living wage ratios is a key driver of change. Where sufficient public interest is present, it is reasonable to expect communities to insist on such disclosures as part of annual reports, tax returns, and permit applications. One prominent example of the impact of such practices is U.S. Superfund legislation, which requires companies to report annually on the amount of hazardous chemicals within each of their facilities. As Savitz and Weber note in *The Triple Bottom Line*, "companies suddenly faced with the simple disclosure requirement immediately began to take dramatic, unprecedented steps to redesign their processes to eliminate the need for these chemicals at all." The result was a 59-percent reduction in the amount of hazardous chemicals stored on-site by U.S. companies, the most dramatic voluntary environmental improvement in history—"all because of a simple disclosure requirement."[38]

Innovations like these need to be acknowledged and publicized, so that one good measure leads to another. No one indicator can capture all the components of sustainable development. Instead, governments should back a suite of creative indicator initiatives, giving the world a better and more holistic portrait of progress being made in the twenty-first century toward both happy people and a happy planet.

CHAPTER 3

Rethinking Production

L. Hunter Lovins

In 1999, executives at DuPont boldly pledged to reduce the company's greenhouse gas (GHG) emissions 65 percent below their 1990 levels by 2010 as part of a company-wide strategy to lighten its environmental impact. The plan, in part, was to diversify the product line—shedding divisions such as nylon and pharmaceuticals to focus on materials that reduce greenhouse gases, such as Tyvek house wraps for energy efficiency. The plan worked: by 2007 DuPont had cut emissions 72 percent below 1991 levels, reduced its global energy use 7 percent, and, in the process, saved itself $3 billion. DuPont now plans to go beyond mere efficiency improvements to make products that mimic nature, including plant-based chemicals like Bio-PDO that can replace petroleum in polymers, detergents, cosmetics, and antifreeze.[1]

DuPont's actions—and similar ones in dozens of other firms—reflect a recognition that the way goods and services are produced must be radically rethought in this sustainability century. Over the past 100 years, the way humans made and sold goods and services took a heavy toll. Now, smart companies recognize the need to move beyond business as usual to meet people's needs in sustainable ways.

Every year the world digs up, puts through various resource crunching processes, and then throws away over a half-trillion tons of stuff. Less than 1 percent of the materials is embodied in a product and still there six months after sale. All of the rest is waste. This pattern of production and the consumption it engenders now threaten every ecosystem on Earth. In March 2005, U.N. Secretary-General Kofi Annan observed that "the very basis for life on earth is declining at an alarming rate."[2]

By the time most human artifacts have been designed but before they have been built, 80–90 percent of their lifecycle eco-

---

L. Hunter Lovins is president and founder of Natural Capitalism Solutions and a professor of business at the Presidio School of Management.

nomic and ecological costs have already become inevitable. For example, this book you are holding, the seat in which you are sitting, the airplane in which you may be flying, the terminal at which you will land, the vehicle in which you will continue your trip are all the result of myriad choices made by policymakers, designers, engineers, craftspeople, marketers, distributors, and so on. Each step represents opportunities to deliver the idea, the part, or the production process in ways that use more or fewer resources and result in a superior or suboptimal end-result. Thinking in a more holistic way and choosing more wisely at each step can reduce the impacts of these choices on the planet and its inhabitants.[3]

This is the foundation of Natural Capitalism, the framework of sustainability that describes how to meet needs in ways that achieve durable competitive advantage, solve most of the environmental and many of the social challenges facing the planet at a profit, and ensure a higher quality of life for all people. It is based on three principles:

- Buy the time that is urgently needed to deal with the growing challenges facing the planet by using all resources far more productively.
- Redesign how we make all products and provide services, using such approaches as biomimcry and cradle to cradle.
- Manage all institutions to be restorative of human and natural capital.[4]

The good news is that meeting human needs while using less stuff can be more profitable and can deliver a higher standard of living than continuing with current practices. Combined with efforts to lower consumption (see Chapter 4), practices that raise resource efficiency, circulate materials rather than dump them, and imitate nature offer a new model of prosperity for an environmentally degraded and poverty-stricken planet.

The Solid Foundation of Eco-efficiency

The ability to produce cheap goods and ship them around the planet derived in part from abundant supplies of cheap energy. Using this inexpensive oil, gas, and coal has polluted the planet and dangerously warmed the climate. In a carbon-constrained world, survival depends on finding ways to produce goods and services in dramatically more energy-efficient ways.

The concept of making things using fewer resources is far from new, but it remains the cornerstone in producing goods and services more sustainably. Critics such as William McDonough disparage eco-efficiency as simply doing less bad, but therefore still bad. Greater resource productivity alone will not deliver a sustainable society, but the criticism misses the significance of using as few resources as possible. The foundation of a building is far from sufficient to house a family, but without a solid underpinning no structure can long stand. Without eco-efficiency, no system of production can be said to be sustainable.[5]

More important, however, given the challenges facing the world, is the fact that using less stuff buys the critical time necessary to solve such daunting problems as climate change and to develop and implement production methods that meet humanity's needs in ways that do not cause more problems.

Eco-efficiency is the easiest component of the transition to sustainability to implement. It is increasingly profitable, and psychologically it is far more familiar to industrial engineers than are such concepts as biomimicry or the human dimensions of implementing the changes necessary. It is therefore a great place to start.

It is now cost-effective to increase the efficiency with which the world's resources are used by at least fourfold—dubbed "Factor Four" in a 1997 book. The European Union has already adopted this as the basis for sustainable development policy and practice. Some countries like Australia have set this and even greater efficiency as a desirable national goal. The Environment Ministers of the Organisation for Economic Co-operation and Development, the government of Sweden, and various industrial and academic leaders in Europe, Japan, and elsewhere have gone even further, adopting Factor Ten improvements as their goal. The World Business Council for Sustainable Development (WBCSD) and the U.N. Environment Programme have called for Factor Twenty, which involves increasing efficiency 20-fold. There is growing evidence that even such ambitious goals are feasible and achievable in the marketplace. They may, in fact, offer even greater profits.[6]

One of the foremost proponents of eco-efficiency is the World Business Council for Sustainable Development, which introduced this term to the world right before the 1992 Earth Summit in Rio de Janeiro. WBCSD defines eco-efficiency as:

- reduction in the material intensity of goods or services,
- reduction in the energy intensity of goods or services,
- reduced dispersion of toxic materials,
- improved recyclability,
- maximum use of renewable resources,
- greater durability of products, and
- increased service intensity of goods and services.[7]

WBCSD is a CEO-led network of more than 200 companies promoting market-oriented sustainable development and greater resource productivity. It enables its members to share knowledge, experiences, and best practices on energy and climate, development, ecosystems, and the role of business in society. It maintains initiatives in sustainable value chains, capacity building, water, and energy use in buildings. WBCSD conducts sector-specific studies on how to reduce resource use in such areas as cement, electric utilities, mining and minerals, mobility, tires, and forestry. The group is led by an executive committee featuring leaders of such companies as Toyota, DuPont, Unilever, Lafarge, and Royal Dutch Shell.[8]

Member companies have implemented profitable resource productivity to lower their costs and reduce their environmental footprint. For example, AngloAmerican/ Mondi South Africa increased the production capacity of one of its pulp mills by 25 percent. This enabled it to accommodate a 40-percent increase in timber supply from more than 2,800 small growers, while increasing the efficiency of using waste wood to power the plant, decreasing the use of bleach chemicals, and reducing the use of coal from 562 to 234 tons per day—all while significantly cutting costs. The measures achieved reductions in:

- 2,177 tons of sulfur dioxide—a 50-percent reduction;
- 509 tons of nitrogen oxide (NO_x)—a 35-percent reduction;
- 297,121 tons of carbon dioxide (CO_2)—a 50-percent reduction; and
- total sulfur emissions—down approximately 60 percent.

Energy-efficient technologies also reduced water consumption and purchased energy. These enabled the pulp mill to use 44 percent less purchased energy in 2005 than in 2003. During 2005, one mill cut its energy and water costs by 27 percent.[9]

Increasingly, companies are implementing eco-efficiency to drive their innovation and enhance their competitiveness. STMicroelectronics (ST), a Swiss-based $8.7-billion semiconductor company, set a goal of zero net GHG emissions by 2010 while increasing production 40-fold. ST's GHG emissions were traced to facility energy use (45 percent), industrial process (perfluorocarbon and sulfur hexafluoride) emissions (35 percent), and transportation (15 percent). The company undertook to reduce on-site emissions by investing in cogeneration (efficient combined heat and electricity production) and fuel cells (efficient electricity production).[10]

By 2010 cogeneration sources should supply 55 percent of ST's electricity, with another 15 percent coming from fuel switching to renewable energy. ST will reduce the need for energy supply through improved efficiency and implement various projects to sequester carbon. This commitment has improved profitability. During the 1990s its energy efficiency projects averaged a two-year payback—a nearly 71 percent after-tax rate of return.[11]

Making and delivering on this promise has also driven ST's corporate innovation and increased its market share, taking the company from the twelfth to the sixth largest microchip maker by 2004. By the time ST meets its commitment, it expects to have saved almost $1 billion.[12]

What is true in microchip manufacturing holds true in consumer retailing as well: things can be done more efficiently. In October 2005, Wal-Mart, the world's largest retailer, announced a corporate commitment to cut greenhouse gas emissions and reduce waste, pledging to be supplied 100 percent by renewable energy, to create zero waste, and to sell products that sustain resources and the environment.[13]

To achieve this, Wal-Mart is working with its 60,000 plus suppliers to help them learn how to produce "affordable sustainability, and become more sustainable businesses in their own right." The company began by reducing waste, announcing a goal of a 5-percent reduction in overall packaging by 2013. It estimated that the impact would be the equivalent of removing 213,000 trucks from the road and saving about 324,000 tons of coal and 77 million gallons of diesel fuel a year.[14]

Reducing packaging in the company's Kid Connection line of toys let Wal-Mart use 427 fewer containers to ship the same number of items, saving $2.4 million in shipping costs, 3,800 trees, and 1,300 barrels of oil annually. The company estimates that a similar effort globally could save nearly $11 billion. Wal-Mart's supply chain alone could save $3.4 billon.[15]

> Companies are implementing eco-efficiency to drive their innovation and enhance their competitiveness.

Wal-Mart has pledged to implement an "Ethical Supplier Initiative" and is seeking more long term and sustainable partnerships with the factories that supply its stores. One such program in a candy factory in Brazil that lacked a system for processing, recycling, and disposing of waste enabled the factory to install a waste management program, which in turn let the supplier generate $6,500 a year in new profits.[16]

Wal-Mart is working with suppliers to design more-efficient products to offer to its customers. A partnership with the Eco-magination program of General Electric (GE) will produce light-emitting diodes (LEDs). LED lights last longer, produce less heat, contain no mercury, and use significantly less energy than other bulbs. Lighting accounts for about one third of Wal-Mart's electricity use. Since 2004 Wal-Mart has invested about $17 million in developing LED lighting systems for its own refrigerator cases in more than 500 stores. It projects that this will save about $3.8 million a year and reduce the company's CO_2 emissions by 65 million pounds. Wal-Mart's purchase will be sufficiently large that it will bring GE's production costs for LED lighting down to levels competitive with ordinary lamps.[17]

The company is also taking a closer look at how some of the products on its shelves are made, in line with WBCSD's emphasis on reducing the dispersion of toxic chemicals as one component of eco-efficiency. At the March 2007 quarterly meeting of senior management and major suppliers of Wal-Mart, CEO Lee Scott indicated that the company would begin phasing phthalates out of the plastics used in children's toys. By July, Wal-Mart announced that it would no longer ship infants' toys containing these endrocrine-disrupting compounds.[18]

A number of frameworks aim to help companies use resources more efficiently. Lean manufacturing arose from the Toyota Production System and was popularized in the 1996 book *Lean Thinking* by James Womack and Dan Jones. It emphasizes reduction in process variability as a way to identify and eliminate inefficiencies that reduce quality. Waste is eliminated as a byproduct of enhancing the smoothness of the process. Similarly, the Six Sigma system trademarked by Motorola and fanatically implemented by hundreds of companies seeks to cut waste by eliminating any variability in the production of items.[19]

These two systems are valuable approaches, but management needs to understand their limits. Manufacturers have found that both have the drawback of inhibiting creativity. The mental model that seeks to eliminate any defect or deviation from a given standard is inimical to the sort of intellectual curiosity, tolerance for ambiguity, spirit of experimentation, and appetite for risk that characterizes great invention. Many companies now insulate their creative staff from the salutary dis-

cipline of Six Sigma. But once the invention is conceived, lean manufacturing enables a company to deliver exceptional quality, squeeze out waste, and scale up production to efficiently deliver a predictable product.

Lean manufacturing, as implemented by Toyota, features an almost manic dedication to reducing the "seven wastes" as a way to enhance customer satisfaction. It identifies any part of an operation that does not contribute to customer satisfaction as waste, specifically targeting product design, supplier networks, and factory management. It seeks to eliminate the production of more items than are demanded by the customer, the movement of people or machines, any idle time of people or machines, the movement of material or product, inefficient processing (see Box 3–1), excess inventory of input or product, and the need to rework or throw out anything.[20]

As lean manufacturing caught on in the United States, it was logical that it would be combined with clean production, which is what the U.S. Environmental Protection Agency, the Chicago Manufacturing Center (CMC), and others did.

CMC sponsored the GreenPlants Sustainable Leadership Program to help a group of Chicago area manufacturers implement lean, clean, more-sustainable production, in order to enhance the competitiveness of manufacturing companies threatened by foreign companies. Working with Natural Capitalism Solutions, the program helps local manufacturers implement more-sustainable production techniques as the basis for retaining globally competitive manufacturers in the Chicago area. The 84 CMC clients surveyed in fiscal 2004 reported that they hired 194 people for newly created jobs, saved 527 jobs, and did not lay off anyone due to improvements.[21]

PortionPac Chemical Corporation is using

Box 3–1. The Robot Versus the Hair Dryer

A *Wall Street Journal* article exploring why Toyota was outcompeting Detroit and its suppliers stated that the Japanese manufacturer was able to "produce vehicles with one-third the defects of mass-produced cars using half the factory space, half the capital, and half the engineering time. Elements of lean production, such as 'just-in-time' shipments of supplies, are familiar to most U.S. manufacturers. But adapting the whole Toyota system, and the cultural changes that go with it, has proven difficult for many American companies."

The article tells one of the classic Toyota stories of an engineer making wasteful reliance on expensive high technology look silly. Painting processes are one of the auto industry's more polluting activities.

Armed with a $12 dryer from a discount store, Mr. Oba proved to engineers from Michigan's Summit Polymers Inc. that their $280,000 investment in sleek robots and a paint oven to bake the dashboard vents they produce actually was undermining quality and pushing up costs. The fancy equipment took up to 90 minutes to dry the paint and in the bargain caused quality flaws because parts gathered dust as they crept along a conveyor.

Mr. Oba's hair dryer did the job in less than three minutes. Chastened, Summit's engineers replaced their paint system with some $150 spray guns and a few light bulbs for drying and integrated the painting into the final assembly process. Family-owned Summit cut its defect rate to less than 60 per million parts from 3,000 per million.

Source: See endnote 20.

CMC's program to develop sustainable cleaning systems. The cleaning industry has traditionally wasted energy in manufacturing, shipping, and disposing of cleaning formulations that were 90 percent water; these were shipped in steel pails and multigallon drums that were then discarded. Many cleaning formulations being used were extremely hazardous, and few janitors understood how to apply the solutions correctly. To address these problems, PortionPac Chemical Corporation was founded in 1964 to eliminate the water and instead ship small plastic packets of concentrated, portion-controlled solutions. PortionPac helped Boeing reduce costs and simplify its cleaning process by reducing a thousand different brands of cleaning products to just 10, with PortionPac products as 3 of those 10.[22]

PortionPac has gained market share because of its sustainability campaign. It has also shifted its business model to sell customers the service of a cleaner facility, in addition to selling chemicals that others can use. In 1999, the company helped schools in Tacoma, Washington, save 627,000 hours of labor, including moving drums around, and $102,000 in chemical purchases by implementing this system. Now more than 7,000 schools have signed on to PortionPac's set cost fee, which includes the cleaning products the schools need plus proper education on how to clean, proper mixing, and safe usage. PortionPac works with correctional facilities, schools, hotels, hospitals, and industrial plants to limit the number of products and ensure proper usage.[23]

The company has also helped such clients as Cornell University earn Leadership in Environmental and Energy Design (LEED) certification from the U.S. Green Building Council by using PortionPac's Green Seal–certified products. Dale Walters, General Manager of Facilities Operations at Cornell, notes that "over time, Cornell saved costs by using the right amount of product and going from twenty cleaning products to four. It also reduced safety risks involved with handling chemicals. When we sought to create LEED certified buildings, we worked with PortionPac to establish a green housekeeping strategy." Walters reports that "PortionPac products reduced chemical waste through both the proper use of cleaning chemicals and the sheer reduction of packaging (small packets versus large jugs or plastic containers). PortionPac products are a main component of our sustainable cleaning strategy." By helping organizations find better ways to motivate their janitors and clean their facilities, while reducing the use of chemicals, PortionPac is winning contracts and expanding its business.[24]

Cradle to Cradle: Extending a Product's Life

"Cradle to cradle" is a concept introduced by Walter Stahel more than 25 years ago in Europe. In 1976, as Director of a project on product life extension at Battelle research laboratories in Geneva, Stahel embarked on a program to return products to useful lives. He analyzed cars and buildings on microeconomic and macroeconomic bases and concluded that every extension of product life saved enormous amounts of resources in contrast with turning virgin material into a new product, and it also substituted the use of people for the expenditure of energy.[25]

Stahel found that 75 percent of industrial energy use was due to the mining or production of such basic materials as steel and cement, while only about 25 percent was used to make the materials into finished goods like machines or buildings. The converse relationship held for human labor: three times as much labor was used to convert materials into higher value-added products as in the original mining. He suggested that increasing the kinds of businesses that recondition old equipment as opposed to those that convert virgin resources into new goods would sub-

stitute labor for energy. And he pointed out that such work could be conducted in small workshops around the country where the products that needed rebuilding were located—something like car repair shops that are located in every village. This sort of job creation would address both unemployment and resource waste.[26]

In the early 1990s Walter Stahel, by then widely recognized in Europe as a founder of the new sustainability movement, proposed that sustainability rests on five pillars, each of which is essential for the survival of humans on Earth. None of these pillars is a higher priority, he observed, or subject to tradeoffs. Stahel's pillars roughly mirror the history of the sustainability movement.

The first pillar is the conservation of nature as the underpinning of a prosperous economy. This involves the need to preserve intact ecosystems as the basis of all life-support systems. It applies to such planetary systems as a stable climate or the ability of the oceans to support life, as well as to local carrying capacities and the ability of regions to assimilate waste. The second pillar is the need to preserve individual health and safety that may be jeopardized by economic activities. This seeks to limit toxicity and pollution by such things as heavy metals and endocrine disruptors.

The first two pillars form the domain of the original environmental movement. They are characterized by command-and-control legislation and by minimalist compliance by industry. They tend to be dominated by technical experts and agency bureaucrats. This approach to protecting the environment costs money and created the belief that environmental protection, actually the basis of durable prosperity, is incompatible with economic success.

The third pillar adds resource productivity, innovation, and entrepreneurship to the sustainability approach. It assumes a Factor

Ten increase in efficiency as the way to forestall such threats as climate change and the loss of ecosystems. This is the approach of eco-efficiency in industrial as well as developing countries.

Stahel argues that implementing the first three pillars is the basis of a sustainable economy. But, he says, "a sustainable economy is only part of the objective to reach a sustainable society. A distinct border-line exists therefore after these first three pillars, which separates techno-economic issues from societal ones. The coming 'Quest for a Sustainable Society' must be much broader and include social and cultural issues."[27]

Thus the fourth pillar adds social ecology to the mix. This is the first element of the human dimension of sustainability and includes, in Stahel's words, "peace and human rights, dignity and democracy, employment and social integration, security and safety, the constructive integration of female and male attitudes. Key words here are: the commons, 'prisoners' dilemma', sharing and caring, barter economy."[28]

The fifth pillar Stahel calls cultural ecology. This encompasses how different cultures view the concept of sustainability and how to achieve it. It includes attitudes toward risk-taking and a sense of national heritage. For example, American engineers may see a good business case for eliminating waste, but the Japanese have an almost visceral distaste for waste. It offends them. The fifth pillar includes the critical aspects of corporate culture, whereby, for example, in 1995 DuPont called for 100-percent yield rather than zero waste. This pillar also considers the human part of the equation, such as whether people should be retrained rather than fired.

The First Industrial Revolution, the forerunner of modern manufacturing, arose at a time in history when there were relatively few skilled people to run the new machines that

were revolutionizing production. There was an apparent abundance of nature and its services. Profit-maximizing capitalists "economized on their scarce resource" (people) and substituted the use of natural resources and ecosystem services (the ability to spew pollution into the air that everyone breathes and pour wastes into rivers) to drive profits. From this the modern world was born. This transformation enabled a Lancashire weaver to spin 200 times as much fabric on the new machines as his predecessor did on a spinning wheel.[29]

The Holy Grail of prosperity was believed to be labor productivity, and indeed still today people believe that increasing labor productivity will increase well-being— as if the goal of the economy is one person doing all the work and everyone else out of work. But in today's world of relative scarcity, the tables are turned. About 10,000 more people arrive on Earth every hour, and every major ecosystem is in peril. Greater use of ecosystem services impoverishes everyone, and people need work. Yet the whole mental model of how to run the economy is based on the 200-year-old perception of the basis of prosperity: penalize the use of people, subsidize the use of resources, and increase labor productivity.[30]

Stahel describes how in 1993, as U.S. companies faced hard times, the corporate world made heroes of such restructurers as Al Dunlap and Jack Welch. Dunlap, in the name of "creating shareholder value" gained the nickname Chainsaw Al: in 20 months as CEO of Scott Paper, he devastated the 115-year-old company by terminating 11,000 people—35 percent of the labor force— including 71 percent of the staff at corporate headquarters. He, of course, made enormous personal gain. His counterpart at GE, dubbed Neutron Jack Welch, cut GE employment from 380,000 to 208,000.[31]

The logic of capitalism, the greatest known

system in human history for the creation of wealth, has not changed. But the relative scarcities have. In today's world, the recipe for prosperity is to encourage, as Stahel has outlined, the use of people and to penalize the use of resources.

Stahel describes how, also in the early 1990s, Honda used its workers to maintain and repair its own machines rather than suffer layoffs that would damage worker morale and lead to work stoppages. Increasingly, European and Japanese policymakers are considering the approach of tax shifting: eliminating taxes on employment and income, things people want more of, and replacing them with taxes on pollution and depletion of resources, things the world wants less of.[32]

Stahel cautions that of the five pillars, social and cultural ecology are the weakest underpinnings. To the extent that the social fabric breaks down, the other pillars soon collapse. The current focus on eco-efficiency, clean production, green products, and the use of technology to implement sustainability are necessary, but it is equally important to consider the human dimension, including such issues as meaningful employment, sustainable development, and enabling people to achieve their full potential.

Sustainability, Stahel notes, has little application in the short term. Its value is as a vision. He tells the story of the three stonecutters who are asked what they are doing. One says that he is putting in his eight hours. The second replies that he is cutting this limestone into blocks. The third answers that he is building a cathedral. Sustainability, says Stahel, is the cathedral we are all creating.[33]

Following Nature's Lead

Biomimicry, the conscious emulation of life's genius, is an even more profound approach to making manufacturing sustainable. Janine Benyus, author of the groundbreaking book *Biomimicry*, asks the simple question, How would nature do business? She points out that nature delivers a wide array of products and services, but very differently from the way humans do. Nature, for example, runs on sunlight, not high flows of fossil energy. It manufactures everything at room temperature, next to something that is alive. It makes very dangerous substances, as anyone who has been in proximity to a rattlesnake knows well, but nothing like nuclear waste, which remains deadly for millennia. It creates no waste, using the output of all processes as the input to some other process. Nature shops locally and creates beauty. Buckminster Fuller once pointed out that "When I am working on a problem I never think about beauty. I only think about how to solve the problem. But when I have finished, if the solution is not beautiful, I know it is wrong."[34]

The discipline of biomimicry takes nature's best ideas as a mentor and then imitates these designs and processes to solve human problems. Dozens of leading industrial companies—from Interface Carpets and AT&T to 3M, Hughes Aircraft, Arup Engineers, DuPont, General Electric, Herman Miller, Nike, Royal Dutch Shell, Patagonia, SC Johnson, and many more—use the principles of biomimicry to drive innovation, design superior products, and implement production processes that cost less and work better. (See Box 3–2.)[35]

Biomimicry invites innovators to turn to the natural world for inspiration, then evaluate the resulting design for adaptiveness in the manufacturing process, the packaging, all the way through to shipping, distribution, and take-back decisions. It ensures that the energy used, production methods chosen, chemical processing, and distribution are part of a whole system that reduces materials use, is clean and benign by design, and eliminates

Box 3–2. Biomimicry and Carpets

Industrialist Ray Anderson, chair of the billion-dollar-a-year carpet company Interface, tells the story of the creation of his product Entropy. David Oakey, the head product designer of Interface, sent his design team into the forest with the instruction to find out how nature would design floor covering. "And don't come back," he instructed, "with leaf designs—that's not what I mean. Come back with nature's design principles."

So the team spent a day in the forest, studying the forest floor and streambeds until they finally realized that it is total chaos there: no two things are alike, no two sticks, no two stones, no two anything....Yet there is a pleasant orderliness in this chaos.

They returned to the studio and designed a carpet tile such that no two tiles have the same face design. All are similar but all are different. Interface introduced the product into marketplace as Entropy, and in 18 months the design was at the top of best-seller list. This was faster than any other product in the company's history. How different is that from the prevailing industrial paradigm of every mass-produced item? A typical industrial product must be cookie-cutter the same.

The advantages of Entropy were astonishing: almost no waste and off quality in production. The designers could not find defects in the deliberate imperfection of having no two tiles alike. Installers could put the carpet in quickly without having to take time to get the pile net all running uniformly. They could take tiles from the box as they came and lay them randomly, the more random the better—like a floor of leaves. The user can replace individual damaged tiles without the "sore thumb effect" that comes with precision perfection and uniformity and can rotate tiles just like tires on cars in order to extend useful life. Moreover, dye lots now merged indistinguishably, which means sellers do not have to maintain an inventory of individual dye lots waiting to be used.

Yet one wonders: could there be more to explain the success of entropy? Perhaps there is.

A speaker on an environment lecture circuit begins every speech by having her audience close their eyes and picture that ideal comfort zone of peace and repose, of solitude, creativity, security—that perfect place of comfort. She then asks, how many of you were somewhere indoors? Almost no one ever raises their hand. This quality has a name, biophilia—humans gravitate to nature for the perfect comfort zone.

And somehow, subliminally, Entropy seems to bring the outdoors indoors. That is its real appeal.

Entropy is made with recycled content in a climate-neutral factory; 82 of Interface's products are now designed on the principle of no two alike. These represent 52 percent of Interface's sales. Using principles like waste minimization and biomimicry has enabled Interface to bring the company's CO_2 emissions to roughly 10 percent of their 1996 levels.

Source: See endnote 35.

the costs that last century's technologies imposed on society and the living world.[36]

EcoCover Limited of New Zealand used the concept that in nature there is no waste—the output of all processes is food for some other process—to develop an organically certified, biodegradable mulch mat to substitute for black plastic sheeting used in agriculture to prevent moisture loss and weed growth. Using shredded waste paper that would otherwise have gone to landfill, bound together with fish waste, the material is produced by previously unemployed people.[37]

The product uses waste to improve soil productivity, conserve soil moisture, and cut water use. It cuts the use of chemical fertilizers, pesticides, and herbicides that contaminate soil and groundwater. It reduces weeds; increases plant growth, quality, and yield; and keeps paper and fish waste out of landfills. The cover is left in the soil as improved organic and nutrient content. This is not recycling. It is "upcycling" waste back into productive soil.[38]

The humble abalone sits in the Pacific Ocean and in seawater and creates an inner lining immediately next to its body that is twice as strong as the best ceramics that humans can make using very high temperature kilns. The overlapping brick-like structure of the seashell makes it very hard to crack, protecting the abalone from sea otters and the like. Dr Jeffrey Brinker's research group at Sandia Labs found out that the iridescent mother-of-pearl lining of the abalone self-assembles at the molecular level when the animal excretes a protein that causes sea water to deposit out the building blocks of the abalone's beautiful shell.[39]

The researchers mimicked the manufacturing process of the mollusk to create mineral/polymer layered structures that are optically clear but almost unbreakable. This evaporation-induced, low-temperature process enables the liquid building blocks to self-assemble and harden into complex "nano-laminate" structures. The bio-composite materials can be used as coatings to toughen windshields, airplane bodies, or anything that needs to be lightweight but fracture-resistant.[40]

Companies are using biomimicry to match not only the form of natural products but also the function of larger ecosystems. In July 2007, Toyota Motor Corporation announced plans to increase the sustainability of its production operations. The Tsutsumi Prius production plant will add a 2-megawatt solar electric array. It will also paint some of its exterior walls and other surfaces with a photo-catalytic paint that breaks down airborne NO_x and sulfur oxides. This will do as much to clean the air as surrounding the plant with 2,000 poplar trees would have.[41]

The plant's impressive biomimicry program is coupled with a strong foundation of eco-efficiency. The plant is installing innovative assembly-line technology and further streamlining current production systems such as the Global Body Line and Set Parts System to greatly improve both productivity and energy efficiency. By 2009, the plant is expected to achieve an annual CO_2 reduction effect of 35 percent.[42]

The practice of using nature as model, measure, and mentor lies at the heart of the change in the industrial mental model that will be essential if humans are to survive. Nature runs a very rigorous, 3.8-billion-year-old testing laboratory in which products that do not work are recalled by the manufacturer. As Janine Benyus says: "Failures are fossils, and what surrounds us is the secret to survival."[43]

The First Industrial Revolution was based on brute force manufacturing processes that inefficiently heat, beat, and treat massive amounts of raw materials to produce a throwaway society. The next Industrial Revolution will rise upon the elegant emulation of life's genius, a survival strategy for the human race, and a path to a sustainable future. "The more our world looks and functions like the natural world," Benyus notes, "the more likely we are to endure on this home that is ours, but not ours alone."[44]

Riding the New Wave of Innovation

Business success in a time of technological transformation demands innovation. Since the First Industrial Revolution, there have been at least six waves of innovation (see Figure 3–1), each shifting the technologies that underpin economic prosperity. In the late 1700s textiles, iron mongering, water-power, and mechanization enabled modern commerce to develop.[45]

The second wave saw the introduction of steam power, trains, and steel. In the 1900s, electricity, chemicals, and cars began to dominate. By the middle of the twentieth century

Figure 3–1. Waves of Innovation

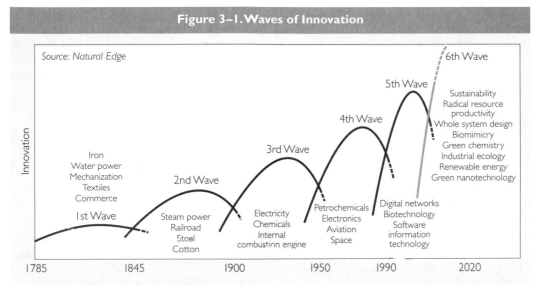

Source: Natural Edge

it was petrochemicals and the space race, along with electronics. The most recent wave of innovation brought computers and ushered in the digital or information age. As the Industrial Revolution plays out and economies move beyond iPods, older industries will suffer dislocations unless they join the increasing number of companies implementing the array of sustainable technologies that are making up the next wave of innovation.[46]

Perhaps the tipping point in corporate movement to greener production came when General Electric announced Eco-magination. As part of the initiative, GE board chairman Jeffrey Immelt promised to double the company's investment in environmental technologies to $1.5 billion by 2010. He also announced that GE would reduce the company's greenhouse gas emissions 1 percent by 2012; without action, emissions would have risen 40 percent. Immelt stated: "We believe we can help improve the environment and make money doing it."[47]

Critics charged that GE was greenwashing, simply labeling some of its existing products as green and changing very little. Hypocrisy,

however, is often the first step to real change. A little less than a year after the campaign's launch, Immelt announced that his green-badged products had doubled in sales over the prior two years, with back orders for $50 billion more, blowing away his initial prediction of $12 billion in sales by 2010. Over the same time frame, the rest of GE products had increased in sales only 20 percent. GE also announced that it had reduced its GHG emissions by 4 percent in 2006, dwarfing its 2012 target of 1 percent.[48]

Companies that increase resource productivity and implement sustainable production strategies such as biomimicry and cradle to cradle, especially in the context of a broader whole-system corporate sustainability strategy, improve every aspect of shareholder value. What constitutes shareholder value? What enhances it?

Traditionally, the "bottom line" measured whether a company was profitable. More recently, a company's profits and stock value had to increase over the next quarter or the firm was considered unworthy of investment. This highly questionable metric is so incompatible with management of an enterprise for long-term value that even the Financial Accounting Standards Board has undertaken to rewrite financial reporting to encourage alternatives to such short-sighted behavior. (See also Chapter 2.)[49]

Sustainability advocates have urged companies to manage a "triple bottom line": achieve profit but also protect people and the planet. While this is a tempting formulation, it has had the effect of bolting concern for the environment and social well-being onto companies as cost centers that reduce the traditional measure of profit. A much more useful approach is that of the "integrated bottom line." This recognizes that profit is a valid metric, but only one of many that give a company enduring value.[50]

Other aspects of shareholder value include enhanced financial performance from energy and materials cost savings in industrial processes, facilities design and management, fleet management, and operations. Reduced risk is another key point to consider, tied to insurance access and cost containment, legal compliance, reduced exposure to increased carbon regulations and price, and reduced shareholder activism. Finally, core business value is enhanced through:

- sector performance leadership;
- greater access to capital;
- first-mover advantage;
- improved corporate governance;
- the ability to drive innovation and retain competitive advantage;
- enhanced reputation and brand development;

- increased market share and product differentiation;
- ability to attract and retain the best talent;
- increased employee productivity and health;
- improved communication, creativity, and morale in the workplace;
- improved value chain management; and
- better stakeholder relations.

The validity of this management approach is borne out by a recent report from Goldman Sachs, which found that companies that are leaders in environmental, social, and good governance policies have outperformed the MSCI world index of stocks by 25 percent since 2005. Seventy-two percent of the companies on the list outperformed their industry peers.[51]

It is daunting to realize that achieving a sustainable society will require changing how we manufacture and deliver all our products and services. But the evidence increasingly shows that companies taking a leadership role in using resources more efficiently, in redesigning how they make products, and in managing their operations to enhance people and intact ecosystems have found a better way to make a bigger profit. Solving the challenges of implementing a transition to a sustainable society can unleash the biggest economic boom since the space race. There has never been a greater opportunity for entrepreneurs to do well by doing good and for communities to enhance energy security, improve the quality of life, and enable people to join the transition to a more sustainable future.

CHAPTER 4

The Challenge of Sustainable Lifestyles

Tim Jackson

In a small apartment in the sprawling suburbs of Mumbai, the financial capital of India, 35-year-old George Varkey wakes at dawn to the sound of his newborn baby's uneven breathing. Already the apartment is hot and humid, the air stirred rather than cooled by small electric fans. His wife, Binnie, is preparing breakfast. His elderly parents, four-year-old son, and younger brother are all still in bed. George is keen to be ready early. Today a news team from the BBC in London is coming to visit.[1]

George's apartment has three rooms and a tiny kitchen. The modern apartment block has running water and electric power. There is a small fridge in the kitchen and a TV in every other room. The family's latest acquisition is a DVD player. Outside is George's Suzuki sedan, essential to his small advertising business. He takes home 55,000 rupees (a little under $1,200) a month. Together with his brother's earnings as a mechanic and

his wife's part-time nursing, the family lives reasonably well on just over 1 million rupees ($24,000) a year, well above the average household income in India of $3,000 a year.[2]

George and his family are part of a rapidly growing consumer market—India's "bird of gold." In the last two decades, household income has roughly doubled. In the next two decades, average incomes are expected to triple. By 2025 India will be the fifth largest consumer market in the world, surpassing even Germany in terms of overall spending. On a per capita basis, however, India will still be poor. Each person will still spend on average less than 50,000 rupees, a little over $1,000, a year. Yet in only 20 years the share of the population classified as "deprived" will be more than halved—from 54 percent today to 22 percent by 2025. And this is in spite of the fact that by then India will nearly have passed China to become the most populous nation on Earth.[3]

Dr. Tim Jackson is Professor of Sustainable Development at the University of Surrey in the United Kingdom.

Someone who might benefit from this economic "miracle" is 26-year-old Vidya Shedge, another participant in the BBC program. Vidya lives with 10 members of her family in a single room in the considerably poorer outskirts of Mumbai. There is no running water, no fridge, and no DVD player. But they do now have electricity—enough to burn three incandescent lightbulbs and a couple of fans during the hottest part of the day. Vidya's ambition is to save enough from her 7,500 rupees ($160) a month job in a bank to afford a car. She, too, is looking forward to her visit from the BBC. They want to talk to her about "carbon footprints."

Perhaps surprisingly, both George and Vidya already know something about climate change. They understand that human activities are responsible for global warming. George has even discussed what his household can do to reduce their carbon emissions. Every room in the apartment has energy-efficient lightbulbs. A little more surprisingly, and in spite of believing that the industrial world must lead the way, both George and Vidya are relatively optimistic that something can be done to halt climate change.

A recent international survey confirms these counterintuitive findings. In June 2007 the HSBC Bank published a Climate Confidence Index. People in India showed the highest level of concern about climate change—60 percent of respondents placed it at the top of their list of concerns—the highest commitment to change (alongside Brazil), and the highest level of optimism that society will solve this problem. Skepticism and intransigence, it seems, are mainly the domain of industrial nations. The United States and the United Kingdom scored lowest on commitment. France and the United Kingdom scored lowest on optimism. India's optimism in finding solutions is driven in particular by the younger age groups. A whole new generation of Indians see hope in the future.[4]

Justifying that hope will not be easy. For George's family, life has clearly improved since his parents' generation. And yet his standard of living—measured in conventional terms—is modest at best. Vidya's family has a massive hill to climb. Eleven people living in one small room with a combined income of $16 a day is a level of poverty long consigned to history in the West. So how is it going to be possible for George, Vidya, 1 billion other Indians, and great numbers of Chinese (not to mention people in Africa, Latin America, and the rest of Southeast Asia) to achieve the standard of living taken for granted in the United States—and still "solve the problem" of climate change?

How can a world of finite resources and fragile environmental constraints possibly support the expectations of 9 billion people in 2050 to live the lifestyle exemplified for so long by the affluent West? That is the challenge that guides and frames this chapter.[5]

The Math of Sustainability

Broadly speaking, the impact of human society on the environment is determined by the number of people on the planet and the way in which they live. The math of the relationship between lifestyle and environment is pretty straightforward. It was set out several decades ago by Paul Ehrlich of Stanford University and has been explored in detail in many other places since. In essence, the lesson is simple. Reducing the overall impact that people have on the environment can happen in only a limited number of ways: changing lifestyles, improving the efficiency of technology, or reducing the number of people on the planet.[6]

The question of population is clearly critical. Population is one of the factors that "scales" humanity's impact on the planet.

Another is the expectations and aspirations of the increasing population. This chapter focuses primarily on the latter. But a simple example based on George and Vidya's carbon footprints helps illustrate the relationship.

In George's household, the carbon footprint is around 2.7 tons of carbon dioxide (tCO_2) per person. In Vidya's, it is less than a fifth of this, under 0.5 tCO_2 per person. (The average carbon footprint in India is 1 tCO_2 per person.) The difference is mainly due to the different level and pattern of consumption in the two households, since the efficiency of technology providing goods and services is pretty much the same. Basically, George's household enjoys a much higher standard of living in conventional terms. If India's 1 billion people all lived as George does now, that country would have moved from fifth place in the list of carbon emitters in 2004 to third, below only the United States and China. (See Table 4–1.) Their personal carbon footprints would still be low by western standards, however.[7]

The technological efficiency of providing goods and services is higher in the European Union (EU) and the United States than it is in India. All other things being equal, then, this should lower the carbon footprint in industrial nations. So huge regional disparities in per capita footprint are almost entirely due to the pattern and level of consumption—to differences in lifestyle.

Clearly, western nations have been the key driver of climate change so far. Between 1950 and 2000, the United States was responsible for 212 gigatons of carbon dioxide, whereas India was responsible for less than 10 percent as much. So it is clear that the richest people

Table 4–1. Population and Carbon Dioxide Emissions, Selected Countries, 2004

Country or Region	Population	CO_2 Emissions	Emissions per Person
	(million)	(million tons)	(tons of CO_2)
United States	294	5,815	19.8
China	1,303	4,762	3.7
Russia	144	1,553	10.8
Japan	128	1,271	10.0
India	1,080	1,103	1.0
Germany	83	839	10.2
United Kingdom	60	542	9.1
France	62	386	6.2
Bangladesh	139	35	0.3
European Union (15 countries)	386	3,317	8.6
World	6,352	26,930	4.2

Source: See endnote 7.

on the planet are appropriating more than their fair share of "environmental space." Yet this lifestyle is increasingly what the rest of the world aspires to.[8]

Much is made of efficiency improvements. And some relative improvements in the carbon intensity of growth are evident in some countries. (See Figure 4–1.) But these gains are slow at best, and in China they have been reversed in recent years. This is one reason that China's carbon dioxide emissions recently surpassed those of the United States. Across the world as a whole, greenhouse gas emissions grew by 80 percent between 1970 and 2004 and could double again by 2030.[9]

In summary, any gains in technological efficiency are simply being swamped by the sheer scale of rising aspirations and an increasing population. If everyone in the world lived the way Americans do, annual global CO_2 emissions would be 125 gigatons—almost five times the current level—by the middle of the century. In stark contrast, the Intergovernmental Panel on Climate Change has esti-

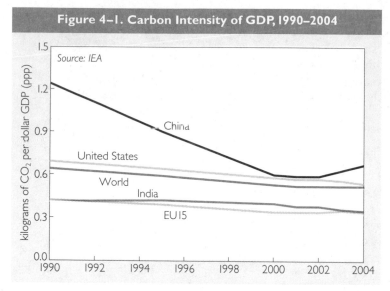

Figure 4–1. Carbon Intensity of GDP, 1990–2004

product (GDP) has become one of the principal policy objectives in almost every country. Rising GDP symbolizes a robust and thriving economy, more spending power, richer and fuller lives, increased family security, greater choice, and more public spending. The rise of India's "bird of gold," its consumer class, is heralded in financial markets with huge delight. China's vigorous economy has led to an equally striking sense of market optimism.[11]

mated that the world needs to reduce global emissions by as much as 80 percent over 1990 levels by 2050 if "dangerous anthropogenic climate change" is to be averted. This would mean getting global emissions below 5 gigatons and reducing the average carbon footprint to well under 1 ton per person, lower than it now is on average in India.[10]

This challenge clearly calls for an examination of assumptions about the way people live. What is it that drives and frames people's aspirations for the "good life"? What lies behind the runaway aspirations that seem so unstoppable in the West and are rapidly becoming the object of desire in every other nation?

The "Science of Desire"

In the conventional economic view, consumption is the route to human well-being. The more people have, the better off they are deemed to be. Increasing consumption leads to improved well-being, it is claimed.

This view goes a long way toward explaining why the pursuit of the gross domestic

Economics has remained almost willfully silent, however, on the question of why people value particular goods and services at all. The "utilitarian" model has become so widely accepted that most modern economic textbooks barely even discuss its origins or question its authenticity. The most that economists can say about people's desires is what they infer from patterns of expenditure. If the demand for a particular automobile or household appliance or electronic device is high, it seems clear that consumers, in general, prefer that brand over others. Their reasons for this remain opaque within economics.[12]

Fortunately, other areas of research—such as consumer psychology, marketing, and "motivation research"—have developed a somewhat richer body of knowledge. This "science of desire" has mainly been dedicated to helping producers, retailers, marketers, and advertisers design and sell products that consumers will buy. Little of the research concerns itself explicitly with the environmental or social impacts of consumption.

Indeed, some of it is downright antithetical to sustainability. But its insights are extremely valuable for a proper understanding of consumer motivation.[13]

For a start, it is immediately clear that consumption goes way beyond just satisfying physical or physiological needs for food, shelter, and so on. Material goods are deeply implicated in individuals' psychological and social lives. People create and maintain identities using material things. "Identity," claim consumer researchers Yiannis Gabriel and Tim Lang, "is the Rome to which all theories of consumption lead." People narrate the story of their lives through stuff. They cement relationships to others with consumer artefacts. They use consumption practices to show their allegiance to certain social groups and to distinguish themselves from others.[14]

It may seem strange at first to find that simple stuff can have such power over emotional and social lives. And yet this ability of human beings to imbue raw stuff with symbolic meaning has been identified by anthropologists in every society for which records exist. Matter matters to people. And not just in material ways. The symbolic role of mere stuff is borne out in countless familiar examples: a wedding dress, a child's first teddy bear, a rose-covered cottage by the sea. The "evocative power" of material things facilitates a range of complex, deeply ingrained "social conversations" about status, identity, social cohesion, and the pursuit of personal and cultural meaning.[15]

Material possessions bring hope in times of trouble and offer the prospect of a better world in the future. In a secular society, consumerism even offers some substitute for religious consolation. Recent psychological experiments have shown that when people become more aware of their own mortality, they strive to enhance their self-esteem and protect their cultural worldview. In a consumer society, this striving has materialistic outcomes. It is almost as though people are trying to hold their existential anxiety at bay by shopping.[16]

At a recent Consumer Forum organized for the Sustainable Consumption Roundtable in the United Kingdom, people were asked to talk about their hopes and fears for the next decade or so. They spoke about their desire to do well for their children and grandchildren. There was a strong wish to live in safe, sociable communities. People expressed spontaneous concern about others, about poverty in the developing world, and—without being told the interests of the sponsors—about the environment: climate change, resource scarcity, recycling. Shot through these expressions of concern, however, like a light relief, were recurrent, persistently materialist themes: big houses, fast cars, and holidays in the sun. Getting on and getting away pervades narratives of lifestyle success.[17]

This deep reliance on material goods for social functioning is not unique to the western world. George and Vidya also say they want to see a good future for their children. They want to do well and be seen to do well among their peers. Just below the surface, these aspirations are cashed out in broadly western terms. Vidya's overriding ambition is to afford a car. For the first time in their lives, George and Binnie are planning a holiday outside India. Getting on and getting away means as much there as it does in London, Paris, New York, and Sydney.[18]

Very similar values and views are clearly discernible in China, Latin America, and even parts of Africa. The consumer society is now in effect a global society—one in which, to be sure, there are still "islands of prosperity, oceans of poverty," as Indian ecologist Madhav Gadjil puts it. But one in which the evocative power of material goods increasingly creates the social world and provides the dominant arbiter of personal and societal progress.[19]

The Paradox of Well-being

In the conventional view, the recipe for progress is simple: the more people consume, the happier they will be. A close look at what motivates consumers uncovers a whole range of factors—family, friendship, health, peer approval, community, purpose—known to have a strong correlation with reported happiness. In other words, people really do consume in the belief that it will deliver friends, community, purpose, and so on. But there is a paradox at work here that at one level is tragic. People have a good grasp of the things that make them happy but a poor grasp of how to achieve these things. The assumption that more and more consumption will deliver more and more well-being turns out to be wrong.[20]

Using data collected in the World Values Survey, Ronald Inglehart and Hans-Dieter Klingemann examined the hypothesis that happiness (or life satisfaction) is linked to income growth. The good news is that the equation just about works for George and Vidya. There is an increasing trend in life satisfaction at lower levels of income. (See Figure 4–2.) The bad news is that the relationship will begin to diminish as their incomes rise further. Across most industrial countries there is at best only a weak correlation between increased income and reported happiness. And in countries with average incomes in excess of $15,000, there is virtually no correlation between increased income and improved life satisfaction.[21]

The same paradox is found within individual nations over time. Real income per head has tripled in the United States since 1950, but the percentage of people reporting themselves to be very happy has barely increased at all—in fact, it has declined since the mid-1970s. In Japan, there has been little change in life satisfaction over several decades. In the United Kingdom, the percentage reporting themselves very happy dropped from 52 in 1957 to 36 today.[22]

Some key aspects of people's well-being, far from improving, appear to have declined in western nations. Rates of depression have been doubling every decade in North America. Fifteen percent of Americans age 35 have already experienced a major depression. Forty years ago, the figure was only 2 percent. One third of people in the United States now experience serious mental illness at some point in their lives, and almost half of these will suffer from a severe, disabling depression. During any single year, about 6 percent of the population will suffer from clinical depression; suicide is now the third most common cause of death among young adults in North America.[23]

Teasing out the underlying causes of this unhappiness is not particularly easy. But there are two fairly compelling sets of data suggesting that consumerism itself is partly to blame. The first set suggests a negative correlation between materialistic attitudes and subjective well-being. Philosopher Alain de Boton has shown how an unequal society leads to high levels of "status anxiety" in its citizens. Psychologist Tim Kasser and his colleagues have shown how people with more materialistic attitudes—people who define and measure their own worth through money and material possessions—report lower levels of happiness. Striving for self-esteem through material wealth appears to be a kind of "zero-sum game" in which the constant need for betterment and approval only serves to entrench people in an almost neurotic spiral of consumption.[24]

A second, equally compelling set of evidence relates rising unhappiness to the undermining of certain key institutions. Subjective

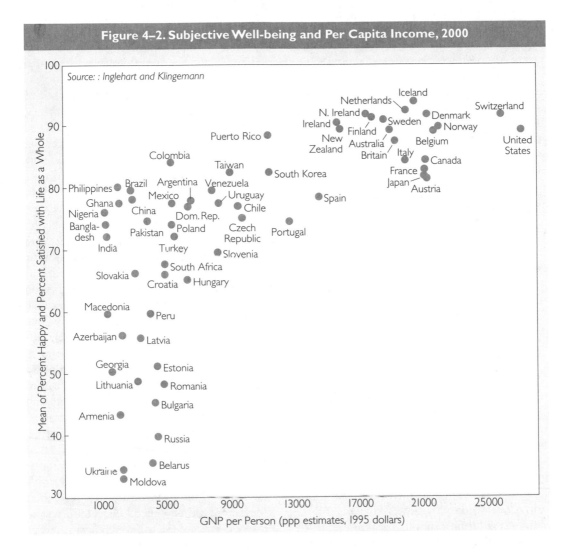

Figure 4–2. Subjective Well-being and Per Capita Income, 2000

well-being depends critically on family stability, friendship, and strength of community. But these aspects of life have suffered in the consumer society. Family breakdown, for example, has increased by almost 400 percent in the United Kingdom since 1950. The percentage of Americans reporting their marriages as "very happy" declined significantly over just 20 years during the latter part of the last century. People's trust and sense of community have fallen dramatically over the last 50 years.

In the middle of the twentieth century, more than half of all Americans believed that people were "moral and honest." By 2000 the proportion had fallen to little over a quarter. Participation in social and community activities declined markedly over the same period.[25]

In other words, there appears to be a correlation between rising consumption and the erosion of things that make people happy—particularly social relationships. This correlation does not necessarily mean, of course, that one thing "causes" the other. But in practice, as described later, there are some pretty compelling reasons to take seriously the idea that the structures and institutions that are needed to maintain growth simultaneously erode social relationships. As economist Richard Layard describes it: consumption growth has "brought some increase in happiness, even in rich countries. But this extra happiness has been cancelled out by greater misery coming from less harmonious social relationships."[26]

One tragic result of this elusive search for happiness is that industrial societies are closing off options for other people, both now and in the future, to lead fulfilling lives—without even being able to show reward for it in the here and now.

Live Better by Consuming Less?

The paradox of well-being begs the question, Why do people continue to consume? Why not earn less, spend less, and have more time for families and friends? Couldn't people live better—and more equitably—this way and at the same time reduce humanity's impact on the environment?

This idea has provided the motivation for numerous initiatives aimed at living more simply. "Voluntary simplicity" is at one level an entire philosophy for life. It draws extensively on the teachings of Mahatma Gandhi, who encouraged people to "live simply, that others might simply live." In 1936, a student of Gandhi's described voluntary simplicity in terms of an "avoidance of exterior clutter" and the "deliberate organisation of life for a purpose." Former Stanford scientist Duane Elgin picked up this theme of a way of life that is "outwardly simple, yet inwardly rich" as the basis for revisioning human progress. More recently, psychologist Mihály Csíkszentmi-

hályi has offered a scientific basis for the hypothesis that people's lives can be more satisfying when they are engaged in activities that are both purposive and materially light.[27]

Sociologist Amitai Etzioni has identified three kinds of people pursue simplicity. "Downshifters" are those who, having achieved a given level of wealth, make a conscious choice to reduce their income; they then moderate their lifestyle so they can spend more time with family or pursuing community or personal interests. "Strong simplifiers" are those who give up highly paid, high-status jobs altogether and accept radically simpler lifestyles. The most radical contingent are the "dedicated, holistic simplifiers," who embrace radical change and adjust their entire lives around an ethical vision of simplicity, sometimes motivated by spiritual or religious ideals.[28]

Some of these initiatives, such as the Findhorn community in northern Scotland, emerged initially as spiritual communities, attempting to create space in which to reclaim the contemplative dimension of living that used to be captured by religious institutions. Findhorn's character as an eco-village developed more recently, building on principles of justice and respect for nature. Another modern example is Plum Village, the "mindfulness" community established by an exiled Vietnamese monk, Thich Nhat Hahn, in the Dordogne area of France, which now provides a retreat for at least 2,000 people. At one level these initiatives are modern equivalents of more traditional religious communities like those of the Amish in North America or Buddhist monasteries in Thailand, which every young male is expected to spend some time in before going out into professional life.[29]

Not all networks have this explicit spiritual character, however. The Simplicity Forum, for example, launched in North America in 2001 is a loose secular network of "simplicity leaders" who are committed to "achieving and honoring simple, just and sustainable ways of life." Downshifting Downunder is an even more recent initiative, started following an international conference on downshifting in Sydney in 2005; its aim is to "catalyze and co-ordinate a downshifting movement in Australia that will significantly impact sustainability and social capital."[30]

The downshifting movement now has a surprising allegiance across a number of industrial economies. A recent survey in Australia found that 23 percent of respondents had engaged in some form of downshifting in the preceding five years. A staggering 83 percent felt that Australians are too materialistic. An earlier study in the United States found that 28 percent of those surveyed had taken some steps to simplify and 62 percent expressed a willingness to do so. Very similar results have been found in Europe.[31]

Research on the success of these initiatives is quite limited, but existing studies show that simplifiers really have less materialistic values and show greater respect for the environment and for others. More important, simplifiers appear to show a small but significant increase in subjective well-being. Consuming less, voluntarily, can improve well-being—completely contrary to the conventional model.[32]

The backlash against consumerism bears witness to an emerging counterculture that recognizes the limits of the consumer society and is looking for something beyond it. Buy Nothing Day every November—dedicated to persuading people to resist consumerism—is now an international phenomenon. In 2006 there were initiatives on the streets in almost 30 countries and in scores of cities, including, for the first time, a demonstration on the streets of Mumbai.[33]

Equally striking is the rise of the Transition Towns concept—towns and cities that have declared unilateral action against the twin threats of peak oil and climate change. Launched in September 2006 in the small town of Totnes in southwest England, the U.K. network expanded to over 20 towns and cities in only a year. In the United States, 400 cities have signed the U.S. Mayors Climate Protection Agreement, which pledges to meet the Kyoto Protocol targets on reducing CO_2 emissions, in spite of the federal government's refusal to ratify the protocol.[34]

It is important not to get too carried away with this evidence. Simple living communities remain marginal. The religious basis for them does not appeal to everyone, and the secular versions seem less resistant to the incursions of consumerism. Downshifting Downunder generated a flurry of activity in Australia for six months or so, for instance, but barely functions as a working network only two years later. Some of these initiatives depend heavily on individuals having sufficient personal assets to provide the economic security needed to pursue a simpler lifestyle. Finally, it is clear that forced or involuntary simplicity is quite another story. Subjective well-being plummeted in the "transition economies" (former Soviet states) during the 1990s.[35]

As the evidence on global consumerism makes abundantly clear, mainstream consumer values show little sign of slowing down the pace of material and environmental profligacy. Existing attempts to live better by consuming less remain marginal at best. So the question remains, Why do people continue to consume, knowing the social and environmental consequences, even beyond the point at which it adds to their satisfaction?

Competing for Status— and for Survival

Is the urge to consume somehow "natural," hardwired through evolution? Certainly, the desire for comfort, a decent home, good relationships with friends and family, doing well in the community, and perhaps broadening horizons through experience appear to be very widespread. The emerging field of evolutionary psychology suggests that human desires do indeed have their roots in ancestral origins.[36]

Genetic succession depends on two critical factors: surviving long enough to reach reproductive age and finding a mate. So human nature is conditioned by the need to get the material, social, and sexual resources required for these tasks. In particular, argues evolutionary psychology, people are predisposed to "position" themselves constantly in relation to the opposite sex and against their sexual competitors. As a (male) reviewer of one book on evolutionary psychology noted with some glee: "Animals and plants invented sex to fend off parasitic infection. Now look where it has got us. Men want BMWs, power and money in order to pair-bond with women who are blonde, youthful and narrow-waisted."[37]

To make matters worse, this fundamental element of sexual competition never abates. People adapt to any given level of satisfaction and continually expand their aspirations. This response may be conditioned by the fact that everyone else is engaged in the same unending struggle. There is an evolutionary advantage in never being satisfied. But the result is that people find themselves condemned to run faster and faster, like the Red Queen in Lewis Carroll's novel *Through the Looking Glass*, just to maintain their position in the race.[38]

The idea that consumerism may have something to do with sex has a clear resonance with common wisdom. Advertisers and media executives are extraordinarily creative in using sex and sexual imagery to sell their products. In a recent study of people's behavior in three completely different cultures, researchers found that consumer moti-vations are almost inextricably entwined in the language and imagery of sexual desire. The fact that material things play a role in creating and maintaining desire is central here. As a respondent in the study remarked: "No one's gonna spot you across the other side of a crowded room and say: 'Wow! Nice personality!'"[39]

Survival itself is mediated by social status. This is most graphically illustrated by the plight of India's 170 million Dalits. Literally translated, Dalits means "the broken people," and life at the bottom of India's caste system is tough. Infant mortality and undernourishment are high; literacy, access to health care, and life expectancy are all significantly lower than the national average. Workers in the stone trade—almost exclusively Dalits—can have a life expectancy as low as 30 years, compared with a national average of 62.[40]

This effect is by no means confined to poorer countries. Recent evidence has shown how closely health and well-being are related to social status in industrial countries. A fascinating example of this was revealed by the U.K. government's research on life satisfaction across different "life domains." (See Figure 4–3.) Poorer people reported lower life satisfaction in almost all domains. One notable exception was higher satisfaction with their community. People employed in higher-status jobs pay a price, it seems, in terms of social relationships. Being poor may have some limited advantages in this one area. On the whole, however, inequality favors the rich. Though it might undermine social relationships, reduce overall well-being, and even corrupt values in pathological ways, the evidence suggests that being better off really does pay in terms of individual well-being.[41]

The problem for society is threefold. First, at the aggregate level, this intense status competition leads to less happy societies. Unequal societies systematically report higher levels of "distress" than more equal ones. Second, this mechanism for achieving happiness appears to have no endpoint. There is no getting off the "hedonic treadmill" of rising income and increasing consumption. Third, the environmental and resource implications of this unproductive "race to the top" are quite simply unsustainable. Taken together with the vast inequalities—the "oceans of poverty"—that still persist across the world, these three problems represent an enormous challenge to consumerism. But they also begin to point toward the importance of social structure in determining whether or not society is sustainable.[42]

Figure 4–3. Domain Satisfaction by Social Group, England

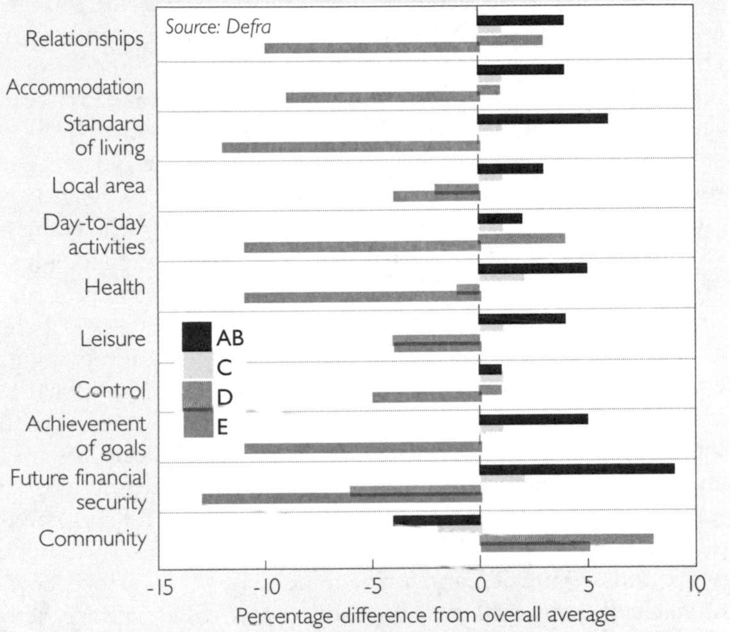

Source: Defra

Percentage difference from overall average

Key (examples of occupations in each social group)
AB: doctor, lawyer, accountant, teacher, nurse, police officer
C: junior manager, student, clerical worker, foreperson, plumber
D: manual worker, shop worker, apprentice
E: casual laborer, unemployed

The "Iron Cage" of Consumerism

Left to their own devices, it seems, there is not much hope that people will spontaneously behave sustainably. As evolutionary biologist Richard Dawkins has concluded, sustainability just "doesn't come naturally" to humankind. But it is a mistake to assume that evolutionary motivations are all selfish. Evolution does not preclude moral, social, and altruistic behaviors. Social behaviors evolved in humans precisely because they offer selec-

tive advantages to the species. An important lesson from evolutionary psychology is that the balance between selfish and cooperative behaviors depends critically on the kind of society they occur in.[43]

Social behavior can exist—to some extent—in all societies. In very competitive societies, self-serving behavior tends to be more successful than cooperation. But in a society characterized by cooperation, altruistic behaviors tend to be favored over selfish ones. In other words, the balance between altruism and selfishness is not hardwired in people at all. It depends critically on social conditions: rules, regulations, cultural norms and expectations, government itself, and the set of institutions that frame and constrain the social world.[44]

So there are some searching questions to ask about the balance of the institutions that characterize modern society. Do they promote competition or cooperation? Do they reward self-serving behavior or people who sacrifice their own gain to serve others? What signals do government, schools, the media, and religious and community institutions send out to people? Which behaviors are supported by public investment and infrastructure and which are discouraged?

Increasingly, it seems, the institutions of consumer society encourage individualism and competition and discourage social behavior. Examples are legion: private transport is encouraged through incentives over public transport; motorists are given priority over pedestrians; energy supply is subsidized and protected, while demand management is often chaotic and expensive; waste disposal is cheap, economically and behaviorally, while recycling demands time and effort. These kinds of asymmetry represent an "infrastructure of consumption" that sends all the wrong signals, penalizing pro-environmental behavior, making it all but impossible even for highly motivated people to act sustainably without personal sacrifice.[45]

Increasingly, it seems, the institutions of consumer society encourage individualism and competition and discourage social behavior.

Equally important are the subtle but damaging signals sent by government, regulatory frameworks, financial institutions, the media, and education systems. Salaries in business are higher than those in the public sector, particularly at the top; nurses and those in the caring professions are consis-

tently poorly paid; private investment capital is written down at high discount rates, making long-term costs invisible; success is counted in terms of material status; children are becoming a "shopping generation"—hooked on brand, celebrity, and status.[46]

At one level, the task facing sustainability is as old as the hills: balancing individual freedoms against the social good. This relies crucially on being able to make prudent choices, at the individual and the social level, between the present and the future. Rampant individualistic behavior that seeks short-term gratification ends up undermining well-being not just for the individual but for society as a whole. So the task for sustainability—indeed, for any society—is to devise mechanisms that prevent this "undermining of well-being" and preserve the balance between present desires and future needs.

Oxford economic historian Avner Offer addresses exactly this task in *The Challenge of Affluence*. Unaided, argues Offer, individual choices tend to be irredeemably myopic. People favor today too much over tomorrow, in ways that—to an economist—are entirely inexplicable under any rational rate of discounting of the future. Offer's unique contribution is to suggest that this fallibility has (or in the past had) a social solution. And that solution is precisely what affluence is in the process of eroding.[47]

To avoid trading away long-term well-being for the sake of momentary pleasures, society has evolved a whole set of "commitment devices": social and institutional "mechanisms" that constrain people's choices in ways that moderate the balance of choice away from the present and in favor of the future. Savings accounts, marriage, norms for social behavior, government itself in some sense—all these can be regarded as examples of mechanisms that make it a little easier for people to curtail their evolutionary appetites for immediate arousal and protect their own future interests. And, indeed, the interests of affected others.

The "challenge" Offer addresses is that affluence is eroding and undermining these commitment devices. The increase in family breakdown and the decline in trust have already been noted. Parenthood has been placed under increased financial and social pressure in industrial countries. And in terms of economic commitment, it is telling that savings rates fell worldwide in the second half of the last century, declining by 5–10 percentage points across the United States and Europe. Meanwhile, consumer debt has soared, rising from $1 trillion to $2.5 trillion in the United States alone between 1995 and 2007. The role of government itself has been increasingly "hollowed out" as politicians on both left and right sought to bolster economic output and free up the "invisible hand" of the market.[48]

The drivers behind these trends are complex, but a key responsibility, argues Offer, lies with the relentless stream of novelty inherent in consumption growth. Evidence seems to bear this out. "Accelerating the rate of innovation is a top priority for technology managers," notes the U.S.-based Industrial Research Institute. The rate of innovation is driven in turn by the structural reliance of businesses and the economy on growing consumption. Novelty keeps people buying more stuff. Buying more stuff keeps the economy going. The continuing expansion of the market into new areas and the continuing allegiance of consumers appear to be vital to this process—even as they erode commitment devices and undermine well-being.[49]

The end result is a society "locked in" to consumption growth by forces outside the control of individuals. Lured by humanity's evolutionary roots, bombarded with persuasion, and seduced by novelty: consumers are like children in a candy store, knowing that sugar is bad to eat, but unable to resist the temptation. This is a system in which no one is free. People are trapped by their own desires. Companies are driven by the need to create value for shareholders, to maximize profits. Nature and structure combine to lock people firmly into the "iron cage" of consumerism.[50]

Living Well— and Within Limits

Put simply, sustainability is about living well, within certain limits. For this to happen, across a global population approaching 7 billion and expected to reach 9 billion by 2050, people's patterns of consumption have to change.[51]

Achieving this is a colossal task. But it is not an impossible one. A proper understanding of the relationship between individual desires and the social good is vital here. As noted earlier, consuming comes naturally to humankind. Restraint does not. Change requires a supportive social environment. People are torn constantly between self-enhancement and self-transcendence. There is little individuals can do to shift their underlying nature. But the balance between self-serving and social behaviors is malleable at the social level. In one social context, selfishness will imprison us, impoverish people's lives, and may ultimately destroy the living environment. In another, the common good will prevails and people's lives will be richer, more satisfying, and more fulfilling.

There is clear evidence of an appetite for change. During an 18-month project, the Sustainable Consumption Roundtable in the United Kingdom identified a strong desire for collective action. *I Will If You Will*—the title of the Roundtable report—was a common theme emerging from a range of social research. This effect is not confined to the United Kingdom. The evidence on downshifting and simplicity, reactions against consumerism, the high levels of commitment to change (even in developing countries) found in the HSBC survey, a rising interest in alternatives to consumerism: all these are real, demonstrable effects. But good intentions are not enough, and they will continue to be undermined unless physical infrastructure, institutions, and social structures change.[52]

Who is capable of influencing these wider structures? Ultimately, of course, all sections of society must take responsibility for change. Government, business, and consumers all have some role to play; the media, community groups, religious institutions, and traditional wisdom are all essential influences on the social environment. But without strong leadership from government, change will be impossible. Individuals are too exposed to social signals and status competition. Businesses operate in competitive markets. A transition from self-interest to social behaviors requires changes in underlying structures— changes that strengthen commitment and encourage social behavior. Government is the principal agent in protecting the social good. A new vision of governance that embraces this role is critical.

Two or three key tasks are vital here. In the first place, policies need to support an infrastructure of sustainability: access to reliable public transport, recycling facilities, energy efficiency services, maintenance and repair, re-engineering and reuse. Systematic biases against these facilities have to be dismantled and policies to encourage them brought into place.[53]

The second key task lies in establishing fiscal and institutional frameworks that send consistent signals to businesses and consumers about sustainable consumption. A core example of this is the role of a "social cost of carbon" in providing incentives for investments in low-carbon technologies and behaviors. The Stern Review on the economics of climate change suggests that this cost might be as high as $85 per ton of CO_2. There is no doubt that internalizing this cost in market prices and investment decisions would have a major influence on reducing carbon emissions. The review also cast doubt on prevailing discounting practices, suggesting that zero or even negative discount rates might be appropriate when looking at projects with long-term impacts on the environment.[54]

But the role of government is not confined to fiscal frameworks. The way energy industries are regulated, for instance, has a profound effect on the incentives for demand management and energy service companies. Product policy can have a significant influence on access to durable, efficient products that minimize environmental harm. Recent EU legislation, for example, has already led to progressive improvements in the efficiency of energy-consuming appliances. Australia pledged early in 2007 to outlaw incandescent lightbulbs before 2010. The 27 EU nations have now followed that example. Surveying evidence of policy successes, the Sustainable Consumption Roundtable found that progressive standards, clearly signaled to manufacturers in advance, are a particularly effective instrument for moving toward more-sustainable consumption.[55]

The influence of government on social norms and expectations is, at first sight, less obvious. Policymakers are uncomfortable with the idea that they have a role in influencing people's values. But the truth is that governments intervene constantly in the social context. Myriad different signals are sent out, for example, by the way education is structured, by the importance accorded to economic indicators, by guidelines for public sector performance, by public procurement policies, by the impact of planning guidelines on public and social spaces, by the influence of wage policy on the work-life balance, by the impact of employment policy on economic mobility (and hence on family structure and stability), by the effect of trading standards on consumer behavior, by the degree of regulation of advertising and the media, and by the support offered to community initiatives and faith groups. In all these arenas, policy shapes and helps create the social world.

As this chapter suggests, the drift of these influences over the last few decades has been away from encouraging commitment and in favor of encouraging consumption. But there are some striking counterexamples: places where strenuous efforts have been made to rein in consumerism and focus more specifically on well-being. Several nations, including the United Kingdom, Canada, and China, have begun to develop "well-being accounts"—new ways of measuring national progress alongside or in place of the GDP. (See Chapter 2.) In late 2007, the Organisation for Economic Co-operation and Development, the European Commission, and several nongovernmental groups cohosted a major international conference, "Beyond GDP," designed to look at more effective measures of social progress.[56]

A crucial arena for action lies in advertising, particularly ads directed at children. Global advertising expenditures now amount to $605 billion (with the United States alone accounting for $292 billion). The figure is growing at the rate of 5–6 percent a year, with online advertising growing faster than any other sector, at between 30 percent and 40 percent a year. The impact of this, particularly on children, is pernicious. Marketing pressure has been linked explicitly to rising childhood obesity.[57]

At an international conference in 2006, the World Health Organization stopped short of banning advertising to children, but Scandinavian nations have taken a more proactive stance. In Sweden, TV advertising to children under 12 is banned. Norway, too, has restrictions on children's advertising, and the Consumer Ombudsman has an educational role in Norwegian schools. Recent advertising guidelines in Norway include a ban on advertising cars as "green," "clean," or "environmentally friendly." Although a Norwegian plan to develop anti-consumption adverts failed to attract funding in the United Nations, the nongovernmental group Adbusters, based in Vancouver, Canada, remains a focus of resistance to commercial advertising. Perhaps most striking of all, São Paulo, Brazil, the fourth largest city in the world, has recently become the first city outside socialist economies to ban outdoor advertising.[58]

Australia pledged early in 2007 to outlaw incandescent lightbulbs before 2010.

Religious leadership has declined substantially in industrial countries. But traditional wisdom is still an important influence on the debate about living well. In less secular societies, religion plays a number of roles. It warns against material excess; it provides a social and spiritual context for self-transcendence, altruism, and other-regarding behavior; and it offers a space for contemplation in which to make sense of people's lives in deeper and more meaningful ways than those provided by the fleeting consolations of consumerism.

One thing is clear: if a part of the function of consumerism is to deliver hope—as indicated earlier—then countering consumerism means building new avenues of hope that are less reliant on material goods. In countries where religious institutions are still strong, this task is much easier. In Southeast Asia, for example, in response to the economic crisis of the mid-1990s, the King of Thailand revived the traditional concept of the Sufficiency Economy, built on Buddhist principles, and provided a much-needed frame of reference to help countless microenterprises in rural villages survive the economic shocks of the recession and build a sustainable future in its aftermath. In the mountain Kingdom of Bhutan, progress is being reconceived in part as a spiritual endeavor. In many Islamic nations, the framework for moral restraint is already in place. From a western perspective, this framework is often seen as oppressive of individual freedoms, particularly for women. But Islam—and other religious traditions— are important sources of understanding the limits of relying on human nature to protect the public good.[59]

In the final analysis, the consumer society offers neither a durable sense of meaning in people's lives nor any consolation for losses. The erosion of religious participation in the West offers one more example of crumbling commitment devices. The examples in this chapter bear testament to the desire for change and the visionary courage of individuals, communities, and a handful of political leaders prepared to initiate that change. Millions of people have already discovered that treading more lightly allows them to breathe more easily. And it offers a new creative space for social change—a place where family, friendship, community, and a renewed sense of meaning and purpose are possible.

A sustainable world is not an impoverished world but one that is prosperous in different ways. The challenge for the twenty-first century is to create that world.

CHAPTER 5

Meat and Seafood: The Global Diet's Most Costly Ingredients

Brian Halweil and Danielle Nierenberg

Walk into any kitchen around the world and there's a good chance that meat or seafood sit neatly at the center of the meal. This is especially true at any top restaurant in New York, Rio, or Beijing. But billions of people all over the world have hamburgers or pork chops or fish fingers with their families at home every night. Even the poorest people often spend their extra income on some odd cuts of meat or fish bones for soup. In fact, meat and seafood are the two most rapidly growing ingredients in the global diet. Yet in terms of resource use, these are also two of the most costly.

In 2006 farmers produced an estimated 276 million tons of chicken, pork, beef, and other meat—four times as much as in 1961. On average, each person eats twice as much meat as back then, about 43 kilograms. And the fishing industry harvested about 141 million tons of seafood globally in 2005, the last year for which data are available. That was eight times as much as in 1950, with each person on average eating four times as much seafood as before. (See Fig-ure 5–1 and Table 5–1.)[1]

For people living in wealthy nations, seafood is an increasingly popular health food option; with its high levels of fatty acids and trace minerals, nutritionists recognize seafood as essential to the development and maintenance of good neurological function, not to mention a reduced risk of cancer, heart disease, and other debilitating conditions. In poorer nations in Asia, Africa, and Latin America, people are also eating more fish if they can afford it. And Chinese consumers now eat roughly five times as much seafood per person as they did in 1961, while total fish consumption in China has increased more than 10-fold. For more than a billion people, mostly in Asia, fish now supply 30 percent of their protein, versus just 6 percent worldwide.[2]

The good news is that there are methods of raising beef, pork, and chicken that do not create mountains of toxic manure and consume huge amounts of grain and water, as well as techniques for catching fish that do not end up destroying coral reefs and ensnaring

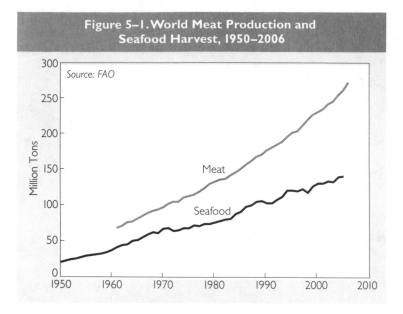

Figure 5–1. World Meat Production and Seafood Harvest, 1950–2006

Source: FAO

breeding and farm structure and with the rise of corporate agribusiness. Before World War II, cattle were raised on the open range, eating a grass-based diet. Chickens—raised mostly for their eggs, not meat—were allowed to forage outdoors for grass and insects. Pigs, while usually enclosed in open air pens, were given sufficient space to nest and root, as well as access to fresh air and sunlight. And the manure these animals produced was used efficiently to fertilize crops.[3]

seabirds and turtles. These innovations will be much cheaper in terms of energy and resource use as well as health impacts. But the price that consumers pay at the store or market will likely rise. Rethinking how fish and meat are produced will mean that consumers in industrial countries will have to eat fewer of these products—surf-and-turf dinners for executives may become a thing of the past, as will cheap fast-food meals of fried fish and hamburgers that have become a dinnertime staple for busy families. Eating less of these foods now, however, is a sort of investment in the future, since it will mean saving family farms, improving rangeland, reducing water pollution, and—in the case of wild fish—preserving a catch that is increasingly scarce.

Changing Production Methods

How did the meat and seafood that people eat change so dramatically? Industrial meat production took off in the early twentieth century with a series of changes in animal

But starting in the 1930s farmers began raising chickens for meat as well as eggs. Researchers developed new, higher-efficiency feed for these meat chickens, now called broilers. Then scientists discovered that adding antibiotics to feed caused these birds—and other farm animals—to gain weight quicker. Since the 1950s, the time it takes to raise broiler chickens decreased by half, from 84 to 45 days. Today broilers eat less than half as much feed and reach a weight of 2 kilograms in about one third as much time. By the 1960s, pigs and cows were also being raised in feedlots and confined animal feeding operations—indoor enclosures that can hold thousands of animals.[4]

In the case of fishing, the technologies were different but the broad changes in the industry were largely the same. Fishing fleets became larger, more powerful, and better at extracting fish from ever more remote corners of the ocean. Boats now depend on devices such as sonar technology, satellite navigation

Table 5–1. Meat and Seafood Consumption in Top Five Countries or Regions, 2005, and Increase since 1961				
Country	Meat		Seafood	
	(kilograms per person)	(percent increase since 1961)	(kilograms per person)	(percent increase since 1961)
China	55.5	14.6	25.8	5.4
Japan	91.0	1.7	66.5	1.4
European Union	44.3	5.9	26.5	1.5
United States	123.5	1.4	23.2	1.8
India	6.0	1.6	4.9	2.6
World	42	1.8	23.5	1.8

Source: See endnote 1.

systems, depth sensors, and detailed maps of the ocean floor. Enormous nets made out of synthetic fibers and huge winches give boats access to previously unreachable deep-sea areas where fish gather and spawn. Some fishing boats in the Atlantic Ocean use spotter planes, while in the Pacific fishers use helicopters to seek out schools of prized fish and scoop them up in huge quantities. These technologies are part of the reason that the wild fish catch holds steady at about 70 million tons even though scientists estimate that the fishing industry has eliminated 90 percent of the large fish in the ocean.[5]

When these practices first emerged in fishing ports and rural farming areas, they might have seemed like a good idea—more seafood harvested by bigger boats and fewer fishers; more meat on a more reliable schedule at a lower price. Agribusiness executives saw profits jump. Politicians supported the shift in the interest of competing better with other nations, having more abundant food supplies, and in some cases lowering food prices.

But these lower prices were an illusion. By raising meat in factory farms and grabbing fish and other seafood from the ocean with huge

trawlers and other industrial fishing techniques, current production methods are endangering people's health while also threatening the long-term stability of the land, oceans, and genetic diversity that sustain production itself.

In one particularly ironic case, producing meat in midwestern factory farms may actually be reducing the fish harvest from one of the most productive U.S. fisheries. The fertilizers used to grow corn for animal feed run off into surface water and eventually make their way down into the Gulf of Mexico, where they have created a "dead zone" the size of New Jersey. The nitrogen-based fertilizers encourage algae blooms that rob other ocean life of oxygen. This area produces some $662 million worth of seafood each year, nearly one fifth of the entire fishing yield from the United States. And although there is only anecdotal evidence of a decline in fisheries harvests in the Gulf, experience from other less severe dead zones around the world shows that catches can drop precipitously.[6]

Emerging concerns about these two food sources—including avian flu and other new diseases in the case of meat and outright depletion and contamination in the case of seafood—are prompting consumers, fishers, farmers, and agribusiness to search for better alternatives.

Going Back to Nature

Part of the reason that livestock and fish farms have become ecological disasters is that they have moved away from mimicking the environment in which animals exist naturally. Decades ago, before the big jump in production, livestock played a symbiotic role on most farms—grazing on cropland before or after production and providing essential fertilizer in the form of manure. Fish ponds occupied a similar place on most farms, feeding off of agricultural waste and helping to enrich soil. But once farmers removed livestock and fish production from the land, the need for inputs jumped and the manure began to pile up.[7]

In places as diverse as the Philippines and Iowa, some farmers are going back to more traditional methods of farm animal production. Outside Manila, for example, innovative farmers have learned from the centuries-long practice of raising livestock and fish together. By rearing hogs, chickens, and tilapia and by growing rice, these farmers have created a self-sustaining system: the manure from the hogs and chickens fertilizes the algae in ponds needed for both tilapia and rice to grow. And in central Iowa, pig farmers are remodeling "conventional" concrete sheds for raising pigs into open areas with deep bedding and outdoor access and raising heritage pig breeds, like Berkshires and Tamworths. These breeds are more used to living outdoors, and because they are allowed to forage, their meat is tastier and healthier than factory-farmed pork.[8]

Outside Manila, innovative farmers have learned from the centuries-long practice of raising livestock and fish together.

These farms produce very little waste, provide a diversity of food, and give farmers a much needed sense of both food and economic security if prices for meat or fish fluctuate. The farms also cut down on veterinary costs: Animals that are raised outdoors rarely suffer from the respiratory ailments and other illnesses common in factory farms. And because farmers raising grass-fed animals have fewer of them than factory farms do, they are much better at spotting and treating sick and injured animals and at preventing potential pandemics like avian flu.[9]

Of course, going back to a more traditional way of raising meat and fish is not completely practical. Many people who used to farm have moved away from the countryside, and farms are bigger and more concentrated than they once were, all of which makes it hard to return to a more integrated form of production. But meat and seafood farmers around the world are mixing a dose of old-time practices with certain lessons from modern ecology and showing that they can raise just as much food, while greatly reducing the harm caused by their farms.

For years, for example, the pig industry has said that gestation crates—concrete stalls that do not allow pigs to move much, turn around, or act in other natural ways—are the most economical way of meeting demand for pork products. But recent Iowa State University research that compared the costs of raising sows (female pigs) in gestation crates and alternative structures found otherwise. Instead of confining pigs in crowded factory farms, the researchers reared sows in group hoop houses—pens that allow the animals to nest in straw and walk around freely. A two-year study found that sows in hoop houses had more live births than those in confinement facilities. Researchers also found that group housing could reduce production costs by as much as 11 percent compared with gestation crates. Pigs are not only very social creatures, but when allowed to nest together they can better control their own temperatures, which can improve overall health and performance, the researchers claimed.[10]

This type of mangement-intensive farming will also create more jobs. According to agricultural economist William Weida, one reason factory farms claim that they are profitable is that they need fewer people to take care of the animals. But recent evidence indicates that when animals are well cared for they perform better. Smithfield, for example, the world's largest pork producer, found at one of its hog farms in Mexico that productivity increased when they had more people tending the pigs. These practices are part of a much wider movement toward humanely raised and environmentally sustainable products from animals that were raised on grass.[11]

Raising cattle, cows, pigs, and chickens—and raising fewer of them—in more natural environments also has some significant benefits for what is likely the most pressing environmental issue today: climate change. Researchers at the University of Wales are looking at how introducing different grasses—which are what ruminants are meant to eat—into cattle diets can help reduce the methane emissions from belching, flatulent cows. While the diet fed to cattle and dairy cows on factory farms encourages them to gain weight quickly, it also leads to a variety of digestive problems. Scientists believe that more-digestible feed will reduce these problems and thus help curb methane emissions. Not surprisingly, some of the grasses found commonly in U.K. pastures and meadows—including white clover, rye, and a flower called bird's foot trefoil—are highly digestible. And a Swedish study in 2003 found that beef cattle raised organically on grass emit 40 percent less greenhouse gases and use 85 percent less energy making beef than cattle raised on grain.[12]

While improving meat farming largely means moving animals out of grain-focused feedlots and back onto the land, the simplest way to reform fish farming is by moving back down the food chain toward species that do not require as much fish feed. As seafood producers have begun farming fish to compensate for the depletion of wild fish stocks, farmed fish have grown to account for 40 per-

cent of all seafood eaten around the world. Industry analysts suspect this share will be well above half in the next few years. But much like the move to concentrated factory farms for meat, fish farming has been transformed from its ancient roots of efficiently reusing vegetable scraps, weeds, and manure to raise a few carp or catfish.[13]

The closely confined fish on industrial farms require massive inputs of feed, energy, and biocides to control disease, while also generating large amounts of manure. Today, fish farmers raising tuna, salmon, striped bass, shrimp, and other carnivores consume considerably more fish—anchovy, herring, capelin, and whiting--in the form of feed than they produce. In 1948, only 7.7 percent of total marine catch was reduced to fishmeal and fish oil. Now about 37 percent of global landings are reduced to feed, eliminating an important historical and future source of human sustenance.[14]

Understandably, farmers raise carnivorous fish like salmon, tuna, and cod in large open-ocean pens because of the high prices these fish command. Only a shift in taste by consumers will help push farmers toward raising more-efficient species like carp and catfish as well as shellfish. In the short term, however, fish farmers are at least starting to move—in line with the urgings of various concerned citizens' groups—in a better direction.[15]

Consider salmon, the first species to be raised in fish farms on a large scale. Several decades of production in nations like Chile, Norway, and the United States have shown that such farms also lead to large amounts of coastal pollution from waste and excess feed, the use of antibiotics and other chemicals to control disease, and the occasional escape of millions of salmon into nearby waters, where they often spread disease to remaining wild salmon.[16]

In response, the National Environmental

Trust and other conservation groups, fishing organizations, and marine scientists launched the Pure Salmon Campaign. The group has eight primary areas—such as waste, disease, and escapes—that they encourage salmon farms to address. In particular, the campaign has been lobbying for a move toward closed-container farms, so that water can be reused and any pollution from the fish can be treated and kept out of the surrounding waters. And they have started lobbying the world's largest salmon farming companies—including Marine Harvest, which controls more than 20 percent of global production—with a combination of shareholder resolutions and direct negotiations with corporate boards. Most recently, they helped convince Marine Harvest's largest shareholder (an avid angler for wild salmon) of the importance of closed-container farms.[17]

In many densely populated Asian nations, where demand for seafood is growing fastest, fish farming is a natural addition to existing rice farming operations.

But what about the high feed requirements in salmon, shrimp, and other carnivorous fish farms? Borrowing principles from ancient fish farms that raised several species of carp that each fed on a different plant or that combined ducks, fish, snails, and other organisms that fed off each other, integrated farms can reduce feed requirements and waste while generating more edible seafood than a fish monoculture does. While large-scale applications are still relatively few and far between, raising salmon with bottom-feeding fish, mussels, sea urchins, or algae can help eliminate most nitrogen "leakage" from the salmon, while also producing other harvestable crops. (Mussels actually grow 50 percent faster near salmon pens.)[18]

In Norway, several large farms have found that introducing cleaner fish—a species that cleans parasites and leftover food off other fish—into salmon pens dramatically reduces lice (the major disease of farmed salmon, which also has been spreading to and decimating wild salmon throughout the world) and feed wastage (as the cleaner fish scavenge what the salmon miss) and that the cleaner fish can later be harvested to turn into fishmeal. Salmon production remains the same while waste drops by more than half, the incidence of disease drops, and the farm harvests two or three additional crops.[19]

Because oysters, clams, scallops, mussels, and other shellfish eat algae and can help filter and reduce excess nutrients that run into the water and promote algae blooms, coastal communities around the world are using shellfish farms to remove nutrients from bays, rivers, and coastal waterways. Studies have shown that enhancing shellfish beds is a cheaper way to remove nitrogen from the water than sewage treatment plants. This allows sunlight to reach the bay bottom so that grasses and the other bases of the food chain thrive. "By providing these three services—filtration, stabilization and habitation—oysters engineered the ecosystem," wrote shellfish expert Rowan Jacobsen in *A Geography of Oysters* when describing the historic role of oysters in places like the Chesapeake Bay on the east coast or Puget Sound in the west.[20]

A return to oyster farming could not only result in lots of new jobs and shellfish to eat. It might actually be the best way to restore inland estuaries, coral reefs, and coastal ecosystems damaged by pollution, including the more than 200 large dead zones that have been caused by excess nutrient runoff. Moreover, the metal cages that hold the shellfish in these operations function as artificial reefs. Fishers have learned that striped bass, shad, and other species congregate around them.[21]

In many densely populated Asian nations, where demand for seafood is growing fastest, fish farming is a natural addition to existing rice farming operations. This isn't new. Archeological evidence shows that Chinese farmers have been raising fish in rice paddies for nearly 3,000 years. Vegetable scraps and crop residues are fed to fish, which in turn produce waste that is used to fertilize the fields. Farmers can also use fewer pesticides and herbicides, since fish help control pests by consuming the larvae and eating weeds and algae that compete with rice for nutrients. (Fish farming also helps to control malaria, since fish eat mosquito larvae.)

Farmers practicing rice-field culture in Bangladesh have managed to reduce production costs by 10 percent, and the average farm income has increased by 16 percent in just three years, buoyed by sales of fish fry and fingerlings as well as of fish that farmers do not eat. One hectare of rice field typically produces between 250 and 1,500 kilograms of fish. Thousands of rural Bangladeshis have already adopted this form of affordable aquaculture. And researchers suggest that farmers could quickly adapt this integrated system on about 40,000 hectares, generating 10,000–60,000 tons of fish, worth roughly $40 million a year.[22]

Such benefits are not restricted to Asia. A recent project that focused on increasing production at several hundred small-scale fish farms in Cameroon found that basic technical assistance—including regularity of feeding, proper stocking densities, and a harvest schedule—boosted production from 498 kilograms to 2,525 kilograms of fish per hectare and increased cash returns 16-fold. The researchers estimated that in areas with good market access, similar investments could add 5,300 tons of fresh fish to the food supply, put an additional $50 million into the local economy, and produce profits for each farm in the range of $2,000 a year—twice the average income per person.[23]

A Change in Incentives

For governments interested in being ahead of the pack in promoting ecological meat and seafood farms, the biggest priority is changing the major financial incentives they give to farmers and fishers. Right now, most subsidies keep farming and fishing mired in the status quo of destructive production. For instance, governments give farmers nearly $300 billion each year to grow a handful of commodities like corn and soybeans, which not only encourages chemical use and discourages diversity on the farm—since farms get paid based on how much of these crops they harvest—it also brings down the prices of these crops and turns corn and soybeans into a very cheap way to fatten animals.[24]

The Washington-based Environmental Working Group reports that direct subsidies for livestock between 1995 and 2005 totaled $2.9 billion in the United States alone. During the same time, corn and soybean producers—who provide, in effect, the fuel for confined animal feeding operations—received approximately $50 billion and $13 billion respectively.[25]

The estimated $30–40 billion in fisheries subsidies each year goes mainly to low-interest loans to replace old boats with more powerful, newer ones, to fishing port development, and to payoffs from wealthy nations that wish to gain access to the fishing grounds of poorer countries. As one historic analysis of fisheries subsidies noted, "in the 1950s and 1960s, the more boat-building subsidies you gave, the more fish you got." But since more than two thirds of ocean fisheries are now fully exploited, continued subsidies mean that too many fishers are going after too few fish.[26]

As Daniel Pauly of the Sea Around Us Project at the University of British Columbia notes, the public pays for these subsidies with tax dollars and is rewarded with cheaper fish only in the short term. As in agriculture, the wealthiest nations and the largest boats reap most of the benefits: the United States, the European Union, and Japan account for 75–85 percent of fisheries subsidies.[27]

In both farming and fishing, subsidy reform does not have to mean fewer jobs and less food.

Because this support structure favors larger, less diverse, more capital-intensive operations, the prevailing policy actually discourages more diverse and humane livestock farms and less destructive fishing operations.

Subsidies have proved particularly resistant to reform as the recipients have amassed political clout on a par with the payouts they receive. But a first approach would be to go after the most egregious subsidies, including fuel subsidies for fishing fleets. Ships that have to travel farther to find fish gobble up tremendous amounts of energy keeping the fish cool on the long trips back to shore. In 2000, fisheries around the world burned about 13 billion gallons of fuel to catch 80 million tons of fish. In other words, the world's fleets use about 12.5 times as much energy to catch fish as the fish provide to those who eat them.[28]

Consider bottom trawling. Dragging a net across the ocean bottom has been likened to clearcutting a forest in search of squirrels and chipmunks. Such fishing is energy-intensive and destroys habitat, including sensitive deep-sea areas that can harbor future populations of fish. Governments still give bottom trawlers about $152 million in subsidies. That is about 25 percent of the total value of the boats' catch, even though this fleet only yields about 10 percent of the catch in profits. In other words, the subsidies are the only reason fishers are still using the technique.[29]

Or consider subsidies in many developing nations that either directly or indirectly favor raising exotic breeds of animals The Farm Animal Genetic Resources Division of the U.N. Food and Agriculture Organization reports that subsidies for veterinary drugs can encourage raising animals that are not suited to particular climates or that have resistance to certain pests. But if these subsidies were removed and replaced with compensation for farmers who raised their animals outdoors on grass or who worked to conserve rare breeds, the environmental and public health benefits could be wide-ranging.[30]

In both farming and fishing, subsidy reform does not have to mean fewer jobs and less food. Redirecting subsidies that go to the largest operations can actually create more jobs, since small livestock farms and fishing vessels both employ more people per unit of food harvested. A study in Norway found that small-scale fisheries generate five times as many jobs per unit of landed value as large-scale ones. Small-scale fishers are also likely to use more selective and less destructive fishing practices—catching tuna with handlines, for instance, instead of long lines that snag sharks and seabirds or using passive traps to only catch certain fish instead of dragging, which kills everything in the net.[31]

And despite the fears of farmers and governments that eliminating subsidies would destroy agriculture, farmers and agribusiness can actually thrive with zero subsidies. In New Zealand, in 1984 a newly elected government stopped paying farmers for growing crops and raising animals. It was a shock to rural communities. But instead of destroying them, production of milk quadrupled.[32]

Without subsidies for fuel and grain, New Zealand dairy farms have turned to nurturing the nation's abundant pasture. Farmers shifted away from Jersey cows, with milk rich in butterfat, to larger Friesians, which provide more protein-rich milk. A "Kiwi cross" of the two breeds resulted in a higher-protein milk in a more compact, hardier animal. Today, cows in New Zealand cost less to feed and yield more milk solids, making them more profitable. Sheep farmers also responded, reducing their huge herds of mostly small and fatty lambs, importing breeds from Finland and Denmark to improve the fertility of their ewes, and producing larger, leaner lambs that were both less expensive to raise and more appealing to health-conscious consumers.[33]

In other cases, subsidies can help jumpstart a completely different regulation of the oceans. Some maritime nations, including Belgium, Canada, China, Germany, New Zealand, and the United Kingdom, are beginning to shift their fisheries subsidies toward establishing marine reserves in which a swath of ocean is made off-limits to any fishing.[34]

In contrast to the current system, which regulates fish species by species and which sets sometimes controversial limits on how much of each can be caught in a given time, marine reserves do not require expensive data collection programs in order to gain a detailed understanding of the fish stock. Nature manages itself; the entire ecosystem gets protection rather than just one species, and fish have a safe place to get big, spawn, and produce young fish that migrate out of the preserve. Evidence shows that fish populations recover rapidly in such reserves and that nearby fish catches and sizes increase dramatically after a reserve is set up.[35]

A recent study estimated that establishing reserves for all the world's major fisheries would cost $5–19 billion each year and create about 1 million jobs. Beyond increasing the fish catch, these reserves make ideal centers for tourism and help restore coral reefs, mangroves, and other ocean ecosystems, yielding other benefits to society. Delegates at the 2002 World Summit on Sustainable Development and the 2003 World Parks Congress called for the establishment of a global system of marine protected areas, and scientists estimate that making just 20 percent of the oceans off-limits to fishing would be sufficient. Today only 1 percent of the world's ocean area is currently protected.[36]

Embracing the Ethical

Governments and policymakers can shift policy and enact regulations on food, but it is consumers and big buyers who can rapidly reshape the market and make the most impact by voting with their food dollars. From farm-friendly companies like Niman Ranch and Heritage Foods U.S.A. to major corporations like Whole Foods, and even Smithfield Foods, business is starting to meet consumer demand for safe, humane, and sustainable meat production. The same is happening in the seafood supply chain—from fishing cooperatives whose members are returning to less destructive artisanal methods to large supermarket chains that are marketing sustainable seafood as the healthier choice.

There are two sides to this innovation—a move by the food industry to embrace ecologically sustainable food and label it as such and a reciprocal response from shoppers who seek out this choice. In some cases consumers help set the relationship in motion. Heritage and rare breeds of livestock are coming back in vogue because of their unique qualities: healthier meat, milk, and eggs and better flavor. More sustainable fish also are often the ones that have a lower risk of mercury contamination, because they tend to be lower on the marine food chain.

These markets for ethical meat and seafood cannot grow without clear labels and certification programs that ensure that one farmer or fisher is different from another—and that consumers are really getting what they pay for. In the case of seafood, the impetus for such certification actually came from Unilever, the Dutch food and consumer products giant. In the 1990s, Unilever—then the world's largest seafood buyer—faced considerable pressure from its customers and from environmental groups to rethink its seafood purchases. But the company needed some guidance on which species to avoid and which to favor.[37]

Working with WWF, Unilever helped create the Marine Stewardship Council (MSC) in 1997 to certify fish populations as sustainable and to provide direction for the nascent sustainable seafood market. The MSC is now supported by at least 100 corporate, environmental, and consumer organizations in more than 20 nations, all of whom have a stake in the future of the global seafood supply. Certified fisheries can use the group's "Fish Forever" ecolabel, signifying that their product was caught using environmentally sound, economical, and socially responsible management practices. More than 300 seafood products bearing the MSC blue ecolabel are available in supermarkets in nearly 30 nations.[38]

Certain seafood companies are beginning to base their entire business on "the story behind the fish"—how it was raised, caught, and processed—just as many supermarkets and agribusinesses now capitalize on rising global interest in organic produce, grass-fed beef, and other "environmentally friendly" food choices. Consider EcoFish, a distributor based in the state of New Hampshire. Founded in 1999 as the only company in the world whose sole mission was to identify and market seafood originating from environmentally sustainable fisheries, EcoFish's products are now found in more than 1,000 stores and 150 restaurants throughout the United States. Another U.S. firm, CleanFish, specializes in finding a market for seafood caught by smaller-scale fishers around the world, whose artisanal techniques are less likely than large-scale fishing fleets to harm the marine environment (and the quality of the fish flesh).[39]

In contrast to certification through the MSC, an expensive process that can take some time and begins in response to requests from fisheries, EcoFish and CleanFish seek out seafood supplies from around the world and then assess whether they meet certain standards. This has allowed the two firms to offer a wider range of seafood—including farmed seafood—and to offer products years before they receive MSC certification. EcoFish recently received an investment grant that it hopes will allow its sales to grow fivefold in the next three years, to $15–20 million. EcoFish products are now available in 243 branches of Loblaws, Canada's largest seafood retailer.[40]

These innovations in sales pitch have a way of being contagious, particularly when they involve big players in the market. In June 2007 Tyson Foods—one of the largest meat processors in the world—decided to quit doing something that has been a hallmark of industrial animal agriculture since the 1950s. The company announced that the birds it sells to grocery stores and restaurants all over the country would no longer be treated with antibiotics. This move was not altogether altruistic or even based on health concerns about antibiotics resistance. Instead, Tyson was reacting to consumer demand for antibiotic-free meat products.[41]

Once one major industry player makes the shift, its competitors often must do the same or risk losing business. In early 2006, Darden Restaurants—parent company of Red Lobster, the top seafood restaurant chain in the United States, with 1,300 locations—

announced plans to certify all its farm-raised shrimp "to ensure it is grown in a sustainable way, with minimal impacts on the environment." And Wal-Mart, the world's largest retail store and the largest food seller in the United States, announced that within three to five years it would be certifying that all its seafood for the North American market was raised sustainably. Critics suggest the standards could be stiffer, and implementation is far from assured.[42]

Other big companies are also jumping on the natural, organic, or humanely raised bandwagon, partly for economic reasons. Smithfield announced in 2005 that it would only buy from suppliers who did not use antibiotics on their animals. Burger King—the second largest fast-food company—has said that it will try to buy animals that are given more living space. Natural foods giant Whole Foods will introduce labeling criteria in 2008 that give consumers detailed information about how the meat on their plates was raised, treated, and slaughtered.[43]

Consumers are also looking to connect directly with livestock producers. A few years ago it was hard for consumers to find farms where they could buy grass-fed and pasture-raised eggs, meat, and milk. Today there are more than 800 U.S. and Canadian farms listed on the Web site Eatwild.com, an organization that promotes grass-raised animal products.[44]

Fishing communities are a growing ally in this movement. Fishers are often the first to know that a given fish supply is endangered. So it is not surprising that fishers are using the newfound consumer awareness about the state of the world's fisheries to redefine their own role. In some cases this means returning to older fishing techniques that are less destructive and that help preserve the quality of the seafood. The Cape Cod Commercial Hook Fishermen's Association, faced with depletion of the cod stock that his-

torically sustained its members, decided to promote "old fashioned" hook lines that mean considerably less bycatch and fish that are less likely to get damaged, so that their texture and taste are usually superior.[45]

In other cases, like Alaska's wild salmon fishery or wild shrimp harvesters off Viet Nam's coast, fishers are forming cooperatives to manage a given fishery collectively and perhaps even to cut down on the total catch. When it is their own survival at stake, they are proving to be quite innovative. And just as seafood companies are beginning to see fish as a form of wildlife rather than just a commodity, fishers are making a similar shift in mindset, adopting a marketing strategy that treats the fish as a higher-value product rather than a low-cost raw material for processing.[46]

Moving Down the Industrial Food Chain

For the poor, whose diets might be confined to starchy staple crops, meat and seafood bring both increased status and added nutrition. For the wealthy, a meal is not complete unless it includes chicken, pork, or beef, while health-conscious consumers often replace the traditional meat serving with tuna, swordfish, or some other seafood. But consumers need to rethink their relationship with all these foods in order to keep them on the menus in fine restaurants as well as on the plates of people in the developing world.

Under this new food paradigm, people will need to reconsider the place of meat in their diets. Raising animals outdoors on grass will necessarily mean that there are fewer of them to eat, and higher prices for sustainably and humanely raised meat will mean shifting this from the center of each meal. The same is true for seafood. Fish, especially the big, carnivorous species, will not be as readily available, and consumers will have to eat fewer of them and more of certain other fish. Chefs, large food buyers, and consumers will need to explore less well known fish species and choose seafood that is lower on the marine food chain.

Many consumers are giving up meat altogether as the health and environmental benefits of doing so become clearer. And it is becoming easier to obtain meat alternatives. Researchers at the Vrije University of Amsterdam, for example, are developing alternative meats based on peas and other legumes that are highly nutritious, extremely economical, easy to prepare, and—perhaps most important—tasty. And consumer perception of these products has been positive, especially when people learn more about how their meat is raised and the ecological impact of raising animals in a densely populated nation like the Netherlands.[47]

Slow Food offers an alternative to fast-food culture by celebrating regional cuisines, distinct crop varieties, and forgotten food traditions.

While the growth of industrial meat and seafood production is likely inevitable in the developing world, livestock producers and fishers everywhere have an opportunity to improve meat and seafood. When it comes to producing meat, eggs, milk, and seafood, bigger does not necessarily mean better—or even more profitable.

For both meat and seafood, eating lower on the food chain generally reduces the harm done by these products. In the case of fish, the smaller, herbivorous species (shellfish, anchovies, catfish, and tilapia) are less endangered and fished in a less destructive way than the larger, carnivorous species (tuna, swordfish, and shark). For meat, eating fewer animal products in general and eating eggs, beef,

pork, and chicken from animals raised on a natural diet of grass is healthier for people, for the animals, and for the environment.

Many of the innovations that will reduce the ecological burden of meat and seafood can also help make these foods more available to poorer communities. Adding fish ponds to rice paddies and coastal agriculture is an easy way to boost a farmer's income and dietary options. Setting up no-fish zones around coral reefs and spawning grounds boosts the fish catch for both rich and poor fishers. And while cows or pigs bred for industrial-scale production may not thrive in poor areas where farmers cannot provide feed and veterinary inputs, hardier, indigenous breeds may be the best hope for adding milk and eggs to the local diet.

Rather than burden consumers with lengthy lists of "good" and "bad" food, a group called Slow Food International has tried to give seafood lovers, as a start, some basic rules of thumb that depend on a more holistic understanding of what is happening in the oceans. With a membership that includes 100,000 people in more than 80 nations, Slow Food offers an alternative to fast-food culture by celebrating regional cuisines, distinct crop varieties, and forgotten food traditions.[48]

The organization held a meeting in 2007 called Slow Fish that brought together small-scale fishers, chefs, and seafood companies to suggest how people could continue enjoying seafood without compromising responsibility. Participants called for support of "small-scale inshore fishing and ancient methods of fishing, processing and preserving which are sustainable and produce outstanding products that form part of our cultural identity." They urged people to eat fish lower on the food chain—such as the smaller, spinier fish that have long been part of Mediterranean cuisine—and to support traditional, low-impact types of fish farming, such as oyster farming and low-density freshwater pool systems.[49]

In Peru, several marine scientists have taken this message to heart and have launched a campaign to change the image of the *anchoveta* from something that only poor people eat to a fish that could be turned into a gourmet item consumed by connoisseurs. The Peruvian anchovy accounts for about one tenth of the wild fish netted around the globe each year. And yet nearly all of these small fish—chock full of the same beneficial fatty acids found in tuna, salmon and other big fish—get ground into fish meal and fish oil that will be used to fatten pigs and chickens in factory farms in North America, Europe, Japan, and other areas.[50]

As part of Discover the Anchovy Week in 2006, some 18,000 people tasted anchovies at 30 restaurants in Lima. Fresh anchovies are now available in many of the nation's markets, and the government is supplying the fish as part of its hunger programs. Researchers estimate that Peru could employ many more people and generate 10 times the revenues if the high-volume, low-value fishmeal industry were retooled to carefully package the anchovy as a fresh fish for local consumption and export.[51]

Part of the global impact of this gastronomic shift is that it would make much better use of beleaguered fish populations. "We can still savor seared ahi and grilled swordfish steaks—they have the best meat and few bones, after all—but we must reserve them as a luxury product," notes Martin Hall, chief scientist of the Dolphin Tuna Program at the Inter-American Tropical Tuna Commission. He explains that "it takes close to 60 million metric tons of potentially edible fish per year to feed the three million metric tons of the three major tropical tuna species we harvest annually. If we could replace some of our tuna sandwiches with the anchovies, sardines, squids, and other species the tuna eat, we would open up a substantial supply of protein that could feed millions more."[52]

In Japan, recent reductions in tuna catch quotas and soaring prices have prompted sushi chefs and home cooks in this fish-loving nation to search for substitutes. The Japanese consume about three quarters of the world's annual tuna catch. As the *New York Times* reported in the summer of 2007, Tadashi Yamagata, vice chairman of Japan's national union of sushi chefs, has been experimenting with tuna alternatives at Miyakozushi, his family's busy lunchtime restaurant in Tokyo. His most successful substitutes were ideas he "reverse imported" from American sushi bars, like "smoked duck with mayonnaise and crushed daikon with sea urchin."[53]

Other groups, like Heritage Foods USA, encourage customers to eat antique or heritage breeds of cows, pigs, chickens, and other foods in order to save them from extinction. The most well-known example is the turkey variety known as Bourbon Reds. These birds were almost extinct because of industrial farming practices that favor fast-growing but flavorless, big-breasted birds. Such birds are raised on factory farms, are never allowed to mate (they reproduce by artificial insemination), and are pumped full of antibiotics. But thanks to a consumer awareness campaign promoting the hearty, distinctive flavor of Bourbon Reds, these birds are in high demand—last year Heritage Foods sold 3,000 Bourbon Reds in the United States for Thanksgiving—and more and more farmers are raising them.[54]

In the developing world, groups such as GRAIN and the League for Pastoral Peoples are working hard to ensure that livestock genetic diversity is on the agenda of policymakers worldwide. Corporate agribusinesses, says GRAIN, have "dramatically increased their control over the livestock industry in recent years," and this makes the food system "dangerously dependent on a few corporations and a vulnerable, narrowing genetic base." The group also warns that the vast knowledge attained by livestock keepers over millennia is quickly disappearing and that there is an urgent need for pastoralists and livestock keepers to "reclaim their rights."[55]

Such a historical view is useful. Meat and seafood have long been a part of the human diet, but the form they take has changed as wild populations of fish have waxed and waned, as hunted game gave way to domesticated livestock, and as human desires and culinary fads shifted and spread. The meat of sharks was not in wide demand until recently, for example, when shark fin soup—an ancient Chinese dish that can cost $200 a bowl and was once reserved for the kitchens of the wealthy—became a more common menu item in economically booming China. The roaring market in these fins, which can fetch $700 a kilogram and entice shark hunters from as far away as Ecuador, is driving the killing of roughly 100 million sharks each year and the extinction of most major shark species.[56]

As part of a recent shark awareness campaign, the conservation group WildAid released several graphic videos of sharks being "finned" that were later aired on television in Taipei, Hong Kong, and Singapore. The group also features Asian celebrities like film director Ang Lee and Taiwan's President Chen Shui-bian in public service announcements asking people not to eat shark fin soup. These efforts seem to be paying off. Both Thai Airways and Singapore Airlines pulled shark fin soup from their first-class services in 2000, for instance. And in late 2005, several high-profile institutions in Hong Kong, including Disneyland and Hong Kong University, stopped serving shark fin soup following protests by animal rights and marine conservation groups.[57]

Following their lead would mean breaking with long-standing tradition, but it is not unprecedented. Stark white veal flesh has become a symbol of cruel caging techniques, while "rosey veal" from calves allowed to walk with their mothers is now showing up on menus. Savvy seafood processors are starting to favor wild harvested shrimp over shrimp raised on patches of deforested mangroves. Shark fins, like so many ecologically taxing food items that the planet can tolerate only on a small scale, are something people will need to give up.[58]

But we know that not all meat and seafood is created equal. And innovative farmers, fishers, and food companies have already shown that providing safe, tasty, and humane food does not have to cost our health and the environment so much.

CHAPTER 6

Building a Low-Carbon Economy

Christopher Flavin

Over the past half-million years, the world's climate has seen four ice ages and four warm periods separating them, with extensive glaciers engulfing large swaths of North America, Europe, and Asia and then retreating, thousands of species displaced, and the shape of coastlines rearranged as sea levels rose and fell. Yet throughout these hundreds of thousands of years, the atmospheric concentration of carbon dioxide (CO_2), which plays a key role in regulating the climate, has never risen above 300 parts per million.[1]

In 2007, the atmospheric concentration of CO_2 passed 382 parts per million—and it is already at the equivalent of 430 parts per million if the effect of other greenhouse gases is included. (See Figure 6–1.) Humanity is at risk of creating a climate unlike any seen before—unfolding at an unnatural, accelerated pace—more dramatic than any changes in the climate since Earth was last struck by a large asteroid nearly a million years ago. Unless greenhouse gas emissions begin to decline within the next decade, we risk triggering a runaway disruption of the world's climate, one that could last centuries and that our descendants would be powerless to stop.[2]

The world is entering uncharted territory. Fossil fuels made the modern economy and all of its material accomplishments possible. But building a low-carbon economy is now the central challenge of our age. Meeting that challenge will require restructuring the global energy industry through technological, economic, and policy innovations that are as unprecedented as the climate change it must address.

Avoiding Catastrophe

Only recently have scientists understood that changes in the concentration of carbon dioxide, methane, and other less common gases could trigger an ecological catastrophe of staggering proportions. The climate, it turns out, is not the vast, implacable system it appears to be.

Past climate changes have been caused by tiny alterations in Earth's orbit and orientation to the sun—providing, for example, just

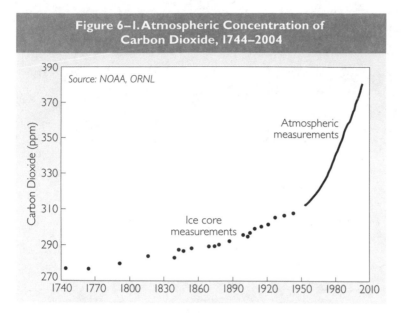

Figure 6–1. Atmospheric Concentration of Carbon Dioxide, 1744–2004

Source: NOAA, ORNL

Atmospheric measurements

Ice core measurements

point—or whether it already has—is not known. But it is already clear that ecological change of this magnitude would lead to unprecedented disruptions to the world's economies. A groundbreaking 2006 study led by former World Bank chief economist Nicholas Stern concluded that climate change could cut global economic output by between 5 and 20 percent. In his 2007 book, *The Age of Turbulence*, Alan Greenspan, the leading free-market economist of the day, included climate change as one of five forces that could derail the U.S. economy in the twenty-first century. The uneven and disruptive nature of these changes could set off an even more serious crisis as conflict within and between societies undermines their stability.[5]

enough added energy to warm the planet over thousands of years, increasing the concentration of carbon dioxide in the atmosphere, and in turn triggering even larger changes in the temperature, which scientists call a positive feedback. Today's massive release of CO_2 and other greenhouse gases is leading to far greater changes to the atmosphere in a period of decades.[3]

Scientists now project that within the decades immediately ahead, the capacity of the earth and ocean to absorb carbon emissions will decline, while vast changes in the Arctic may further accelerate warming. Melting tundra will release millions of tons of methane, a greenhouse gas more powerful than CO_2. And as the Arctic ice pack disappears in summer—nearly half is already gone—it will be like removing a large air conditioner from Earth's northern hemisphere. This will further warm the climate and could mean the end of the million-year-old Greenland ice sheet—which by itself contains enough water to raise worldwide sea levels by more than seven meters.[4]

When the world will reach such a tipping

In 2006 the combustion of fossil fuels released 8 billion tons of carbon to the atmosphere—nearly a million tons every hour—with coal and oil contributing roughly 40 percent each and natural gas accounting for the rest. (The manufacture of cement released nearly another 350 million tons, while deforestation and agriculture contributed roughly 1.6 billion tons.) Global fossil fuel carbon emissions have increased fivefold since 1950 and are up 30 percent just since 1990. Today, fossil fuels provide four fifths of the energy that powers the global economy.[6]

Burning fossil fuels on this scale is a vast and risky experiment with Earth's biosphere; scientists are still not sure when the world will cross an invisible but catastrophic threshold of no return. But growing evidence suggests that it may be close. James Hansen, Director of the NASA Goddard Institute of Space Studies, is among a growing group of climate scientists who believe that the world should make every effort to avoid pushing the atmospheric concentration of CO_2 beyond 450 parts per million and the effective concentration (including methane and trace gases) beyond 500 parts per million. This would limit the increase in the average global temperature to 2.4–2.8 degrees Celsius above pre-industrial levels. The increase so far is just under 0.8 degrees Celsius.[7]

To keep the world's climate within the range it has occupied for at least a million years, current emission trends will need to be quickly reversed, according to the complex models used by scientists and included in the report of the Intergovernmental Panel on Climate Change (IPCC) released in early 2007. The IPCC scenario that most closely matches likely ecological limits suggests that global carbon emissions will need to peak before 2020 and be reduced by 40–70 percent from the current emissions rate by 2050, eventually falling to zero.[8]

The magnitude of the challenge is clear when the emissions path needed to stay below an atmospheric CO_2 concentration of 450 parts per million is compared with the current path. (See Table 6–1.) The U.S. Department of Energy forecasts that both world energy use and carbon emissions will grow nearly 60 percent by 2030—an average rate of 1.8 percent per year. This would take emissions to nearly 12 billion tons in 2030 and, assuming continued growth at that rate, to almost 16 billion tons in 2050—nearly four times the annual emissions of 4 billion tons that would

Table 6–1. Global Energy Use and Carbon Emissions in 2006 and in 2050 Under Two Scenarios			
		2050	
Indicator	2006	Business as Usual	Stabilization Scenario
CO_2 concentration (parts per million)	382	~550	< 450
Energy (billion tons oil equivalent)	12	22	16
Energy-related carbon emissions (billion tons)	8	16	4

Source: See endnote 9.

be needed to keep the CO_2 concentration below 450 parts per million.[9]

Complicating the challenge is the fact that the energy needs of poor countries such as India and China have accelerated in recent years as they entered the most energy-intensive stages of their development—building industries and infrastructure at an astonishing pace. In 2006, industrial countries, with less than 20 percent of the world's population, contributed roughly 40 percent of global carbon emissions, and they are responsible for more than 60 percent of the total carbon dioxide that fossil fuel combustion has added to the atmosphere since the Industrial Revolution began. But this picture is now changing rapidly, particularly in China, where emissions are now rising at 10 percent a year—10 times the average rate in industrial nations. By 2006, China's fossil fuel emissions were only 12 percent below the United States—and gaining rapidly. (See Table 6–2.) Emissions are also growing quickly in the Middle East, where rapid population growth, rising oil wealth, and low, subsidized energy prices have led to skyrocketing energy demand.[10]

At the G-8 Economic Summit in Ger-

Table 6–2. Energy-Related Carbon Emissions, Selected Countries, 2006

Country or Region	Carbon Emissions*	Carbon Emissions, Per Capita	Carbon Emissions, Per $ GDP
	(million tons)	(tons)	(kilograms per $1,000 GDP (PPP))
United States	1,600	5.3	120
China	1,400	1.1	140
Western Europe	930	2.2	71
India	400	0.4	97
Japan	330	2.6	78
Africa	300	0.3	130
World	8,000	1.2	120

*Does not include emissions resulting from gas flaring, cement making, or land use change.
Source: See endnote 10.

many in June 2007, Canada, France, Germany, Italy, and Japan called for a 50-percent cut in global emissions by 2050—consistent with the trajectory needed to keep atmospheric concentrations below 450 parts per million. Although Russia and the United States abstained from that portion of the final statement, it is clear that the need for drastic cuts in emissions is increasingly accepted by political leaders as well as scientists. This is an ambitious goal, and achieving it will mean reversing an upward trend in carbon dioxide emissions that has been under way for a century and a half.[11]

Providing energy services for the much larger global economy of 2050 while reducing emissions to 4 billion tons of carbon will require an energy system that is very different from today's. For the world as a whole to cut emissions in half by 2050, today's industrial countries will need to cut theirs by more than 80 percent. Getting there depends on three elements in a climate strategy: capturing and storing the carbon contained in fos-

sil fuels, reducing energy consumption through new technologies and lifestyles, and shifting to carbon-free energy technologies.[12]

A variety of combinations of these three strategies can in theory do the job. Princeton scientists Robert Socolow and Stephen Pacala have broken the task down into 15 1-billion-ton "wedges" of reductions—including such options as improved fuel economy or massive construction of wind farms—that policymakers can choose from. The key question is which combination of strategies will minimize the substantial investment cost but also provide a healthy and secure energy system that will last.[13]

Phasing out oil, the most important fossil fuel today, may turn out to be the easiest part of the problem. Production of conventional crude oil is expected to peak and begin declining within the next decade or two. By 2050, output could be a third or more below the current level. Reliance on natural gas, which has not been as heavily exploited as oil and which releases half as much carbon per unit of energy as coal, is meanwhile likely to grow.[14]

But the slowdown in the rate of discovery of oil and gas is pushing world energy markets toward dirtier, more carbon-intensive fossil fuels. The greatest problem for the world's climate is coal, which is both more abundant and more carbon-intensive than oil, and the "unconventional" energy sources such as tar sands and oil shale, which at current oil prices have become economically accessible.

The central role of coal in the world's climate dilemma has led policymakers and industrialists to focus on so-called carbon capture and storage (CCS). Although it is only likely to be feasible for large, centralized uses of fossil fuels, many energy planners are counting on it. They hope to build a new generation of power plants equipped with devices that capture carbon either before or after the combustion of fossil fuels and then pipe the CO_2 into underground geological reservoirs or into the deep ocean, where it could in principle remain for millions of years.

Coal can either be gasified (as it already is in some advanced power plants), with the CO_2 then separated from the other gases, or it can be directly burned in a super-critical pulverized plant that also allows the capture of carbon dioxide. Three significant CCS projects are in operation in Algeria, Canada, and Norway. The facilities in Algeria and Norway simply capture CO_2 that is extracted together with natural gas, which is much easier than capturing CO_2 from coal combustion. A better demonstration of technical feasibility is offered by the sequestration project in Weyburn, Canada, which captures CO_2 from a coal gasification plant. However, even these advanced facilities lack the modeling, monitoring, and verification that are needed to resolve the many outstanding technical issues.[15]

The United States, the European Union, Japan, and China have all launched government-funded CCS programs in the last few years, but the pace of the programs is surprisingly lethargic, given the urgency of the climate problem and the fact that much of the power industry expects CCS to allow continued reliance on the hundreds of coal-fired power plants that today provide over 40 percent of the world's electricity. A 2007 study by the Massachusetts Institute of Technology (MIT) concluded that the U.S. Department of Energy's main program to demonstrate large-scale CCS is not on track to achieve rapid commercialization of key technologies.

Locating, testing, and licensing large-scale reservoirs where carbon dioxide can be stored is a particularly urgent task.[16]

In light of the lead times required for technology development and demonstration, it will be 2020 at the earliest before significant numbers of carbon-neutral coal plants come online. Nor is it guaranteed that CCS plants will be competitive with other carbon-free generators that are likely to be in the market by that date. But the bigger question is whether that would not be too late, considering the hundreds of new coal-fired power plants that are currently being considered in China, the United States, and other nations. To have any hope of halving carbon emissions by 2050, it is hard to avoid the conclusion that the uncontrolled burning of coal will need to be eliminated—and soon. In the meantime, a growing number of climate experts are calling for a moratorium on building new coal-fired power plants unless or until CCS becomes available.

The Convenient Truth

Many energy industry executives argue that reducing carbon emissions as rapidly as scientists now urge would risk an economic collapse. According to conventional wisdom, the available alternatives are just too small, unreliable, or expensive to do the job. In 2001, for example, Vice President Dick Cheney described saving energy as a moral virtue but not important enough to play a major role in the national energy policy proposals he was developing at the time. The World Energy Council, which represents the large energy companies that dominate today's energy economy, declared in 2007 that renewable energy has "enormous practical challenges.It is unlikely to deliver a significant decarbonisation of electricity quickly enough to meet the climate challenge."[17]

A thorough review of studies that assess the potential contribution of new energy options, as well as the rapid pace of technological and policy innovation now under way, points to the opposite conclusion. Improved energy productivity and renewable energy are both available in abundance—and new policies and technologies are rapidly making them more economically competitive with fossil fuels. In combination, these energy options represent the most robust alternative to the current energy system, capable of providing the diverse array of energy services that a modern economy requires. Given the urgency of the climate problem, that is indeed convenient.

The first step in establishing the viability of a climate-safe energy strategy is assessing the available resources and the potential role they might play. Surveys show that the resource base is indeed ample; the main factors limiting the pace of change are the economic challenge of accelerating investment in new energy options and the political challenge of overcoming the institutional barriers to change.

Energy productivity measures an economy's ability to extract useful services from the energy that is harnessed. From the earliest stages of the Industrial Revolution, energy productivity has steadily advanced; in the United States, the economy has grown 160 percent since 1973, while energy use has increased 31 percent, allowing the nation's energy productivity to double during the period. Germany and Japan, starting with higher productivity levels, have achieved comparable increases. But even today, well over half of the energy harnessed is converted to waste heat rather than being used to meet energy needs.[18]

This suggests enormous potential to improve energy productivity in the decades ahead. Light bulbs, electric motors, air conditioners, automobiles, power plants, computers, aircraft, and buildings are among the hundreds of systems and technologies that can be made far more efficient, in many cases just by using already available technologies more widely—such as compact fluorescent light bulbs and hybrid electric vehicles. Further gains can be made by altering the design of cities—increasing the role of public transport, walking, and cycling, while reducing dependence on automobiles.

A global assessment by the McKinsey Global Institute of the potential to improve energy productivity concluded that the rate of annual improvement between now and 2020 could be increased from 1 percent to 2 percent, which would slow the rate of global energy demand growth to just 1 percent a year. If these gains are extended to 2050, the growth in world energy use could be held to roughly 50 percent, rather than the doubling that is projected under most business-as-usual scenarios. This large difference represents the combined current energy consumption of Europe, Japan, and North America.[19]

The greatest potential turns out to lie in the most basic element of the energy economy—buildings—which could be improved with better insulation, more-efficient lighting, and better appliances, at costs that would be more than paid for by lower energy bills. With technologies available today, such as ground-source heat pumps that reduce the energy needed for heating and cooling by 70 percent, zero-net-energy buildings are possible that do not require fossil fuels at all. All countries have untapped potential like this to increase energy productivity, but the largest opportunities are found in the developing nations, where current energy productivity tends to be lower. Future increases in energy productivity will not only reduce consumption of fossil fuels, they will make it easier and more affordable to rapidly increase the use of carbon-free energy sources.[20]

On the supply side, one of the post-carbon

energy sources receiving much attention these days is nuclear power, which already plays a major role in some countries but faces considerable obstacles to its expansion in the decades ahead. (See Box 6–1.) Renewable energy, in contrast, relies on two primary energy sources—sunlight and the heat stored below the earth's surface—that are available in vast abundance. The sunlight alone that strikes Earth's land surface in two hours is equivalent to total human energy use in a year. While much of that sunlight becomes heat, solar energy is also responsible for the energy embodied in wind, hydro, wave, and biomass, each with the potential to be harnessed for human use. Only a small portion of that enormous daily, renewable flux of energy will ever be needed by humanity.[21]

Several studies have assessed the scale of the major renewable resources and what their

---

Box 6–1. What About Nuclear Power?

Nuclear power is a largely carbon-free energy source that could in theory help phase out fossil fuels. More than 300 nuclear plants currently provide 15 percent of the world's electricity. But this energy source has been plagued by a range of problems, most fundamentally high cost and the lack of public acceptance, that have halted development for more than 20 years in most of Europe and North America. Over the past decade, global nuclear capacity has expanded at a rate of less than 1 percent a year; in 2006, the world added 1 gigawatt of nuclear capacity but 15 gigawatts of wind capacity.

Major efforts are now under way to revive the nuclear industry—driven by a combination of high natural gas prices, concern about climate change, and a large dose of new government subsidies. Technology advances have led several companies to develop modestly revamped plant designs that are intended to make nuclear plants easier to control, less prone to accidents, and cheaper to build. The most important innovations are to standardize designs and streamline regulatory procedures. So far, two nuclear plants are being built in Europe, several are under construction in China, and the United States is expecting as many as 32 plants to be ordered by the end of 2008. Unfortunately for the industry, several different plant designs are being promoted by different companies, limiting the potential for standardization.

It is too early to tell whether these nuclear plants will be economical enough to launch a wave of construction. The first new European reactor has been under construction in Finland and is already two years behind schedule and $1 billion over budget. A study by a Keystone Center panel composed of academics, energy analysts, and industry representatives estimated the cost of new nuclear power at 8–11¢ per kilowatt-hour—more expensive than natural gas- and wind-powered generators. And because of large capital requirements and long lead times, nuclear plants face a risk premium that other generators do not.

Energy planners will also have to reckon with the scale and pace of construction that would be needed to make a serious dent in the world's climate problem. MIT researchers estimate that 1,000–1,500 new reactors would be needed by 2050 for nuclear to play a meaningful role in reducing global emissions—a construction pace 20 times that of the past decade and five times the peak level in the 1980s.

Many advocates of nuclear power argue that given the urgency of doing something about climate change quickly, it must be pursued. Speed, however, is not one of nuclear power's virtues. Planning, licensing, and constructing even a single nuclear plant typically takes a decade or more, and plants frequently fail to meet completion deadlines. Due to the dearth of orders in recent decades, the world currently has very limited capacity to manufacture many of the critical components of nuclear plants. Rebuilding that capacity will take a decade or more.

Source: See endnote 21.

practical contribution to the energy economy might one day be. One study by the National Renewable Energy Laboratory in the United States, for example, concluded that solar thermal power plants built in seven states in the U.S. Southwest could provide nearly seven times the nation's existing electric capacity from all sources. And mounting solar electric generators on just half of the suitable rooftop area could provide 25 percent of U.S. electricity. In the case of wind power, the Pacific Northwest Laboratory found that the land-based wind resources of Kansas, North Dakota, and Texas could meet all the nation's electricity needs, even with large areas excluded for environmental reasons.

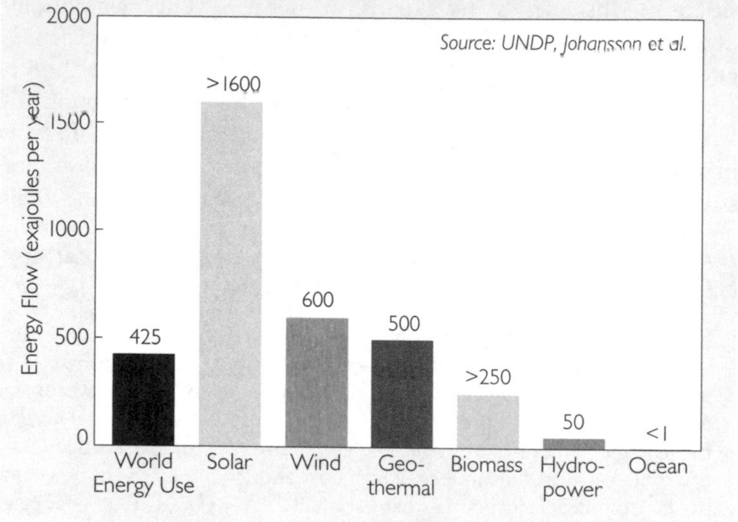

These reports demonstrate that resource availability will not be a limiting factor as the world seeks to replace fossil fuels. With improved technologies, greater efficiency, and lower costs, renewable energy could one day replace virtually all the carbon-based fuels that are so vital to today's economy. (See Figure 6–2 and Table 6–3.)[22]

Designs for a New Energy Economy

The greatest challenge for the widespread adoption of renewable energy sources is fitting them into an energy system that was designed around fossil fuels—fuels that have the advantage of being concentrated and easily stored.

Figure 6–2. Estimates of Available Energy Resources Using Today's Technology

Source: UNDP, Johansson et al.

To seriously de-carbonize the energy economy, ways must be found to power everything from transportation to the latest electronics on seemingly ephemeral energy sources such as solar energy and wind power.

Electricity is the single most important element of today's energy system, essential for lighting, cooling, electronics, and many industrial processes; its role will only grow as new technologies allow grid electricity to be used for plug-in hybrid cars and to heat and cool homes efficiently through ground-source heat pumps. Electricity also happens to be the output of the largest and most easily replaced contributor to carbon emissions: coal-fired power plants. It is therefore fortuitous that solar, wind, geothermal, ocean, and bioenergy are all able to produce electricity.

From the generator's viewpoint, the main disadvantage of most of these electricity sources is their intermittency—wind and solar, for example, tend to be available only 25–40 percent of the time, depending on the tech-

Table 6–3. Estimates of Potential Contribution of Renewable Energy Resources

Energy Source	Potential Contribution
Solar water heaters	Could provide half the world's hot water
Solar cells	Could supply 10 percent of grid electricity in the United States by 2030
Solar power plants	Seven states in U.S. Southwest could provide more than 7,000 gigawatts of solar generating capacity—nearly seven times U.S. electric capacity from all sources
Wind power	Could provide 20 percent of world's electricity; offshore wind farms could meet all of European Union's electricity needs
Biomass	One billion tons could be available for energy conversion in the United States in 2025, replacing one third of current oil use
Geothermal heat	Could provide 100 gigawatts of generating capacity in the United States alone
Wave and ocean thermal energy	Long-run contribution could be on same order of magnitude as current world energy use

Source: See endnote 22.

nology and site. Intermittency turns out, however, to be not as big a problem for renewable electricity as utility engineers once anticipated. Power companies are already accustomed to dealing with fluctuating demand, and even conventional power plants are sometimes shut down unexpectedly. So intermittency is not a new concept, though dealing with it does take planning and a willingness to make adjustments in grid operation as penetration levels rise.

Power companies in some regions have already gained experience in operating grids that include a sizable number of wind turbines. Several U.S. utilities have found that when wind turbines meet 10 percent of peak power demand, only minimal adjustments to grid operations are needed. And in areas of northern Europe, where wind contributes over 20 percent of peak power, only minor strengthening of grids and adjustments to the operations of other generators are required. Utilities with substantial hydropower capacity have the ability to quickly ramp up power generation when needed, but most use gas turbines to provide

"peak power" when demand is particularly high (or when other generators are not working.) Strengthening weather forecasting capabilities and interconnecting multiple, dispersed wind farms also enables utilities to avoid most problems related to high levels of dependence on wind power.[23]

As reliance on coal is reduced in the decades ahead, it is likely that many regions will move well beyond the 20 percent threshold for wind, solar, and other intermittent power sources. To do this, they can pursue some combination of three strategies: add local generating capacity using microturbines and fuel cells, move to digital "smart" grids that are more flexible in their ability to balance demand and supply, and develop the capacity to store energy economically so that it is available when needed.

The digital grid would allow the electricity system to operate much the way the Internet does—an electronically controlled grid that responds in real time to decisions made by users, providing the same kind of efficiency, interconnectivity, and precision as the digital devices that it powers. One advantage of such a system is that the electricity meter can be transformed into a consumer gateway that transmits price signals instantaneously and allows unneeded devices to be turned off when prices are high or renewable resources are not as available. Kurt Yeager, who directs the Galvin Electricity Initiative, believes that the introduction of digital grids will increase the ability to achieve higher levels of reliance on intermittent renewable generators.[24]

The ability to store energy is also developing rapidly. Wind farm operators' desire to qualify for the "capacity credits" earned when power can be generated during peak periods has pushed some to explore storage options, notably in the form of compressed air that can be kept in underground steel pipes or in geological formations. One company plans to mount a compressor under the structure that houses the generating components and send the compressed air down the tower, where it will be stored underground; when electricity is needed, the compressor is reversed, generating electricity. TXU, a large electric power company in Texas, recently canceled eight coal-fired power plants and is planning instead to build a 3,000-megawatt wind farm—larger than any now in operation—that may include compressed air storage.[25]

The development of less expensive, longer-lived batteries will further ease the way to greater reliance on renewable energy. Portable electronic devices and hybrid electric cars are rapidly increasing demand for advanced batteries made of nickel metal hydride and lithium; as they become less expensive and more widely used, these will allow power companies and consumers to complement distributed micro-solar generation with distributed storage. And the planned introduction of plug-in hybrid cars by General Motors and Toyota in the next few years will allow automobiles to run on sunlight and wind power as well as renew-

able biofuels, while the cars themselves can be plugged into the grid and used as "peaking plants" when demand is high.[26]

Flexible, secure electricity grids will be further aided by a new generation of micro-power generators that is being developed. Small-scale gas turbines, sterling engines, and fuel cells can easily generate up to a third of the total electricity supply, with the waste heat available for use in the buildings in which they are located. And unlike the large power plants that dominate today's power system, micro-generators will be able to respond quickly to shifts in demand. In the longer run, the natural gas that currently courses through the world's gas pipelines may be replaced by hydrogen or ammonia that is produced from a broad range of renewable resources.

The ability to integrate new energy sources into the existing energy infrastructure will speed the transition and reduce its cost. Already, wind power is being blended into many electric grids, while ethanol is being added to gasoline. In Brazil, most new cars are designed to run on any mixture of ethanol and gasoline. In Germany, local producers have begun to add biogas (methane) to natural gas pipelines. And in Japan, many homeowners are generating electricity with solar cells—sending power to their local grids as well as drawing from them.[27]

The Economics of Change

When oil was first discovered in western Pennsylvania in the 1860s, it was virtually useless—far more expensive than coal and, prior to the development of the refinery or internal combustion engine, useless for transportation. Even as oil became widely used for lighting in the late nineteenth century, the idea that it would become a dominant energy source—let alone reshape the global economy—was inconceivable.

The history of economic transformation follows a familiar path. Dominant technologies and businesses are generally reliable and economical, and over time they develop a network of institutional and political support that effectively resists change. New technologies and businesses generally enter a niche of the broader market, offering a higher cost service that meets specialized needs. But over time the new competitor becomes more economical and widens its share of the market, eventually undercutting the cost of the dominant player and gradually remolding the institutional infrastructure to meet its own needs. The transition from one generation of technology to another is often gradual at first, but then speeds up as the economic advantage flips.

According to conventional wisdom, the energy sector is far from such a transformation. New renewable energy sources represent less than 2 percent of the total energy supply, and in 2007 total U.S. government support of renewable energy R&D came to little more than $600 million—about what the government spent in Iraq in a single day. What these figures fail to capture is the recent infusion of private- sector capital and technology and the fact that today's renewable energy pioneers are not limited to "energy technology" but rather draw on fields as diverse as semiconductor physics, biotechnology, aerodynamics, and computer engineering.[28]

Over the past five years, the manufacture of wind turbines has grown at 17 percent annually, and solar cells at a 46-percent annual rate. This rapid growth has turned these industries into lucrative businesses, with demand outrunning supply and profits soaring. Some $52 billion was invested in renewable energy in 2006, up 33 percent from 2005. (See Figure 6–3.) At that level, investment in renewable energy is already one quarter that of the oil industry—and gaining ground rapidly. Some of the world's leading corporations have made major investments in renewable energy, including Applied Materials (solar photovoltaics (PV)), BP (wind and solar PV), General Electric (wind), DuPont (biofuels), Goldman Sachs (wind, and central solar), Mitsubishi (wind), Royal Dutch Shell (wind, hydrogen, and solar PV), Sharp (solar PV), and Siemens (wind).[29]

Corporate R&D on clean energy technologies reached $9.1 billion in 2006. A single company, Vestas Wind Systems, spent $120 million on R&D in 2006, while the U.S. government spent less than $50 mil-

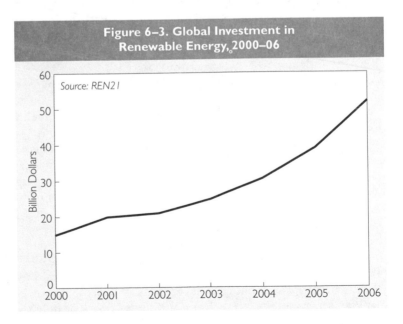

Figure 6–3. Global Investment in Renewable Energy, 2000–06

Source: REN21

Billion Dollars

lion on wind R&D. Even these numbers understate private R&D, which is often embedded in commercial projects, and exclude R&D investments by privately held companies, many of them funded with venture capital and other forms of equity investment. Venture capital and private equity investment in clean energy totaled $8.6 billion in 2006, 69 percent above the 2005 level and 10 times the 2001 level. (See Chapter 13.) By early 2007, these investments had helped create 146 clean energy start-up companies with names such as Nanosolar, Celunol, SunPower, E3 Biofuels, and Miasole, most of them working to develop and commercialize new energy technologies.[30]

These tiny firms may be the real game changers in the new energy industries, following in the footsteps of companies like Microsoft and Google, which quickly came to dominate their more established competitors—bringing a level of innovation that larger firms are rarely capable of.

In Silicon Valley, clean energy is helping drive a post-dotcom revival. Although it is regrettable that serious investment in renewable energy did not begin earlier, the science and technology available today will allow the industry to achieve performance and cost goals that would not have been possible in the past.

One example is photovoltaics, where producers are pursuing a host of strategies for reducing materials requirements, raising efficiency, and lowering manufacturing costs of the crystalline cells that dominate the market. Other companies are developing new thin-film photovoltaic materials that hold the promise of dramatic cost reductions. With demand outrunning supplies of PV materials in the past two years, price trends have temporarily reversed their usual downward course. But the industry is planning to increase its manufacturing capacity as much as eightfold

over the next three years, and dramatic price declines are likely, spurring the industry to develop new applications and markets that would not be feasible today.[31]

Beyond the advance in technology, the economics of renewable energy will further improve as the scale of production rises—the same phenomenon that has successively turned televisions, personal computers, and mobile phones from specialty products for high-income technology pioneers into mass-market consumer devices. An analysis of production costs in several manufacturing industries by the Boston Consulting Group found that each time cumulative production of a manufactured device doubles, production costs fall by 20–30 percent.[32]

The annual production of wind turbines is now doubling every three years—and wind is already competitive with natural gas–fired power in the United States. It would be competitive with coal-fired power plants if they had to pay the current European CO_2 price of $32 per ton. Solar electricity is still twice as expensive as retail grid electricity in most markets, but annual production is doubling every two years—which should cut costs in half in the next four to six years.[33]

Making Energy Markets Work

Advancing technology, rising energy prices, and the growing move to place a price on carbon emissions in many parts of the world have created an extraordinarily favorable market for new energy technologies. Reaching a true economic tipping point will depend on more than these simple variables, however. Energy markets virtually everywhere are regulated, complex, often inefficient, and rarely predictable. What happens to the energy economy, and to the world's climate, in the years ahead will be heavily influenced by hundreds of policy decisions made at international, national, and local levels—and whether these new policies can be sustained.

Many energy economists argue that the reason fossil fuels dominate today is their inherently lower cost compared with the alternatives. This suggests that putting a price on carbon—likely through a carbon dioxide tax or a regulatory cap on emissions such as the one in Europe—would solve the climate problem. Getting the price signals right is an essential step, but its limits are demonstrated by the modest impact that the $50 increase in the cost of a barrel of oil has had on petroleum consumption in the past five years. That is equivalent to a carbon dioxide price of $120 per ton; the current price of a carbon credit in Europe is $32 per ton, while one of the leading climate bills before the U.S. Congress would cap the price of carbon at $12—equivalent to $5 per barrel of oil.[34]

The neoclassical economic view assumes an economically frictionless world in which buyers and sellers have all the information and capital they need, and there are no serious barriers to the introduction of new technologies. At the extreme, neoclassical economists sound like economic fundamentalists, envisioning an idealized, mechanistic economy that is never found in the real world. Economic research beginning in the 1920s has shown that the costs of transactions can greatly limit the effectiveness of markets, while other research suggests that people's behavior often fails to follow neoclassical rules. Nobel laureate economist Douglass North has shown that laws, customs, and social priorities greatly influence the working of the economy. Without them, most markets would work inefficiently if at all.[35]

Because energy markets have been shaped more than most others by government policy, institutional constraints, and the power of large industrial enterprises, simple economic theory provides minimal insight about how to spur change. The electric power industry is particularly far from the neoclassical model, governed as it is by extensive government regulation that is intended to facilitate development of large, reliable electric systems, with one company dominating most local grids and in some cases owning the transmission lines and power plants as well.

Although this economic model has been broadly successful in delivering affordable electricity to billions of people, it has done so mainly by making it easy to add energy supply—but providing much less incentive or opportunity to improve energy efficiency. Regulations have also favored large fuel-intensive generators at the expense of smaller, capital-intensive units. The result is an electricity system that is far from the economic ideal—and that will require major reforms if it is to maximize economic efficiency, let alone account for the massive environmental externalities represented by global climate change.

The profits of most electric utilities are determined by regulators based on the amount of power sold. This naturally makes them proponents of growth—the more electricity consumers buy, the more profitable the utility is. And as long as the regulator approves, there is no risk in building a power plant since there are no competitors, and costs are borne by the consumer. The utility also bears little risk if the plant burns a fuel whose price is volatile—fuel adjustment clauses allow price increases also to be passed to the customer.

Although consumers should in theory be interested in making investments in energy efficiency whenever it is economical, they face many obstacles, including a lack of capital to invest in conservation and a lack of information about which investments make sense. Perceiving the lack of demand, potential manufacturers and installers of energy-efficient equipment have little incentive to scale up production or build businesses that would facilitate efficiency improvements.

One of the easiest ways to overcome these kinds of market barriers is government mandates. Since the 1970s, many governments have required that home appliances, motor vehicles, and buildings meet minimum efficiency standards in order to be sold, and these standards have been gradually ratcheted up over time. Additional tightening is now in order, and many governments are moving quickly in that direction. Average auto efficiency standards, for example, will soon move to 47 miles per gallon in Japan and 49 miles per gallon in Europe, and the U.S. Congress is considering tightening the U.S. standard, which has been stuck at 27.5 miles per gallon for over two decades. Another approach to requiring efficiency can be seen in the law recently passed in Australia to phase out the use of most incandescent light bulbs, which would be replaced by compact fluorescent bulbs that are four times as efficient.[36]

Government mandates are also being used to compel the construction of more energy-efficient buildings and to require the introduction of renewable energy into electricity grids as well as the markets for liquid fuels. Several national governments and 24 states in the United States now have binding "renewable portfolio standards" requiring that specified amounts of renewable electricity be added to their grids. In Spain, a recent update of building codes requires all new buildings to incorporate solar water heaters. As of April 2008, the state government of Baden-Wurttemberg, Germany, will require that 20 percent of new buildings' heating requirements be met with renewable energy. Brazil, the United States, and the European Union are among the jurisdictions that require that a minimum proportion of biofuels be blended with gasoline and diesel fuel, spurring growth in their use.[37]

Such mandates can patch over some of the holes in a market economy, but they are at best blunt instruments that do not harness the full power of the market to effect change. While they are a useful backstop to ensure that minimal rates of change occur and to remove the very worst technologies from the market, it is also essential that markets reward innovation and investment that strives to achieve the best possible performance. One important step in this direction is to de-couple electric utilities' profits from the amount of power they sell by introducing a regulatory formula that instead rewards utilities for providing the best service at the least cost. California regulators have already made this change; as a result of this and other policies, Californians use less than half as much electricity per person as other Americans do. (See Figure 6–4.)[38]

John Hoffman, an energy efficiency expert and former U.S. Environmental Protection Agency official, has proposed an additional strategy for spurring efficiency investments—a "transaction bridge" that allows manufacturers and installers to share in the savings derived from installing more-efficient equipment in buildings. This would motivate them to continually develop better technologies, to work with utilities to accelerate the development of new markets, and to scale up both production and installation in order to lower cost. This mechanism could also be used to spur introduction of micro-power technologies such as photovoltaics, as well as ground source heat pumps. And Hoffman has proposed a similar system for motivating the production and sales of efficient vehicles.[39]

European governments have developed another economic tool to spur investment in renewable energy. Beginning in the early 1980s, Denmark decided to reduce its dependence on oil-fired generation by encouraging its agricultural industry to enter the power

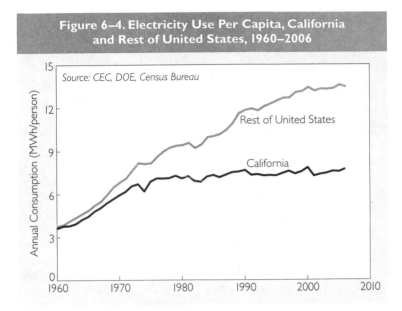

Figure 6–4. Electricity Use Per Capita, California and Rest of United States, 1960–2006

Source: CEC, DOE, Census Bureau

investment, and policy reform have led to a pace of change unseen since men like Thomas Edison and Henry Ford created the last great energy revolution a century ago. But is it enough? Will the coming years bring the accelerated change and trillions of dollars of investment that Nicholas Stern estimates is needed to reverse the tide of climate change?[42]

business by selling wind- and biomass-based electricity to the utilities at prices set by government. This stopped the utilities from thwarting potential competitors, and over two decades it reduced Denmark's dependence on fossil fuels and made it a leading generator of renewable power.[40]

Germany and Spain adopted similar market access laws in the 1990s, and they too moved quickly into the leading ranks of renewable energy development. Over time, the prices governments set have been adjusted downward as the cost of renewable technologies has fallen. As a result of this law, Germany now holds the pole position in solar PV and wind-generating capacity—despite the fact that it has modest resources of sun and wind.[41]

The Final Tipping Point

There are good reasons to think that the world may be on the verge of a major transformation of energy markets. The powerful interaction of advancing technology, private

The answer to that question will likely be found not in the messy world of economics but in the even messier world of politics. Can the enormous power of today's industries be set aside in favor of the common good? Time is growing short. In the United States alone, 121 coal-fired power plants have been proposed. If built, they could produce 30 billion tons of carbon dioxide over their 60-year lives. China is building that many plants every year.[43]

There were growing signs in 2007 that the years of political paralysis on climate change may be coming to an end, spurred by the warnings of scientists and the concerns of citizens. One sign of the changing times is that many of the planned coal plants are under attack by local and national environmentalists, and some have already been scrapped. Germany recently announced that its centuries-old hard coal industry will be closed by 2018. Several potentially game-changing political developments in 2007 are worth noting:

- Twenty-seven major U.S. companies—from Alcoa and Dow Chemical to Duke Energy,

General Motors, and Xerox—announced support for national regulation of CO_2 emissions.

• The European Union committed to reducing its carbon dioxide emissions 20 percent below 1990 levels by 2020, and member states are ramping up their energy efficiency and renewable energy programs in order to achieve these goals.

• China announced its first national climate policy, pledging to step up its energy efficiency and renewable energy programs and acknowledging that earlier policies were not sufficient.

• Seventeen states in the United States moved toward adopting regulations on CO_2 emissions, increasing pressure on the U.S. Congress, which was considering national legislation.

• Brazil recognized the threat that climate change poses to the country's economically crucial agriculture and forestry industries and signaled a new commitment to strengthening international climate agreements.[44]

As negotiations begin on the international climate agreement that will supplant the Kyoto Protocol after 2012, the world's political will to tackle climate change will be put to an early test. The politics of climate change are advancing more rapidly than could have been imagined a few years ago. But the world has not yet reached the political tipping point that would ensure the kind of economic transformation that is required. And the divide between industrial and developing countries over how to share the burden of action must still be resolved.

As people around the world come to understand that a low-carbon economy could one day be more effective than today's energy mix at meeting human needs, support for the needed transformation is bound to grow. Urgency and vision are the twin pillars on which humanity's hope now hangs.

CHAPTER 7

Improving Carbon Markets

Zoë Chafe and Hilary French

In financial capitals across the world, brokers are hard at work trading a key commodity of the twenty-first century: carbon credits. These are allowances or offsets that represent a quantity of carbon dioxide (CO_2) or other greenhouse gas (GHG) measured in tons of carbon dioxide equivalent.[1]

Regions, countries, and states are setting limits or caps on the amount of greenhouse gas that can be emitted each year—limits that are typically passed on to large emitters such as power plants and factories in certain industries. If these plants reduce their emissions—by installing low-carbon technologies or improving the energy efficiency of their production processes, for example—and emit less than their allowed limit under the cap, the companies can sell unused allowances to utilities or companies that are emitting more gas than legally allowed. The effect is to put a price tag on greenhouse gas emissions—and to create an economic incentive to look for ways to reduce them.

The platforms for exchanging such credits are part of a rapidly growing global carbon market. They take several forms, including cap-and-trade systems in countries meeting Kyoto Protocol emissions targets and credit exchanges for energy-related industries. Recent years have also seen the rapid growth of voluntary carbon markets, in which individuals, businesses, and communities invest in projects that offset their emissions.

There is little question that carbon markets are here to stay: some analysts project that they will constitute the world's largest commodity market in the years ahead. But carbon markets are in their infancy. There are major challenges, such as adequately addressing verification, certification, and monitoring. And these markets must be scaled up substantially if they are to significantly decrease the concentration of greenhouse gases in Earth's atmosphere. Despite the remaining hurdles, today's burgeoning efforts by businesses, governments, and individuals to reduce carbon emissions and exchange credits are critical first steps toward ensuring that future generations inherit something priceless: a stable climate.[2]

The Shape of Carbon Markets Today

In the last few years, carbon markets moved from the realm of economic theory into that of practical reality—due in no small measure to the Kyoto Protocol to the U.N. Framework Convention on Climate Change. Under this accord, 38 industrial countries agreed to cut their greenhouse gas emissions to, on average, 5.2 percent below 1990 levels between 2008 and 2012. This commitment became legally binding on participating countries in early 2005, after the protocol had been ratified by the required number of countries. By October 2007, the protocol had been ratified by 174 countries and the European Union (EU).[3]

The emissions reductions required under the protocol are just a small fraction of what scientists now believe will be needed to limit global average temperature increases to 2 degrees Celsius and to avoid crossing potentially catastrophic thresholds in Earth's climate system. (See Chapter 6.) Still, the reductions made under Kyoto represent a critical first step.[4]

The inspiration for today's rapidly growing carbon markets comes from a successful U.S. experiment with trading sulfur dioxide and nitrogen oxide credits. This market was created in the early 1990s primarily to address the problem of acid rain. As a result of this experience, the U.S. government successfully pushed for the inclusion of similar provisions in the Kyoto Protocol, overcoming initial skepticism from other countries. Ironically, the U.S. government has so far refused to ratify the protocol that contains the very provisions it championed, while the EU has created the most ambitious trading system to date.[5]

The protocol created three innovative market-based instruments to encourage its cost-effective implementation:
• The Clean Development Mechanism (CDM) allows countries with emissions reduction commitments under Kyoto to reduce their burden by investing in emissions reductions in developing countries that are party to the protocol but not held under it to any specific reductions.
• Joint Implementation (JI) allows countries to meet their reduction targets by investing in projects that reduce emissions in other countries bound by Kyoto targets, usually those in Eastern Europe and the former Soviet Union.
• Emissions trading allows parties with emission targets to trade portions of their national emission allocations among themselves.[6]

So far, most of the credits generated under the terms of the Kyoto Protocol have involved the CDM, although some projects under Joint Implementation have also begun. Trading of emissions allocations between countries has not yet started, but it could begin as early as 2008—the first year of the Kyoto Protocol's initial commitment period.[7]

Carbon trading in all of the major markets reached an estimated total value of $30.1 billion in 2006, almost triple the amount traded in 2005. The EU Emissions Trading Scheme (EU-ETS) accounted for more than 80 percent of the total value of carbon credits traded in 2006, with credits related to the Clean Development Mechanism coming in a distant second. (See Table 7–1.)[8]

Within the broad category of carbon credits, there are two distinct segments: allowances and project-based transactions. Allowances are allotted through a government cap-and-trade system or by a financial institution with a binding emissions reduction schedule, such as the Chicago Climate Exchange (CCX). Global trade of allowances has increased rapidly, from 328 million tons of CO_2 equivalent in 2005 to 1,131 million tons in 2006. The value associated with these trades rose

	2005		2006	
Market	Volume	Value	Volume	Value
	(mill. tons of CO_2 equiv.)	(million dollars)	(mill. tons of CO_2 equiv.)	(million dollars)
EU Emissions Trading Scheme	321	7,908	1,101	24,357
New South Wales	6	59	20	225
Chicago Climate Exchange	1	3	10	38
Primary Clean Development Mechanism*	351	2,638	475	4,257
Joint Implementation	11	68	16	141
Other compliance	20	187	17	79
Other voluntary markets	6	n/a	13	55
Total	716	10,863[†]	1,652	30,153

Table 7–1. Carbon Transactions, Selected Markets, 2005 and 2006

* *Primary sales of credits generated through the CDM are distinguished from the secondary market, which exists when these credits are resold through a market mechanism such as the EU-ETS.* [†] *Excludes over-the-counter voluntary market.*
Source: See endnote 8.

from just under $8 billion in 2005 to $24.6 billion just one year later.[9]

Project-based transactions are associated with specific carbon reduction projects. Companies and governments can acquire credits from international emissions reduction projects and count the reductions toward their national caps using the Clean Development Mechanism or Joint Implementation. And individuals, businesses, universities, municipalities, or organizations can seek to reduce their own "carbon footprints" by voluntarily investing in specific emissions reduction projects.

In sum, carbon trading can be described as either allowance-based (under a cap-and-trade scheme) or project-based, and it can be part of a compliance market (such as the EU-ETS) or a voluntary transaction.

Capping and Trading

Measured by both volume and value, allowance-based systems dominate today's carbon markets. At least three such systems are currently operating—the European Union Emissions Trading Scheme, the New South Wales Market in Australia, and the Chicago Climate Exchange in the United States—and more are being formed.

The EU-ETS has grown to become the largest carbon trading platform. Established as an important component of the European Union's strategy for achieving its Kyoto-mandated emissions target, the EU-ETS allows European reduction credits to be bought and sold alongside credits created through projects in developing countries (through the CDM) or in economies in transition (through JI). The EU-ETS includes the 15 countries that originally committed through the protocol to collectively reduce their greenhouse gas emissions by 8 percent from 1990 levels by 2012 under what is known as the "European bubble." An EU Directive translated this commitment into specific emissions reduction targets for each member country. The EU-ETS also allows newer EU member states to participate in the trading scheme in order to meet their national reduction targets of 6–8 percent, as agreed under the protocol.[10]

The EU-ETS has recorded strong growth since it began operations, more than tripling the tons of CO_2 equivalent traded in its first two years—from 321 million in 2005 to 1,101 million in 2006. The value of the traded carbon also tripled over that time, climbing from $7.9 billion in 2005 to $24.4 billion. The program currently involves at least 12,000 companies across the EU whose allowances and transactions are recorded in registries. These registries are vital for keeping track of legitimate transactions and making sure that credits are not double-counted or resold.[11]

During its initial test phase, from 2005 to 2007, the EU-ETS traded only CO_2 emission allowances associated with power and heat generation and select industries, including oil refineries, iron and steel plants, and factories making cement, glass, bricks, ceramics, and pulp and paper. These sources account for 45 percent of CO_2 emissions in the EU. The second phase corresponds with the Kyoto Protocol's first emissions reduction commitment period, which runs from 2008 to 2012. It is expected that this phase will integrate additional emissions sources, such as aviation, and other greenhouse gases beyond carbon dioxide.[12]

The New South Wales market is the second largest allowance-based market to date. Australia's most populous state, New South Wales, set mandatory emissions reductions targets in 2003; its market whirred into motion two years before trading began on the EU-ETS. Targets apply specifically to the state's power sector—meaning that large electricity buyers or sellers must reduce or offset emissions from production of the electricity they supply or use. They can buy certificates from low-emission generation of electricity, improved generator efficiency, reduced electricity consumption, or forestry carbon sequestration projects to meet their targets. (So far, this market does not include credits generated through the CDM or JI.) In 2006, 20 million tons of carbon dioxide equivalent were traded on this market, worth $225 million.[13]

The third largest allowance-based market is the Chicago Climate Exchange. Started in 2003, the CCX differs from the other two markets described here in that it was not established by a government. Any entity that joins the CCX does so voluntarily. CCX members must, however, legally adhere to the emissions reduction schedule stipulated by the exchange. Trading volume on the CCX surpassed its 2006 total in the first half of 2007, putting it on course to double its trading volume over one year.[14]

Businesses and organizations join CCX at different membership levels: full members have significant direct emissions, including industrial companies, states, and municipalities. They can purchase or sell credits. Associate members are organizations, universities, and companies with negligible direct emissions that agree to buy credits to offset 100 percent of the emissions associated with their energy purchases and business travel. CCX members have a range of motives for joining, such as to respond to public demand for action on climate change or to gain early experience with emissions trading on the assumption that mandatory U.S. systems will sooner or later be created.[15]

While the Chicago Climate Exchange grows, pressure is building within the United States for federal regulation of greenhouse gas emissions through a cap-and-trade system. Prospects for some form of national legislation improved in January 2007 with the formation of the United States Climate Action Partnership, an alliance of major U.S. companies and prominent environmental organizations. The partnership, which has grown to include more than 30 businesses and organizations, is calling for national legislation on "significant reductions" of GHG emissions using a multi-pronged strategy based around a cap-and-trade program. More than a dozen competing pieces of legislation are currently being considered by the U.S. Congress.[16]

In the absence of effective federal action on emissions reductions, several other allowance-based carbon markets have been proposed or are in the process of being created by states and provinces within the United States and Canada. (See Box 7–1.) Meanwhile, the central government in Australia has announced that it will develop a national cap-and-trade market for greenhouse gas emissions by 2012. Legislators and regulators working to develop

these systems are carefully studying the European experience.[17]

One of the biggest surprises as the EU Emissions Trading Scheme was the precipitous drop in the price of emissions contracts for credits to be counted in 2007 (known as December 2007 contracts); the price sank from a peak of $34 per ton to nearly zero in early 2007. The second phase will have more stringent emissions caps, so future contracts are currently trading at higher prices. (See Figure 7–1.) (Emissions contracts have an assigned date, according to the date the credits will be produced; contracts can be traded several years in advance, for delivery at future dates.) The price crash for December 2007 contracts coincided with the announcement that more permits had been allocated through the EU National Allocation Plan process than

---

Box 7–1. North American Carbon Trading Systems under Development

Regional Greenhouse Gas Initiative (RGGI): This program was initiated in 2005 through the support of state governors in the northeastern United States. Cooperation between at least 10 states will lead to a regional cap-and-trade system that will regulate the emissions associated with most power plants in the region. Collectively, participating states have agreed to cap regional CO_2 emissions at 1990 levels by 2014 and to reduce them to 10 percent below that level by 2018. When the program gets going in 2009, some 188 million carbon credits representing one ton of carbon each will be distributed to participating states, which will in turn allocate or auction them to power plants within their borders. The program could be extended beyond power plants to include other large emitters after the initial trading period is completed.

California: The state passed landmark legislation in 2006 that mandates a 25-percent reduction in CO_2 emissions by 2020, with emissions reductions expected to reach 174 million tons of CO_2 equivalent. It is expected to establish a

cap-and-trade system based largely on emissions reductions among major emitters in-state. Emissions trading is scheduled to begin in 2012. California stands to benefit from the establishment six years ago of the California Climate Action Registry—a voluntary system of GHG emissions accounting that was set up to protect and reward companies that chose to take early action in anticipation of future regulatory requirements. (Other states, including Florida, Minnesota, New Jersey, and Oregon, have since passed similar legislation.)

Western Climate Initiative: Created in February 2007, this scheme involves California, five other western states, and the Canadian provinces of British Columbia and Manitoba. Modeled somewhat on RGGI, the initiative has set a regional emissions reduction goal of 15 percent below 2005 levels by 2020 and is establishing a market mechanism for achieving it. (Three other states and three provinces have also joined as observers.)

Source: See endnote 17.

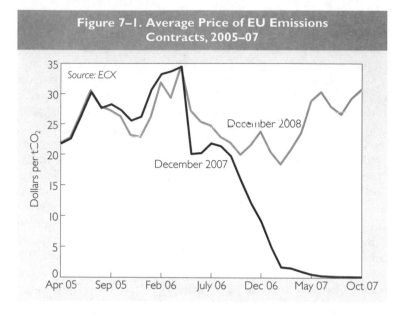

Figure 7–1. Average Price of EU Emissions Contracts, 2005–07

Source: ECX

December 2008

December 2007

Dollars per tCO₂

were needed, resulting in an oversupply for the first phase of the EU-ETS. Political and special interests lobbying led in part to overly generous permit allocations, combined with inadequate historical emissions data. This highlights the key importance of establishing high-quality baseline data if cap-and-trade markets are to function effectively.[18]

A significant problem in the recent EU-ETS experience was that the vast majority of emissions permits were distributed for free to large emitters rather than offered for sale through an auction. (See Box 7–2.) Whether permits are allocated or auctioned, the right to emit carbon gains a value when a carbon cap exisits—and that value is reflected in increased electricity prices. Because large emitters were given permits for free, they reaped windfall profits when electricity prices rose while their production costs did not. British power companies, for example, made an estimated $1.5 billion in profits as a result of the carbon permits they were issued for free by the U.K. government, and German utili-

ties are expected to enjoy windfall profits worth $44–91 billion between 2005 and 2012 as a result of emissions credits granted to them under the EU-ETS.[19]

There is a good side to the price rises, though: in general, consumers react to higher electricity prices by increasing energy efficiency and buying less electricity. Jörg Haas of the Heinrich Böll Foundation and Peter Barnes of the Tomales Bay Institute explain that "as emissions trading is meant as a way of internalizing external costs, it is necessary that prices reflect these new costs." But they and other critics nonetheless question whether large emitters should profit from free allocations of a public good: the atmosphere's capacity to absorb carbon. While allocating permits amounts to a subsidy for electricity companies, auctioning can encourage a more equitable distribution of permit revenues.[20]

The EU-ETS allows large emitters to meet their caps in part by purchasing credits via the Clean Development Mechanism and Joint Implementation program; this provision has also elicited criticism. Some groups worry that wealthy countries will fail to make significant in-country reductions, relying instead on the relatively cheap credits generated in developing countries or economies in transition. This fear is one reason that forestry-related credits have so far been banned from the EU-ETS. The World Wide Fund for Nature–UK (WWF–UK) recently

Box 7–2. Who Gets Permission to Emit?

When carbon trading began under the EU-ETS, European governments had to decide how many emissions permits each company covered by the EU-ETS would receive. There were two major options: to auction permits or to allocate permits to companies based on their historical emissions. In an auction, companies list the amount they are willing to pay for a given quantity of permits, and a market price is established. Under allocation, or "grandfathering," companies receive permits for free based on the amount they emitted in past years.

Governments decided that in the first phase of EU-ETS (2005–08), no more than 5 percent of permits could be auctioned in each member country. (Only four countries used auctions at all.) In Phase II (2008–12), up to 10 percent of permits will be auctioned.

Prices will rise anytime carbon emissions are restricted—whether through allocation or auctioning. When permits are allocated to com-

panies, production costs usually remain about the same, despite the rise in electricity prices, because the permits are basically given as a subsidy—so businesses and associations favor this option. When permits are auctioned, the average cost of production can increase, and the revenue from the auction is redistributed either through tax breaks for consumers, assistance to energy-intensive sectors, or investments in low-carbon technologies. In general, economists support auctioning permits.

Some 80 percent of businesses polled said that the EU Directive should not allow for more auctioning in the future, in part because they are worried they will not be able to compete with sectors not covered by the EU-ETS or with companies abroad—worries that researchers say are largely unfounded due to domestic protections covering many industries.

Source: See endnote 19.

reviewed nine National Allocation Plans for the second phase of the EU-ETS, concluding that up to 88 percent of the EU emissions reductions required by 2012 could take place outside of the European Union. WWF–UK argues that this is contrary to the Kyoto Protocol and EU directives, both of which specify that Kyoto mechanisms be supplemental to domestic actions.[21]

Some lessons from Europe are already being incorporated there and elsewhere. Current prices indicate that the prices of contracts for the second phase of the EU-ETS will rise, with more-aggressive emissions caps making permits scarcer. As of early October 2007, EU-ETS contracts for December 2008 (for delivery just before emissions levels are evaluated for 2008) were trading around $30 per ton of carbon dioxide equivalent.[22]

And U.S. policymakers appear increasingly convinced that auctioning is the best approach

for allocating permits. Under the Regional Greenhouse Gas Initiative in the northeastern part of the country, all participating states with announced rules have opted for 100 percent auctions, and California is considering a similar requirement for its climate registry. Most of the cap-and-trade proposals before the U.S. Congress call for a share of permits to be auctioned and for a percentage of the revenue generated to be allocated for public benefit.[23]

Under the auctioning systems being considered in the RGGI program, earned revenues would be used in part to finance public spending on climate-related programs, such as the promotion of energy efficiency. Federal proposals currently under consideration also envision investing auction proceeds in alternative energy development (including clean coal), cleaner transportation technologies, and climate-related initiatives to lessen the impacts of climate change on low-income communities in the United States and elsewhere. Peter Barnes has gone further, proposing that all citizens should share benefits from carbon emissions permits. When permits to "use" atmospheric capacity are auctioned, the revenues would be placed in a public trust. Through a mechanism similar to the Alaska Permanent Fund, which distributes royalties to Alaskans for oil extracted from the North Slope, citizens would receive their fair share of the trust's value. (See Chapter 10.)[24]

The Kyoto Mechanisms in Action

The Kyoto Protocol's flexibility mechanisms link countries that have a shared interest in creating projects to reduce greenhouse gas emissions—harnessing industrial countries' interest in investing in lower-cost efficiency projects overseas and pairing that with developing countries' interest in receiving financing and cleaner technologies. International carbon finance flows to developing countries could climb as high as $100 billion a year in coming decades, according to U.N. estimates, roughly equivalent to total spending on foreign aid in 2006.[25]

Investments in project-based transactions funded through the Clean Development Mechanism and Joint Implementation have grown rapidly since the protocol's flexibility mechanisms became operational. Since 2002, CDM credits worth 920 million tons of CO_2 equivalent have been generated—equal to one fifth of the EU's total emissions in 2004. In 2006 alone, CDM projects led to certified emissions reductions (CERs) of 475 million tons of carbon dioxide equivalent, with a total value of more than $4 billion. Joint Implementation projects have gotten off to a slower start. Nonetheless, 16 million tons of CO_2 equivalent were transacted through JI

in 2006, worth $141 million.[26]

Since the creation of CDM credits began in 2002, China has registered 118 projects, accounting for the highest share of expected CERs (75.4 million, 45 percent of the global total). While India has registered the most projects (282), these projects are expected to generate 27.8 million CERs (about 17 percent of the global total). China's domination of the CDM market is expected to continue: adding up all the CDM projects that are in the process of being verified and registered, it is expected that by 2012 China will generate almost 53 percent of all CERs and India will be home to 16 percent. (See Figure 7–2.)[27]

By contrast, Latin America as a whole has only registered 290 CDM projects worth 33.6 million CERs, and sub-Saharan Africa has issued 13 projects worth 3.8 million CERs (just 2.3 percent of the global total). Though there are 33 sub-Saharan African CDM projects now in the pipeline, they are expected to account for about the same low percentage of the global total by 2012.[28]

Despite Africa's opportunities to gain outside investment for sustainable development through the Kyoto mechanisms, the continent has thus far received an abysmally low share of CDM investment. To counteract this worrying trend, six U.N. agencies have formed the Nairobi Framework, an initiative aimed at improving CDM implementation in Africa by building the capacity of countries in the region to develop and implement projects.[29]

The largest volume share of CDM projects to date involves "fugitive emissions"—that is, those that trap and dispose of fuel emissions, halocarbons, and sulfur hexafluoride. Projects that destroy the greenhouse gas HFC-23 (a potent byproduct created during the manufacturing of a class of refrigerant gases known as HCFCs) have generated the largest share of CDM credits to date, accounting

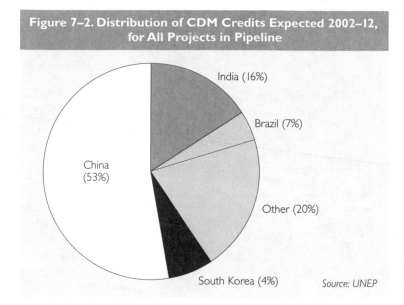

Figure 7–2. Distribution of CDM Credits Expected 2002–12, for All Projects in Pipeline

India (16%)

Brazil (7%)

China (53%)

Other (20%)

South Korea (4%)

Source: UNEP

for 50 percent of all issued credits.[30]

There are significant concerns about these projects, however, including that the lure of earning CDM credits has created a perverse incentive for countries to produce more HCFCs than they would otherwise, despite the fact that HCFCs are both an ozone-depleting substance and a greenhouse gas. An added problem is the high price of buying these credits relative to directly subsidizing needed technology. By one estimate, installing the equipment needed to eliminate HFC-23 emissions at the 17 remaining refrigerator plants producing HFC-23 in developing countries would cost only $142 million—$6.5 billion less than purchasing CDM credits generated by capturing the HFC-23.[31]

In any event, a decline in new HFC-23 projects in 2007 suggests that these opportunities have largely been exploited. A shift is under way toward other projects, including energy efficiency, hydroelectric, and methane capture from landfills. (See Figure 7–3 and Table 7–2.)[32]

In 2001, the parties to the Kyoto Proto-col agreed that countries could work toward their emissions targets by encouraging carbon sequestration in vegetation and soil through forest management, cropland management, grazing land management, and revegetation. Now the CDM is beginning to approve projects from the sector known as LULUCF, for land use, land use change, and forestry. This sector includes projects started since 1990 that focus on afforestation (planting new trees) or reforestation (planting replacement trees).[33]

Despite their potentially important role in stabilizing the climate, forestry and land use projects have been tightly restricted under CDM rules. As of September 2007 one project was registered—a reforestation project in China's Pearl River Basin. (Eleven other forestry projects, in seven countries, were being evaluated.) The World Bank is seeking to expand forestry and agriculture project funding through its BioCarbon Fund and its new Forest Carbon Partnership Facility, with the aim of helping countries gain credits by protecting existing forests—a concept known as "avoided deforestation." Although countries cannot yet generate credits through this approach, it is likely that avoided deforestation will be included under the CDM in the future.[34]

Voluntary standards are now being developed to help guide the LULUCF sector in the future and to maximize the benefits of forestry projects. The Climate, Community and Biodiversity Alliance (CCB) is a group of

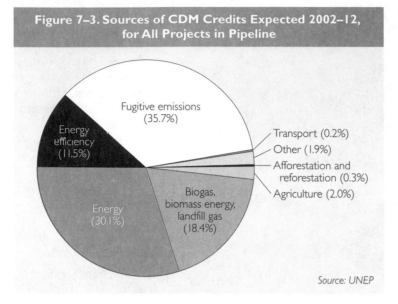

Figure 7–3. Sources of CDM Credits Expected 2002–12, for All Projects in Pipeline

Fugitive emissions (35.7%)

Energy efficiency (11.5%)

Transport (0.2%)

Other (1.9%)

Afforestation and reforestation (0.3%)

Agriculture (2.0%)

Biogas, biomass energy, landfill gas (18.4%)

Energy (30.1%)

Source: UNEP

percent). Russia (19 percent) and Bulgaria (18 percent) are also home to many JI projects.[36]

European buyers lead both the CDM and JI markets, with 86 percent market share. This reflects the fact that the European Union is party to the Kyoto Protocol and can use emissions credits purchased under the CDM and JI to meet its emissions reductions targets.[37]

Elaborate rules governing the CDM and Joint Implementation have been painstakingly negotiated among the parties to the Kyoto Protocol over the last several years to ensure that projects meet key quality-oriented criteria. For example, in order to be approved a project must be certified to be "additional"—in other words, that it would not have taken place if the CDM did not exist. A second requirement relates to a concept known as leakage: businesses and governments proposing CDM projects must show that they are not simply shifting activities from one place to another.[38]

Although these requirements were created with the best of intentions, they have led to some unanticipated problems. One difficulty has been that the transaction costs associated with the CDM are so high that only large projects can absorb them. It typically costs $50,000–250,000 to shepherd a project through the approval process—or on average some 14–22 percent of the projected revenue from the sale of the carbon credits. This is a particular obstacle for the world's poorest countries, such as those in Africa,

12 companies and nonprofit organizations that are working together to implement standards for carbon ventures. Projects must meet 15 standards—addressing land tenure, community impacts, and biodiversity impacts, among others—in order to be certified. They may earn additional points if they satisfy 8 other standards, on issues like capacity building, adapting to climate change, and native species use. Both CDM and voluntary market projects can earn CCB certification.[35]

With Joint Implementation projects, energy projects dominate the overall portfolio in both number and overall volume. Between 2003 and 2006, energy projects accounted for nearly two thirds of the volume of JI projects, with energy efficiency and projects switching from carbon-intensive fuels to renewable energy accounting for 28 percent of the total, biomass for 13 percent, wind energy for 12 percent, and hydroelectric projects for 8 percent. Projects financed through JI are predominately located in Eastern Europe, with Ukraine accounting for the largest volume between 2003 and 2006 (21

Table 7–2. Selected Clean Development Mechanism and Joint Implementation Projects

Project	Host Country/ Authorized Participants	Other Parties	GHG Reductions	Description
			(million tons of CO_2 equiv. per year)	
Clean Development Mechanism				
Reforestation for Guangxi watershed management in Pearl River Basin	China: Xinghuan Forestry Development Company	BioCarbon Fund, IBRD Italy Spain	25,795	First forestry project registered under CDM; 4,000 hectares of new forest will sequester carbon, conserve soil and water, and generate revenue for local farmers from sale of CDM credits.
BRT Bogotá, TransMilenio Phase II to IV	Colombia: TransMilenio S.A.	Netherlands: Corporación Andina de Fomento	246,563	First transportation project to be registered under CDM; a Bus Rapid Transit system will increase efficiency of public transportation.
Lawley Fuel Switch Project	South Africa: Corobrik	Netherlands: Statkraft Markets BV	19,159	Corobrik's Lawley brick factory located in Gauteng province of South Africa will switch from using coal to natural gas.
Osório Wind Power Plant Project	Brazil: Ventos do Sul Energia	Spain: Enerfin Enervento S.A.	148,325	The wind power complex, the largest in Latin America, will generate 150 megawatts, enough power to meet the needs of 650,000 residents.

where potentially eligible projects tend to be smaller in scale and thus less able to afford the high transaction costs. However, the World Bank and private brokers are working to aggregate smaller projects and reduce transaction costs. Africa also stands to benefit from the expected future inclusion of more LULUCF projects.[39]

The CDM has been criticized for lax oversight on its rules. For the first several years of operation, every project proposed was approved. Since then, there has been tighter scrutiny by the CDM Executive Board, and some projects have been rejected. In August 2007, for example, a large gas-capture project slated for Equatorial Guinea was turned down on the grounds that it was unclear that the project would not have happened anyway—meaning the project developers may have been trying to cash in on what was in fact business as usual.[40]

Assessing Voluntary Carbon Markets

In the absence of government caps on carbon dioxide emissions—or sometimes alongside them—businesses, organizations, and individuals are voluntarily purchasing credits that aim to mitigate greenhouse gas emissions. Often referred to simply as "carbon offsets," these credits are bought and sold over the

	Table 7–2. continued			
Project	Host Country/ Authorized Participants	Other Parties	GHG Reductions	Description
			(million tons of CO_2 equiv. per year)	
		Joint Implementation		
Rehabilitation of the district heating system in Donetsk Region	Ukraine		826,875 (total by 2012)	Old boilers will either be replaced or upgraded; switch to natural gas from coal/oil; pipe length will be decreased and pipe insulation will be enhanced; introduce combined heat and power plants; reduce heat loss, improve efficiency, and decrease fuel consumption.
Switch from wet to dry process at Podilsky Cement	Ukraine	Ireland-based CRH plc, Dublin	750,000	Cement will be produced through dry process rather than through energy-intensive wet process.
Landfill gas recovery in Moscow	Russia		4,122,016 (2008–12)	A landfill gas recovery and flaring system will be constructed to reduce release of landfill methane.
RBTI Biomass Waste-to-Energy Project	Latvia		5,337	Boilers will be introduced at the Baltic Timber Industries so bark and wood waste can be used to generate electricity for the company.

Source: See endnote 32.

counter or through an established trading mechanism such as the Chicago Climate Exchange. Ecosystem Marketplace, a U.S.-based group that tracks markets for a variety of ecosystem services, estimates that in 2006 at least 23.7 million tons of CO_2 equivalent were exchanged in voluntary carbon markets, with 10.3 million tons moving through the CCX. Many more voluntary credits were exchanged in so-called over-the-counter trades—transactions made outside of formal market structures, often between an offset provider and a private citizen.[41]

People in North America or Europe are increasingly encouraged to buy carbon offsets to negate the climate impacts of their everyday activities. The airline ticket consolidator Expedia, for example, teamed up with carbon credit broker TerraPass to offer customers the opportunity to offset the carbon dioxide generated during their flights; TerraPass, in turn, uses the fees it collects to buy carbon credits produced by verified wind, biomass, or industrial efficiency projects. And Jiva Dental in the suburbs of London advertises itself as the first "carbon-neutral" dental practice in the world; the office buys carbon offsets created by projects in India, Mexico, and the United States. Jiva Dental is just one of many institutions, events, and enterprises to claim "carbon neutrality." (See Box 7–3.)[42]

One specific type of renewable energy offset sometimes traded on the voluntary market is the renewable energy credit (REC), which represents power generated from renewable sources and fed into the grid. Use of RECs as carbon offsets is controversial because the energy sources are not tested for additionality—in other words, it is difficult to know if they represent renewable energy products that would not have occurred anyway without financing from the purchase of the credits.[43]

Forestry and tree-planting projects are a prevalent but controversial method of sequestering carbon and producing voluntary offset credits. A recent report from the Amsterdam-based Transnational Institute questions the claims of several well-known organizations or companies that sell forestry-based carbon offsets. The report documents incidents in which groups advertised that buying their offsets would support the planting of new forests when, in reality, consumers' money was going toward purchase of carbon sequestration rights to existing forests.[44]

The report also calls attention to an incident in which a community was displaced by a forestry project and then moved to another forested location, clearing the area to build their new homes. This allegedly happened with a project unfortunately located at a disputed boundary area in a Ugandan national park—the site of ongoing forced evictions and conflicts over resource rights. Some residents forced to move away from this site had little choice but to fell trees at their new location, perhaps cancelling the intended beneficial effects of the offset project. While some of the examples in the report are quite

---

Box 7–3. Carbon Neutrality—Not a Neutral Term

When "carbon-neutral" became the *Oxford American Dictionary*'s 2006 Word of the Year, many hailed it as the mainstreaming of an important environmental topic. But what does it really mean to be carbon-neutral? Is it at all possible to document such a claim? Businesses, organizations, conferences, sporting tournaments, concerts, and individuals are certainly trying to.

Some critics argue that carbon neutrality is an empty descriptor, in part because it sometimes takes years for the emissions being offset to really be neutralized. Offsets based on forestry projects, for example, often calculate a 99-year lifespan, during which the tree will absorb carbon dioxide at varying rates. Trees are by no means guaranteed to live for this amount of time, and there are still uncertainties about the carbon emissions associated with their decay.

There are also significant questions about the often-opaque algorithms used to determine the emissions that a person or organization would need to offset in order to truly erase their impact on the global atmosphere, especially for emissions associated with air travel. Although several well-recognized methodologies do exist, such as the World Business Council for Sustainable Development (WBCSD)/World Resources Institute GHG Protocol, not all voluntary offset sites use this methodology.

While the term carbon-neutral is surely alluring, buyers do need to beware when purchasing offsets and using this term. Some critics argue that offsets are a cheap way of pushing aside more serious questions about ongoing consumption patterns. Others urge that people should go beyond carbon-neutral and look toward a "carbon-positive" future—one in which people are proactively repairing damage to the climate through lifestyle changes, business practices, and everyday purchases.

Source: See endnote 42.

old, the authors' main points remain valid: without proactive legislation, concerns over land tenure could easily escalate as forestry projects increase in frequency and size.[45]

Given the frequent changes in scientific findings, certification systems, and due diligence that affect carbon credits, purchasers need to ask about the origins of carbon offsets and how they are verified. By understanding the differences among various offset products, their certifiers, and the available standards, buyers can get a sense of whether they are getting value for their money. This will clarify the process involved in offsetting carbon emissions and will put pressure on those generating and brokering the credits to ensure that customers are truly getting the "offsets" they believe they are paying for.[46]

By understanding the differences among various offset products, their certifiers, and the available standards, buyers can get a sense of whether they are getting value for their money.

A note of caution: while carbon offsets offer some positive benefits, they are not a panacea. The carbon emissions associated with high-consumption lifestyles will not be neutralized by simply buying carbon offsets. (Nor would it even be possible to produce and offer for sale enough credits to attempt that feat.) Improving energy efficiency and decreasing consumption are key first steps to decreasing carbon emissions.

With the energy sources currently used to generate electricity, the building standards that dictate construction of houses and offices, and the industrial regulations that influence how appliances and clothes are manufactured, it is clear that government rules and regulations have great power over the emissions associated with everyday lives.

With the right legislation, people will be able to purchase better products and there will be less need to consider buying carbon offsets on a voluntary basis. Until that happens, carbon offset purchases will be made more meaningful by simultaneously lessening consumption and lobbying for more effective national legislation.

The Future of Carbon Markets

As emissions reduction projects and carbon trading increase rapidly, financial analysts, environmental researchers, and human rights advocates will jostle to fine-tune the implementation. Perhaps the most crucial issue to improve is the ability to prove that GHG reductions are indeed happening as marketed. Several recent cases spotlighted by the media make this clear. In one case, Toby Nichol, communications director at EasyJet, a low-cost airline in Europe, warned carbon offset buyers to beware the "snake oil salesmen" that lure do-good customers into paying exorbitantly high fees for offset services. EasyJet had originally intended to offer its passengers credits from carbon offsetting brokers, but the company found that the quality of the credits offered was questionable and the markup was high, so it decided to purchase the credits from the CDM instead.[47]

Reliable emissions calculators and reputable certification and verification schemes will help ensure that carbon credit purchasers are getting what they paid for. These tools are crucial to the continued success of this nascent market. Several protocols help project managers ensure that they are correctly calculating the environmental benefits they market. Perhaps best known is the WBCSD/World Resources Institute GHG Protocol, which standardizes accounting methods. The International Organization for Standardization has also released a useful methodology (ISO 14064) with four components: organization reporting, project reporting, validation and verification, and accreditation of validation or verification bodies. But there is concern that these tools do not sufficiently address the key issue of additionality.[48]

While lack of certification and oversight continues to be a problem in some sectors of the carbon market, a new problem is emerging: there may be too many competing certification and registration schemes. Ecosystem Marketplace counted at least 15 major certification programs and standards available for the U.S. voluntary carbon offset market alone.[49]

Several certification systems stand out in the crowd, however: The Gold Standard developed by WWF is one of the most focused certification schemes. Endorsed by more than 40 organizations, it certifies only renewable energy and energy efficiency projects, excluding any forestry or land use projects. It was originally developed to spotlight exceptional CDM projects when there was widespread skepticism regarding the CDM governing body's ability to screen projects adequately. The Gold Standard has created a registry for emissions reductions traded on the voluntary market to ensure that the same credits are not sold multiple times. At the same time, an increasing number of certification and standard programs are focusing not only on the quantifiable environmental aspects of offset projects but on larger social and biodiversity characteristics as well. The Climate, Community and Biodiversity Standards and Social Carbon are two examples of this approach.[50]

Other initiatives target one specific segment of the market, such as voluntary offsets. In 2007 a consortium of organizations—including the International Emissions Trading Association, the Climate Group, WBCSD, and the World Economic Forum—continued work on the Voluntary Carbon Standard Framework, a global standard for project-based emissions reductions. The goal of this standard is to ensure uniformity, additionality, and registration in an extremely varied voluntary offsets market.[51]

While the inner workings of the global carbon market are being refined, it is important not to lose sight of the larger picture: how to best integrate emissions trading into the architecture of future international climate governance. It is widely agreed that the current Kyoto target is not stringent enough to meet the overall goal of the 1992 climate change treaty—preventing dangerous levels of human interference with the climate system. Kyoto was always intended as simply a first step. The initial phase of Kyoto emissions targets comes to an end in 2012, and governments will soon begin formal negotiations over what should come next. A post-2012 target is needed, among other reasons, to provide a clear signal to the market. As British economist Nicholas Stern explains: "Creating an expectation that a policy is very likely to be sustained over a long period is critical to its effectiveness." Belief in the future viability of an effective global carbon market, underpinned by strong emissions reduction targets, is key to behavior change.[52]

Countries already bound by the Kyoto Protocol have recently recognized that global emissions must be reduced 25–40 percent below their 1990 levels to avoid catastrophic levels of climate change. But this goal has not been agreed to by countries that are not party to the Kyoto agreement—notably the United States, which is alone responsible for some 20 percent of global carbon dioxide emissions from fossil fuel burning. In upcoming negotiations, governments will consider strengthening the reduction targets included in the protocol in the post-2012 period. They will also likely discuss the possibility of adding targets for developing countries, where emissions are growing rapidly but from a small per capita base.[53]

The future of the CDM is linked closely to these discussions of post-Kyoto targets. There is widespread agreement that the current design, while an interesting experiment, is not putting a meaningful dent in the rapid increase in greenhouse gas emissions in many developing countries. One way to restructure the CDM would be to allow developing countries to obtain credits for implementing broad-based policy reforms rather than piecemeal projects. As a move in this direction, the CDM Executive Board recently approved new procedures for a "programmatic CDM," in which countries can initiate a number of small projects under one larger program. It is hoped that this will result in greater emissions reductions and will make the investment more commercially attractive by reducing high transaction costs.[54]

Some critics ask whether limits should be placed on countries' ability to purchase CDM credits to meet domestic reduction targets, particularly while developing countries are not subject to binding emission limitations. Another remaining issue is whether a global emissions trading system will eventually be created, building on and linking today's ongoing experiments with instruments as diverse as the EU-ETS, the regional trading blocs developing in North America, the Clean Development Mechanism, and the many voluntary offset programs now available.[55]

Whatever the future may hold for international carbon markets, they are properly viewed as only one of many strategies that will be needed to help reverse the powerful forces fueling steadily rising greenhouse gas emissions. A range of other tools will also be important, including carbon taxes and policy reforms to reduce carbon emissions in key sectors such as buildings, transportation, and forestry. (See Chapter 6.) Individual actions to reduce carbon emissions are also essential—from shortening trips to using public transportation whenever possible, purchasing local goods, improving energy efficiency at home and in the office, and lobbying for more effective government emissions reduction policies.[56]

Although far from a magic bullet, carbon markets will be a significant feature of the global economic landscape in the years and decades ahead. One of their most important benefits is political: they are creating powerful economic constituencies that favor stricter international action to stabilize Earth's climate. This development stands poised to fundamentally alter the political calculus surrounding climate change negotiations in the years ahead—perhaps finally breaking the logjam that has so far stalled global efforts to reduce greenhouse gas emissions.[57]

CHAPTER 8

Water in a Sustainable Economy

Ger Bergkamp and Claudia W. Sadoff

Water is as essential to economies as it is to human life. Clean drinking water is needed for the health of productive populations, but only 10 percent of global water use is actually for household consumption. Agricultural water is needed to produce food and fiber. Water is a direct input in virtually all industrial production processes, and it is needed to produce hydropower and to cool thermal power plants, which together account for the vast majority of world energy supplies. In lakes and rivers it is used for transportation, fisheries, and recreation.

Water is also essential, however, to sustain the ecosystems people live in and depend on. It must be recognized for its value as an environmental resource that underpins economies and societies. Consider the findings from a disparate set of recent economic analyses:

- Wastewater treatment services provided by the Nakivubo Swamp to the citizens of Kampala, Uganda, are worth $363 per hectare of swamp area per year.
- Wetland products in the Zambezi basin in Southern Africa—including crops, livestock, fish, and tourism—are valued at an average $48 per hectare.
- The net market value of downstream flood protection given by avoiding upstream deforestation through the establishment of the Mantadia National Park in Madagascar is estimated at $12.67 per hectare per year.[1]

Recognition of water's full range of values comes at a time when societies are confronted with mounting water shortages and the fact that clean and reliable water can no longer be taken for granted, even for those who can afford it. Over the last century water usage increased sixfold, twice the rate of population growth. Fifty years ago people did not perceive water as a globally scarce resource. But

Dr. Ger Bergkamp is head of the Water Programme at IUCN–The World Conservation Union. Claudia W. Sadoff is Economic Adviser at IUCN and Principal Economist at the International Water Management Institute.

today competition for clean water is becoming the norm in many regions. Experts estimate that by 2025 over three quarters of the people in the world will face some degree of water scarcity. Already 2.8 billion people—40 percent of the global population—live in basins with some level of water scarcity. Nearly half of the world's river systems are degraded to some degree, and the flows in some rivers no longer reach the ocean.[2]

In some locations and economies water scarcity is a matter of physical shortage; in others, it is an issue of economic or sociopolitical access. Physical water scarcity can be defined as a situation in which water use is approaching or exceeding sustainable limits—that is, where more than 75 percent of

flows are withdrawn for agriculture, industry, or domestic purposes. (See Figure 8–1.) In this sense, dry areas may not be water-scarce if there is adequate water to meet all demands, while wetter areas may be effectively water-scarce. Economic water scarcity occurs when human, institutional, infrastructural, or financial limitations prevent people from gaining access to water even though there is enough available locally in nature to meet human demands. The existence of water resources and the management and delivery of water services are dual but distinct constraints.[3]

Shortages in water stem from growing economies, rising populations, and changing lifestyles. The result: ever increasing

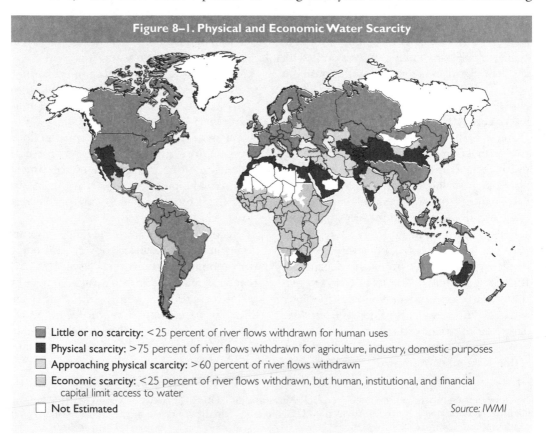

Figure 8–1. Physical and Economic Water Scarcity

■ **Little or no scarcity:** <25 percent of river flows withdrawn for human uses

■ **Physical scarcity:** >75 percent of river flows withdrawn for agriculture, industry, domestic purposes

■ **Approaching physical scarcity:** >60 percent of river flows withdrawn

■ **Economic scarcity:** <25 percent of river flows withdrawn, but human, institutional, and financial capital limit access to water

☐ **Not Estimated**

Source: IWMI

demand and competition for water. Newspapers are filled with warnings of a "global water crisis" and impending "water wars." Although these headlines may be hyperbole, there is simply no question that the way water resources are managed today is unsustainable. The resource is vulnerable to overexploitation and pollution and increasingly scarce relative to current and future demands. Uncertainties associated with climate change are adding to communities' vulnerability to an unreliable and scarce water resource.

Growing demands and rising competition over water mean that choices must be made—choices over allocating water for different purposes. Drinking water and sanitation, food and fiber production, hydropower generation and industrial production, river transportation and the maintenance of ecosystems and their services: all these need water. Choices must also be made in the ways water is used—whether it is wasted or conserved, polluted or protected, overextracted or managed sustainably, valued for all its uses or simply exploited for a few.

The increased recognition of the value of water for economies and the impending water shortages present, surprisingly, an opportunity to move toward a more sustainable global economy. As economies are closely linked to the way water is used, managing water wisely becomes an economic imperative rather than a luxury available only to those who can afford it. Moving in this direction, however, requires significant changes in the way water is viewed and managed. The practical steps needed include more inclusive and transparent decisionmaking, investments in new technologies to enhance water use efficiency and water productivity, and a careful alignment of economic signals and incentives.

Water in Today's Economy

More than 70 percent of the world's water is used for food and fiber production in agriculture (see Table 8–1), a source of livelihood for some 80 percent of the world's poor. Industry consumes an additional 20 percent, and less than 10 percent of global freshwater abstraction is used for drinking water and sanitation. Water used to sustain ecosystem services is left out of these global calculations, as are navigational, recreational, and other direct and indirect uses that do not involve monitorable withdrawals of water from rivers, lakes, or groundwater reserves.[4]

As the primary user of water, agriculture is at the heart of the water management challenge. While the average person requires two to five liters of water a day for drinking, average daily food intakes embody some 3,000 liters of water. Diets in wealthier countries involve even higher water usage. A single hamburger requires over 10,000 liters of water, taking into account what is used to produce corn to feed the cows. The International Water Management Institute recently completed a five-year comprehensive assessment of water management in agriculture to determine whether there will be sufficient water to grow enough food in 2050. It found that this will only be possible with real changes to the way in which the world produces food and manages the environment.[5]

Table 8–1. Water Use by Sector			
Region	Agriculture	Industry	Domestic and Residential
		(percent)	
Developing countries	81	11	8
Industrial countries	46	41	13
World	70	20	10

Source: See endnote 4.

A number of global trends related to agricultural production are set to have profound effects on the global water balance. Growing populations and changing diets are the primary drivers, likely tempered to some degree by gains in land and water productivity. Trade in food and fiber products could either ease or aggravate water scarcity. A surge in biofuel production may help mitigate climate change, but it will certainly consume great volumes of water. In many places, agricultural water constraints are beginning to pinch, while in growing economies the competition for water from industries and municipalities is rising.[6]

As agriculture, industry, and households vie for ever larger shares of water, ecosystems risk being the greatest losers.

Water use for energy production, industry, and services is the next largest user of water globally and the most rapidly growing one. Typically, developing economies tend to be highly dependent on agriculture, with the relative share of industrial production rising as the economy grows. Water use patterns mirror these trends: industries in industrial economies withdraw twice the global average (over 40 percent), while those in developing countries account for roughly 10 percent of national water usage.[7]

While drinking water and sanitation claim a relatively modest share of the global water resource, access to safe drinking water is recognized as an urgent global priority. The challenge of providing these services, however, is daunting. Worldwide, more than 1.1 billion people currently lack access to improved water supplies, and over 2.7 billion lack sanitation. These people are, of course, the very poor. Two thirds of those without access to water earn less than $2 a day. In 2000, at least 1.7 million deaths were attributed to unsafe water, sanitation, and hygiene practices—all, in theory, preventable.[8]

In September 2000 the global community agreed to a set of Millennium Development Goals (MDGs) that includes reducing by half the proportion of people in the world living without access to water and sanitation by 2015—at an estimated cost of some $30 billion a year. At this time it appears that this target can be achieved, although not uniformly in all countries. But the MDG goal for drinking water is not an end point. World population—today over 6.5 billion people—is expected to reach around 9 billion by 2050. Clean, potable water will need to be provided to all. Moreover, the challenge of ensuring sustainable access will remain long after the MDG investment targets are (or are not) met. In industrial countries, for example, it is estimated that $200 billion a year is needed just to replace aging water supply and sanitation systems, reduce leakage rates, and protect water quality.[9]

As agriculture, industry, and households vie for ever larger shares of water, ecosystems risk being the greatest losers. To continue to provide a range of provisioning, regulating, and cultural services, ecosystems need clean water. This demand, however, is often not taken into account when water is abstracted from aquifers or rivers are used as sewers. To maintain downstream ecosystems and their services, societies need to keep (semi-) natural river flows and leave water of sufficient quality in the river. This is referred to as the "environmental flow." Maintaining or restoring environmental flows forms a real challenge when economic growth and development intensify the competition for increasingly scarce water resources.[10]

It is clear that some level of tradeoff needs to be made between economic development and water for ecosystems. Increasingly, however, efforts to enhance economies and the environment go hand in hand. People are now defining dual benefits from keeping rivers alive and investing in economic sectors toward greater water use efficiency. Citizens are calling for action to protect water, air, and forests. Consumers are demanding "greener" businesses practices, which creates direct economic returns for sustainable management of natural resources and ecosystems. Growing recognition of the value of ecosystems and their services for economies is often behind these changes.

Managing water across scales. Water shortages are most clearly seen at local levels, but managing water is a challenge at all scales. Because water is bulky and expensive to store and move, it is generally managed and allocated at a fairly local level. Integrated water resources management—a process promoting the coordinated development and management of water, land, and related resources—focuses on the basin level and tries to reconcile various water users and demands to arrive at a sustainable system. Working at basin level is often difficult, however, because political and administrative boundaries rarely correspond with hydrological ones.[11]

At the national level, reservoirs and pipelines are built that store and transport water to where it is needed, potentially enabling water management on a country-wide scale. Most countries aspire to integrated water resources management at the national level, but this requires significant coordination across a range of institutions and stakeholders.

At the international level, integrated approaches are being proposed in transboundary river basins. Transboundary rivers join countries, so uses in one country are likely to have direct impacts on others. There are more than 260 such rivers in the world, posing potential conflicts over water but also real potential for cooperation. Transbound-

ary basin management initiatives are increasingly being seen, with many positive results.[12]

Trade in goods that embody significant amounts of water can also transcend this resource's local nature. Rather than moving water itself from scarce to plentiful regions, "virtual water" can be traded by exporting water-intensive goods from wet to dry regions. In these ways, while water is managed locally, it can have impacts on (and be affected by) water management and economic policies at many scales.[13]

Water management and equity. Water policies and investments can have important equity impacts through the opportunities and risks they create for different groups and individuals within an economy. The availability of and access to reliable water of good quality in a particular region will help spur that region's growth, whereas absence of water or lack of access to it can reduce economic opportunities and investments. Providing access to water of good quality at an affordable price creates incentives and opportunities for different sorts of economic activities in different places. Not doing so effectively forecloses opportunities or makes them unprofitable. Thus the mix and character of economic activities undertaken in a region—the structure of the regional economy, in other words—is influenced by water policies and infrastructure investments, whether intentionally or incidentally.

Great wealth has been built in many countries where early settlers and entrepreneurs obtained valuable water rights or passed the cost of pollution and natural resource degradation on to others or to future generations. In other countries, millions of people remain in poverty due in part to the burden of waterborne diseases and a lack of reliable water for agriculture or other forms of economic development.

The *Human Development Report 2006*

prepared by the U.N. Development Pro-gramme highlighted the fact that the water crisis is a challenge of poverty, inequality, and unequal power relationships as much as it is about physical water scarcity. The issues of equity and power, in addition to the strong spiritual and cultural associations that societies have with this vital resource, give rise to an extremely complex and often emotive polit-ical economy around water.[14]

Valuing Water for Sustainability

The value of water as a resource that under-pins economic activities is evident in all economies, but it is much less evident in eco-nomic statistics. Its value and that of related ecosystem services are poorly understood and rarely explicitly factored into tradeoffs and decisionmaking. Prices virtually never reflect water's full value, so water users do not see its full value or the need for conservation. These flawed "market signals" guide everyday eco-nomic decisions. If they do not recognize the value of water, then—broadly speaking—neither will the economy.

The value of water is also obscured in measures of macroeconomic performance such as the gross domestic product (GDP). In the System of National Accounts, from which the GDP is calculated, water for con-sumption or as an input into production is universally undervalued by using the price actually paid for its use. Unlike other inputs that are sold in competitive markets, this price is generally far less than water's real economic value and often even less than the cost of supplying it. Under these circum-stances, neither producers (who receive price signals that do not value water) nor policy-makers (who receive economic analyses that do not value water) can know whether they are using water beneficially or simply squan-

dering it.

Furthermore, the costs of degradation of water resources and related ecosystem services are not accounted for in national income accounts. Whereas investment in manufac-tured capital, such as a water treatment plant or a dam, is reflected as an increase in a coun-try's wealth, investments in "natural assets" such as wetlands, watersheds, or groundwa-ter aquifers are not included at all, even if they serve equivalent functions as produced cap-ital. (See Box 8–1.) In fact, quite the oppo-site tends to be true: the inflated income derived by overexploitation or degradation of natural assets is reflected as (apparently) strong growth. At the macroeconomic level, there-fore, decisionmakers are receiving perverse signals regarding the impacts—and, in par-ticular, the sustainability—of their develop-ment strategies.

Since the 1970s, many people have worked to reintroduce the value of the envi-ronment and natural resources into eco-nomics and thereby promote more sustainable economic decisionmaking. (See Chapter 2.) These perspectives are grounded in the recognition that natural resources, while once abundant, are now clearly a con-straint in some circumstances. Again, water provides an excellent demonstration. The use of deep groundwater was once con-strained by the technology and capital needed for pumps and fuel. Groundwater abstrac-tions since the 1950s, with the advent of motorized drilling rigs and pumps, have increased from 100–150 cubic kilometers per year to 950–1,000 cubic kilometers. Today groundwater is significantly overex-ploited in many countries. As a consequence, water tables fall, wells run dry and no longer provide water for human and agricultural needs, and fragile ecosystems such as wetlands are degraded. The constraint is no longer capital or labor, but the resource itself.[15]

Box 8–1. Water as Capital

Fifty years ago sustainability was simply not a part of the vocabulary, and water was not a particular consideration for economists. Classical economists recognized land (meaning all natural resources), labor, and produced capital as the basic sources of wealth. Neoclassical economists focused only on labor and capital, with "land" treated as just another interchangeable form of capital. The general view was that natural resources were abundant relative to demand and therefore not an important focus for the economist, whose task it was to allocate scarce resources—those whose use constrained alternative economic opportunities. There was little appreciation of the fact that the environment is used not only as a "source" of valuable inputs but also as a "sink" for the waste and pollution of the economy. Neither was there much thought about the possibility that the world might reach a scale of resource exploitation at which the capacity of both the "source" and "sink" functions of the environment could become a binding constraint

on well-being and economic growth.

The focus on produced rather than natural capital is particularly stark when it comes to water. Prices are typically related to the capital outlays required to deliver water (that is, the infrastructure and the operations and maintenance charges) without any component of value attributed to the resource itself. Not only does an undervalued water resource tend to be overused, it also induces distorted prices that provide poor information about whether investments make sense. It provides no insight into whether economic activities are actually creating value or whether the resource is running out and needs to be conserved. It must be said, though, that water delivery is highly capital-intensive, and produced capital will therefore remain a crucial focus for financial and economic analyses of water investments. The point to recognize is that the value of water resources also matters, and that water's availability, quality, and timing cannot simply be "assumed."

Total economic value (TEV) has become a recognized means of capturing both the market values (those that can be observed through market trades) and the nonmarket values of natural resources. (See Box 8–2.)[16]

While efforts are being made to ensure that the value of water is better incorporated into economic decisionmaking, similar efforts are being made to ensure that the economic value of the resource is recognized in water management decisions. In January 1992, in advance of the U.N. Conference on Environment and Development in Rio, the International Conference on Water and the Environment was held in Dublin, Ireland. Some 500 participants—government experts and representatives from nongovernmental groups around the world—endorsed the Dublin Principles, which distilled global good practice in water management and were a

milestone in the area of sustainable resource management. (See Box 8–3.)[17]

Principle 4, on water's economic value, unleashed a spirited debate. Many people held the view that water was a "gift of nature" or a "basic human right" and that it should therefore be provided free of charge. "Water as an economic good" was seen as a denial of water as a social or environmental good and an effort to "capture" and "commodify" the world's water. Yet Principle 4 was not intended as anything quite that radical and was not meant to deny the environmental or social aspects of water—these features were in fact underscored in the very first principle. Nor was it intended to call into question whether access to water for basic human needs would remain a priority relative to other economic uses. There was, and still is, a strong global consensus that this is the case.

Box 8–2. Total Economic Value

Total economic value has become a widely used framework for looking at the value of ecosystems. TEV is typically disaggregated into two categories, use values and non-use values.

Use value has three elements:

Direct use value, which is mainly derived from goods that can be extracted, consumed, or enjoyed directly. Examples include drinking water, fish, and hydropower, as well as recreation activities.

Indirect use value, which is mainly derived from the services that the environment provides, including regulation of river flows, flood control, and water purification.

Option value, which is the value attached to maintaining the possibility of obtaining benefits from ecosystem goods and services at a later date, including from services that appear to have a low value now but could have a much higher

value in the future because of innovations in management or new information.

Non-use values, on the other hand, derive from the benefits that ecosystems may provide that do not involve using them in any way, whether directly or indirectly:

Bequest value is the value derived from the desire to pass on ecosystems to future generations.

Existence value is the value people derive from knowing that something exists even if they never plan to use it. Thus people place value on the existence of blue whales or pandas even if they have never seen one and probably never will, as demonstrated by the sense of loss people would feel if these animals ever became extinct.

Source: See endnote 16.

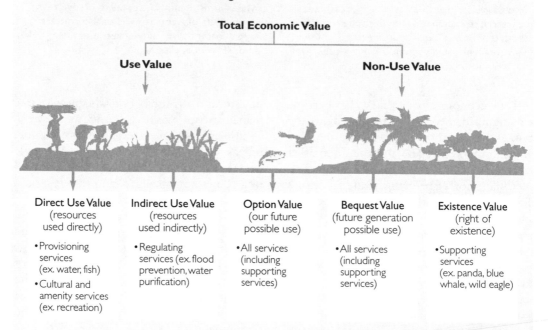

Total Economic Value

Use Value — **Non-Use Value**

Direct Use Value (resources used directly)	Indirect Use Value (resources used indirectly)	Option Value (our future possible use)	Bequest Value (future generation possible use)	Existence Value (right of existence)
• Provisioning services (ex. water, fish) • Cultural and amenity services (ex. recreation)	• Regulating services (ex. flood prevention, water purification)	• All services (including supporting services)	• All services (including supporting services)	• Supporting services (ex. panda, blue whale, wild eagle)

Principle 4 was included to highlight the importance of recognizing the full range of economic values that can be derived from water, of allocating all water resources efficiently and equitably, and of delivering water services (including sanitation and wastewater treatment) cost-effectively.

Recognizing water as an economic good

Box 8–3. The Dublin Principles

Fresh water is a finite and vulnerable resource, essential to sustain life, development and the environment. Since water sustains life, effective management of water resources demands a holistic approach, linking social and economic development with protection of natural ecosystems. Effective management links land and water uses across the whole of a catchment area or groundwater aquifer.

Water development and management should be based on a participatory approach, involving users, planners and policy-makers at all levels. The participatory approach involves raising awareness of the importance of water among policy-makers and the general public. It means that decisions are taken at the lowest appropriate level, with full public consultation and involvement of users in the planning and implementation of water projects.

Women play a central part in the provision, management and safeguarding of water. This pivotal role of women as providers and users of water and guardians of the living environment has seldom been reflected in institutional arrangements for the development and management of water resources. Acceptance and implementation of this principle requires positive policies to address women's specific needs and to equip and empower women to participate at all levels in water resources programmes, including decision-making and implementation, in ways defined by them.

Water has an economic value in all its competing uses and should be recognized as an economic good. Within this principle, it is vital to recognize first the basic right of all human beings to have access to clean water and sanitation at an affordable price. Past failure to recognize the economic value of water has led to wasteful and environmentally damaging uses of the resource. Managing water as an economic good is an important way of achieving efficient and equitable use, and of encouraging conservation and protection of water resources.

Source: See endnote 17.

brought the value of water itself to the foreground. When water was abundant relative to demand, the challenge of water management was to raise the capital and find the skilled engineers to deliver the service. Where there was a demand for water, engineers created supply by developing new sources and designing delivery systems. The resource was not perceived as a constraint. Economists were involved in water resources development only to the extent that they could assist in defining a least-cost approach to delivering new water supplies.

Highlighting water's economic value in other uses, including ecosystem uses, helped shift the paradigm of water management from a supply-side focus on an unlimited resource to one that also includes demand management of a limited resource. Today, calls for new water supplies are questioned and water conservation is increasingly seen as one of the options to "fulfill" future water demands. Can people do more, or better, with the water already in use? Is it really necessary to tap "untapped" resources, and for what purpose? What will these additional abstractions cost, and how will they affect ecosystems and current water users? Do benefits justify economic, environmental, and social costs? These questions, in turn, prompt innovations in the way water is managed.

Innovations That Turn the Tide

Fortunately, given the pressures on water supplies and quality described earlier, innovations are constantly being made in the ways water is used and managed. Innovations occur in the way water is stored and distributed, allocated and priced, and used and reused for productive and ecosystems purposes. Massive investments are being made in new water storage and delivery systems, while established water systems and management practices are being reassessed in light of climate change predictions. New technologies are changing the ways in which water is used, cleaned, and reused to meet human, economic, and environmental needs. Serious efforts are also being made in the "software" of water management, to make better use of currently available water, to safeguard the quality and integrity of water resources, and to clarify goals and risks by involving stakeholders in design and decisionmaking.

Innovations in technology. Technological innovations already offer many ways of managing water more efficiently, productively, and sustainably. Industries are investing in new technologies and processes that diminish water use and wastewater discharges. Household consumers are being offered water-saving technologies such as low-flush toilets, low-flow showers, and faucet aerators to diminish demand. Agricultural productivity is being leveraged by drip irrigation and other targeted water delivery technologies and by soil fertility and conservation techniques. Moreover, the adoption of established agronomic good practices could lead to real gains in water productivity in many countries. In rainfed agriculture, which accounts for some 80 percent of global cropland and the livelihoods of most of the world's poor, adoption of already proven technologies could at least double current crop yields. Innovations in agriculture are particularly beneficial because agriculture is such a large consumer of water that a relatively small percentage decline here could allow a relatively large percentage increase in other uses.[18]

Water supplies are being enhanced in many countries using innovative wastewater treatment and reuse techniques. Break-throughs continue in desalination, where advances in technologies and energy efficiency have brought costs down dramatically in the past decade so that desalination is now an economic option for water supplies in the coastal cities of industrial countries. Singapore, a recognized leader in urban water management, has diversified its water sources by leveraging innovations in water reuse, desalination, stormwater management, multipurpose water storage, and high-quality recycled water. Singapore has also pursued demand management measures, such as reducing water losses due to leakage in pipes and restructuring its water pricing and access policy to encourage more-efficient water use while ensuring low-cost water for poor households.[19]

Managers are increasingly looking at investments in and management of "natural water infrastructure" such as watersheds, wetlands, lakes, and floodplains to be used as complements or even substitutes for infrastructure like dams, weirs, and wastewater treatment plants—all while providing biodiversity, aesthetic, and recreational benefits that are all increasingly valued. In Costa Rica, for example, the water utility of the Heredia region pays landholders to protect forest on the hill slopes from which they derive their water, which has proved to be very beneficial for both landowners and municipal water customers. In the United States, the government is considering converting strategic tracts of the coastal areas that were battered by Hurricane Katrina into public wetlands, to help mitigate the impacts of future hurricanes.[20]

Innovations in management. Water management practices are evolving. Integrated water resources management is now a universal aspiration—albeit one that is quite challenging to implement. River basin organizations are being established to manage water holistically at the basin level, some using highly sophisticated computer models to grapple with the complexity of their river systems. Stakeholder consultations are considered routine good practice these days in order to better understand the social and livelihood impacts of water management decisions, although structuring these consultations to have meaningful impact is a continuing challenge. Environmental flows is an innovative framework for ensuring that adequate instream water is allocated to sustain the health of river systems, with much work ongoing as to how to establish and institutionalize environmental flow regimes.[21]

The range of current innovations include finding better options for water management and also better ways of making choices among those options. The importance of better decisionmaking in water management was highlighted in 2000 in the report of the World Commission on Dams. Built on an awareness of the range of interrelated interests and impacts of water management, multistakeholder consultations are increasingly being used to strengthen policy design and implementation. This apparently obvious innovation—to consult the people who will be affected—has proved essential in enhancing sustainability.[22]

The private sector is also innovating. Motivated both by consumer demand for "greener" products and the recognition that sustainable strategies can be extremely cost-effective, many corporations now find that sustainability makes good business sense. Increasingly, progressive companies are working with community and stakeholder groups to create water management partnerships. The Sustainable Agriculture Initiative (SAI) is an example of a major food industry effort: some 30 partners are actively supporting the development and implementation of sustainable agricultural practices to safeguard the future availability of natural resources and enhance their efficiency. Nestlé, a founder of the SAI, has recently begun targeted trainings in water management for farmers who supply the company with its primary commodities.[23]

Innovations in market-based tools. Market signals and incentives, which have often led to overexploitation and degradation of water resources, can and are increasingly being used to enhance the sustainability of water management. One way this can be done more effectively is through water prices and wastewater fees. These can signal the true value of water to every user, so that people are aware of—and bear—the full costs they incur when using or degrading water. Prices set to reflect the full costs of sustainable water management should also, by definition, generate sufficient revenues to accomplish this.

> Integrated water resources management is now a universal aspiration—albeit one that is quite challenging to implement.

Water managers are beginning to construct better-targeted pricing schemes based on a range of tariff structures, on survey techniques to determine consumers' willingness and ability to pay for services, and on more sophisticated monitoring and information systems. Prices can be structured to meet multiple objectives: allocate water resources efficiently; ensure financial viability so that reliable service can be delivered; provide affordable access to clean water for drinking, cooking, and washing requirements; and encourage water conservation. Wastewater fees are being targeted to ensure water quality and to encourage industries to minimize overall volumes of water use. Water pricing, however, tends to be a controversial topic. (See Box 8–4.)[24]

Water pricing, however, is not a panacea.

Box 8–4. Water Pricing and Water Prices

Economic water pricing does not necessarily require charging the very poorest users the full cost of water. There are likely to be cases where targeted subsidies will be needed to meet the basic water needs of the poor. But it is essential to understand the actual level of subsidy embodied in water prices—that is, the difference between the price paid by the consumer and the true value of the water and its associated delivery costs—and to make transparent policy decisions based on those full costs. It is also absolutely essential to understand who receives those subsidies.

Governments have traditionally subsidized all water use rather than just targeting poorer people. When this happens, those who use the most water receive most of the subsidy. So a poor family who uses, say, 50–100 liters of water each a day for basic needs would receive a subsidy on that volume of water. Meanwhile, a wealthy family might consume 10 or 100 times that amount of water to wash cars, water lawns, and fill swimming pools and would receive 10 or 100 times that amount of subsidy. By subsidizing (undervaluing) all water, all users are effectively encouraged to overuse it. Underpricing water also means that utilities cannot recover their costs, which often leads to poor service and an inability to extend municipal systems and provide water to new users.

"Getting the prices right" does not mean that water should be made unaffordable to the very poor, who consume just a very small share of the water governments deliver. Rather, it means pricing the vast majority of water in a way that encourages productive use and conservation, and carefully structuring and targeting pro-poor subsidies as the exception rather than the rule in water pricing.

Source: See endnote 24.

In some countries cultural practices and beliefs hamper or even forbid the use of water pricing. In some cases it may be uneconomical or infeasible to recover water fees at all. Fortunately, there are numerous market-based tools, as well as legal, regulatory, and participatory ones, that can aid the sustainable management of water. In all cases, good governance and consumer and environmental protection will be crucial for the sustainable management of water.

Water markets, tradable water rights, and water quality credits are increasingly being used to enhance the efficiency of water use and allocation within and across sectors. Water markets are arrangements in which users are granted water rights—sometimes rights of ownership but more often time-bound use rights (called usufruct rights)—which they can sell or trade. In a functioning market, water can thus be "moved" to higher value uses in a transparent transaction that both increases the productivity of water and diminishes tensions among competing users. Appropriate and capable institutions are necessary to ensure transparency, enforcement, and protections for vulnerable groups and ecosystems.

Efforts are being made to explicitly incorporate water into calculations of GDP, to ensure that macroeconomic indicators provide more rational guidance about the impact of water use on economies. These efforts are part of a broader movement toward environmental accounting that began in the late 1980s and was consolidated in 2003 with the System of Environmental and Economic Accounting. The United Nations recently developed a more detailed, specialized System of Environmental-Economic Accounting for Water. There appears to be a good deal of interest in these accounts but little systematic adoption to date, particularly in developing countries.[25]

The concept of "genuine savings" is another innovation in conceptualizing macroeconomic measures of sustainable wealth.

(See also Chapter 2.) Rather than focusing on economic production (like GDP), this approach looks at an economy's creation or depletion of wealth—broadly defined. Genuine savings takes net savings measures for an economy and subtracts the value of resource depletion and environmental degradation (and adds the value of investment in human capital) to arrive at a measure that more fully reflects the changes in the real sources of wealth of an economy. By this measure, many countries are being progressively impoverished by negative genuine savings patterns. Using this to identify losses in wealth can help direct policymakers toward a more sustainable development path, economically and environmentally.[26]

Trade can also influence water management decisions, both positively and negatively. Global trade in agricultural goods can diminish water stress and take pressure off ecosystems if, for example, water-intensive goods are exported from water-rich areas and imported by water-poor regions, as noted earlier. Recent studies suggest that such trade in virtual water could reduce worldwide water use in agriculture by 6 percent. It must also be kept in mind, however, that packaging, storing, and transporting large volumes of goods also carries its own environmental footprint.[27]

Health and safety standards, such as water quality standards imposed on traded agricultural products, can be drivers for reform and investment in environmental protection. (On the other hand, in some instances standards can effectively create trade barriers against poor countries.) Diminished barriers to trade in environment-enhancing or water-saving technologies and services can help spread state-of-the-art solutions. The World Trade Organization's current Doha Round of negotiations includes the first multilateral negotiations on trade and environment, with a specific call to diminish barriers to water provision and wastewater treatment services. (See Chapter 14.)

In the absence of effective national regulation frameworks and enforcement, however, global markets can aggravate water stress and ecosystem degradation by creating strong incentives for individuals or corporations to produce inappropriate products (such as water-intensive exports from water-scarce regions) using destructive practices (polluting or overabstracting water sources, for example), which can result in overexploitation of resources, excessive pollution, and the degradation of ecosystem services on which the poor and the environment rely.

Paying for ecosystem services is another market-based tool that seeks to create incentives for maintaining a water resource or paying for watershed services. (See Table 8–2.) These payment mechanisms are differentiated by the degree of government intervention in administration of the schemes and the characteristics of the buyers and sellers. Four types of approaches are distinguished:
• private payment schemes;
• cap-and-trade schemes, under a regulatory cap or floor;
• certification schemes for environmental goods; and
• public payment schemes, including fiscal mechanisms.
In practice, many initiatives are a mix of these approaches, adapted to local needs and context. (See also Chapter 9.)[28]

Private payment schemes have the lowest level of government intervention. In these, private entities agree among themselves to provide payments or rewards in return for maintenance or restoration of a watershed service. The actual transaction mechanisms in such schemes can take many forms; the most popular ones are transfer payments, land purchases, cost sharing, and the purchase of

Table 8–2. Selected Examples of Payments for Watershed Services

Location	Activities Compensated	Watershed Services Provided	Service Buyer	Service Seller	Price Paid (per hectare per year)
Murray Darling Basin, Australia	Reforestation	Salinity control Freshwater supply	Downstream farmers' association	Government and upstream landowners	$45
Sarapiqui watershed, Costa Rica	Protecting, sustainably managing, and replanting forests	Hydropower Regulation of flows Sedimentation control	Energia Global (hydropower company) and National Fund for Forest Financing (FONAFIFO)	Private upstream landowners	$48
Costa Rica	Protecting, sustainably managing, and replanting forests	Freshwater supply Wildlife habitat Cultural heritage and identity	National Forest Office and FONAFIFO	Private upstream landowners	$45–116
United States	Soil conservation	Soil protection Sedimentation control Water quality control Regulation of flow	U.S. Department of Agriculture	Farmers	$125
State of Paraná, Brazil	Watershed restoration	Freshwater supply Wildlife habitat	State of Paraná	Municipalities and private landowners	$170
Rhine-Meuse Basin, France	Reduced-input farm management	Water quality control Freshwater supply	Perrier Vittel (private bottler of mineral water)	Upstream farmers	$230

Source: See endnote 28.

development rights to land.

With transfer payments, a service seller receives money from a service buyer in return for the protection or restoration of a watershed service. For example, a hydroelectric power company experiencing increasingly irregular water flows might decide to pay landowners upstream to change their management practices. Here the company assumes that a different management practice will improve water supply.

In a land purchase, a private party may decide to buy land from another private party with the aim of safeguarding the watershed services provided there. Strictly speaking, this is a mechanism for payment for watershed services only if the land is purchased and then leased back to the former owner under a contract stipulating how the land can be used or managed.

In the third type of private payment scheme, beneficiaries of watershed services can agree among themselves to share the costs that must be met by service sellers upstream to maintain or restore watershed services. For example, if conversion of nat-

ural vegetation upstream is affecting water quality, downstream landowners can agree to share the costs of compensating or rewarding upstream landowners for maintaining or establishing preferred land uses in certain areas.

In cap-and-trade schemes, a cap is established for, say, the release of pollutants or abstraction of groundwater. In the case of pollution, the cap is the aggregate maximum amount of pollution that can be released by participating entities. (See also Chapter 7.) Tradable pollution permits or credits are then allocated by dividing up the allowable overall total among polluters. Industries or companies can sell permits they do not need to other participants who need more than they were allocated. This rewards companies able to cut their pollutant discharge and penalizes those who pollute more heavily, creating an incentive for them to invest in pollution control. Trading increases the economic efficiency of water and environmental management by enabling companies or landholders to buy permits from those able to comply in a cheaper way.

Certification or eco-labeling schemes are a third payment mechanism for watershed goods and services. Transactions occur between private parties, but payment is embedded in the price paid for a traded product, such as certified timber, fish, or organic produce. Payments under this approach can be made to suppliers as, for example, a fixed sum, a fixed sum per hectare, or a price premium on products sold.

Public payment schemes are the most common form of payment scheme for environmental services and have the highest level of involvement by public agencies. Service buyers in these schemes are public authorities such as municipalities or national governments who are typically motivated by the need to provide safe drinking water or regu-

late river flows. Mechanisms for payment in these schemes include user fees, land purchase, and land easement, which are rights to the specific use of land owned by others.

Environmental taxes are fiscal mechanisms that can be used to ensure that some or all of the external costs of land use are internalized in the decisionmaking process. They create direct price signals for producers and consumers. Taxes can be used as a positive incentive when people are exempted from paying them. Taxes can also be used negatively—to discourage consumption or activities that are detrimental to the environment.

Aligning Economic and Water Policies

Water management and economic management is a two-way street. Water management affects the performance and structure of economies—and economic policies have an impact on the condition of water resources. The sustainability of economies and water-related ecosystems could be strengthened by better aligning the two and by looking for more-efficient and more-equitable uses of water resources across various sectors and users.

On the one hand, water management should be designed with due consideration for its economic implications. What sorts of economic activities will be encouraged or discouraged? Are these prospective changes consistent with broader economic, environmental, and social goals? Are they likely to enhance growth or sustainability? Who will benefit and who will be harmed? How will this affect poor people and the broader distribution of wealth?

On the other hand, those making economic policies should consider the implications for water management. Will sectoral and macroeconomic policies encourage more-efficient and sustainable water management or lead to waste, overexploitation, and degradation of the water resource and aquatic ecosystem? Can policies be modified or compensatory mechanisms put in place so that economic incentives are aligned to promote sustainable water management?

In a sustainable economy, social, economic, and regulatory incentives need to be aligned to promote:

• water use patterns that are sustainable;
• water allocations that enhance current and future welfare; and
• water investments, technologies, and practices that promote efficiency, water quality, conservation, and ecosystem integrity.

Today's water use patterns are clearly not sustainable. There is strong evidence that under a business-as-usual scenario there will not be enough water to produce the food needed to feed the world in 2050. Current practices are also depleting and degrading many ecosystems, raising serious concerns for the future of the natural environment and the sustainability of ecosystem services. Grappling with environmental and ecosystem dynamics remains the main challenge for sustainable water resources management in industrial and developing countries alike.[29]

There is reason for both optimism and activism. We are not on a straight-line path to the future, and the best available information suggests that over the coming decades the world can make the changes necessary to feed the planet and sustain it at the same time. As described in this chapter, a range of innovations in technologies and management practices are increasing the potential productivity of water in all its various uses. The supply of water available for people and the environment is also effectively being enhanced through increasingly sophisticated management and technologies. Ecosystem diagnostics and management techniques are demonstrating cost-effective means for sustaining and even strengthening ecosystem health.[30]

Broader consultations and more structured and transparent decisionmaking is helping water managers to capture the range of water's value and to avoid many of the environmental and social missteps of the past. Increasing recognition of the need to sustain ecosystem services and the desire to conserve the natural environment are also leading to a closer alignment of economic signals and incentives with sustainability.

Together these innovations, and those still to come, can help ensure the sustainability of water management, ecosystems, and economies. The challenge is to change.

CHAPTER 9

Banking on Biodiversity

Ricardo Bayon

Protecting the world's biodiversity requires answers to a few not entirely rhetorical questions: Assuming agreement of the need to protect Earth's biological wealth, how much would you be prepared to pay to protect an endangered fly? Would you spend $1.50, $15, $150,000, or more? How about society as a whole, how much should society spend on the protection of this fly? Does the answer depend on the nature of the fly itself? On its role in the ecosystem? Or is the calculus based on something else—perhaps on what you must give up to save the fly, or your standard of living, or your priorities?

The questions may seem crass and materialistic—and in some ways they are—but they are essential if the world is to conserve the species and ecosystems that sustain humankind. The reason is simple: like many other important matters, the staggering loss of biodiversity is really a matter of values—and not just the principles that allow people to dis-

tinguish right from wrong, but also the more mundane concept of economic values.

In a way, the issue boils down to the fact that the world is losing species and ecosystems because the economic system has a blind spot. It sends signals that cutting down a rainforest to grow soybeans or palm oil plantations makes more economic sense than leaving that forest intact. It says that building a shopping mall to sell iPods is more valuable than having a wetland that buffers coasts against storms, filters water, and provides nesting ground for birds. Is it, therefore, any surprise that people take such signals seriously?

Or, to put it another way, the fact that the U.S. suburban landscape appears to have more bowling alleys than wetlands is simply a symptom of an economic system that has its values—used here in the sense of its prices—wrong. It is what economists call a problem of externalities. Some values—like

Ricardo Bayon is Director of Ecosystem Marketplace, a leading source of information on market and payment schemes for ecosystem services.

that of a species of woodpecker or of a particular ecosystem such as a rainforest or a wetland—do not enter into the economic system. They are external to it, and so they are not taken into account when economic decisions are made.

Indeed, for eons the price of nature has been woefully close to zero. Supply outstripped demand, and priceless came to mean worthless. But that equation is changing. Priceless nature is becoming increasingly scarce (see Box 9–1) and therefore needs to be made valuable once again. Giving some economic value to biodiversity would make it easier to protect. At the very least, standing rainforests would not compare so unfavorably when considered against soybean fields and palm oil plantations. Their value would no longer be zero.[1]

It may sound strange, even counterintuitive, but the solution to the loss of biodiversity may actually lie in the very same markets that appear to be causing the problem. It may lie in creating payment schemes for biodiversity, mechanisms that give nature a value and that force the economy to look into its blind spots. Luckily, a good number of countries—from Australia and Brazil to the United States—have been experimenting with such schemes, sometimes for more than 20 years, and there is much to be learned.

Countries use a variety of mechanisms for giving value to ecosystems and the services they provide. In essence, these can be summarized as follows:

- *Government sets the price*: This is done either by fining those who damage the ecosystems (through endangered species laws, for instance) or by paying those who conserve it (providing tax breaks or subsidies for conservation, for example). While these systems are useful and play an important role in protecting biodiversity, they suffer from a fundamental flaw: they do not send

the right signals to the economy; they do not permit society, via markets, to determine and understand the actual value (the price) of biodiversity.

- *Voluntary transactions set the price*: Users of ecosystem services voluntarily agree on the value with those who provide the services. These "self-organized private deals" are sometimes mislabeled as "markets," but true markets depend on multiple buyers and multiple sellers meeting regularly to exchange goods and services. In contrast, in most cases these are one-time-only deals. They may also take the form of "voluntary biodiversity offsets," in which an individual or company that damages biodiversity pays to "protect, enhance, or restore" an equivalent amount of biodiversity somewhere else.

- *A hybrid system sets the price*: In this case scarcity of a traditionally "public" good is established through government regulation, which then forces buyers and sellers to negotiate in order to set a price for the good or service in question. Examples of this include various "cap-and-trade" schemes in the United States for sulfur dioxide and in Europe for greenhouse gases (see Chapter 7). These schemes create true markets because they generate demand for services from multiple buyers and therefore lead to the provision of services from multiple sellers.

This chapter focuses mainly on the third of these mechanisms, regulatory cap-and-trade systems. While government payment schemes and voluntary biodiversity offsets are extremely useful and are likely to account for the majority of global payment schemes for biodiversity in the near future, they tell more about where we are now than where we might be in the future. The new and emerging regulated markets for biodiversity offsets hold the key to that future.

Box 9–1. The Escalating Problem of Biodiversity Loss

The loss of biodiversity is tremendous and disturbing, and it continues to grow at an exponential rate (see Figure)—even though scientists for decades have been saying that species and ecosystems are important, that they provide invaluable goods and services, that they keep people fed and clothed and Earth habitable.

The Millennium Ecosystem Assessment, one of the most comprehensive scientific assessments of the world's biodiversity ever undertaken, came to this sobering conclusion: "Human actions are fundamentally, and to a significant extent irreversibly, changing the diversity of life on Earth, and most of these changes represent a loss of biodiversity." The authors cited ample evidence to support their conclusion. For example:

• Virtually all of Earth's ecosystems have now been dramatically transformed through human actions. More land was converted to cropland in the 30 years after 1950 than in the 150 years between 1700 and 1850.

• Some 35 percent of mangroves have been lost in the last two decades in countries where adequate data are available.

• Over half of the 14 biomes assessed have experienced a 20–50 percent conversion to human use, with temperate and Mediterranean forests and temperate grasslands being the most affected.

• There are approximately 100 well-documented extinctions of birds, mammals, and amphibians over the last 100 years—a rate 100 times higher than background rates.

• Some 12 percent of bird species, 23 percent of mammals, and 25 percent of conifers are currently threatened with extinction. In addition, 32 percent of amphibians are threatened with extinction, but information is more limited and this may be an underestimate.

Sociobiologist E. O. Wilson attributes the loss of biodiversity to five forces summarized in the acronym HIPPO—habitat loss, invasive species, pollution, population growth, and overexploitation of species for consumption (essentially overconsumption). While he is correct in singling out each of these forces, they are in many ways interconnected: the first three are byproducts of the last two. They are essentially the result of human numbers multiplied by human greed. And given that human population is expected to go from 6 billion in 2000 to 9 billion in 2050 and that per capita consumption of everything from water and energy to oil and food is growing at practically exponential rates, the pressures on biodiversity are likely to become unbearably intense.

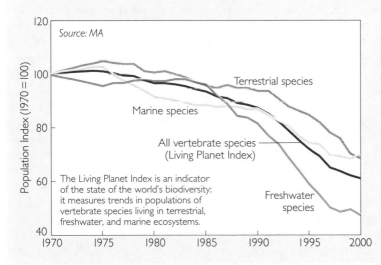

Source: MA

Population Index (1970 = 100)

Terrestrial species

Marine species

All vertebrate species (Living Planet Index)

The Living Planet Index is an indicator of the state of the world's biodiversity: it measures trends in populations of vertebrate species living in terrestrial, freshwater, and marine ecosystems.

Freshwater species

Source: See endnote 1.

The Fly in the Ointment

Before delving too deeply into these issues, however, a story: There is a small town nestled in the sand dunes east of Los Angeles—Colton, California—that provides some idea of the new world that may be emerging as a result of regulated markets for biodiversity offsets. Colton is smack in the economic center of San Bernadino county, one of the fastest-growing counties in the United States.

But there is a fly in Colton's ointment of future economic growth. The city is currently involved in a series of legal battles over how much it should be prepared to pay to save an endangered fly: the Delhi Sands Flower-loving Fly, a rather pretty insect that, like a butterfly, hovers and sips nectar from local flowers. This tiny creature has the distinction of being the first fly—and only the seventeenth insect—to be declared an endangered species in the United States.[2]

According to the U.S. Endangered Species Act (ESA), no individual or entity, public or private, can harm an endangered species—not even a fly—without a permit from the government. Thus shortly after this fly was listed as an endangered species, construction of a hospital in San Bernadino county ground to a halt. The hospital had planned to pave over seven acres of occupied fly habitat, but that all of sudden became illegal. The hospital then had to spend $4 million redrawing its plans, moving its parking lot 250 feet, and making a few other minor changes. All so it wouldn't harm a fly.[3]

How much is a fly worth? Do you judge by what the fly does? With this fly, scientists do not know the answer to that question. They know that pollinators, such as this fly, tend to have important and symbiotic relationships with the plants they feed on. In some cases, without the pollinator the plant cannot reproduce. Perhaps the flower-loving fly plays that role. Or it could be a cornerstone species, without which an entire ecosystem could collapse. Or maybe protecting this fly will protect dozens of other species, some of which may not even have been discovered yet. Or maybe not.

E. O. Wilson has written: "I will argue that every scrap of biological diversity is price-less, to be learned and cherished, and never to be surrendered without a struggle." The state of California, in contrast, has a more moderated view. Having determined that the fly should be protected, it decided to let the market decide what it costs to conserve it. And the market determined that the going rate in California for Delhi-sands fly habitat is currently somewhere between $100,000 and $150,000 an acre.[4]

This story is interesting not so much because it is hard to believe that people are buying fly habitat—let alone paying $150,000 for it—but rather because it forces society to answer that crass and materialistic question: How much is nature really worth? Some would argue that the question should not even be asked. And yet society answers this question "by default" every day. Every time people buy soybeans, for example, they are putting a value on the Amazonian rainforests that were cleared to grow them. At least in the case of the fly, the price tag is clear, evident, and visible. If a developer wants to pave over fly habitat, it will cost the company (in today's market) as much as $150,000 an acre.

If that were all there was to this story, the concept of putting a price on endangered species would be quite troubling. It implies that someone could pay the price set by the marketplace and then go ahead and destroy the last surviving population of a species. But that is not what is happening. The $150,000 paid to pave over the fly's habitat is actually being used to protect or create habitat for that same fly somewhere else. It is, in other words, an "offset"—not unlike the carbon offsets people are buying to counteract their greenhouse gas emissions. (See Chapter 7.)

As the money goes into legally and financially protecting the flies forever (at least in theory), in a way it is a market, or at least a market-like mechanism. It puts a value on endangered species and habitat, turning them into marketable assets. It puts a cost on the fly for those who would harm it, and at the same time it creates a value for those who would conserve it. It is this marvelous alchemy—turning cost into value, liability into asset—that may ultimately allow society to preserve biodiversity. But does it work? And, if so, how does it work?

Wetland Mitigation Banking

Since the mid-1980s the United States has had a series of functioning biodiversity markets worth more than $3 billion a year. This system is currently the largest and most well established experiment on Earth on creating biodiversity markets. Although these are markets and they involve the private sector, it is government that makes these markets possible. The system that makes the flower-loving fly worth real cold, hard cash begins with government regulation. Indeed it has its roots in two very important U.S. laws: the Clean Water Act (CWA) and the Endangered Species Act, both passed in the 1970s.[5]

Although the Clean Water Act is basically designed to prevent the dumping of chemicals into the nation's rivers, it is also in some respects a rather innovative biodiversity law—thanks to section 404, which attempts to prevent the placement of dredged and filling materials into the "waters of the US." Anyone wishing to dredge or fill a wetland considered of national importance in the United States must first obtain a permit through a program administered by the U.S. Army Corps of Engineers and the U.S. Environmental Protection Agency (EPA).[6]

In considering whether to award this permit, EPA and the Corps are supposed to follow a process known as "sequencing," in which the first step is to determine if the damage to the wetlands can be avoided. If it

cannot, the next step is to minimize the damage. Finally, the developer is supposed to offset, mitigate, or compensate for any damage that cannot be minimized. This hierarchy should be considered in all forms of offsets, but it is not usually codified into law. Section 404 of the CWA is an exception.[7]

The law is also quite clear on what is considered appropriate compensation for the damage to wetlands: developers must "create, enhance, or restore" an amount equal to or greater than the amount being damaged in a wetland of "similar function and values" in the same watershed. In some special cases, protecting a similar wetland is considered suitable compensation, though this is rare. The law recognizes that not all wetlands are equal. Someone cannot damage a wetland in California and protect one in New Jersey. In short, the law is trying to ensure "no net loss" of wetlands.[8]

The compensation for any development projects that harm wetlands—whether done by private developers or the government—can be undertaken by the developers themselves or by third parties. And the Army Corps of Engineers and EPA are charged with overseeing this process and making sure the compensation happens.

One of the most interesting repercussions of this law is that there are now private, for-profit, wetland mitigation bankers who make money by creating, enhancing, and restoring wetlands and then selling the resulting "wetland credits" to needy developers. (See Box 9–2.) They buy wetland areas in parts of the United States that are likely to experience economic growth; they work with the Corps and EPA to get "credits" for their "creation, enhancement, and restoration" of wetlands (hence creating a "wetland bank"); and then they sell these wetland credits to developers who find themselves in need of compensation. In other words, wetland mitigation banking

Box 9–2. The Evolution of a Wetland Banker

Steve Morgan is a duck hunter who now makes a living as a wetland banker. He came to this business via a strange and somewhat circuitous route. In the late 1980s, Morgan and a few colleagues bought a piece of land in central California to create a "hunting club," a place where streams and wetlands would attract the ducks they so loved to hunt. Unfortunately for Morgan—or perhaps fortunately—the wetlands that served as a rest stop on the ducks' flyway were also slated to serve as the site of a major highway bypass. Under the U.S. Constitution, the government can force private landowners to sell their land (assuming adequate compensation) when it is deemed in the "public interest." In legal jargon, the law is called "eminent domain."

Naturally, Morgan was furious. But in discussions with the local authorities, he found out that while it was perfectly legal for the U.S. government to strip him of his duck-hunting grounds in order to make a highway, it was not legal—thanks to the Clean Water Act—for anyone to damage the wetland without "minimizing and mitigating" (or offsetting) that damage.

Morgan decided to take advantage of this situation. He bought 315 acres of his neighbor's farm across the street and then "enhanced and restored" the existing wetland complex by removing invasive species and returning water to the system of streams and channels that had in the past been dammed, dredged, or filled (thus attracting his beloved ducks). With the approval of the U.S. Army Corps of Engineers and EPA, he then turned around and sold the wetland credits from this land (for tens of thousands of dollars an acre) to the Department of Transportation that was building the highway on his former hunting club, allowing them to offset the damage to the wetland they wanted to pave over by protecting the restored wetlands on his new property. The end result was that Steve Morgan had created the first "wetland mitigation bank" west of the Mississippi.

Based on this success, Morgan went on to found a wetland mitigation company called Wildlands Inc. Two decades later, this has become a multimillion-dollar business that employs some 100 people and manages thousands of acres of restored wetlands. (It is also involved with species mitigation banking.) In March 2007, Wildlands received a major capital infusion from Parthenon Capital, a private equity investment firm that manages some $1.5 billion.

In destroying his wetlands, the government had upended Steve Morgan's life, but that gave him a whole new way of making a living and pushed him to become an accidental pioneer for a whole new industry.

Source: See endnote 9.

is possible because the government is restricting supply and allowing the market to set a price—a value—on this particular aspect of biodiversity.[9]

In a way, it amounts to governments tinkering with the economic infrastructure in order to protect those aspects of biodiversity that should be valued, the externalities. And it is no small matter: Although there are no reliable figures on the size and value of wetland banking, the best guess is that there are more than 400 wetland banks throughout the United States, that the market for wetland mitigation is worth more than $3 billion a year, and that entrepreneurial wetland mitigation bankers account for about one third of that business. The rest is composed of people doing their own wetland mitigation in order to obtain permits or paying the government or nonprofit groups a fee instead of compensation.[10]

Although wetland mitigation banking has proved to be a rather innovative concept—fueling the growth of a new "nature management industry"—it is important to point out that it is by no means perfect. Like all innovations, it has come in for some serious criticism. Some of these critiques are really about a reticence to assign a dollar value to biodiversity, reflecting an inherent dislike for the use of markets and capitalist tools to protect nature.[11]

The critics often argue that the only way to protect nature is for government to restrict its use and strongly enforce this restriction. Although there is clearly a place for this type of protection, there are other powerful tools that should be used as well. Besides, without wetland banking U.S. wetlands would be worth little or nothing, and they would continue to disappear under strip malls, airports, and highways. With banking, their loss has at least a very real monetary cost and can generate funds that may actually lead to the creation of new, very similar wetlands. More important, this cost sends a signal: developers who want to develop a site that has wetlands will spend considerably more per acre, so they had better be absolutely sure they must have that particular site.

Two other criticisms do merit concern, however. The first has to do with the fact that it is notoriously difficult to "create, enhance, or restore" wetlands, so the wetland acre used as compensation may be inherently "less valuable" in terms of biodiversity than the acre being damaged. Partly for this reason, many of the U.S. wetland banking systems require that each acre damaged be compensated with two, three, or more acres of wetland "created, enhanced, or restored." It is a form of overcompensation or insurance and, while it alone does not resolve the matter, it does help.

So far the studies on the quality of the wetlands created as compensation are mixed. In one study conducted in Ohio, scientists looked at the 12 oldest of the state's 25 wetland mitigation banks. Although these had been studied and monitored by the Army Corps and EPA, the study found that many were not up to standard when checked against stringent scientific criteria. Indeed, against these measurements only three banks scored in the "successful category," while five passed in some areas and failed in others. The remaining four failed nearly every assessment, functioning more like shallow dead pools than wetlands. More disturbing, none of the government agencies charged with oversight were taking the bank managers to task for this fact. Overall, however, the study found that the banks were most successful when they maximized the areas defined as wetland, minimized areas of open water, and had similar plant and animal life to natural wetlands.[12]

Despite its implicit criticism of banking, the study's author, wetland ecologist John Mack, remains one of the more steadfast supporters of mitigation banking. He says that the conclusion from his study should not be that banking as a concept is flawed but rather that, when done properly, it can succeed. He argues that by using better designs, performance standards, enforcement, financing, and an appropriate watershed approach, wetland mitigation banking can produce high-quality wetlands.[13]

The second important criticism centers on how wetland mitigation banks are monitored and implemented. How is it possible to ensure that an acre of wetland protected today will still be there tomorrow, the day after, and the day after that? There is also a related question: Will funding be ensured to maintain the newly created wetland? To address these issues, the Corps and EPA require that wetland bankers provide both legal and financial assurances that the "created, enhanced, or restored" wetland will last (presumably) in perpetuity. The legal assurances usually take the form of conservation easements (legal restrictions on the use of land) held by third parties (usually a non-profit or the government). The financial assurances can take a variety of forms. They are either trust funds set up to produce the interest necessary to run the bank or bonds or letters of credit that hold the bank financially liable for the protection of the wetlands.[14]

In addition to these assurances, wetland mitigation banking requires a considerable amount of enforcement and verification. It needs the government agencies overseeing the system to continuously monitor and ensure that the promised wetland protection is delivered. Such "perpetual oversight," however, is costly and is usually very difficult for understaffed and underfunded government agencies. Nevertheless, as the mitigation industry grows it may generate the funds needed to monitor itself.

Despite these warranted criticisms, wetland mitigation is still probably a better system than the alternative—which, realistically, amounted to little or no real protection. Even if there were no wetland banking, roads would still be built, airports would still be constructed, and shopping malls would still go up. Wetlands, in other words, would still be damaged. History shows that society has not been very good at blanket prohibitions on the use of land.

And even if all further damage to biodiversity could realistically be prohibited, the problems of government enforcement and monitoring would still exist. It just would be spread out across tens of thousands of projects, and tens of thousands of acres of damaged wetlands, rather than across hundreds of wetland banks. In fact, numerous government officials report that the existence of wetland mitigation banking makes it easier for them to carry out their monitoring, enforcement, and protection work.[15]

Endangered Species: From Liabilities to Assets

If endangered species are so important, so valuable, why does the economic system see them as liabilities? The perverse unintended consequence of the Endangered Species Act—forcing people to see endangered species as a liability—is nothing new. Ever since the act was passed some 30 years ago people have been complaining that listing an endangered species places an unfair burden on the private landowners whose land harbors these species. In such cases, they argue, the incentive is not to protect an endangered species but rather to get rid of it fast, before anyone knows it is there. (See Box 9–3.) This is what some have called the "Three Ss Approach to Endangered Species Management": shoot, shovel, and shut up.[16]

Critics of the ESA have often used this attitude to argue that the act needs to be revised or even dismantled. But rather than throw the legislative baby out with the bathwater, there are other, less drastic approaches. One of these involves a process known as conservation banking. In the 1990s, people began looking for a better way to accomplish the ESA's objectives—one that instead of penalizing private landowners for harboring endangered species would perhaps reward them.

To do this, they created a system reminiscent of wetland banking. Under this system, landowners with an endangered species on their land can get a permit to harm that species (known as an "incidental take" permit in the euphemistic language of the government) if they can show they have compensated for it by creating habitat for that same species somewhere else. Again, as with wetland banking, this has paved the way for private, for-profit, species bankers to create habitat for endangered species, get credit from the government for any new members

Box 9–3. Perverse Incentives on Endangered Species

Ben Cone is a tree farmer in North Carolina. He owns 7,200 acres of pine forest that he was managing on an 80–100 year rotation. The system made sense for him because he could harvest different portions of his land at different times and take the largest, most valuable trees. And it was good for a wide variety of species that lived on his land. In particular, it was good for red cockaded woodpeckers, which like to make their nests in pine trees that are at least 80 years old. These woodpeckers are endangered, however. So when they were discovered on Cone's land, the U.S. government prohibited him from harvesting some 1,500 acres of forest. This ban alone is alleged to have cost Cone some $1.8 million in lost revenues.

Following the prohibition, Cone did what any rational landowner would do: he started har-

vesting the trees on the rest of his land on a much quicker rotation schedule (around 40 years). Understandably, he did not want those trees to be still standing after 80 years and thereby become a tempting home for the endangered woodpeckers. It wasn't Cone's preferred modus operandi, since the trees were less valuable and needed to be harvested on a quicker rotation, but he could not afford to have more of his land placed "off-limits" by endangered woodpeckers. And, ultimately, it was bad for the woodpeckers and many other forms of biodiversity that would have probably preferred the more mature (and presumably more diverse) forests made up of 80-year-old trees.

Source: See endnote 16

of that species found on their land ("new" meaning above an initial baseline), and sell those credits to other developers who intend to damage that species' habitat or harm the species somewhere else.[17]

Not much is known about the size and breadth of species banking across the United States, though it appears that there are more than 70 species banks and that these might trade anywhere from $100 million to as much as $370 million in species credits each year. Whatever the size, the use of conservation banking means that species banking, also known as "conservation banking," can turn a species liability into a species asset.[18]

This is just what one company in Colton, California, discovered. While the municipal government there sued the federal government over the Delhi Sands Flower-loving Fly, saying the government had no place regulating where people can build their houses, a sand and gravel company called Vulcan Materials Corporation acquired 130 acres of prime fly habitat—the largest remaining contiguous

area of it in the Colton dunes. But instead of hiring lawyers and attacking the fly's endangered species status, Vulcan decided to see if it could make the fly pay.[19]

Working with the U.S. Fish and Wildlife Service and the Riverside Land Conservancy, Vulcan set up a conservation easement on the land, created a management plan for the fly habitat, established a baseline for flies on its land, and obtained the right to sell "fly habitat credits" above that baseline to needy developers. The bank opened in June 2005 and by December had already sold three of its credits. Although Vulcan will not officially release the sale prices, reliable sources estimate that at least one credit sold for $100,000, although they also say the price has now risen to $150,000 per acre, as mentioned earlier.[20]

According to Kevin Klemm, the owner of the development company that was Vulcan's first customer, the credits were worth it: "The Vulcan Materials people were tremendous. They were business-like and accommodating. They didn't waste any time. The bank is a tremendous value... I spent six years of my life trying to build 18 buildings." And presumably he got nowhere because the government made it illegal for him to harm the flower-loving flies. Now, with a bank from which to buy offsets, he has an option. To people like Klemm, the rapid response mitigation solution now offered by the Vulcan bank is no doubt a blessing.[21]

And Vulcan is not alone. There are now conservation banks in the United States that sell credits on everything from vernal pool fairy shrimp and valley elderberry longhorn beetle to tiger salamanders, Gopher Tortoises, and prairie dogs. As noted, these markets may be worth as much as $370 million a year. The conservation of endangered species has thus become a very real, and very profitable, business opportunity.[22]

Government Programs: Benefits and Drawbacks

Outside the United States, several other countries are also experimenting with regulated biodiversity offsets. (See Table 9–1.) For instance, the Australian states of Victoria and New South Wales either already have or are setting up schemes similar to the U.S. system, although with a few important differences. The BioBanking system in New South Wales has proposed a scheme whereby some areas would be deemed too sensitive for development. These would be "red-flagged" and would ideally be the sites where species banking would occur. In other words, the Australians are looking at addressing one of the main pitfalls of the U.S. system: a lack of broad-based, landscape-level planning to determine which areas are most needed for conservation. For now, it looks like the BioBanking scheme will be voluntary, but the hope is that, since compensation for damage is obligatory, BioBanking will be cheaper

than the alternatives.[23]

In the state of Victoria, the BushBroker scheme is mandatory and applies to native vegetation. The principle is simple: whoever harms native vegetation in Victoria needs to offset that damage by creating or protecting the same type of vegetation in the same bioregion. Applying this scheme, on the other hand, is extremely complicated. There are literally dozens of vegetation systems and bioregions, which makes finding the right match a daunting task. To address this problem, the government of Victoria is building a sophisticated computer matching system that it expected would be operational by the end of 2007.[24]

While cap-and-trade regulated offset schemes to protect biodiversity can indeed create real markets and can be extremely powerful when used correctly, they also require strong government oversight, effective legal systems, enforcement of rules and regulations, and robust financial institutions. These conditions may be found in some industrial countries, but they are not the conditions of much of world—especially in those parts that hold most of the world's biodiversity, places like parts of Central and South America, Congo, China, Indonesia, Madagascar, and Mexico. So what can be done in those parts of the world?

Fortunately, the underlying concept behind both conservation banking and wetlands mitigation banking—that is, putting a value on biodiversity—applies in all countries, even if the exact systems for providing these payments may not. Even the U.S. government has a multimillion-dollar-a-year program to help farmers and private landowners conserve. It comes in the form of Farm Bill payments such as the Wetlands Reserve Program, the Conservation Security Program, the Conservation Reserve Program, and the Environmental Quality Incentives Program.[25]

Table 9–1. Examples of Legal Requirements for Biodiversity Offsets

Country or Region	Program	Legislation	Policy goal
United States	Species Mitigation (of which conservation banking is one tool)	Endangered Species Act 1973 as amended and the Guidance on Establishment, Use and Operations of Conservation Banks	To offset adverse impacts to threatened and endangered species
	Wetland Mitigation	Clean Water Act 1972 Chapter 404(b)(1) and the US Army Corps of Engineers regulations (33 CFR 320.4(r))	"No overall loss of values and functions" (1990); "net gain" (2004)
Australia, New South Wales		Green Offsets for Sustainable Development: Concept Paper (2002); Native Vegetation Act (2003) and subsequent regulations (2005); the Threatened Species Conservation Amendment (Biodiversity Banking) Bill 2006	"Net environmental gain"
Australia, Victoria		Native Vegetation Management Framework (2002) and subsequent amendments to related Acts; BushBroker— native vegetation credit registration and trading: Information Paper (2006)	"A reversal, across the entire landscape, of the long-term decline in extent and quality of native vegetation, leading to a Net Gain"
Western Australia		Native Vegetation Act (2003); Environmental Offsets: Position Statement No. 9 (2006)	"Net environmental benefit"
Brazil	Forest Regulation and National System of Conservation Units	Lei No. 4771 of 1965; Lei No. 14.247 of 22/7/2002, Lei No 9.985 of 18/7/2000, Decreto No. 4.340 of 22/8/2002	No net loss of habitat under a defined minimum forest cover for private landholdings
Canada	Fisheries Act	R.S. 1985, c. F-14, Policy for the Management of Fish Habitat (1986), and the Habitat Conservation and Protection Guidelines, Second Edition (1998); see especially Subchapter 35(1) and Subchapter 35(2) of the Fisheries Act	No net loss in capacity of habitat to produce fish
European Union	Habitats and Birds Directive	Council Directive 92/43/EEC of 21 May 1992 on the conservation of natural habitats and of wild fauna and flora and Council Directive 79/409/EEC	Maintain overall (ecological) coherence of the sites

Source: See endnote 23.

In Brazil, the government requires that a minimum amount of a landowner's territory be kept in forest cover. There is also a law on Brazil's books that requires compensation for damage to biodiversity, although the laws to determine that compensation are not adequately established yet. Similarly, in places as far afield as South Africa, Colombia, and the European Union, laws requiring or encouraging biodiversity offsets are either being considered or already being implemented.[26]

The Chinese government has long had a program known as Grain for Green (the official title translates as the Sloping Lands Conversion Program, or SLCP) that pays farmers to keep forest cover on hillsides. Its aim is to help conserve watersheds and prevent floods, but it also affects biodiversity conservation. This is not a market-based system, however; it is a system of government subsidies and payments. The money comes directly from tax revenues and is redistributed based on certain established criteria. While the SLCP system does help increase the value of standing forests (and has an astounding budget of $43 billion over 10 years), it does not directly link the users of the biodiversity services with the providers of those services. Government mediates the transaction, so the users of the service are not receiving information on the cost of their use.[27]

Private landowners in Costa Rica who protect their forest cover receive a payment from the National Forestry Trust Fund.

Mexico is introducing a similar system. It was modeled on a program for water conservation in the country known as Pago por Servicios Ambientales Hidrológicos (PSAH, or Payment for Environmental Hydrological Services). The PSAH is interesting in that it collects a fixed amount of revenues from water users and then redistributes it to key targeted forested watersheds across the country. The principle here is that by helping protect forested areas in key watersheds, the payments will help support the provision of water-related ecosystem services throughout

the country. The program started in 2003 and pays between $30 and $40 a hectare for forest conservation, depending on the type of forest being protected. Currently the program is paying for the management of close to a million hectares.[28]

Building on its success with water services, Mexico has received a grant from the Global Environment Facility to establish a similar program to make payments for biodiversity conservation. The problem with this approach is twofold. First, as in China, the money is coming from philanthropic sources or the government. Second, the payment and the payer are severed from the actual service being received. In other words, while all Mexicans contribute a bit of the money they pay for water to the PSAH, they often do not know they are making this contribution. And the money they pay is not necessarily used in the watersheds that supply those individuals with water. Again, the link between buyer and seller is not direct. This makes it difficult for users of the service to make decisions based on the economic costs of their use.[29]

One of the most talked about payment for ecosystem services programs, as these are often called, is the Pago por Servicios Ambientales (PSA) program created by Costa Rica in 1996. Private landowners in Costa Rica who protect their forest cover receive a payment from the National Forestry Trust Fund. These payments are made at a base rate of $40 per hectare but can vary depending on type of forest cover. Most of the money for this trust fund comes from a tax added to fuel sales in Costa Rica, but this is supplemented by "environmental credits" sold to businesses and other sources of international finance. Between 1996 and 2003, the Costa Rican PSA program had enrolled more than 314,000 hectares of forested land, transferring more than $80 million to landowners in the process.[30]

Once again, this is a government-run program where the user and provider of the biodiversity services are not closely linked. Also, like China's Grain for Green program and Mexico's PSAH, the price per hectare of [...] ment, not via a [...] nism. They are [...] nopsonies (one [...], the opposite of [...] services, and as [...] little or (though [...] for the conser- [...] price is largely [...] he government's [...] on supply and

[...], the programs in [...] Rica have been [...] iving added eco- [...] rsity and, some [...] een successful in [...] asing forest cover. [...] ing and different [...] r biodiversity ser- [...] oria in Australia. [...] there—known as [...] der—the state has [...] ion system for pro- [...] yments to private [...] e local biodiversity

[...] nder took place in [...] according to Mark [...] chitects, it "used an [...] bute environmental [...] o were interested in improving terrestrial biodiversity on their properties. The implementation of Bush-Tender led to 5,000 hectares of native vegetation on private land being secured under management agreements. In economic terms, it created the supply side of a market for nature conservation and generated significant cost savings when compared with pre-

vious grant-based systems for distributing conservation funds to landholders."[31]

BushTender's success is now being followed up with EcoTender, in which the state is inviting local landholders to submit competitive "bids" for government funding to pay for improved management of remnant vegetation and revegetation on their properties. "Where BushTender focused on a single environmental outcome (increasing terrestrial biodiversity), EcoTender aims to achieve multiple environmental benefits, including improvements in saline land and aquatic function," explains Eigenraam.[32]

What is interesting about BushTender and EcoTender is that they use government's monopsony buying power to invite bids that effectively serve to discover the "best" price at which biodiversity conservation will be achieved. Nevertheless, the buyer is once again the government using tax revenues, so the connection between the buyer or user of the biodiversity services and the seller is still not direct.

Voluntary Biodiversity Offsets

Beyond government regulation, numerous companies have begun to set up biodiversity offsets voluntarily in places like Qatar, Madagascar, and Ghana because they think it makes good business sense to do so. Like the voluntary carbon markets described in Chapter 7, the number and investment in such offsets is presently modest. But they are likely to become much more widely used as a part of standard business practice. Some observers believe that they could serve as the precursors to larger, more broad-based biodiversity markets in the long term. Essentially, they demonstrate that there can be a business case for investing in biodiversity conservation.

To understand whether, when, how, and where voluntary biodiversity offsets should be undertaken, the Washington-based nongovernmental group Forest Trends established the Business and Biodiversity Offsets Program (BBOP). This is a partnership of over 50 companies, governments, conservation experts, and financial institutions from many different countries and led by Forest Trends and Conservation International. The BBOP partners believe that biodiversity offsets may help achieve significantly more, better, and more cost-effective conservation outcomes than normally occur in the context of infrastructure development. The program aims to demonstrate conservation and livelihood outcomes in a portfolio of biodiversity offset pilot projects; to develop, test, and disseminate best practice on biodiversity offsets; and to contribute to policy and corporate developments on biodiversity offsets so they meet conservation and business objectives.[33]

Companies undertake biodiversity offsets for one or more of three reasons: they are required to by national legislation (as in the United States, with wetland mitigation banking and conservation banking), they are encouraged to or facilitated by Environmental Impact Assessment legislation or other planning procedures, or they find a legitimate business case to get involved. BBOP staff have identified numerous benefits for companies in doing this; namely, voluntary offsets can help companies:

- ensure continued access to land and capital and to the license to operate;
- bring competitive advantage or favored status as a partner;
- increase investor confidence and access to capital;
- reduce risks and liabilities;
- ensure strong and supportive relationships with local communities, government regulators, environmental groups, and other important stakeholders;
- influence emerging environmental regula-

tion and policy;
- assure "first mover" advantage for innovative companies; and
- maximize strategic economic opportunities in emerging markets (for instance, establishing companies to implement offsets).[34]

Currently BBOP is working with partners on projects in a variety of countries, including Ghana, Kenya, Madagascar, Qatar, South Africa, and the United States, and is exploring projects in Argentina, China, Mexico, and New Zealand. Some of the companies the program is working with or in discussions with include Newmont Mining, Rio Tinto, Shell, and AngloAmerican.[35]

As these experiences mount up, and as case studies become available on best-practice biodiversity offsets, it is likely that both the supply and demand for these offsets will grow. Countries that establish clear policies may improve land use planning and use market mechanisms to create aggregated offset areas that achieve significant conservation outcomes in high biodiversity-value areas.

How Much Is Nature Worth?

Whether through voluntary offset mechanisms, government-mediated payment schemes, or full-fledged markets in offsets, the concept of payment for biodiversity services is beginning to take hold. More important, these approaches are beginning to subvert the current economic model that is blind to the value of biodiversity, to the services that species and ecosystems provide, and to the costs inherent in destroying the natural wealth on which human well-being depends.

The problem these systems are trying to address is self-evident: When iPods are valued over whale pods, the economic system will deliver ever more species of iPods and wipe out yet another species of whales. When wetlands are seen as nothing more than mosquito-infested swamps, they will lose out to shopper-infested malls. And as land becomes ever more scarce, the problems will simply be aggravated. The economic system is not broken. It is doing exactly what it was set up to do: deliver more of what people value—or at least more of what the imperfect price signals say people value—and less of what they don't.

As this chapter documents, the solution to the problem may actually lie in using markets and the economic system to our advantage. Imagine how powerful it would be if market forces—the same market forces that have inexorably pushed for the destruction of rainforests and the extinction of countless species—could be used to protect species, to give them a real value in people's everyday decisions of what to eat, what to wear, and what to buy.

To return to the questions at the start of this chapter: How much should society be prepared to spend to protect nature? The answer will in large measure determine whether humanity ends up living in a world of whales, wild tigers, and wetlands or a world of pavement, iPods, and pollution. Better yet, we can hope that through a form of economic jiu-jitsu these market mechanisms will make it possible for the pavement and the iPods to co-exist comfortably with the whales and the wetlands.

CHAPTER 10

The Parallel Economy of the Commons

Jonathan Rowe

It is an article of faith among economists that a resource without a private property regime is destined for overuse. Yet on Bali, an island in the Indonesian archipelago, that is not the case. For centuries rice farmers there have coordinated their use of scarce water through social networks built on the innate human capacity to manage such resources in a cooperative manner.[1]

The system is based on what anthropologists have called "water temples," which enfold the water sharing within a context of traditional Balinese religion. But actually the networks function through a form of bottom-up cooperation in which the temples provide a venue through which producers can coordinate their water use. Modern computer analysis has found that the resulting allocation is close to ideal in terms of the productivity of the farms. It defeats pests naturally and uses the available water to maximum effect.[2]

Bali's water sharing system is a textbook example of commons management—a traditional property arrangement that has worked effectively for centuries in a wide variety of resource contexts but that economists today either disparage or ignore. That was the case in Bali, when in the late 1960s the government decided to push rice farmers into the modern age. It bypassed the water temples, hired hydrologists to install modern water systems, and pushed Green Revolution techniques, complete with heavy pesticides, upon the farmers.[3]

The result was a disaster. Insects soon developed resistance to the chemical pesticides. Crop yields plummeted. In the end, the government had to relent, and the farmers returned to the social productivity arrangements that the experts had deemed relics of an unenlightened past.[4]

Fast forward to 2001 in the United States, when Jimmy Wales set out to create an encyclopedia online. He thought first of the corporate *Britannica* model, only staffed by

Jonathan Rowe is a fellow at the Tomales Bay Institute and is founding codirector of West Marin Commons.

volunteers. He established panels for peer reviews, assigned articles to recognized experts, and then waited for something to happen. Not much did. Economists might see the problem right away—a kind of corollary of the problem they would see in Bali. Writers lacked a property right in their output and therefore a monetary "incentive" to activate their dormant mental assets. Wales was familiar with that lure; he was a refugee from the world of options trading and understood the role that incentives play in business. But instead he went in a different direction.[5]

He tried writing an entry himself (on option trading) and discovered it was like "handing in an essay at grad school." It just wasn't any fun, and the top-down corporate structure was the reason why. So Wales shifted gears. He abolished the expert peer-review panels and put informal teams of coordinators in their place. More important, he dropped the idea of assigning entries and let users write them on any topic they desired. Then these same users would check one another for accuracy and bias. A discussion page for each entry would provide a forum in which to hash these issues out and a written record that every user could retrace.[6]

In other words, Wales created—or rather, seeded—a social network instead of an economic mechanism in the conventional sense. People were engaged not as profit seekers from the economics texts but as social beings who get a kick out of producing in this way. Within two weeks the project had generated more articles than it did in two years of the top-down model.[7]

The result is Wikipedia, the free online encyclopedia that now has almost 2 million articles in English and smaller numbers in about 250 other languages—for a total of almost 8 million articles. *Nature* magazine compared a sample of science articles from Wikipedia with corresponding ones in *Bri-*

tannica. It found that the difference in accuracy was "not particularly great."[8]

Technophiles attribute this social productivity to the magic of silicon chips and the Web. Tech leads and people follow. Yet in reality the Web is just a new venue for the same human capacity that found expression in the water temples of Bali. It is a long way from one to the other, in time as well as space. But in both the rice fields and on the Web, social structures and social norms are doing jobs—creating and managing resources that are held in common—that conventional economic wisdom says only monetary incentives and private property rights can do.

Moreover, both draw on a side of human nature that does not exist in the economics texts and that has fallen off the radar in western economic life. People are not supposed to produce something for nothing. They are not supposed to be able to manage a scarce resource without a regime of private property rights to keep them in line or else the edicts of an authoritarian state. They are not supposed to but they are—and with results that equal if not surpass those produced by the prevailing economic model.

The rice farmers on Bali are an example of a mode of local resource management that has worked for eons, from the alpine pastures of Switzerland to the irrigated rice fields of the northern Philippines. Today this model is reappearing in many precincts of the economy at large—from the revival of traditional main streets, public spaces, and community gardens to the resistance to the corporate enclosure of university research and the genetic substrate of material life.[9]

It is as though something latent in human nature is breaking through the concrete of the corporate economy and the bureaucratic state. The result is not just effective and generative use of the asset, but also a dividend in the form of social cohesion and trust that can be as important as the product itself. A new field called "behavioral economics" (a phrase that ought to be redundant but revealingly is not) has been rediscovering and giving empirical shape to this. Researchers have demonstrated, for example, that people seek fairness in economic dealings and not just their own gain. They seek stability over the long term and not just a quick buck.[10]

Such insights are not really news to most people. But recognition of them by at least a part of the economics profession helps put policies that derive from them into play in the high-level debate. In particular, it gives new legitimacy to the commons—a form of property that is neither the market nor the state, public nor private, but rather that people hold jointly and together rather than separately and apart. (See Box 10–1.) As governments look for models for conserving natural resources for the long haul, a large part of the answer could lie here.[11]

How Tragic Are the Commons?

To most economists, a commons is by definition "tragic" because it is prone to overuse. Their standard reference point is an article that appeared in *Science* in 1968 called "The Tragedy of the Commons." Though the author, Garrett Hardin, was a biologist, his article was strangely lacking in scientific inquiry. It was more like economics—that is, a logical

---

Box 10–1. Property: A Social Construct

Property is not a metaphysical absolute. It is an instrument that societies design to advance particular ends. There are many different kinds—corporate, marital, municipal, partnership, cooperative, and so forth—all of which are defined socially for different purposes. Today, two categories of property dominate the public debate: public and private. This follows from an ideological spectrum that offers the public and private "sectors" as the only options from which to choose.

Yet a third kind of property—common property—is neither public nor private in the usual sense. Historically it has served well for organizing the use of natural resources of many kinds and for defining the rights and responsibilities of people regarding these. In England, much agricultural land was held in common until the eighteenth and nineteenth centuries. In practice this was similar to community gardens today. Individuals had their own plots, but the underlying ownership was in common.

The concept permeated the early thinking about property generally, including what today are called the public and private realms. In the early U.S. colonies, private woodlands typically were regarded as commons for purposes of subsistence, such as hunting, fishing, and even cutting wood. The woodland commons sustained slaves during their bondage. To resubordinate them after emancipation, the southern planters closed the commons and thereby shut off a key part of their livelihoods.

Residues of the earlier thinking exist today in regards to wildlife and more broadly in the legal doctrine of the public trust. Ancient Roman law declared that some things are common by their very nature—primarily air, sky, wildlife, and navigable waters. Government did not own these and therefore could not privatize them, even if legislators wanted to. Much like trustees of an estate, governments have a legal obligation to maintain the asset for the benefit of the public at large.

Today the public trust prohibits governments from turning over to private parties the coastlines and navigable waters (and perhaps other things as well) that they have a responsibility to protect for future generations. Common property is encoded for the long haul.

Source: See endnote 11.

---

extrapolation from assumptions about reality rather than an actual investigation of it.[12]

Hardin simply assumed that all commons are free-for-alls, and he took no account of the human capacity to create rules to govern access and use. He bid his readers to "picture" a hypothetical pasture, which he peopled with hypothetical herders enlisted from the economics texts. These individuals existed outside of any social structure and tradition and lacked a capacity even to talk to one another. They all behaved as the texts said they would and according to what they call "rationality." They let their herds loose in the pasture in a single-minded effort to maximize their own gain, with no thought for the future or for anybody else. The pasture was depleted, and the tragedy was born.

There is a large irony here. Hardin was assuming the psychology of the large corporation and projecting it onto the pasture. This is the very institution that free market advocates, who cite Hardin as gospel, want to entrust the pasture to through privatization. They are purporting to solve the problem by embracing a purer version of it.

What Hardin overlooked is that people do not necessarily behave as economists assume they do. As historian E. P. Thompson observed, Hardin failed to grasp "that commoners themselves were not without common sense." Thompson was referring specifically to the common-field agriculture of his own England. Households had their own plots, but the rights to these were a matter of custom rather than of legal title, and the same was true of access to other lands for hunting, foraging, and grazing.[13]

Commoners pooled their implements and labor for joint maintenance and the like. They combined their herds to fertilize their respective plots. The destruction that Hardin declared to be an axiom simply did not happen. To the contrary, the system worked well

for those who constituted it.

The historical and anthropological literature is full of examples of commons-based management of limited resources. Regarding water, the irrigation systems in Bali are not exceptional. Spain has had similar systems, called *huerta*, for almost 600 years. The farmers whose land adjoins each canal elect their own chief executive, called a *syndic*, who resolves disputes between them in a tribunal held twice a week. They get water from the canal on a rotating basis. During droughts, the crops with the greatest need get first priority.[14]

Especially suggestive are the *zanjera* of the northern Philippines. Tenant farmers there join together and build irrigation systems on dry private land in exchange for use rights to that land. In effect they become joint semi-owners through sweat equity. It is grueling work. The dams break routinely during the monsoon season and must be rebuilt sometimes three or four times in a single year. Members typically work something like 40 days a year on the *zanjera* and in some cases close to double that.[15]

There are more than a thousand of these in the province of Illocos Norte, according to one estimate. They have an ingenious system for allocating water to make sure everyone gets a share. They divide the land into three or more sections and members get a plot in each section, in differing sequences along the canals. This way each member can have a plot that is close to the front of an irrigation line. Even in times of drought, everybody gets something. In addition, officials of the *zanjera* get extra land at the tail end of the line. This gives them extra motivation to ensure prudent use so that at least some water makes it that far.[16]

There are many examples of common pastures working effectively as well. In the alpine region of Switzerland, for example, the grazing pastures typically are commons, as are forests, irrigation systems, and paths and roadways connecting private and common property. Farmers generally have private land for their own crops. The commons and the private exist in symbiosis, a little like the common areas of a co-op or condominium apartment building. Each form of property serves the purpose for which it is suited best.[17]

In the Swiss village of Törbel, residents formed a commons association over 500 years ago. They established a rule that members could graze no more cattle on the common pasture than they could feed during the winter. As of a decade or so ago the rule still was in effect. It is general practice throughout the Alps—another example of the common sense that Hardin and others assumed that commoners lack.[18]

Hardin practically could have looked outside his California window, at the western plains, to test his hypothesis against reality. The early cattle ranchers there were not saintly people. But they also were not stupid. They found ways to cooperate rather than destroying the habitat that sustained their herds and themselves. They adopted the practice of branding from Mexicans, to distinguish different herds. They cooperated on roundups and cattle drives. Most important in the present context, these ranchers limited their cattle herds and worked to keep out newcomers. It was not always pretty. But it also was not the tragedy that the "tragedy thesis" assumes is inevitable in a pasture not enclosed by a property regime.[19]

Hardin's essay won applause in environmental quarters, mainly because it was not really about the commons. It was a case for population control, and the tragedy thesis served merely as a grim parable to that end. From the start, however, anthropologists and others who actually studied commons-based social arrangements objected to Hardin's broad-brush dismissal of the commons. Even-

tually, Hardin himself had to modify his stance. He acknowledged that the problem is not common ownership per se but rather open access—that is, commons in which there are no social structures or formal rules to govern access and use.[20]

Such cases do exist, of course. The fisheries on the East Coast of the United States are an obvious example of an open access regime; Earth's atmosphere is another. When tragedies occur, there generally has been a breakdown in the social structure that once governed use, or else a scale at which such structures are not possible, or new technologies of exploitation for which the existing rules are not sufficient. Population pressures have played a role as well, as in the mountain forests of the Philippines.[21]

But population generally has not worked alone. There also has been the invasion of a corporate, governmental, or other external and exploitive force. Native Americans did not eradicate the buffalo on the western plains; fur hunters from outside did. Local residents have not sliced the tops off mountains in Appalachia or befouled the land and water in quest of coal bed methane gas in the Rocky Mountains. Outside corporations have. When the fishery off of Brooklyn and Queens in New York City began to collapse in the 1960s, it was not because of local fishers alone. Rather it was a combination of garbage barges and factory trawlers that brought this fishery to the brink.[22]

It is strange that the reigning policy focus is on the tragedy of the commons when actually the tragedy of the corporate is probably a greater threat.

The Tragedy of the Corporate

Privatization of the commons usually means corporatization of them. When a government sells resources, such as oil rights or ocean plots, individuals rarely have the means to buy them. To free-market believers, this is a distinction without a difference. Corporations are really just economic persons, they say, only bigger. But that is like saying that a federal bureaucracy is no different than a town meeting democracy, because both are "government."

As Adam Smith observed often, humans are social beings. They have a capacity for empathy and a desire to be esteemed by their peers. "Nature, when she formed man for society," Smith wrote in his *Theory of Moral Sentiments*, "endowed him with an original desire to please, and an original aversion to offend his brethren." This desire actually goes deeper, Smith said, because we aspire truly to be "what ought to be approved of." Right or wrong, that is an assumption on which his theory of a benign and generative market was based. The modern corporation does not fit this model.[23]

The corporation is a creature of lawyers rather than of nature. It embodies the pure financial calculus of the ciphers that inhabit the economics texts. The bottom line really is the bottom line. This is not because corporations are run by bad people. On the contrary, the financial calculus is built into charters through which corporations acquire legal life—fixed in the operating system, as it were.

This institutional machinery was designed for an era in which resources seemed limitless and the consumption of them the only urgent mandate. It was set loose on this landscape and did what it was supposed to do—dig mines, drill wells, build factories, lay tracks, generally eat like an adolescent and consume everything in sight. Today, however, it has become like an appetite without a shut-off switch, the adolescent who never grew up. It has no built-in capacity to say "enough."

The main internal constraints are financial,

in the form of quarterly earnings statements, the demands of shareholders and creditors, and the like. These push generally toward liquidating nature, not husbanding it. Speaking of a rival who controls his own company and so can think "long term," Richard Parsons, the CEO of Time Warner, observed, "If almost anybody else did it, they'd get killed" by shareholders and Wall Street analysts.[24]

> The problem is not common ownership per se but rather open access—that is, commons in which there are no social structures or formal rules to govern access and use.

The paradigmatic case is that of Pacific Lumber, a California company that in the 1980s owned most of the major old-growth redwood forest still in private hands. Pacific Lumber was unusual. The chief executive was a lifelong timberman by the name of A. S. Murphy, who believed in harvesting no more than the forests could replace. "Their approach," said David Harris, author of *The Last Stand*, "was basically to treat the forest as capital and try and live off the interest."[25]

This virtue did not go unpunished. Pacific's self-discipline meant its forests were ripe for less conscientious plucking. Its clean balance sheet—Murphy believed in pay-as-you-go—left plenty of room for a raider to load up the company with debt. This is exactly what happened. During the leveraged buy-out boom of the 1980s, a corporate chief by the name of Charles Hurwitz teamed up with Michael Milken and Ivan Boesky, two of the more infamous financiers of the era, to take over Pacific Lumber. They mortgaged the company to the hilt to finance the purchase.[26]

Then Hurwitz began to liquidate the forests that Murphy had conserved, in order to pay off the debt. Finance trumped husbandry, as it most often does. External restraints are vulnerable at best, given the political influence of those whom they are supposed to restrain.[27]

But there is a more fundamental problem—namely, the way the modern corporation lies outside the constitutional structure that the nation's founders erected to keep institutional power in check. The corporations of today did not exist when the United States was founded. Adam Smith actually dismissed them as inherently too cumbersome and bureaucratic, their managers too given to "negligence and profusion." Individual entrepreneurs, nimble and resourceful, would outwit them every time.[28]

Smith was talking about the joint stock companies of his day, which were government-sanctioned monopolies such as the East India Company. He did not know that free incorporation laws soon would release the corporation from its legal strictures and obligations. He could not have known that these lawyer-created entities then would acquire the constitutional protections intended for human beings, through a Supreme Court procedure that was irregular at best.

The result is an institution that has outgrown both its legal and conceptual containers, including the ones of Smith's own theory. Although this is especially the case in the United States, it is true to some degree in most nations in which corporations operate. Even a diligent U.S. Congress can go only so far in terms of regulation. Nor have organized labor and consumer interests been an effective counterweight. Labor unions represent only some 12 percent of the workforce in the United States and often side with employers on resource issues, as when autoworkers oppose fuel efficiency standards for cars.[29]

The companies that own the resources—oil, coal, gas, and so forth—and those premised on their use have an insatiable

hunger that drives—indeed, requires—the invasion of the commons. The appetite requires more, and the commons is where that more lies. This institutional engine is programmed to take whatever in nature and society did not have a protective shell around it. There are efforts to reform the corporation from within, by rewriting the charters under which they operate. Whether that succeeds or not, there still will be a need to establish a new kind of outer boundary, so that corporations cannot claim everything.

Reclaiming Common Spaces

Enclosure is the process by which a commons is taken for private use and gain. It has a long history. War and conquest excepted, the original enclosures in Anglo-American history largely were the work of the British Parliament, which parceled out the common lands to private owners, often with inadequate compensation—if any—for the commoners whose rights and subsistence were taken in the process.

The U.S. government followed the example of its British parent on many fronts. The Dawes Act in 1887 broke up the tribal commons for many Native Americans and imposed on them a private ownership regime, as did the Alaska Native Claims Settlement Act a century later. The North American Free Trade Agreement, enacted in 1994, declared the water commons a private commodity for purposes of international trade. It also helped erode the *ejido* system of land tenure in Mexico, which was based on communal rather than market values.[30]

The parceling out of the broadcast airwaves to private corporations was part of this same lineage. In recent decades the process has metastasized from discrete acts into a wholesale assault. From the microcosm of the gene pool to the far reaches of space, corporations have been transgressing all boundaries and laying claim to that which previously was assumed to belong to all.

Often corporations have direct help from government, such as the expansion of the intellectual property laws that made possible the patenting of seeds and genes. The Bush administration has worked to parcel out tracts of ocean to corporate fish farmers. There are efforts in Congress to privatize outer space as well, for the purpose of advertising. The momentum now is so great that corporations often need no direct help at all.[31]

The escalating enclosures of recent decades have prompted a response that is almost like an autoimmune reaction. Spontaneously, all over the world, people are seeking to re-establish boundaries and to reclaim territory that has been lost. The environmental movement is one example of this, as are the campaigns against corporate globalism and genetically modified (that is, corporately enclosed) food.

This is a movement that defies standard ideological categories. Genuine conservatives oppose the decimation of traditional main streets by "big box" stores and the commodification of childhood, among other things. Those of a more leftward bent oppose as well the enclosure of university research by a corporate patent regime, the privatizing of water and other resources, and a host of kindred incursions.

Boundaries are not the only issue. There also has been an instinctive groping back to the social dynamic that animated the early commons and made resource sharing in them possible. Community gardens have become increasingly popular in North America, for example. There have been no official surveys, but the American Community Gardening Association estimates there are now roughly 18,000 such gardens in the United States, with 750 in New York City alone. In Toronto, the number increased from 14 to 69 between 1987 and 1997. These operate much the way the original common field agriculture did in England. People have their own plots but often share tools and know-how, and pitch in on maintenance as well. The result is generative socially as well as agriculturally. A study in upstate New York found that a third of the gardens gave rise to broader neighborhood improvement projects such as tree planting and crime watch. "It is very peaceful now," said a resident of Richmond, Virginia, about a community garden reclaimed from a decrepit neighborhood park. "It brings people together." (See also Chapter 11.)[32]

Another example is the revival of common spaces in cities across the United States, from Pioneer Square in Portland, Oregon, to Copley Square in Boston. Three decades ago Detroit tried to renew its decaying downtown with a corporate fortress called Renaissance Center. The Center became a white-collar island, the decay continued, and renaissance never came. In the late 1990s, someone had the idea of taking the opposite approach. Instead of a private corporate space, the city would create an open common one.[33]

The result is Campus Martius, in the heart of downtown. Symbolically enough, Detroit actually rerouted automotive traffic to accommodate it. (The Renaissance Center had housed the corporate offices of General Motors.) Now life is coming back downtown. There are some 200 concerts and events a year, plus ice skating in the winter. People are coming in from the suburbs. Investment is coming too: some $500 million worth. The Compuware corporation has moved 4,000 employees in from the suburbs to be close to this new center of activity.[34]

This actually is how markets began—in common spaces, especially the plazas around churches. Markets were festive social occasions before they became "economic" ones in the narrow modern sense. Farmers' markets today are direct descendents of those early ones, and they are spreading rapidly for much the same reason. According to the U.S. Department of Agriculture, the number of farmers' markets grew by 150 percent between 1994 and 2006. Today there are more than 4,300 in the United States, and people are flocking to them not just for local and organic food. It is also for the festive sociability, the fun of being out among neighbors, the freedom from the hyper-calculated marketing enclosures of corporate supermarkets and malls.[35]

Neighbors are starting to create their own

> At present the institution that best embodies commons functions outside the public sphere is the trust.

common spaces for this kind of spontaneous sociability. In Portland, the City Repair project is turning traffic intersections into public squares. In Baltimore and Boston, neighbors have closed off back alleys and turned them into commons for their blocks. In some cases people actually have shortened their own backyards in order to make the common space larger. The so-called New Urbanism—which is really the old village-ism—expresses a similar desire to restore social content and interaction to the normal flow of daily life.[36]

Such movements are not about expanding the governmental sphere. To the contrary, they are about stopping incursions into the commons sphere and protecting the generative social process (as opposed to the bureaucratized governmental process) that occurs there. They are parallel expressions of the social productivity that is emerging on the World Wide Web. Together they provide a template for a new/old kind of resource management as well.

From Community to Conservation

The lobster fisheries of Maine illustrate how social process can translate into husbandry of a resource commons. These fisheries are organized informally within the state's many harbors, which are small enough to be communities. The fishers that work these waters know and watch one another. Each has a territory that has been worked out informally.

The enforcement of these informal territories, as well as of restrictions on taking undersized, oversized, or egg-bearing lobsters, is a community function more than a bureaucratic one. "As most lobstermen live in the same town, send their kids to the same school, and rely on one another in emergencies," Colin Woodard observed in his book *The Lobster Coast*, "social sanctions can be more effective than a dozen wardens." The wardens do exist. But the social networks that have evolved around these commons make them less needed.[37]

Maine fishers often toss back all the female lobsters in their traps, not just the egg-bearing ones, even though they don't have to. Unlike the hypothetical herders in Hardin's hypothetical pasture, these actual commoners are not without common sense. It is not entirely coincidental that the state's lobster fisheries are thriving, even though the number of fishers making a majority of their income from lobsters more than doubled between 1973 and 1998.[38]

This is the same kind of social structure that makes commons so productive in the alpine pastures of Switzerland, the rice fields of the Philippines, and many other settings. It is an argument for management that is local and community-based, and it raises questions about the assumptions behind a corporate global economy. Such arrangements are not always possible, however, especially in a mobile market culture such as the United States. Then too, some commons are simply too large, such as watersheds, the oceans, and the atmosphere.

The challenge, then, is to devise formal institutions that replicate the essential features of commons even if they cannot include all the social dynamic of local and traditional settings. In other words, it means scaling up commons management just as the corporation scales up business management from the individual entrepreneur. One essential feature is equity and mutual benefit. Commons serve all, either equally or by a just distributional standard, subject to necessary rules for access and use. Central Park is open to all New Yorkers whether they live in Harlem or on Central Park West, so long as they obey the rules.

The second essential feature has to do with time. Corporations are designed to seek short to midterm gain. They move to the metronome of the quarterly earnings statement. The market theory that justifies them, moreover, has no concept of the future in regards to resources. Maximize gain today and the future will take care of itself, the theory goes. The needs of future generations actually are discounted, which means that market calculus always values the present generation more than it does future ones.

Commons, in contrast, turn that assumption upside down. Properly designed, they are encoded to preserve assets for the future rather than to liquidate them for the present. They embody the way neighbors might think about a wooded hillside as opposed to the way developers would. There are times when government management can play this role. Central Park functions admirably as a commons under public ownership.

But government ownership is not always possible—or necessarily the best course. In the United States, continuing pressures on the Arctic National Wildlife Refuge and on national forests illustrate the vulnerability of a system that is ultimately political. Even at the local level there are pressures to invade parks and other public spaces with corporate sponsorships, advertising, and so on. The national parks are treasures, but there is increasing need for an alternative to government ownership that is not so tied to the corporate-government nexus.[39]

No solution is without problems, but some are less problematic than others. At present the institution that best embodies commons functions outside the public sphere is the trust. (See Box 10–2.) Existing trusts are primarily local or regional and have discrete boundaries. The next challenge is to apply the concept to larger commons such as the atmosphere and oceans or with entire watersheds. One possibility is to scale up the trust model one step further and use something that looks like a "market mechanism" but that actually serves nonmarket ends. For example, Peter Barnes of the Tomales Bay Institute has proposed a Sky Trust, which would serve as trustee for the atmosphere much the way a bank serves as trustee for a family trust. To understand the Sky Trust model it helps to consider briefly what it is an alternative to.[40]

The air pollution debate in recent years has focused on something called tradable pollution rights. Under this scheme corporations essentially get grandfathered rights to their past levels of dumping in the sky. If they reduce their emissions they can then sell the air space they are not using to another company—thus reaping a financial bonus for past bad behavior.

This approach is called "market-based" because it involves the buying and selling of dump space as opposed to just regulatory limits. (Such limits still would exist, but they would cap the dump space overall while companies worked out through trading which

Box 10–2. Trusting Commons

Trusts exist by definition to maintain an asset for their beneficiaries, future as well as present. They have all the protections of private property on the outside, but inside they can be designed for opposite ends. It is not surprising that this legal form has emerged as a way to graft commons-type management of limited resources onto an economic system that is not always the most receptive host.

One example is the Pacific Forest Trust, which helps protect private forests in the United States from both clearcutting and development. About four fifths of U.S. forestland is privately owned, and some 6,070 square kilometers (at least 1.5 million acres) of this forest disappears each year. The Pacific Forest Trust is working to halt this trend by acquiring conservation easements, which are a kind of property right in conservation use. Mineral rights give a corporation the right to extract resources; conservation easements give the trust the right to protect the land against uses that would compromise its ecological functions.

The private owners keep the land and the right to harvest it sustainably. They donate or sell to the trust the rights to develop the land. The trust holds these rights so that no one else can use them. In this way the public gets the benefits of living, breathing forests for the long haul, while owners still can harvest timber if they choose. In effect, this harkens back to the time in U.S. history when private forests were deemed commons for purposes of sustenance. Back then sustenance meant cutting trees for firewood. Today it also means refraining from cutting trees to

protect the larger ecological functions of the forest.

A similar example is the Marin Agricultural Land Trust (MALT), which buys development rights to the rolling farm and ranch lands on the western edge of Marin County, California. Ranchers get to keep and work their land and pass it on to heirs. The public gets stunning and unspoiled landscapes, plus active stewards on the land. To date, MALT has protected nearly 15,400 hectares—roughly half the ranchland in the county—on 58 family farms and ranches. Given the development pressures in west Marin and the trophy palaces that Bay Area millionaires are lusting to build, the importance of MALT to one of the nation's most stunning landscapes is hard to exaggerate.

Another example is the Oregon Water Trust, which restores water flow to crucial and endangered streams. It does this by acquiring water rights and by working with farmers and other property owners to find ways to reduce their take from the streams. As with land and forest trusts, the property owners keep their land. All they give up is a portion of their water flow. That in turn becomes a commons that the organization holds in trust for the well-being of people and habitat, present and future.

And in New York City, the Trust for Public Land now holds 70 community gardens. It helped save these from Mayor Rudolf Giuliani's efforts to sell the gardens to developers.

Source: See endnote 40.

ones used how much.) The ability to sell dump space presumably provides an "incentive" for companies to reduce their emissions continually. The problem is that the system rewards most those who polluted the most. It also ignores the equitable owners of the sky—that is, all of us.

A commons-based approach would use a similar market dynamic, but it would start from a different premise and achieve a much

broader beneficial result. The premise is that the sky belongs in some sense to everyone, which is why it is a commons. Corporations should not own it; they only can rent dump space from the owners. Accordingly, under the Sky Trust, there would be annual auctions for the available dump space, within strict and diminishing limits. The proceeds would go into the trust, where it could be used for investment in clean energy, cash dividends to the owners, or some combination of the two. Sky Trust could help finance a long-term solution to climate change, not just reduce emissions.[41]

The Sky Trust would operate much like the Alaska Permanent Fund, which distributes revenues from that state's oil lands. But there would be one crucial difference. The Permanent Fund encourages drilling, because more drilling means more revenues for the owners. Sky Trust, in contrast, would encourage less pollution because it would reward the commons owners—all of us—for tough emission limits. When less dump space is available, the auction price will be higher, as a simple matter of supply and demand.[42]

This commons-based approach has been gaining ground due in part to the failure of a permit trading scheme in the European Union. Even the Deutsche Bank and the Conservative Party in the United Kingdom now back the auction model, as do the governors of New York and Massachusetts. The concept is basically that of parking meters. When you take a scarce resource from the commons, be it parking space on the streets or dump space in the sky, then you have to pay the ultimate owners. And you can take only as much as the natural and social systems can carry.[43]

The approach could be applied to seabed mining, under the Law of the Sea Treaty, and in a host of other ways. It has implications also for public revenues more broadly. Starting from a commons standpoint, rather than a conventional economic one, would bring the ecological and the moral into economic alignment. As Winston Churchill, an advocate of this approach, once put it as a young Member of Parliament: "Formerly, the only question of the tax gatherer was, 'How much have you got?' Now we also ask, 'How did you get it?'"[44]

Churchill was getting at the distinction between income earned by productive investment or toil and income that came from cashing in on something that nature or society already had created. The question is not what people make, he was saying, but rather what they take from the common pool. Specifically he was talking about land.

Land is not just a gift of nature as opposed to a product of human enterprise (with rare exceptions, such as landfills). The value of urban land arises from the investment of the entire society rather than of a particular owner. The difference in value between a parcel in Bridgeport, Connecticut, and one of identical size on Park Avenue in Manhattan has little to do with the efforts of individual owners and much to do with the investment that has gone on around them.

It is a social creation rather than an individual one, and therefore a form of commons. When individuals profit from increases in this location value—that is, the value of the site, as opposed to any buildings or improvements they have made on the site—they are reaping where they have not sown and are expropriating for themselves a gain that rightfully belongs to the society at large.

There is a social component in all gain, of course. But with land the case is almost pure. The consequences of permitting this expropriation from the commons are grim ecologically as well as in terms of justice. The lure of land gains feeds the speculation that drives development far into the hinterland. It encourages sprawling low-density development; when taxes on the site (or socially created) component of real estate are low, there is no need to use the land intensively to generate revenue to pay the tax.

The current property tax includes the value of both land and buildings. Typically the land portion is understated, because commercial owners like to attribute site value to the building so they can depreciate it. Shifting the property tax from buildings to land would encourage more-efficient use of this limited resource. (Zoning is necessary to prevent the high-rising of stable low-rise neighborhoods.) It also would reclaim for society what society had created, thus achieving equity as well as ecological sanity.

Numerous cities have tried this approach: Sydney and Canberra in Australia, Taiwan, and indirectly Singapore and Hong Kong. Almost 20 cities in the state of Pennsylvania have done so too, and the results have been promising. Officials in Harrisburg, Pennsylvania, claim that the number of vacant lots and structures downtown has dropped by 90 percent. Many localities have used the approach in a more limited way, by recouping the value of public improvements from benefited property owners. One study found that the Washington, D.C., metropolitan area could have paid for most of its Metro transit system by recapturing the site value increases along the Metro route.[45]

After a long hiatus, interest in site value taxation is reviving. A computer simulation for King and Clark Counties in Washington state found that taxes on parking lots and vacant building lots—that is, the most wasteful uses—would more than double, while taxes on car-oriented strip development would go up by a quarter. Neighborhood shopping districts would have decreases, as would apartments and most single family residences.[46]

That would be a win both ecologically and politically—and socially as well. It is suggestive, moreover, of the larger possibilities of shifting the tax burden from what people and corporations make or buy in total to what they take from the common weal in the process. Taxing the takings from the commons would encourage people to take better care of it. It would mean less waste of land and other resources and therefore denser patterns of development that are more resource-efficient.

That in turn would increase the occasions for human interaction and community in the course of daily life. Thus the wheel comes full circle. The measures necessary to protect the commons actually would foster the kind of social arrangements that make that protection more feasible.

For decades we have been told that there are only two choices for the management of scarce resources: corporate self-seeking or the bureaucracy of the state. But there is another way. Commons management has worked for centuries and is still working today. It can be adapted to the most pressing global problems, such as climate change. A new phrase is about to enter the policy realm. To "market-based" and "command-and-control" we can now add "commons-based."

CHAPTER 11

Engaging Communities for a Sustainable World

Erik Assadourian

To the west is Vermont Avenue, one of the most congested traffic corridors in Los Angeles, tiled with a mosaic of fast-food chains, nail salons, and dollar stores, all nested in a half-dozen strip malls. To the east lie three auto repair shops, housing, and a giant concrete church that dominates the street. To the north, there are two more auto body shops, three overcrowded schools, and a couple of car dealerships. And to the south, just beyond the Bresee Community and Youth Center, are two giant supermarkets with equally gigantic parking lots, tailored to be one-stop shopping for people commuting along the Vermont Avenue corridor.[1]

In the middle of this car-centric infrastructure—what some might call "sprawl"—lies a little green oasis: the Los Angeles Ecovillage (LAEV). This community, two small apartment buildings with about 55 residents, was started in 1993 as a demonstration project on how a community can transform its surroundings, helping to create a sustainable society.[2]

In its 15 years, the LA Ecovillage has had many impressive victories. Within its grounds, LAEV has facilitated technology and lifestyle changes, such as installing solar panels and composting facilities, providing rent reductions for people who live car-free, and transforming its courtyard into a 7,000-square-foot garden that produces nine types of fruits and many more vegetables as well as a lush common area to sit and relax in. LAEV has also incubated businesses like the Bicycle Kitchen—a shop that repairs bikes and that trains neighborhood children in bicycle maintenance skills. And perhaps most important, the community has influenced the broader political process of Los Angeles, from lending support to "green" mayoral candidates to engaging in public planning processes, such as the restoration of the Los Angeles River, transportation planning, and local redevelopment—all while continuing to be an affordable, accessible place to live, located within a 10-minute walk of two subway stops and 20 bus lines.[3]

Through its built infrastructure, the social relationships it generates, and the way of life it promotes, the LA Ecovillage highlights the powerful contributions that communities can make in helping to facilitate the transition to a sustainable society. (See Box 11–1 for the definition of community used in this chapter.)[4]

Community practices and choices about land use, technologies, and transportation can be used to model sustainable living. The production of social capital—the glue that holds communities together—can be tapped to help community members become leaders in sustainability and can provide the resilience that helps communities weather difficult times. Communities' engagement in economic activities can help localize agriculture and the production of other essential goods. And their unique design can help stimulate new ways to finance sustainability. While national and global-level initiatives will be essential for building a sustainable world, community-level programs may prove indispensable in providing better models and the leadership to drive global-level change.

Modeling Sustainability

Perhaps most concretely, a community manifests its values through its physical design. Local gardens, solar panels on rooftops, and wind turbines spinning on a hilltop are typical signs of an ecologically minded community. Built primarily to reduce ecological and financial footprints of communities, these design features also play a strong role in modeling a sustainable way of living. Many are simple enough to be taken on by practically any community. No matter the size—whether a small town or a neighborhood block—there are immediate opportunities to retrofit a community's design and thereby lower its environmental impact, save money, and model sustainability as well.

Often all that is needed to make these changes is a bit of social support and peer edu-

---

Box 11–1. What Is a Community?

Community typically refers to a wide range of groupings of people: a church, a city, a political party or other affiliation. But more fundamentally, a community suggests a group of geographically rooted people engaged in relationships with each other (though many of the examples of community discussed in this chapter have relevance to broader definitions of community as well). Through these relationships, members in a community have shared responsibilities—as the Latin roots of the word suggest: *com* (with) *munis* (duties).

Source: See endnote 4.

---

cation. This has proved to be the case in Lydney, England, where residents set up a Community Energy Club to help bring energy efficiency measures and small-scale renewable energy projects to the area. Since it started in 2001, the club has grown to 115 members who together have introduced about 500 energy efficiency measures. Altogether these efforts will save 3,865 tons of carbon dioxide (CO_2) emissions over the life of the projects—a significant amount considering that the average U.K. resident produces about 9 tons of CO_2 emissions each year.[5]

Other times, what is needed is not just social support but mobilization of a community's resources—for example, to invest in a community-owned wind farm. In 2006, Findhorn Ecovillage in Scotland completed installation of four wind turbines that have a capacity of 750 kilowatts. Together these produce 40 percent more electricity than the community needs, allowing them to generate revenue by selling some back to the local utility through the broader grid system. Of course, this project took several years to plan and construct, but now the wind farm provides the community with both a source of clean electricity and revenue.[6]

Opportunities to enhance the sustainability of a community when building or just renovating are nearly boundless—limited only by the energy, commitment, and resources of the community. Unlike at the household level, where design options can be limited, nearly the entire metabolism of a community can be adjusted to be more sustainable: from where fresh water is obtained, to how food is produced, to how waste is treated. (See Table 11–1.) Most of these take significant time and effort to implement—or financial resources when built by a contractor—but in the end they can help bring the community together (through the planning and construction of the project), cut costs, and reduce ecological impact.[7]

Table 11–1. How Selected Communities Model Sustainability

Sector	Project	Location	Description
Energy	Micro hydroelectric generator	Inverie, Scotland	In 2002, this remote Scottish community on the Knoydart peninsula finished refurbishing a 280-kilowatt hydro-electric generator, which now provides electricity for at least 65 properties.
Energy	Biomass	ZEGG, Belzig, Germany	The 80 residents of ZEGG obtain their heating from a wood-chip-fired heating plant, with the wood sustainably harvested from the local area.
Energy	Biogas	Hammarby Sjöstad, Stockholm, Sweden	In this Stockholm district 1,000 residences obtain their cooking gas from biogas that is generated from the district's wastewater.
Food Production	Permaculture	Kibbutz Lotan, Arava Valley, Israel	Kibbutz Lotan maintains an array of sustainable agriculture features, including organic gardens, composting, trellising, and community-supported agriculture. It also maintains a migrating bird preserve of five distinct habitats.
Water Catchment	Rainwater harvesting	Christie Walk, Adelaide, Australia	This 27-unit Adelaide community captures all on-site rain-water and uses it to maintain its 870 square meters of rooftop and surrounding gardens.
Sewage Treatment	Ecological machine	Berea College Ecovillage, Kentucky, United States	This community's "ecological machine" processes about 12,700 liters of wastewater each day using a combination of bacteria, snails, and plants. Some of this water is then stored for use on the community's lawns and garden.
Sewage Treatment	Constructed wetlands	Ecoovila, Porto Alegre, Brazil	In this 28-family community, sewage is processed in a bio-logical system that uses reed beds to filter water—water that is then used to irrigate the community's gardens.
Sewage	Water reuse	Solaire Apartments, New York City, United States	In this luxury apartment building, a water reuse system filters wastewater and reuses it for toilet flushing and the building's cooling tower. In 2006, this system recycled about 73,000 liters per day, reducing total water needs by one third.
Transportation	Car sharing	BedZED, London, England	Forty residents subscribe to a community carsharing venture, obtaining access to electric cars that are charged by solar energy.

Source: See endnote 7.

The ecovillage and co-housing movements are perhaps the best illustrations of the opportunities that exist in designing communities to be sustainable through the mobilization of resident energy and resources. An ecovillage, in particular, has the goal of creating "a human-scale, full-featured settlement, in which human activities can be harmlessly integrated into the natural world in a way that is supportive of healthy human development, and can be successfully continued into the indefinite future." While none have achieved this high ideal, many have made great strides. A resident of Findhorn Ecovillage has just half the ecological footprint of an average individual in the United Kingdom. And in Germany's Sieben Linden Ecovillage, per capita CO_2 emissions are just 28 percent the national average.[8]

While co-housing communities are typically more focused on developing a connected community than on reducing environmental impact, they often incorporate many ecological designs as well as adding another important element—namely, clustered homes. Instead of spreading out houses, co-housing communities group homes together, enabling them to preserve more land as open space or farmland and to facilitate community connections by having neighbors within walking distance. At the center of these houses there is also typically a community house, where meetings, dinners, and other activities are regularly held.[9]

Ecovillages and co-housing communities are not the only communities that can implement these changes. Indeed, with 385 registered ecovillages (though the actual number is greater if broader village networks are included) and about 500 co-housing projects worldwide, these serve more as models for other communities than as solutions themselves. Many of the projects these communities implement are readily replicable by any

group of like-minded neighbors. Small groups within a broader setting can come together and start a sustainability project, such as a carpool, community garden, or weekly potluck dinner of locally grown food.[10]

People can even convert their neighborhood into an ad hoc ecovillage—like residents in the neighborhood of Phinney Ridge in Seattle, Washington, did. Phinney Ecovillage members hold regular meetings and gatherings to help neighbors reduce their ecological impact. In spring 2007, the group started a new neighborhood global warming project. This venture, partly funded by a grant from the city government specifically for neighborhood-based climate change efforts, is helping to mobilize residents to change their behavior to reduce fossil fuel use— everything from switching to a push lawn mower that relies on human power rather than fossil fuels to lowering their thermostats and turning off appliances not in use.[11]

Cultivating Community Connections

Not all capital is tangible. Communities generate an often underappreciated asset called social capital, the relational glue that holds communities together, or as political scientist Robert Putnam defines it, "connections among individuals—social networks and the norms of reciprocity and trustworthiness that arise from them." As individuals in a community interact, work together, and trade favors, a level of trust and feelings of reciprocity form. This is what makes a community a community rather than just people living near each other.[12]

In industrial countries, social capital is an increasingly scarce asset, according to Putnam and other social scientists. Since 1985 the average American has lost connection to one confidant each—going from three other people to confide in to just two. Today, nearly a quarter of Americans do not have anyone like that in their lives. But where social capital exists, or where there is the will to rebuild it through regenerating relationships, there is great opportunity to improve opportunity, life quality, and sustainability. Communities, regardless of the obstacles they face, can use social capital to form sustainable community development projects, empowering themselves as they work together on projects that increase their well-being while reducing their ecological impact.[13]

Social capital yields important dividends. Psychological research demonstrates that the breadth and depth of a person's social connections is the single best predictor of happiness. And social isolation translates directly into physical health concerns as well. More than a dozen long-term studies in Japan, Scandinavia, and the United States, for example, show that the chances of dying in a given year, no matter the cause, are two to five times greater for people who are socially isolated than for people with close family, friends, or community ties.[14]

Social capital is generated in a variety of ways. Some communities, particularly ecovillages and co-housing groups, do so by sharing resources. Some have a shared car available that residents can rent or borrow, thus freeing more of the community to live car-free. Many have shared major appliances, including washing machines and dryers. Others have created "tool libraries" for lawn mowers, chain saws, and other implements that may only be needed once a week, month, or year. One community tool is often more than enough and saves members significant cost in purchasing and maintaining these goods. Many people also barter food or goods they produce in exchange for what other residents produce. Along with goods, some communities share services, such as

babysitting and day care, and even elder care. This helps create the ties that bind communities together.[15]

> Sharing within a community also helps to establish a different cultural norm, one based in cooperation instead of conspicuous consumption and competition.

While an economist would regard these shared goods or nonmarket exchanges as a reduction in economic activity (and thus a negative development), they actually may increase community members' quality of life. A recent study of individuals living in ecovillages and co-housing communities found that although they earned significantly less than people in Burlington, Vermont (a town with a similar demographic makeup to the communities studied), members expressed life satisfaction levels equal to Burlingtonians. Indeed, 50 percent of residents had incomes of less than $15,000 a year yet life satisfaction levels equal to Burlingtonians—the majority of whom earned over $30,000 a year. The conclusion of the study was simple: ecovillage members successfully substituted social capital for the possessions they own, thus enjoying a similar quality of life with much less consumption—and as a result a reduced ecological impact as well.[16]

Sharing within a community also helps to establish a different cultural norm, one based in cooperation instead of conspicuous consumption and competition. Indeed, this mental shift can help channel the urge to "keep up with the Joneses" into a more constructive form—namely from one of rivalry over who has the biggest SUV or McMansion to who has the lowest ecological footprint. (See Chapter 4.)

Many communities have even institutionalized these educational efforts, providing schools for community children that maintain an ecocentric curriculum. For example, the Berea College Ecovillage in Kentucky includes the Berea Early Learning Center, for the students' children in day care (most residents of the ecovillage are "nontraditional" students who have children). This eco-friendly day care introduces preschool students to recycling, gardening, and composting.[17]

Throughout history, teahouses and coffeehouses have been a central staging ground to discuss revolutionary action.

Beyond the ecovillage, communities are trying to rebuild community connections in innovative ways, with one of the most interesting being the "third place." This term was coined by sociologist Ray Oldenburg to describe informal public gathering places—the place after home and work (the first and second places) that people tend to spend their time in. Being informal gathering places, they have many important roles: connecting the community, integrating newcomers and visitors, offering staging areas in times of local crisis, and providing a set of local store owners who tend to watch over and help the community.[18]

Over the past several decades, neighborhood hangouts have increasingly been replaced by soulless franchises that are typically identical in design, lack local flavor, and rarely serve community needs. Today, however, many neighborhoods are starting to consciously recreate third places and the community ties that they facilitate. And some are even starting to recognize that these places can not only serve a central role in cultivating social capital, they can also serve as important tools in shaping environmental values.

These "sustainable third places" not only build community ties, they also adopt green business practices and help educate customers about living sustainably—using such tools as periodic lectures, discussion groups, informational guides, and books they sell. Sustainable third places can also synergistically support other sustainable business sectors—particularly food production. Local restaurants, not bound by franchise contracts, can order food directly from local farmers, helping to support local agricultural production. And sustainable third places can encourage their customers to get engaged in sustainability efforts, for example helping to set up volunteer groups to work on a local ecological restoration project or environmental campaign.

One example of a sustainable third place is the White Dog Cafe in Philadelphia. Judy Wicks founded the cafe in 1983 in a 100-year-old house on Sansom Street, after joining with her neighbors to fight to prevent this and other houses from being torn down to make room for a new shopping mall. The White Dog now fills three adjacent houses, serving up local food, running on wind power, and hosting regular "Table Talks" on a variety of social and environmental topics. Wicks was one of the first to serve local food in Philadelphia, a niche she could have attempted to monopolize. Instead, she started a foundation (and supported it with 20 percent of the cafe's profits) that worked to expand local food use in the city, by helping other restaurants to localize and connecting farmers and businesses in the city. And the White Dog is not alone. There are hundreds of sustainable third places around the world, each with its own priorities and projects.[19]

Cafes, in particular, have great potential to shape people's values and mobilize communities. Throughout history, teahouses and coffeehouses have been a central staging ground to discuss revolutionary action, with organizers of both the American and French Revolutions discussing plans and organizing actions in coffeehouses. Today, organizations like the Green Café Network are starting to mobilize cafe owners to use their spaces to "mainstream sustainability"—teaching millions of Americans who visit a cafe each day how they can live greener. The Network, started in San Francisco in 2007, helps locally owned cafes reduce their ecological footprints and become certified green businesses. It also aims to change customer consumption patterns and promote green lifestyle practices by using partner cafes to teach sustainability—through hosting talks, eco-art exhibits, and educational displays and distributing information.[20]

Localizing Economic Production

The dairy at the Cobb Hill Cohousing community in Hartland, Vermont, that produces award winning cheeses, the bakery in the ecovillage of Lakabe near Pamplona, Spain, that bakes bread for 25 stores in surrounding towns, the herbalist business at the Earthaven Ecovillage that makes medicines from herbs found in the surrounding bioregion—there are countless local businesses employing people from the community, providing a sustainable living, and helping to relocalize an economy that has become increasingly globalized and environmentally destructive. The benefits of localizing economic activity have been well chronicled and can include providing a more stable source of jobs and income, a reduction in use of fuel for transportation, businesses more willing to adapt to stricter environmental regulations (as opposed to closing and rebuilding elsewhere), and a larger percentage of profits circulating within the community instead of being concentrated in the hands of far-off investors.[21]

One key sector of the economy ripe for localization (in addition to energy production, discussed earlier) is food production. Farming today depends on massive amounts of petroleum-based inputs: fuel to run the tractors and ship food thousands of kilometers, fertilizers and pesticides, and packaging often derived from petroleum. While oil is cheap and the effects of climate change appear relatively minor, this may not seem to be a problem. But with ramped-up efforts to regulate greenhouse gas emissions, potential disruptions of agricultural production due to climate change, and increasing competition over a finite supply of oil, the cost of far-off food will most likely increase, as will its scarcity.

Local farming can address these problems, reducing oil dependency and the ecological impacts of industrial-scale agriculture while providing many other benefits, such as healthier, tastier food, heightened food security, and increased community interactions. Growing food locally reduces the fuel used to ship goods long distances. From farm to market, fruits and vegetables in the United States travel between 2,500 and 4,000 kilometers on average—generating 5 to 17 times more CO_2 emissions than the equivalent amount of local food. Eating locally produced food can reduce an individual's carbon footprint by about 2,000 kilograms per year.[22]

A study of 200 residents in Philadelphia found that residents who gardened not only had increased access to healthier foods—eating more fresh vegetables and fewer sweets—but also saved at least $100 a year in food costs. Community gardens often help build social capital as well. In a study of 63 community gardens in upstate New York, people in 54 of these worked cooperatively—sharing tools, work, or harvest. Moreover, having a community garden improved many residents' attitudes about their neighborhoods, reducing problems like littering, while also spurring broader community revitalization efforts.[23]

As more local farms and gardens are established, a growing number of farmers' markets and community-supported agriculture (CSA) operations are sprouting up. In the United States, there are now more than 4,300 farmers' markets and 1,100 CSA farms. These tie consumers and producers together—educating consumers about the source of their food, giving farms a better source of income, and, with CSAs, providing working capital to farmers (because CSA members purchase in advance a share of a farmers' annual production). Being part of a CSA or farmers' market can help reconnect consumers directly to the food cycle, obtaining fresh food straight from a farmer. And farmers' markets help increase community interactions: patrons shopping at these markets typically have 10 times more social interactions than those shopping at grocery stores.[24]

To cultivate the local food movement, many community groups and nongovernmental organizations (NGOs) are creating community gardens and small farms. Some are driven by food security concerns, others environmental worries, and still others simply by the facts that local, organic produce usually tastes better and is healthier than food produced in far-off farms or greenhouses and that local gardens can strengthen community ties and give people an opportunity to exercise and reconnect with nature.

In Chicago and Milwaukee, Growing Power is working to create local sustainable food systems through a combination of training local farmers, supporting farmers' markets, setting up local food processing and distribution facilities, and converting the many underused spaces in these two cities—like the 60,000 vacant lots in Chicago—into gardens and farms. One impressive innovation is that the organization is working directly with the Chicago city government, being paid by the city to set up community gardens and urban farms in public parks. This not only sustains the projects but redirects money that would have gone to for-profit landscape businesses toward providing food and job training to underserviced residents. In 2006, one of these projects—a 1,900-square-meter urban farm in Grant Park—trained 25 young people in farming and produced over $15,000 worth of food that was donated to food pantries and soup kitchens.[25]

To expand this beyond certain cities or regions, a national grassroots network called Rooted in Community (RIC) is working to help young people set up community garden, local farms, and other local food projects. Since 1998, at least 75 grassroots groups have been engaged with the network, and RIC has strengthened the skills of hundreds of community leaders through national trainings.[26]

But can gardens and local farms actually supply more than a small fraction of a community's food? Cuba—after reducing annual oil imports from 13 million to 6 million tons in one year because of the collapse of the Soviet Union and the U.S. embargo—proved that the answer to this question is yes. At that time, Cuba had the most industrialized agricultural system in all of Latin America and even used more than twice as much fertilizer per hectare as U.S. farmers did. But the Soviet collapse and subsequent lack of oil, chemical fertilizers, pesticides, and other industrial agricultural inputs forced Cuba to localize agricultural production rapidly. Today, after considerable innovation, the country now delivers much of its agricultural produce from small urban farms and community gardens. In Havana alone, there are more than 26,000 food gardens, spreading across 2,400 hectares of land and producing 25,000 tons of food.[27]

Americans typically have ample space to devote to food gardens. During World War

II, Americans set up 20 million home and community gardens—Victory Gardens—that provided 40 percent of civilians' fresh vegetables, allowing farms to concentrate on providing for the troops. Today, in contrast, Americans maintain 10 million hectares of lawns, often with assistance from toxic pesticides and fertilizers. These lawns could readily be replaced with gardens, producing a new source of local food and reducing toxic chemical usage. The key to this transition will ideally stem from increased support by community groups, NGOs, and government agencies. Realistically, however, a major disruption in food production, like the one Cuba experienced, will also trigger a return to local farming. Future ecological disruptions may also speed the transition to a new model. (See Box 11–2.)[28]

Beyond food production, efforts to localize the economy are taking some novel forms. NGOs are taking a lead in reducing dependence on the globalized economy. One— The Relocalization Network—is helping to

---

Box 11–2. Preparing for the Long Emergency

On the outskirts of Barcelona, a former leper colony now houses a new community. In 2001, a group of 30 squatters took over this property that had lain vacant since the 1950s and created an eco-squatter community, Can Masdeu. While squatters typically are viewed as a problem, this group has taken unused land and is now a model sustainable community—maintaining a composting toilet, a constructed wetlands for processing gray water, homemade solar thermal panels, even a "bici-lavadora" (bicycle-powered washing machine). Moreover, the community provides 28 community garden plots to neighborhood residents, maintains a regular meeting space for a variety of social activist groups, and sets up a sustainable third place on Sunday nights: the Rurbar, selling food and beer that the community produces.

Can Masdeu also offers another benefit: it shows that life can go on in a climate of uncertainty, where community members have no rights to ownership, where police have attempted to expel them by force, and where financial capital to invest is scarce. The leper colony, founded in the seventeenth century, functioned without electricity, obtained its water from mountain springs, and grew its own food. While Can Masdeu has electricity today, its water and sewage treatment and much of its food production are not dependent on it. The community—in pared-down form—could function even if the global economy seized up and died tomorrow.

Communities can play a significant role in helping reduce ecological problems that currently threaten the future of human civilization. But due to a lack of leadership by the worst polluters and positive feedback cycles like thawing permafrost and the melting Arctic ice cap, it may be too late to prevent the worst effects of climate change— such as a sea level rise of 15 meters that the melting of Greenland and western Antarctica would trigger. Add to this growing social disruptions from increased competition over petroleum supplies and the possible breakdown of global governance as new resource rivalries form, and the picture looks bleak indeed. If this scenario— "the long emergency," as author James Howard Kunstler calls it—becomes the new reality, then communities will once again become central in providing for themselves. Local food provision, local energy production, and the basic technologies needed to maintain a water supply and process sewage safely may mean the difference between a high quality of life and abject poverty.

If humanity cannot mobilize to prevent an ecological collapse, any effort by communities to increase their self-sufficiency and reduce dependence on far-off goods that will become scarce as the global economic system falters will help them survive in a less stable future, much as the residents of Can Masdeu are doing now.

Source: See endnote 28.

---

coordinate 166 groups in 13 countries, providing an online learning and networking forum for communities working to lower their reliance on a fragile, globalized economic system. Efforts of these many groups are impressive—ranging from local community education projects to town and city resolutions to reduce dependence on oil.[29]

Networks like BALLE—the Business Alliance for Living Local Economies—are also helping to drive localization forward. BALLE, consisting of more than 15,000 businesses, has 51 networks spread over 26 regions in North America (states and Canadian provinces). These networks help connect local businesses, with the goal of strengthening exchange of goods locally while helping to enact public policies to support decentralized ownership of businesses, fair wages, and good stewardship of the environment.[30]

Some towns and cities are also looking holistically at how they can localize their economies. For example, in Willits, California, the WELL (Willits Economic LocaLization) initiative is educating town residents about the benefits of and opportunities to localize the economy. So far WELL has focused on assessing current resource use in Willits—such as the amount of energy imported and the CO_2 emissions produced per capita—and it is now turning to figuring out how best to reduce the town's ecological impacts and reduce dependence on the global economic system. In the United Kingdom, there are also 21 Transition Towns— towns, neighborhoods, villages, and cities that are setting up "transition initiatives" in which they try to move toward localization, reduce oil dependence, and lower the ecological impact of their economies.[31]

With growing disparities between rich and poor worldwide and the global growth of slums, there is a strong need to merge the empowerment of communities like those just described with efforts to meet people's basic needs independently and sustainably. Community-driven development (CDD) is one strategy to address poverty in this way. With CDD, poor communities are the lead actors in development efforts, not passive recipients of aid, and are empowered to focus on the priorities they choose—whether that be health, education, sanitation, or other pressing issues—and given the assistance they need to succeed.

Sometimes CDD efforts are initiated directly by communities, but many are supported by either NGOs or international agencies that can provide financial or technical assistance. For example, a Zambian NGO, the North Luangwa Wildlife Conservation and Community Development Programme, has worked to reduce poaching in the North Luangwa National Park by empowering communities to make a living through farming and other more sustainable enterprises, while also setting up local clinics and education programs. Started in 1994, this program now reaches more than 35,000 people.[32]

The United Nations and other international agencies are also increasingly using CDD. The COMPACT program (Community Management of Protected Areas Conservation), for instance, is a joint project of the U.N. Development Programme and the Global Environment Facility that provides grants of less than $50,000 to communities in World Heritage Sites to help establish projects that improve community well-being while reducing people's impact on the surrounding ecosystems. Around Mount Kenya, where deforestation is a significant concern, COMPACT has worked with villages to set up a microhydro generator and sustainable food projects like beekeeping and trout farming, and it has worked with schools to provide more efficient cookstoves—all of which help reduce community dependence on firewood while offering new economic opportunities. (For more on CDD in developing countries, see Chapter 12.)[33]

Financing Sustainable Communities

Underlying local economic enterprise there needs to be sustainable community finance, which can mobilize community funds to invest in local green endeavors—an essential element if businesses like local farms and sustainable third places are to thrive. Traditionally, community development financial institutions (CDFIs)—including development banks, credit unions, loan funds, and venture capital funds—finance projects that build affordable housing, create livable-wage jobs, or provide essential services such as health care. (See also Chapter 13.) Although these investments are comparatively small— at just $20 billion in the United States—the effects of community investing are impressive. A survey of 496 U.S. CDFIs found that in 2005 these institutions financed 9,074 businesses that established or sustained 39,151 jobs, and they facilitated the building or renovation of 55,242 units of affordable housing and 613 community facilities in economically disadvantaged communities.[34]

While interest in CDFIs has grown significantly over the past years—with total investments quintupling between 1997 and 2005—few of these investments are targeted toward sustainable community development. If they were, they could have not just an economic impact but an ecological one as well. Some ecovillages have small banks that do just this. In Italy, the community of Damanhur maintains a co-operative that invests members' savings in existing community businesses as well as giving loans and business advice to community members trying to start new sustainable businesses.[35]

On a larger scale, ShoreBank Pacific in Washington State sees itself as a sustainable community development bank. This bank, with assets of $113 million, lends to community businesses while also proactively helping clients in a variety of industries to use energy efficiently, reduce waste, conserve resources, and shift production toward a greener model. This starts with a review of the business by a staff scientist and continues with consultations throughout the course of the loan, offering strategic advice on how to become sustainable.[36]

Instead of creating banks, some communities are actually creating their own currencies. These can take many forms. Some, like Ithaca Hours, are pegged against an hour of labor, thus valuing all work equally. Others are pegged to a national currency. The Berk-Share is one of these. In Great Barrington, Massachusetts, there are about $760,000 worth of BerkShares circulating; they are accepted by some 300 local businesses—from coffeeshops to grocery stores. A local bank is even considering creating a credit card based in BerkShares. And Great Barrington is not alone. There are over 4,000 community currencies around the world.[37]

While the true economic impact of these currencies is relatively minor, they do provide many benefits to communities that use them. Because franchises typically do not trade in community currencies, these systems help create support—and loyal customer bases—for local businesses. They also help build community support networks. According to a U.K. study, local currencies help many users develop a network of people they could call on for help, as well as helping people cope with unemployment. And local currencies can help address specific social needs in a community. In Japan, many areas use *fureai kippu* (caring relationship tickets): helping the sick and elderly with daily living will earn the helper some tickets, which can then be exchanged for help when that person is sick or can be given to sick or elderly relations to use. This has enabled more elderly people to continue living in their homes and communities rather than moving to convalescent homes.[38]

Another innovative way to finance sustainable communities involves harnessing the profits of a new breed of business called "social enterprise." This term refers to businesses that achieve their social missions through their earned income strategies. For example, Greyston Bakery in New York City was founded in 1982 to provide jobs for the chronically unemployed. Today, the profits of this $6.5-million business provide funding for health clinics, day care centers, affordable housing, and other social services that help address poverty in New York City. And in Thailand, the resort and restaurant Cabbages and Condoms uses its five restaurants and two resorts to promote safe sex and AIDS prevention while generating revenue for the Population and Community Development Association, an NGO that works on rural development, AIDS education, population growth, and environmental protection.[39]

Although few social enterprises currently focus on sustainable poverty alleviation, when they do they can make an important contribution to redesigning the economy to serve the needs of communities in an ecologically responsible manner.

Communities Mobilizing Society

Beyond design and helping to rebuild local economies, communities can use members' energy and resources to help green society more broadly—restoring local ecosystems, educating the broader public, or engaging in efforts to reform local or even national political agendas.

One way communities are readily engaging in this effort is helping with ecological restoration projects in their area. The Los Angeles Ecovillage was instrumental in helping the Bresee Center design The Bimini Slough Ecology Park at the end of LAEV's street. Now the runoff from two neighboring streets drains into a small stream in the park. Here the water is cleaned by stream plants on its way back to the watertable instead of moving directly to the ocean, with all of its pollutants, via the storm drain.[40]

An example of a much broader-ranging restoration project comes from the community of Las Gaviotas in Colombia. This village was established on degraded savanna and made it a point to replant 8,000 hectares of surrounding land with forest—an area larger than Manhattan. Along with providing the community with food and tradable forest products, this land now absorbs 144,000 tons of carbon a year and will continue to do so while the forest grows. Gaviotas' efforts are impressive, but the village's decades-long plan is even more ambitious: Gaviotas hopes to replant another 3 million hectares with the help of other villages and towns; that's enough to absorb a quarter of Colombia's annual carbon emissions.[41]

Some communities—in particular ecovillages—are reaching out globally to local leaders to help spread the knowledge needed to make towns and larger regions sustainable. Many ecovillages have regular training courses. At The Farm, an ecovillage in Summertown, Tennessee, the Ecovillage Training Center hosts dozens of training workshops—from how to install solar panels to how to cultivate and build with bamboo. Ecovillages like The Farm also host longer apprenticeships for people wanting to learn about the many aspects of community sustainability. In 2003 many ecovillage and other community sustainability leaders founded Gaia University, which offers accredited bachelors and masters degrees in Integrative Ecosocial Design, in which students learn how to design societal, community, and personal behaviors that are in line with ecological principles.[42]

Communities are also increasingly getting involved in local political efforts. Today in the United States, many of the 300,000 homeowners associations (HOAs) ban their members from hanging clothes outside to dry because of the perception that clotheslines look unsightly and thus reduce property value. Yet if Americans dried just half of their clothes outside instead of in dryers that were powered by coal-fired power plants, they could save enough electricity to shut down eight such plants and reduce CO_2 emissions by 23 million tons. Communities and community

groups are approaching HOAs to get this and other sustainability measures implemented. Project Laundry List is an organization that helps homeowners appeal to their HOAs and that is coordinating broader efforts to change state laws to uphold "the right to dry."[43]

At the town and city level, there are even more opportunities to foster local-level sustainability through policy changes. A key strategy is to push for "smart growth," shifting urban planning away from car-dependent low-density housing to one of walkable neighborhoods with a mix of commercial and residential space. Smart growth is essential for reducing car dependency and for making towns and cities more sustainable. Some communities are joining broader coalitions working on campaigns as varied as increasing public transit, organizing to make cities bicycle-friendly, and lobbying to strengthen urban

Box 11–3. Dockside Green: Developers Taking the Lead

Until recently, the 15-acre Dockside Lands parcel in Victoria, British Columbia—the province's capital on Vancouver Island—was the epitome of an underused property. Purchased by the city for a single dollar in 1989, this prime real estate lay largely ignored for years, crippled by an industrial legacy that left the soil saturated with petrochemicals and toxic heavy metals. Now the site is poised to become the greenest neighborhood in Victoria, thanks to collaboration between the city and two developers, Windmill Development Group and VanCity Enterprises. The first of three distinct neighborhoods, Dockside Wharf, is set for completion in 2009 and will include 268 residential units of varying sizes. By the time it is completed around 2018, the development will accommodate approximately 2,500 people.

The developers have promised to deliver 26 LEED platinum-rated buildings in addition to an impressive green infrastructure and have even pledged to pay penalties up to CDN$1 million if certification goals are not met. One hundred percent on-site sewage treatment is projected to

save CDN$81,000 a year in city fees. On-site energy generation, including solar panels and a biomass gasification system fueled by waste wood, will further reduce pressure on Victoria's infrastructure. Preliminary studies indicate that Dockside Green's goal of carbon neutrality may even produce excess energy that can be sold back to the city. Residents can stroll down a central greenway irrigated only with recycled rainwater, ride mini-transit vehicles that run on biodiesel, and check their personal energy consumption via monitors in each home.

Walkable, dense neighborhoods with a variety of housing units, lively public areas, and commercial space will help foster a sense of community. Planners have also been careful to integrate existing industry, interspersing light industrial space among the housing units, thus preserving Dockside Green's distinctive harbor industry heritage.

—Meghan Bogaerts

Source: See endnote 44.

growth boundaries.

Another innovative strategy is to educate developers about the importance of smart growth. Some developers are starting to recognize the profitability of building developments along these lines, tapping into the growing demand for environmentally friendly communities and the many government incentives that subsidize such projects. (See Box 11–3.)[44]

Eco-municipalities are efforts by community members, local NGOs, and town officials to create long-term comprehensive sustainability plans for towns, villages, or cities.

But the key will be making smart growth the norm for developers. One impressive effort is being led by the U.S. Green Building Council (USGBC). This organization's LEED program (Leadership in Energy and Environmental Design) has helped provide green certification schemes for all type of buildings: commercial, residential, and others.

USGBC is now working on a new "LEED for Neighborhood Development" certification system. This standard, currently in its pilot phase, will provide a grade for planned neighborhood developments, giving points for designs that connect communities, reduce vehicle use, and create local jobs. It also includes prerequisites such that any development that compromises wetlands or agricultural lands, is located in a flood zone, or is built "60 miles from anything" (as Program Manager Jennifer Henry puts it) cannot be certified. For well-planned neighborhoods, developers can receive a high grade (platinum or gold), which may help expedite permission from local planning boards and make developers eligible for tax breaks or other incentives.[45]

Currently 238 projects are involved in the pilot phase of the LEED for Neighborhood Development, ranging from sustainable communities like the Los Angeles Ecovillage to large urban projects. In 2009 the USGBC will finalize the program once the pilot phase concludes and public comments are received. Once finished, new communities that are forming can use these standards, and existing communities can lobby local governments to ensure that these standards are used when new developments are planned.[46]

Another innovative idea that has started to spread around the world is that of the "eco-municipality." In essence, eco-municipalities are efforts by coalitions of community members, local NGOs, and town officials to create long-term comprehensive sustainability plans for their towns, villages, or cities. Over-torneå, Sweden, became the first eco-municipality in 1983. Since then, more than 60 municipalities in Sweden, ranging from villages to cities of 500,000, have followed suit—as have 20 Estonian municipalities and municipalities in 10 other countries.[47]

Because communities are by their nature small, their ability to address global environmental problems is often overlooked by national governments. But with proper support, they can have a dramatic impact. The key will be getting governments to recognize communities' potential and tap into it. The United Kingdom may be the first country to proactively do so. Parliament is close to passing the Sustainable Communities Act, which would provide local councils with direct access to the office of the Secretary of State and fund local sustainability projects—including those that support local businesses, protect the local environment, and build community connections and political activity.[48]

When national policy is changed in the right way, the effects can be impressive. While small-scale wind and other major projects are often difficult to implement because of zoning restrictions, in some countries governments have actually facilitated them. Since the 1970s, Denmark has allowed communities, co-operatives, small companies, and towns to establish small renewable projects and obtain a set price for the electricity they provide to the grid. Today, over 80 percent of wind turbines are owned by co-operatives, local companies, or individuals. Along with triggering a major investment in wind energy (over 20 percent of Denmark's electricity comes from wind), local ownership and the resulting local profits have led to broad public acceptance.[49]

National policy changes have great potential and could take many forms. Imagine the impact of initiatives like California's Million Solar Roofs, which provides financial incentives and other support to individual homeowners to put solar panels on their roofs. Similar efforts could mobilize communities around the world: a 10,000 Town Wind Co-op Project; a 100,000 Neighborhood Energy Club Initiative; a Million Community Garden Program; or a $10 Billion Sustainable Community Investment Initiative could all drive community sustainability efforts to the next level. The key will be mobilizing communities around the world to educate national policymakers on the benefits local efforts can bring—and to challenge them to make these happen.[50]

CHAPTER 12

Mobilizing Human Energy

Jason S. Calder

Niger was all but given a death sentence in the 1970s when drought-propelled desertification, rapid population growth, and unsustainable farming practices threatened ecological collapse and mass human suffering. Women on average each gave birth to more than seven children, and the population was expected to double in the next two decades. Families who had worked their land for generations could see the tell-tale signs: it was taking longer and longer to get to trees and fresh water, and the Sahara desert was getting closer and closer.[1]

Thirty years later there is startling evidence of a turnaround, thanks to changes undertaken beginning in the mid-1980s. (See Figure 12–1.) At that time, farmers in several villages were taught to carefully plow around tree saplings when sowing crops of millet, sorghum, peanuts, and beans. Careful nurturing, along with other simple soil and water conservation practices, saplings became trees,

putting down roots and a buffer against topsoil erosion and crop loss.[2]

The quick-growing native trees became assets that families used to supplement incomes, provide insurance against crop failure, and meet their own needs. The trees provided wood for charcoal, foliage for animal fodder, and fruit for food. News spread through social networks and marketplaces in the more densely populated regions of the country until an area of 7 million hectares, about the size of the state of West Virginia, was re-greening with trees.[3]

Did farmers do this alone? Hardly. Better rains helped, and so did the government. But the standard anti-desertification strategy of massive tree planting projects was not what made the difference. The forest law previously stated that both land and trees were the property of the state. Recognizing that farmers had de facto ownership of the trees and were investing in their regeneration, the govern-

Jason Calder is Director of the Engaging Citizens and Communities in Peacebuilding Project at Future Generations.

Figure 12–1. Farmer-managed Tree Regeneration in Galma Village, Niger, 1975 and 2003

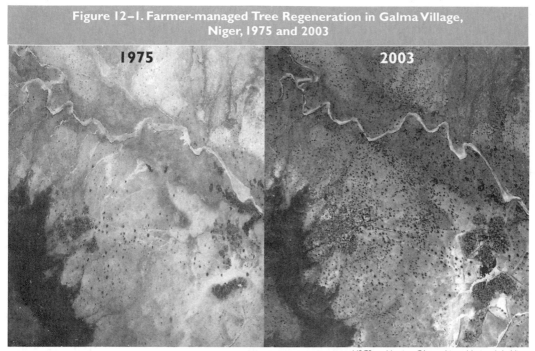

USGS and Institut Géographique National du Niger

ment wisely amended the forest code, giving farmers formal property rights. This additional security helped reinforce a trend and add momentum. The forest service began to change from policing tree cutting and levying fines to partnering with communities to assist regeneration. Nongovernmental organizations (NGOs), the Peace Corps, and donors helped promote the new practices through training programs and farmer-to-farmer visits.[4]

Notwithstanding this support, it was the energy invested by the farmers of Niger that fueled this massive transformation of land and livelihoods. The result is a more complex agricultural system and a more diverse economy that is helping farmers invest in regenerating once-infertile lands. Today farmers credit their efforts with lowering poverty, improving nutrition, and reducing vulnerability to hunger. The average distance a woman must walk for firewood in the Zinder region has declined from 2.5 hours in 1984 to half an hour today. When a regional drought and massive locust invasion hit in 2005, many of the villages in the "green belt" reported no child deaths from malnutrition because they were able to sell wood in local markets to purchase expensive cereals that normally would have been beyond reach.[5]

This success story from Niger demonstrates that the greatest untapped resource in solving the problem of global poverty and environmental decline is the poor themselves. They have the most unambiguous incentive to change their condition, yet this simple fact is all too rarely embraced by governments, aid workers, and the market. In the face of deprivation, discrimination, and oppression, the poor are all too often offered charity, manipulation, and condescension.

But there are signs that this is beginning to

change. Over three decades of grassroots community development experiences that began as a search for an alternative to mainstream economic development have coalesced into new approaches to citizen and community empowerment that embrace partnerships with governments and markets while maintaining an emphasis on self-reliance and self-help.

As with traditional community-based development, this newer community-driven development recognizes that the poor must be the active authors of their own destiny and that development cannot be sustainable if it dislocates people from their communities and resources. Recognizing poverty as much more than a lack of income, the new approaches emphasize building assets, expanding freedoms, and mobilizing the poor to overcome the voicelessness and powerlessness that are defining characteristics of poverty.[6]

Informed by an emphasis on incentives and client knowledge, community-driven approaches are being implemented by NGOs, businesses, and large organizations like the World Bank. Perhaps most promising is that practitioners are tackling the question of how to scale up community-driven change over wide geographic areas involving significant numbers of people.

While the international community sets ambitious development targets like the Millennium Development Goals, it is not clear how to achieve them. So far, the debate is polarized between mobilizing massive financial resources for technical fixes and piecemeal responses sought by entrepreneurs. But financial resources and technology, although important, are not the binding constraints. Experimentation and local solutions are also important, yet the scale of the challenge demands a more ambitious response. As the hopeful case of Niger demonstrates, what is required are ways of tapping into the ultimate resource: human energy.[7]

Grounding Action in Local Realities

Thanks to several encouraging developments in the 1990s (see Box 12–1), there are signs that thinking in international development policy circles is converging around several sensible propositions that could reorient the global poverty fight. The first is that no one-size-fits-all model of development can be applied anywhere. The generally poor record of various western-inspired plans for development has been well documented. Even the World Bank draws this conclusion in its reading of the development experience of recent decades: "The central message...is that there is no unique universal set of rules....we need to get away from formulae and the search for elusive 'best practices.'"[8]

Referring to the standard set of free market reforms promoted by western development institutions since the 1980s, in 2006 development economist Dani Rodrik noted that "the question now is not whether the Washington Consensus is dead or alive; it is what will replace it." It is increasingly accepted that each country's path to success will be different, based on the particular obstacles and opportunities set forth by their histories, cultures, social institutions, political climates, and geographies.[9]

The second sensible proposition is that poverty is about much more than lack of income. The U.N. Development Programme has been publishing annual *Human Development Reports* since the early 1990s; its Human Development Index combines health, education, and income as an alternative measure of national progress. (See Chapter 2.) Informed by the role of social capital and institutions, this is also about more than investing in the "social side" of development. A much broader view is emerging: development is about the expansion of freedoms that

Box 12–1. Reshaping the Development Agenda in the 1990s

The 1990s were a period of momentous change in global affairs, with significant consequences for international development and, in particular, the environment for more holistic, less prescriptive, more locally driven development.

First, with the end of proxy wars between East and West and the historic "third wave" of democracy resulting in greater political openness, it was no longer defensible for rich nations to prop up and defend corrupt and authoritarian regimes with aid dollars (although by no means has that practice ended). This opened discussions about issues of good governance—democracy, accountability, transparency, rule of law, and clean government—that had long been swept under the carpet in official international development. Evidence emerged over the decade that donors slowly but surely were becoming more selective in who received their aid.

As it became more difficult to tolerate unaccountable behavior on the part of aid recipients, the tables were turned on the providers. Developing countries and social activists argued for greater "ownership" of development by those who ultimately lived with the consequences of aid. Society-wide attempts to transform economies from the top down through "structural adjustment" were deeply resented. In an era of political opening and concern for good governance, it became clear that development policies should be the result of public dialogue between citizens and their governments at all levels, and not principally the result of conditions imposed on cash-strapped governments.

The World Bank instituted sweeping changes in the late 1990s requiring governments to consult with citizens on strategies and policies for poverty reduction. There is still plenty of debate on whether governments yet really "own" their development programs, particularly in the macroeconomic arena, but reform of development assistance and "aid effectiveness" are major topics of reform.

Second, it became undeniably clear that the countries that had made the most progress with sustained growth and poverty reduction were following their own unique paths. The good news

was that the absolute number of people living on less than $1 a day worldwide had decreased by 500 million between 1981 and 2001, mainly as a result of growth in China and India. Yet the former had done so without democracy and traditional private property rights, while the latter had a significant government role in the economy.

In addition to these and the well-known East Asian "miracle" economies, countries such as Bangladesh, Botswana, Egypt, Mauritius, Sri Lanka, Tunisia, Viet Nam, and others also achieved progress with "unorthodox" strategies. Meanwhile, countries that had supposedly gotten their macroeconomic fundamentals in order—Bolivia, Brazil, Mexico, Philippines, and Venezuela, for example—had very mixed records. This experience argued for much more humility among policy reformers and international institutions, and much greater attention to the specific conditions within countries.

Third, globalization of trade, investment, technology, and communications accelerated human contacts and shrank the psychological distance between people. Private capital flows outstripped official development assistance by wide margins, although only small amounts went to Africa. Global threats such as climate change, terrorism, and disease, with their various connections to human deprivation, made it increasingly clear that a more robust global engagement on poverty was imperative.

Fourth, the United Nations sponsored a succession of international conferences on the environment, population, food security, social development, women, and housing that shaped a broad international consensus on fighting poverty. These culminated in the adoption of the Millennium Development Goals by the U.N. General Assembly in September 2000, followed by the International Conference on Financing for Development in Monterrey, Mexico, to consider how to fund the goals' achievement through public and private financial flows. This agenda helped establish new norms for international development cooperation.

Source: See endnote 8.

people experience, requiring the interactive engagement of citizens and communities with state and markets.[10]

By the early 1980s, there was growing frustration about the top-down, expert-driven nature of prevailing development models. Many commentators saw that the key to reversing this was to value and build on local knowledge and respond to the "felt needs" of communities, an idea articulated by Brazilian educator and activist Paolo Freire. Later, Robert Chambers helped popularize a series of participatory or community-based development techniques that were effective in stimulating greater community awareness, identifying local needs, highlighting local assets, and mobilizing community action around projects of their own conception that fit with their cultures, ecologies, and local economies.[11]

Use of these techniques exploded in the 1980s and 1990s in NGO projects and began to be adopted by institutions such as the U.S. Agency for International Development, the United Nations, and the World Bank. Much has been learned and accomplished by community-based approaches, but most have not succeeded in igniting fundamental transformation of societies in an age of globalization. (See Box 12–2.)[12]

Several pitfalls have been common. In some cases the use of participatory techniques by donors and NGOs was nothing more than an attempt to co-opt communities into development schemes that had already been fully formulated elsewhere. After all, British and French colonial administrations in Africa and elsewhere had used involvement of "tradi-

---

Box 12–2. Common Critiques of Community-based Development

Scope. Many projects were conceived on a narrow basis, such as helping communities build schools or increase food production. These may respond well to an NGO's particular expertise, a congressional earmark, a bureaucratic priority, or the demand for straightforward quantifiable "results," but they do not reflect the real world of individuals and communities whose problems and challenges are complex and interrelated. Integrated rural development programs in the 1970s and 1980s attempted to combine social and economic needs, but they proved unsustainable and gave little room for local voice. More recent area development programs have had greater success.

Scale. Community-based projects were too small and localized to make much of a difference, given the scale of the problems faced. Despite success, replication "a village at a time'" was not feasible. In addition, many supporters of these projects assumed that eventually someone else—the government, a donor agency—would do the work of replication.

Sustainability. Community-based projects too often failed the "walk-away test" and essentially collapsed or were abandoned by communities when the funding ran out and a sponsoring NGO or aid agency left. There may have been community involvement, but not true community ownership. Communities learned to use outside resources for a one-time effort, not how to seek out, create, and manage partnerships.

Structural change. The obstacle to resolving many community problems lies outside the community in institutions and political and social structures. Community-based projects that dealt exclusively with the local, no matter how participatory, would never achieve fundamental transformation. Until development is understood as an inherently political process of people claiming basic rights, people will never ultimately reshape the structural forces in society that are responsible for the deprivation, discrimination, exclusion, vulnerability, and violence that mark the lives of the poor.

Sources: See endnote 12.

---

tional leaders" and "community participation" as a means of exerting social control. In a reprise of this role, NGOs and private contractors, who were increasingly the conduits of official foreign aid, were driven by donor-mandated results and timetables rather than community needs, capabilities, agency, and vision. Many of these "participatory development" projects weren't all that participatory from the perspective of the poor. Captured by elite interests or simply involving information sharing or consultation but no real control or influence, these were a far cry from the liberating process of local initiative and social movement that their advocates claimed.[13]

Many of these projects also idealized communities in ways that undermined their potential. First, they imagined communities as homogenous and harmonious entities when often they were far more complex units within which needs and interests were mediated by power, caste, ethnicity, age, religion, or gender. Second, many NGOs who supported these projects were ideologically or otherwise antagonistic toward working with government or the private sector. Their efforts at times isolated communities or promoted the naive notion that bottom-up mobilization alone would overcome the powerful and entrenched forces arrayed against them. As a result, many community activities remained essentially local projects and failed to affect or engage wider social and political structures that were driving poverty, environmental degradation, and social injustice.[14]

These criticisms were one helpful reminder of the inherently political nature of poverty. The poor are poor because the rich and powerful have created institutions to serve their interests. The landmark *Voices of the Poor* study, which gathered the views of 60,000 poor men and women from 60 countries, confirmed that the poor saw their humanity

devalued by the world around them. Sustainable routes out of poverty would have to involve the poor not only by building their assets and capabilities but by engaging with the institutions and structures of governance and markets. Engaging this governance agenda involves communities participating in public budgeting decisions, scrutinizing public and private development projects, giving "report cards" to government ministries, and campaigning for greater access to public information.[15]

The Unlimited Resource

Increasing poor people's freedom of choice and action to shape their own lives is critical to achieving development outcomes because it taps into their natural energy and incentive. World Bank research on this topic has dramatically expanded theoretical and practical approaches to understanding and measuring empowerment. It requires the poor to build their individual assets (material, financial) as well as their capabilities (human, social, psychological, political). The poor also require greater collective assets and capabilities, as these provide security, preserve culture, provide meaning, protect the local environment, and expand voice and power. Particularly critical is the role of collective organizations and social movements. Informed by these concepts, efforts to stimulate community-driven development are showing promise in overcoming some key shortcomings of early efforts at community-based development.[16]

A leading example is the Self-Employed Women's Association (SEWA), a 30-year-old grassroots movement that has empowered some of the most marginalized of India's poor women. Where economic growth has outpaced employment growth, many Indian women take up casual labor or self-employment in the informal sector, including load pulling, street vending, and home-based work. In addition to poverty and insecurity, these women are regularly cheated by employers, charged exorbitant interest by moneylenders, and forced to pay bribes to police and public officials to ply their trades. Despite their varied and dispersed occupations, labor activist and SEWA founder Ela Bhatt believed these women could be organized and helped to become more self-reliant.[17]

SEWA today has over 700,000 rural and urban members in seven states. It has organized women to fight for their rights to fair treatment, ranging from better prices for their goods and services to influencing the formation of India's first National Policy on Street Vendors. To secure income and assets, SEWA has formed 76 cooperatives in a variety of fields—from tree growing and handicrafts to milk production and salt farming. It gives women skills training and marketing assistance, helping them to avoid exploitative go-betweens.[18]

The organization helps its members gain access to state-provided services (where they exist) and lobby for improvements of inadequate services. If these approaches do not work, SEWA helps members organize the services for themselves. SEWA today maintains a network of services to meet basic needs such as child care, health care, insurance, and housing. More than 300,000 women have used its primary health services and 110,000 are covered by its insurance program.[19]

The movement has grown and sustained a wide scope of activities and services involving hundreds of thousands because of its organization, values, leadership, and flexibility. SEWA's decentralized structure and strong value system have kept the movement responsive to the women's needs. Bhatt emphasizes the fundamental difference between running an organization and sustaining a movement like SEWA: "The movement flows at times

faster and at other times slower, and may occasionally be deflected around an obstacle, but it always moves in the same direction."[20]

Daniel Taylor and others at the development NGO Future Generations consider community-driven solutions the basis for redirecting globalization, reducing inequality, and preserving and restoring the environment. They maintain that most development projects fail because they seek to control and manage communities rather than unleash energies and potential. Instead of building confidence and resourcefulness, such projects teach dependence on outside actors and funding. When funding runs out and the project ends, communities are left waiting for the next project.[21]

Taylor has developed a simple system of community-driven learning and adaptation called Seed-Scale—a process that helps communities to marshal and direct their energy in ways that fit their economy, ecology, and culture at a pace that is natural and organic. Seed-Scale is based on four simple principles embedded in a seven-step community dialogue and planning process. (See Box 12–3.) These are so intuitive that communities, no matter how daunting their situation, can quickly and easily absorb and use them to mobilize and channel their efforts.[22]

The idea of building purposeful human and social energy is at the center of Seed-Scale. To catalyze it, the poor must believe that a better future is possible and that they can bring about positive change. Arjun Appadurai of The New School has developed the idea of the "capacity to aspire" to understand this aspect of empowerment. It is a cultural capacity based on how the poor learn and understand their "place" in society based on wider cultural norms. It is an ability to navigate the wider world that is developed through experimentation and learning in a way that helps to expand the horizons of

Box 12–3. B[...]
of Se[...]

Build from success[...]
recent or distant succ[...]
for inspiration and ins[...]
munity can work toge[...]

Engage in three-wa[...]
nerships require that [...]
market actors, and ou[...]
facilitators, knowledge[...]
agents) all work togeth[...]

Make decisions base[...]
Objective data can info[...]
measure progress. Lea[...]
techniques gives village[...]
standing of their envir[...]
over information colle[...]

Measure results thr[...]
change in individual[...]
Behavior change happe[...]
perceive something wo[...]
interest to continue.

Source: See endnote 22.

the possible.[23]

In the beginning, [...]
spark that nurtures this [...]
a mother learning to tre[...]
with homemade oral re[...]
farmer learning better [...]
or a group effectively co[...]
industry in its communi[...]
is that the ownership o[...]
deeper meaning resona[...]
munity, which outsiders [...]
build from.

In Seed-Scale, the ini[...]
side assistance is on [...]
methodology and facilit[...]
access to knowledge that [...]
orities in areas such as he[...]
eracy, natural resource [...]
income generation. This [...]

r by taking individuals
[...]er places. People adopt
[...] they see others doing
[...]milar to their own.
[...] Generations has applied
[...]rtheast Indian state of
[...] which shares a border
[...]nd Burma. Arunachal
[...] groups and the center
[...] for all the bananas and
[...]d. In this isolated area
[...] have persisted for cen-
[...]onditions. While the
[...]uccessfully penetrated
[...]al rule, outside inter-
[...] the state today, eye-
[...] for hydropower and
[...]nt has promised the
[...] great deal since inde-
[...] been delivered. Social
[...]rticularly for women.
[...]rriage are entrenched
[...]abor is still practiced
[...]24

[...] sites radiating across
[...]es, communities in
[...]ctively and creatively
[...]ms. Small successes
[...] motivated and mov-
[...]elfare Workers take
[...]ta on health, eco-
[...]al issues; delivering
[...]nd mobilizing the
[...]n a wide scope of
[...] for change. Work
[...] groups but later
[...]. Health improve-
[...]nities learning how
[...]eumonia, improve
[...]hild births, immu-
[...]or child growth.[25]
[...]tially unsupportive
[...]t quickly changed
[...]milies' health and

welfare improved. They have gained access to microcredit and have started small businesses. They also have improved farming techniques and learned how to improve food security and nutrition. Impressed with the success in Arunachal, the state government asked that each new village council be trained in the Seed-Scale methodology so that the 6,000 villages in the state could be equipped to organize a process of local change.[26]

Perhaps the most impressive indicator of community empowerment is demonstrated by what the women have done to change some deep-seated social norms and institutions. Indian law exempts tribal areas from laws banning polygamy and child marriage, so the practices flourish. Some of the women in community action groups were from the lowest rungs of the social hierarchy, as one-time child brides and the third or fourth wives in a household. Once their value to their families and communities was enhanced through new knowledge and practices brought back from village health trainings, they found the voice to argue against child marriage and became part of a gathering community pressure to end the practice voluntarily.

Dialogue started within a few women's groups spread and then percolated up into village council meetings. A petition was drawn up and endorsed by men and women at a series of public meetings and given effect by tribal leaders. When rumors surfaced of an old man planning to take a child bride (his fourth), he was confronted and stopped by the community and reminded that this practice was no longer acceptable. This new attitude has held up throughout an area equivalent to 10 percent of the state. It is noteworthy that this change was the result of an organic process that was directed by the community. For this reason it is likely to be sustained because it reflects changed roles and behaviors.[27]

What has transpired in these cases represents a different way of achieving the Millennium Development Goals. An empowerment approach sees citizens as the authors of their own destiny, not passive vessels awaiting government programs, services, or educational campaigns to catch up with them. While financial resources are an important component of any community development plan, the first question addressed by empowerment approaches is whether the plan can be mobilized from within by using existing assets differently or through partnerships with others. What is perhaps a greater challenge is the fact that this approach requires outside experts and agencies to relinquish control and agree to an iterative effort that starts modestly and will take unexpected directions as well as its own time.

Scaling Up Local Successes

One of the greatest challenges for development organizations is taking a success that is working locally and translating it to the regional or national level. This principally involves understanding why something worked in a particular place and time and then determining how those lessons can be applied elsewhere. In some cases, expansion depends on a quantum leap of investment; in others, it may depend more on removing barriers to entrepreneurial activity or making government agencies more transparent and accountable. Numerous approaches to scaling up successful programs exist. (See Box 12–4.)[28]

Each approach has its place. The biological approach would not be appropriate, of course, to respond to a natural disaster or build a transnational highway system. But the explosion or campaign approach is not appropriate for community-driven development. Yet too often such top-down, expert-

Box 12–4. Common Ways to Scale Up Successful Programs

Blueprint approach. A technical solution that has worked under a set of generally widespread circumstances is codified into a plan for replication on a large scale. Attempts are sometimes made to tailor to local conditions during implementation, but to communities this is essentially a process that operates down from the top or in from the outside. Local actors might comment on proposed implementation but not on the basic plan. Examples include many nature preserves, appropriate technology projects, large-scale microcredit programs, and infrastructure expansion.

Explosion or campaign approach. This involves a large-scale, concentrated effort to marshal resources to deliver commodities or services in response to a generally narrow need. Food, humanitarian aid, and reconstruction assistance after a natural disaster are typical examples. Campaigns focused on disease eradication, such as the global smallpox campaign in the 1970s, are another example. While intensive and generally effective in achieving results, this method is not well suited for systemic change, local variation, or sustainability in terms of local ownership. In fact, some of the favorite disease-specific programs of donors are accused of undermining national health systems, and donated food aid's deleterious impact on local agricultural economies has long been known.

Additive approach. Typical "bottom-up" pro-jects engage in site-specific activity (a community or cluster of villages) for an extended period of time, developing local leaders and change from within. Often implemented by NGOs or religious mission groups, these projects get to know the local circumstances and adapt to local conditions. Replication is additive as success spreads village by village, community by community. Given that these are often pioneering initiatives or demonstration projects, proponents of this approach argue that governments or others with larger budgets have an obligation to adopt and expand these projects. Going to scale with this approach is very slow and dependent on outside resources.

Biological approach. Drawing comparisons to the way species evolve in nature, this approach supports local experimentation and adaptation ("evolutionary adjustments") and then sets an enabling environment for rapid expansion. It combines the local focus of the additive model with the growth potential of the explosion and blueprint approaches, but unlike the latter the impetus comes from within adapting communities. Government plays an important role in removing obstacles and facilitating expansion. The potential for exponential growth, healthy relationships, and balanced and organic growth make this approach more self-sustaining.

Source: See endnote 28.

driven approaches are the favorite of aid agencies and politicians because they deliver tangible goods quickly: school buildings, hospitals, large dams, airports, and the like. These are not undesirable per se, but this approach is not good at engaging the human element. For example, the spread of microcredit programs in Bangladesh used the blueprint approach for expansion initially but was forced to adopt the biological approach when the limitations of the initial model were reached and it became clear that site-specific solutions were needed to ensure that the poor were reached. The Millennium Village Project of the Earth Institute combines a blueprint approach offering villages choices from a list of over 40 poverty reduction interventions with a campaign approach for the distribution of commodities like bednets, but here again it is not clear how much local adaptation, ownership, and integration with local institutions will develop.[29]

Some promising programs to stimulate community-driven development reaching millions of people are being supported by the World Bank using essentially a blueprint approach but still managing to support local collective action and give discretion to communities in the selection of projects to fund. They are designed to institutionalize community participation in decisionmaking. Funding is transferred directly into village bank accounts to be used for the projects selected by elected local committees following extensive public dialogue. The program supports various NGOs to help facilitate community participation and the inclusion of marginalized people. Critical to their effectiveness are built-in systems to promote transparency and control corruption. The Kecamatan Development Program (KDP) of Indonesia and the National Solidarity Program (NSP) of Afghanistan are two examples of the Bank's new approach to scaling up successes.

Governments can institute changes in laws, policies, and practices that reshape institutions and remove obstacles to change.

Between 1998 and 2006 KDP covered 34,233 of the poorest villages in Indonesia—about half the villages in the country. The program is significant for the World Bank, representing almost half its lending portfolio to the country. KDP provides grants in the range of $60,000 to $110,000 to districts for use in projects chosen by the community. Open public meetings are held at the hamlet, village, and *kecamatan* (district) levels to determine priorities; independent facilitators ensure the participation of women and the disadvantaged. Projects are carried out by villages with local labor and materials.[30]

The KDP promotes transparency by using the local media and billboards to publish the amount of funding provided to each community and the details of the contracts. In addition, the media are given unhindered access to information needed to investigate and publicize incidents of corruption. Rigorous evaluations of KDP have shown that it has made important contributions to behavior change and social norms in project areas compared with control sites, even taking into consideration the broader democratic trends in the country during the period. More people are participating in local decisionmaking forums, including more women. In East Java, 67 percent of survey respondents in KDP villages say decisionmaking is more democratic now, compared with 46 percent in non-KDP villages.[31]

The NSP in Afghanistan is implemented through a partnership between the government and NGOs and is the only program to have reached all 34 provinces, affecting 13 million Afghans—two out of every three rural individuals. In rural Afghanistan, where no form of local election has taken place in decades and where some traditional leaders have lost credibility because of their role in 20 years of civil conflict, the NSP organizes elections for community development councils and the key leadership positions. Women's participation in the elections and as candidates is supported by program facilitators. Communities have used NSP resources to build community centers, health posts, and schools, to resurface roads, and to construct run-of-the-river hydropower projects. Community members are learning important civic skills, and community cohesion is being rebuilt.[32]

Innovative blueprint programs such as these, with the backing of government and World Bank resources, are not available to all communities. In addition, their focus has been on providing block grants for small-scale infrastructure, which, combined with the weak coordination within government, has placed limits on community choice.[33]

A biological approach appears most promising for stimulating solutions that evolve to fit a variety of local possibilities rather than being adjusted after the fact. According to Seed-Scale, the process ideally unfolds simultaneously along three dimensions: community, regional, and national. The first dimension is reached when communities have mastered how to build upon their local success. Initial interventions in one area such as community health have stimulated a wider scope of action in other areas such as food security, environmental protection, education, and income generation. Through partnerships with NGOs and government officials, communities gain access to the knowledge and resources necessary to sustain momentum.

The second dimension is pursued when successful communities share their experiences formally and informally with other communities in the same region. As the farmers in Niger showed, this can happen when NGOs facilitate farmer-to-farmer site visits and when farmers meet and share knowledge in markets and social settings. Specifically, the idea is to help transform clusters of communities that have already mastered a series of interventions into formal Action Learning and Experimentation Centers, where experimentation takes place to adapt these interventions to each local area. Visitors from other communities are welcomed to this group of villages to learn and take part in workshops and formal training. The contrast between traditional development—where outside experts design the solution—and truly home-grown approaches could not be stronger.

The third dimension happens at the level of systemic enabling conditions over which governments most often have the greatest influence. They can institute changes in laws, policies, and practices that reshape formal and informal institutions and remove obstacles to change, encouraging people and institutions to respond to new incentives. In Niger, the change in the forest code that gave farmers secure rights to the trees on their land had this effect. It stimulated investments by farmers throughout the country and further experiments that the forest service could support. Alternatively, structural change can happen at the local level and be scaled up to other levels, as when the women of Arunachal brought about the end to child marriage.

Each of these dimensions is an entry point to the other, and all are necessary to see change operate on a regional or society-wide level. Recent developments in Tibet are a good illustration of this. In the early 1980s Tibet faced growing environmental pressures from population growth, increasing fuelwood consumption, and resource pressures from China's economic expansion. One national policy response was the creation of the Qomolangma National Nature Preserve (QNNP), where local people were encouraged to continue living in the preserve and attention was focused on promoting their economic and social development—action that, in the traditional view, would have been seen as antithetical to environmental protection. The regional government provided budgets and staffing for the conservation area—not to police the region but to engage people through education and incentives. Outside partners brought in knowledge and partnered with communities and townships to focus on improving livelihoods rather than expecting people only to protect nature. A participatory model of conservation management emerged reflecting the Seed-Scale principles.[34]

Today the duality of development and conservation success can be seen in the QNNP. In the late 1980s the area had only one bank; by 2006 there were 10. Initially none of the 320 villages had protected water supplies; now 64 villages have them. The number of schools has grown from 5 to 38. The population of the area has swelled, partly from immigration due to the growth of several towns but also because better health means more children are surviving. The conservation side of the ledger is just as impressive. Now 42 percent of the land area is protected under conservation management. Wild animal population numbers are increasing for every species, including the endangered snow leopard, the Tibetan antelope, red ghoral, and argali sheep. Deforestation rates have decreased by over 80 percent, and large-scale tree plantations are being started in fragile river drainages. The use of environmentally friendly solar, geothermal, and hydroelectric generated energy is expanding across Tibet.[35]

Overcoming Obstacles

When considering Earth's potential to sustain growth, the case is often made that the rich and affluent need to reduce their consumption of resources in order to make room for increased consumption by the world's poor as they climb out of poverty. (See Chapter 4.) This proposition stands on its own merits, but it also suggests international action is a zero-sum proposition. Yet poor countries need not repeat the mistakes of the rich or emulate their overconsumptive lifestyles. Sustainable progress on global poverty need not rest on economic growth and resource consumption alone. Attacking poverty as it is conceived by the poor themselves opens up a wider range of possibilities for action.

But for globalization to allow these possibilities to be pursued, the rules of the game need to change at all levels. Needed reforms of the global development architecture of trade, aid, investment, migration, security, and rich-country environmental policies are well documented. For example, international

trade rules are not designed to enhance opportunities for the poorest countries. (See Chapter 14.) In fact, many rich-country policies do just the opposite. U.S. and European Union agricultural barriers and subsidies deny market opportunities to poor countries. Not only do such impediments need to be removed, but Paul Collier, former head of research at the World Bank, argues that the most destitute nations actually require some trade protection (from Asia) to get their economies started.[36]

International aid, held up as a symbol of rich-country concern and generosity to the less fortunate, is hardly accountable to those who receive it. Many rich countries recycle a large percentage of their aid back to influential constituencies of NGOs, consulting firms, and universities. Current estimates are that as much as 57 percent of U.S. development assistance comes back to the United States to pay for good and services. This "tying" of aid reduces its value by up to 25 percent and closes off opportunities to support businesses in poor countries.[37]

A good deal of donor assistance bypasses governments in the name of avoiding corruption and bureaucratic inefficiency, targeting beneficiaries, and supporting civil society. While these goals and concerns are worthy and often legitimate, it means that donors miss the opportunity to build state capacity to deliver services effectively. In an age when the international community is trying to build democratic states that are accountable to their people, the persistent channeling of aid through scattered projects of myriad donors breaks the link between citizen and government. Donors recognize this, and in countries that are reasonably well governed they are attempting to channel more of their aid into budget support rather than stand-alone projects.

If donor nations are to make this investment, developing countries need to make changes too. In return for investments in government capacities, there must be strong efforts toward decentralized and open governance. Deepa Narayan, lead author of the World Bank's *Voices of the Poor*, highlights four priorities: enabling citizen access to public information, promoting policies of participation and inclusion, ensuring democratic and client accountability, and enhancing local organizational capacity. These will help provide the enabling environment.[38]

These and many other systemic changes are critical for unlocking the potential for home-grown development. Development economist Bill Easterly describes it as the need for more "searchers" and fewer "planners." Empowerment frameworks such as Seed-Scale argue for a change in mindset

from control held by experts and officials to one of learning and experimentation among partners. This is often antithetical to the "results-based" mindset that insists on getting things right the first time.[39]

Yet around the world there are many who will be left behind because even the basic conditions for change are absent. Collier argues that the growth engine in many of the more advanced developing countries will eventually pull the poor out of poverty, but it is the weakest states—many caught in conflict and bad governance, where growth is not happening— that need attention and support. The "bottom billion" of the world's poor live in such countries. Perhaps it is here where empowerment-based approaches hold the most promise. Why? Because little more is required to start than a little capacity to aspire.[40]

CHAPTER 13

Investing for Sustainability

Bill Baue

At a United Nations summit on corporate responsibility in July 2007, Goldman Sachs released a report that breathed yet more life into the maturing body of sustainable investing. The venerable investment bank had been nurturing growth in this field over the past several years: in 2004 it released its first sustainable investing report, in 2005 it issued a company-wide environmental policy, and in 2006 it invested $1.5 billion in clean energy. At first glance, it may have disappointed sustainable investing advocates to see Goldman analysts saying that it was too early to correlate sustainability performance directly to financial performance.[1]

Of course, this coy assertion assumed that such a link—considered the Holy Grail by some advocates of sustainable investing—unquestionably exists. In the meantime, until empirical evidence could prove a direct connection between sustainability and financial

performance, Goldman integrated sustainability factors into its traditional financial analysis. The report found that sustainability leaders outperformed the general stock market by 25 percent over the previous two years and outperformed their same-sector peers by almost 75 percent over the same period.[2]

Such numbers turn heads. And more important, they draw ever more money into sustainable investing, as it has come to be known—increasing the amount of capital pegged to environmental, social, and governance performance. (See Box 13–1 for a definition of sustainable investing.) These commitments are increasingly of interest to a broad range of investors—from individual shareholders and businesses engaged in project finance to venture capitalists and nonprofits promoting microfinance. (See Table 13–1.) Together, these investors control significant assets that can steer societies toward

Bill Baue writes on socially responsibility investing for SocialFunds.com and on corporate social responsibility for CSRwire.com. He co-hosts and co-produces the nationally syndicated Corporate Watchdog Radio show and podcast and teaches at the Marlboro Sustainability MBA program in Vermont.

"Investing for sustainability" is an umbrella term used in this chapter for all the various forms of investment that promote sustainability in one way or another. The term "sustainable investing" applies to the most prominent subset of investment practices that promote sustainability: socially responsible investing and mainstream investing that integrates environmental, social, and governance factors into investment decisions. The lion's share of project finance for major infrastructure projects such as dams and mines now operates according to the Equator Principles, which integrates sustainability factors.

Other investment practices that promote sustainability fall outside the definition of "sustainable investing" as it is currently developing, however. "Green" investing, or support for environmentally beneficial companies and projects, is all the rage in private equity and venture capital, though these investments rarely take the full range of sustainability considerations into account. And microfinance is growing rapidly, but it focuses primarily on social factors, with less emphasis on environmental sustainability.

sustainable development.

Indeed, building sustainable economies will necessarily have investment at its core. Currently, modern industrial economies rely on pillaging the past at the expense of the future, burning through solar energy that has fermented for millennia forming fossil fuels that release eons worth of carbon dioxide that turns the atmosphere into a veritable pressure cooker. Changing course requires applying strong leverage from many different directions—especially investment. The scientific consensus, for example, is that carbon dioxide emissions need to be reduced 50–80 percent by 2050 in order to avert catastrophic climate change—essentially requiring a complete overhaul of carbon-intensive economies and lifestyles. (See Chapter 6.) Because investment decisions help shape an economy's infrastructure decades into the future, investor engagement is essential in turning economies away from conventional paths and toward a sustainable one.[3]

Luckily, sustainability and investing share a common horizon: both focus on the future. Sustainability considers how to meet people's needs today as well as in the future.

Table 13–1. The World of Sustainability Investments		
Sector	Description	Contribution to Sustainability
Socially responsible investment (SRI)	Values-based investment opportunities, shareowner advocacy, and community investing	A large share of SRI focuses on environmental and social sustainability; some investments, however, focus on values unrelated to sustainability
Project finance	Funding for major infrastructure or extractive projects such as dams or mines	More than 85 percent of project finance capacity globally falls under the Equator Principles, which factor in social and environmental sustainability
Private equity and venture capital	Speculative financing for promising innovative startups	Attention increasingly focused on green energy and other green products
Microfinance	Very small loans, as little as $50, that help small-scale artisans and craftspeople develop markets for their wares	Largely focused on income generation and poverty alleviation

Investing is essentially a form of delayed consumption that uses current capital to generate future financial support—particularly after retiring from active income earning. Traditional investment strategies in current use support business practices without regard to social or environmental impacts, arguably defeating the purpose of saving, as they contribute to the destruction of the future. Sustainable investing necessitates deep consideration of social and environmental implications, always assessing and measuring whether business practices can sustain social equity and ecological balance while maintaining profitability.[4]

Viewed through this lens, sustainability and investing can reinforce each other. A shift in worldview toward sustainability investments is already well under way, but its continued growth cannot be taken for granted. The challenge is to structure investment options so that outcomes promote both sustainability and strong returns.

Socially Responsible Investing

Some four decades ago, the foundations of sustainable investing were established with the advent of modern socially responsible investing, or SRI, which broke new ground by marrying social and environmental considerations with traditional financial considerations. SRI has since grown by encompassing three elements—shareowner activism, screening, and community investing—all of which now inform sustainable investing.

Modern shareowner activism—where stockholders engage with companies on environmental, social, and governance issues through direct dialogue, campaigns, and nonbinding shareowner resolutions that appear on the corporate proxy and go to vote at annual meetings—dates back to the late 1960s. Since then, shareowner activism

has evolved into a widespread practice, as described in the next section.[5]

The 1971 launch of the Pax World Balanced Fund introduced the second SRI pillar—screening out companies in so-called sin sectors, such as weapons, tobacco, alcohol, and so on. Since the late 1990s, some strands of SRI have been building on this ethical, values-based foundation by adding financial value-seeking approaches typified by so-called positive screens that give priority to companies with best practices in corporate social responsibility. Similarly, "best-in-class" screens reward the best social and environmental performers across all sectors—even those typically avoided by SRI, such as oil. According to this strategy, it is best to encourage better sustainability practices in all companies. More recently, value-enhancing SRI has emerged, arguing that strong environmental, social, and governance management acts as a proxy for strong business management.[6]

In 1973, Chicago-based ShoreBank pioneered community investing, which accepts below-market financial returns in exchange for social returns by supporting community development projects such as low-income housing, minority- and women-owned businesses, and microfinance. However, it wasn't until some two decades later that SRI mutual funds began supporting community investing, when the Calvert Social Investment Fund integrated the practice into its portfolio in 1990.[7]

SRI has moved from a niche practice to the mainstream, with about $1 of every $10 invested in the United States using at least one of the three pillars of social investing, according to the Social Investment Forum. In 2005, $2.29 trillion (9.4 percent) of the $24.4 trillion in total assets under management tracked in Nelson Information's *Directory of Investment Managers* was involved in SRI—up from $2.16 trillion in 2003.[8]

Although SRI growth has been rapid over the past decade, national monitoring bodies measure different attributes of this investment, making growth rates difficult to compare. Still, in Australia SRI funds under management grew 36-fold between 2000 and 2006. In the United States, they grew more than threefold between 1995 and 2005. Canadian SRI increased nearly eightfold between 2004 and 2006. And in Europe, these funds went up by some 36 percent between 2003 and 2006.[9]

Globally, SRI assets stand at about $4 trillion (see Table 13–2), with U.S. growth plateauing somewhat while funds continue to grow more robustly elsewhere around the world. To place this in context, however, the global management consulting firm McKinsey & Company estimates global capital markets at $136 trillion and projects this will reach $228 trillion by 2010. So formal SRI represents a mere 3 percent or so of global capital markets.[10]

Now SRI is shifting terminology, with some leaders in the field advocating for a semantic—and arguably a structural—change, to "sustainable investing." The move seeks to simultaneously broaden and narrow the scope of the practice using this term. It encompasses

Table 13–2. Socially Responsible Investments, by Region, Mid-2000s

Country or Region	Socially Responsible Investments	Year of Data
	(billion dollars)	
United States	2,290.0	2005
Europe	1,224.0	2005
Canada	439.0	2006
Australia and New Zealand	7.0	2005
Japan	2.6	2007

Source: See endnote 10.

SRI or mainstream investments seeking social and environmental sustainability, but it excludes values-based investment strategies that simply involve ethical considerations (such as Catholic screens of companies that produce drugs that induce abortion) that traditionally fall under the SRI umbrella but that do not promote progress toward sustainability.

Spearheading this movement is Pax World CEO Joe Keefe, who believes that sustainable investing has the potential to be a transformative strategy that revolutionizes investing itself—"at a time when market capitalism must of necessity undergo a sustainability revolution equal in significance to the industrial revolution that ushered in the modern period."[11]

Keefe believes sustainability advances a new conception of wealth, with the potential to offer a solution to the crisis in capitalism by aligning financial outcomes with environmental, social, and governance outcomes—"not with 'values,' mind you, but with outcomes," he notes. Achieving sustainability requires companies and markets to shift their behavior and necessitates that wealth-creation strategies live up to the term "sustainable" by eliminating the byproducts that too often flow from market capitalism currently—poverty, injustice, and environmental degradation.[12]

Adoption of the term "sustainable investing" as defined by Keefe represents a mainstreaming for SRI, as it blends the core SRI focus on sustainability outcomes with the mainstream focus on financial outcomes. What is interesting is that the mainstream investment community is converging on the same destination, but from the other direction—integrating sustainability considerations into a traditional focus on financial factors. It is a measure of SRI's success that its methods are now embraced by the very people who previously scoffed at it.

Mainstream asset managers, such as Citi and Neuberger Berman, who buy stocks to fill mutual funds and other portfolios, started practicing SRI long ago to fill a niche demand. Now mainstream investment banks, which sell stocks (a much more lucrative business stream than managing funds) are embracing sustainability, with investment analysts integrating environmental, social, and governance factors into their research.

Now it is standard for mainstream analysts from such firms as Citi, UBS, and Merrill Lynch to incorporate sustainability factors into their research.

This trend dates back to 2003, when the U.N. Environment Programme's Finance Initiative commissioned investment analyst reports from mainstream financial institutions assessing the "materiality" of sustainability issues—in other words, whether they affect stock prices significantly enough to trigger a fiduciary responsibility for investors to take them into account. The result was 11 reports by such venerable firms as Deutsche Bank, Goldman Sachs, HSBC, and UBS—essentially creating a glut of research on the intersection between financial and sustainability issues to fill the dearth that had existed until then. The reports also covered a wide spectrum of sustainability issues, from corporate governance to emissions trading.[13]

In October 2004 this movement received another boost from the Enhanced Analytics Initiative, a global consortium of institutional investors set up by the Universities Superannuation Scheme (one of the largest U.K. pension funds), Generation Investment Management (chaired by Al Gore, the first firm to integrate sustainability analysis directly into financial analysis), and others. Members of the initiative offer 5-percent brokerage commis-

sions to the best research on so-called extra-financial (environmental, social, and governance) factors. The chance to earn real money motivated some financial analysts to become quick studies of environmentalism and humanitarianism.[14]

Now it is standard for mainstream analysts from such firms as Citi, Lehman Brothers, UBS, Piper Jaffrey, and Merrill Lynch to incorporate sustainability factors into their research. JPMorgan has even established a dedicated Web page for its climate change-related research. The Goldman Sachs report released at the July 2007 U.N. corporate responsibility summit exemplifies the strategy of assessing sustainability performance not in isolation but in conjunction with financial metrics.[15]

Many in the SRI community—including Michael Kramer, managing partner and director of social research at Natural Investment Services—consider the mainstream embrace of sustainability a mixed blessing. While Kramer acknowledges that the Goldman Sachs report and others like it are part of the solution due to their influence over the mainstream corporate community, he laments that they advance "such broad interpretations of sustainability now that it renders the concept nearly meaningless." When a major oil company invests modestly in renewable energy while its business model still hinges on fossil fuels, is this really sustainable?[16]

Yet modest support by a giant may do more to advance sustainability than a small renewable energy company with a deeper commitment to sustainability. In practice, in any case, this is not necessarily an either/or equation, as both dynamics are happening simultaneously. In the end, the achievement of true sustainability will require a convergence of both bottom-up and top-down transformations, with investment playing a significant role in both.

One innovative way of moving toward truly sustainable investing from the bottom up is called "regenerative investing," a notion pioneered in 2003 by Michael Kramer. He calls the new investment style "regenerative" because it channels financial resources into projects that mimic the way nature operates within closed-loop systems that recycle matter and energy. Regenerative investing gives priority to far-sighted investments in areas such as clean energy, sustainable agriculture and forestry, recycling, and green real estate development. The strategy also looks for local investment that supports formal barter networks and currency systems, small business incubators, property leasing systems, and land trusts. At this early stage, regenerative investing strategies carry significant risk and so are only open to "qualified" investors with enough assets to buffer the risk.[17]

Shareowner Activism

Shareowner activism, a core strategy of SRI and sustainable investing, is as old as shareownership. The Dutch East India Company was the first enterprise ever to be listed on a stock exchange, in 1602. On January 24, 1609, it received history's first shareowner petition from Isaac Le Maire, the largest minority investor, who railed against the management as "absurd and impertinent" and "a kind of tyranny," according to Stephen Davis, Jon Lukomnik, and David Pitt-Watson in *The New Capitalists: How Citizen Investors are Reshaping the Corporate Agenda*. Dutch religious pacifists followed suit, buying shares in order to protest the company's "generous application of warfare, blockade, piracy, assassination, imprisonment, plunder, terror, slavery, bribery." So began civil society's use of stock ownership as leverage for advancing social justice.[18]

It took almost three-and-a-half centuries for social activists to start using shareownership again as a tool for promoting progressive change. In a 1947 court case, the Securities and Exchange Commission (SEC) confirmed the right of the infamous corporate governance gadflies John and Lewis Gilbert (and all shareowners) to file resolutions with companies, which the brothers had been doing since the 1920s without any legal standing. These rights languished largely unused until social and environmental activists adopted them in the late 1960s. Activist shareowners filed the first social and environmental resolutions in 1967 at Eastman Kodak, addressing racial discrimination against African American employees; in 1969 at Dow, addressing Agent Orange; and in 1971 at GM, addressing apartheid in South Africa.[19]

The year 1971 also saw the founding of the Interfaith Center on Corporate Responsibility (ICCR), which pioneered the modern practice of shareowner activism in the United States—namely, direct engagement with companies through dialogue or the filing of resolutions to advocate for improvements in environmental, social, and governance performance. Since then, ICCR has grown into a coalition of 275 faith-based institutional investors and SRI firms with over $110 billion in assets under management, and the practice it pioneered has brought about significant corporate change.[20]

It is difficult to substantiate the degree of influence shareowners have, however, for two reasons. First, they often work in concert with other activists, such as nongovernmental organizations (NGOs) and campaigners, as well as other intermediaries, making it impossible to attribute success solely to shareowner activists. And second, dialogue most often occurs outside the public eye.

Statistically speaking, the 2007 proxy season (when annual meetings take place, where shareowners present resolutions for all investors in a company to vote on) demonstrated this clearly. According to Institutional Shareholder Services (ISS), which issues voting recommendations on resolutions for investor clients, shareowners filed a record number of proposals: 1,150. And in an indication that companies were making sufficient progress on issues to satisfy resolution filers, a record number were also withdrawn: more than 270. In other words, almost a quarter of all resolution filings prompted acceptable responses to the shareowners' concerns. And this does not even account for shareowner dialogues with companies that progress sufficiently for shareowners to refrain from filing in the first place.[21]

The previous proxy season (the most recent one with complete results) saw record levels of support for shareowner resolutions addressing social and environmental issues. Of the nearly 180 such resolutions that came to a vote through mid-2006, some 27 percent received over 15 percent support from voting shareowners, according to ISS. This almost doubles the percentage of resolutions surpassing the 15-percent threshold in the 2004 and 2005 proxy seasons, and it represents a record high in support since 1973, when this information first began to be tracked by ISS's Social Issues Service.[22]

Perhaps the best indication of the power and success of shareowner activism comes from companies themselves, many of which readily acknowledge the positive though challenging role that shareowners play in promoting the adoption and promotion of corporate sustainability. Indeed, a corporate sustainability executive who wished to remain anonymous has been quietly sending word out to shareowner activists urging them to file a resolution asking her company to produce a sustainability report, as this would provide the kind of pressure she cannot muster internally to get her CEO to approve such an effort.[23]

But shareowner activism as traditionally practiced in the United States is in great peril, as the Securities and Exchange Commission has issued two separate rulemaking proposals addressing shareowners' access to the proxy to file resolutions. Both float suggestions that could seriously curtail shareowners' rights. This is an instance where regulation could stifle the growth of sustainable investing. In response, the Social Investment Forum and ICCR launched a Web site encouraging investors to use the public comment period to oppose any rules that would shrink shareowner rights. The site generated almost 1,700 comments, which contributed to the more than 22,500 comments submitted, a record according to the SEC—all but a handful of which opposed both SEC proposals curtailing investor rights.[24]

Project Finance and the Equator Principles

Project finance—the funding of major infrastructure projects such as dams, oil wells and pipelines, and mines—is one of the most significant investment strategies driving a top-down integration of sustainability principles. Because these projects have such high-profile environmental and social impacts, they expose companies to community and NGO opposition—which has in turn driven corporations to pay more attention to social and environmental management in project finance.

For example, the Rainforest Action Network hounded Citi beginning in late 1999 over its financing of projects considered socially and environmentally destructive, such as the Three Gorges Dam in China. In January 2003, more than 100 NGOs signed the Collevecchio Declaration on Financial Institutions and Sustainability (named after the town in Italy where it was signed), which called on banks to make six commitments, including "doing no harm," sustainability, accountability, and transparency.[25]

A half-year later, 10 financial institutions (including Citi) from seven countries launched their own series of commitments, the Equator Principles (EPs), a voluntary set of guidelines promoting social and environmental responsibility in project finance, particularly in emerging markets. The initiative exemplified a trend in corporate social responsibility toward voluntary action to supplant government regulation, and it showed great promise.[26]

NGOs pragmatically gave their stamp of approval to the principles while maintaining healthy skepticism of the degree of substantive progress that companies can make outside binding mandates. For example, socially and environmentally destructive projects can do an end-run around the Equator Principles by seeking funding from more lax financial institutions—notoriously, banks in China. (See Box 13–2.) By 2007, NGOs were starting to lose patience waiting for companies to deliver on their promises of comprehensive (instead of selective) sustainability. Yet companies defend the EPs, claiming they do have real bite.[27]

The member banks' external commitment to the Equator Principles on a voluntary basis makes them mandatory to implement internally, according to Pamela Flaherty, head of global community affairs at Citi. And when banks incorporate EP guidelines into contracts with clients, the voluntary nature disappears altogether, replaced by legal obligation.[28]

Ironically, financial institutions claim that client confidentiality precludes them from disclosing details on compliance to EP social and environmental covenants, frustrating NGOs who consider this an end-run around transparency and accountability. However, some commentators maintain that NGO scrutiny of the EPs, coordinated by the Bank-Track consortium in Amsterdam, functions as de facto accountability, given the absence of enforceable mechanisms.[29]

The EPs—now with 54 signatory banks, representing over 85 percent of global private project finance capacity—were revised in July 2006 in conjunction with the updating of the social and environmental performance standards of the International Finance Corporation (IFC—the private finance arm of the World Bank) that provided the basis of the EPs. NGOs welcomed some of the revisions as improvements—for example, the lowering of thresholds of projects covered from $50 million to $10 million. But they lambasted the revised guidelines and the underlying IFC standards for retaining significant loopholes.[30]

Take, for example, the issue of the role of communities in approving projects that significantly affect them. NGOs support the right of affected communities to give or withhold their free, prior, informed consent, a concept enshrined in Article Six of the International Labour Organization's Convention 169 concerning indigenous and tribal peoples' rights. The World Bank infamously shifted this concept to free, prior, informed consultation in 2004, and both the IFC and the revised Equator Principles followed suit. Consent and consult may sound very similar, but there is a profound difference in meaning between the two words—a difference with significant human rights implications.[31]

The Greening of Private Equity, Venture Capital, and Hedge Funds

The year 2006 will likely be remembered for the "greening" of the high-stakes upper end of the investment chain—private equity, venture capital, and hedge funds. (See Box 13–3.)

Box 13–2. Importing Sustainability to China

Although China has huge negative social and environmental impacts through exporting, it has the opportunity to integrate sustainability into its burgeoning finance sector. But the task is as big as everything else about the country, and the banks are at least a decade behind their counterparts throughout the rest of the world in this endeavor. The first steps have been taken, however: in May 2006, Bank of China International Investment Managers launched the Sustainable Growth Equity Fund, the first SRI fund in the country.

Even more significant, Chinese banking regulatory authorities have issued notices to all banks in the country that their lending activity must assess borrowers' compliance with environmental laws. How comprehensively is this mandate being followed? The lack of transparency makes it difficult to tell. Only two banks—China Development Bank and the Export-Import Bank of China—have publicly disclosed their environmental financing standards. In addition, the China Construction Bank has issued a corporate social responsibility report.

The Peoples' Bank of China also recently developed a new credit database that includes borrowers' environmental compliance data, allowing Chinese banks to evaluate how well companies have followed environmental laws before offering loans. And finally, in February 2007 the Shanghai Division of the China Banking Regulatory Commission floated a guidance draft document on corporate social responsibility that addresses banks' "shareholders, employees, financial consumers, communities, and other stakeholders, and social development, and environmental protection," according to the Xinhua news agency. Such guidance would be a first in China.

"By adopting world-class environmental financing standards, Chinese banks can play an important role in advancing sustainability on a global level," said Johan Frijns, coordinator of BankTrack, an NGO consortium. "Otherwise, they threaten to drag down whatever progress that has been made in developing such standards for the international banking sector."

Unfortunately, market forces push down on the environmental and social performance of China's banks. The improving sustainability performance of the rest of the world's banks is leaving the socially and environmentally riskier projects to these newer entrants. China's banks are "bottom feeding on those things international banks are not touching," explains Jules Peck, global policy advisor at the World Wide Fund for Nature–UK, in *Ethical Corporation*. For example, a European firm seeking to build a dam in Ecuador that is denied funding due to environmental and social risks can seek (and often receive) capital from a Chinese bank.

International banks are not exactly innocent, however. "International banks have complained that the lack of environmental financing standards at Chinese peers is putting them at a competitive disadvantage," said Michelle Chan-Fishel of Friends of the Earth–US. "But banks like HSBC, RBS, Citigroup, Goldman Sachs, and Bank of America all own large shares in Chinese banks. They must take responsibility for ensuring that high environmental standards, which they all claim to have, are also adopted by their strategic business partners."

The issue of international investment support for Chinese companies operating irresponsibly extends beyond China's banks. The oil company PetroChina has come under intense fire from

The effective death of climate change denial helped drive green investment, as the frenzy to find solutions focused on development of "clean" energy—namely, renewable power sources such as solar, wind, and biofuels. The bonanza extended to clean technology (or cleantech), newly recognized as a distinct investment category encompassing a broad range of eco-friendly products and services—from alternative energy generation to wastewater treatment and more resource-efficient industrial processes.[32]

Market and regulatory forces are also amplifying environmentalists' concerns over

Box 13–2. continued

human rights activists as its parent, the China National Petroleum Corporation, provides significant oil revenues to the Khartoum regime in Sudan that supports the *Janjaweed* militia who are committing genocide, torture, and rape in Darfur. As with Chinese banks, PetroChina holds hefty investments from international investors.

Activists with the Save Darfur Coalition and Sudan Divestment Task Force targeted mutual fund giant Fidelity Investments and Warren Buffett's Berkshire Hathaway in high-profile campaigns urging them to divest their PetroChina holdings. In May 2007, Fidelity divested 91 percent of its U.S. depositary receipt holdings in PetroChina. It was unclear at the time, however, whether the company also divested its shares on the Hong Kong exchange—if not, it would have divested only 38 percent of its overall PetroChina holdings.

Berkshire Hathaway shareowners filed a resolution for vote at the May 2007 annual meeting calling on the company to divest from PetroChina. The "Oracle of Omaha" (as Buffett is known) contended that using his voice as an investor to promote change at Petro-China through divestment or moral suasion was "fruitless" (despite the fact that Berkshire held the largest stake of PetroChina), and more than 97 percent of shareowners voted against the resolution. However, Buffett later quietly divested more than a quarter of Berkshire's holdings in PetroChina—dumping 445 million shares worth over $1 billion between July and September 2007, according to Investors Against Genocide.

Source: See endnote 27.

Box 13–3. Hedge Funds Marry Ecology with Economics

Hedge funds—unregulated portfolios open only to accredited investors that use "sophisticated" strategies such as shorting (profiting from falling stock prices)—have caught the green bug, with the number of hedge funds in this category proliferating. According to Peter Fusaro, founder of Global Change Associates, there are over 600 environmental and energy hedge funds, 50 hedge funds trading emissions in the United States and Europe, and 13 pure green hedge funds.

In other words, there are enough green hedge funds to launch several "funds of funds"—as the name implies, hedge funds that hold a number of hedge funds. The first such meta-fund, the Kenmar Global ECO Fund, which seeks to marry ecology with economics, was launched in July 2007.

There is also enough interest in green hedge funds to get the attention of the world's largest hedge fund management firm. In September 2007, the Man Group announced it had raised almost $400 million in a climate change–related hedge fund. The China Methane Recovery fund will set up subsidiaries to extract methane, a potent greenhouse gas, from Chinese coal mines to generate electricity and also to trade for carbon credits.

Source: See endnote 32.

the viability of traditional energy investments such as coal, according to a July 2007 report from Citi. The report downgraded coal stocks from "buy" to "hold" recommendations due primarily to concerns over impending coal regulations seeking to curb the dirty fuel's contributions to global warming. "Prophesies of a new wave of coal-fired generation [in the United States] have vaporized," writes report author John Hill. "We expect anti-coal politics to intensify, with carbon constraints almost certain to pinch." So carbon regulation is driving investors toward sustainable investing strategies. (See Box 13–4.)[33]

When it comes to green venture capital and private equity investment—namely, large investments to seed startup or early-stage companies—the statistical picture that emerges depends on who is coming up with the numbers. There is a clear consensus on

Box 13–4. TXU Buyout Is History's Biggest—and Greenest

The greening of private equity/venture capital took a surreal turn in February 2007. The major private equity firms Kohlberg Kravis Roberts & Co. and Texas Pacific Group had teamed with Goldman Sachs to buy out TXU. The company had been under intense fire from environmentalists for fast-tracking plans (presumably to get them in place before potential federal carbon legislation kicked in) to build 11 coal plants that would annually dump 78 million tons of carbon dioxide into the atmosphere. SRI activists had filed three separate shareowner resolutions calling the plan into question.

The buyers called in two of the main NGOs campaigning against TXU, Environmental Defense and the Natural Resources Defense Council, to broker agreeable terms over two weeks of intense negotiation. "This will not only be the biggest leveraged buyout ever, it is the only buyout in history made contingent on the approval of environmental groups," said Jim Marston, director of the Energy Program in the Texas Office of Environmental Defense, who led the campaign against TXU and lobbied the buyers.

The $45-billion TXU deal, which also included Lehman Brothers, Citi, and Morgan Stanley as equity investors, committed the company to drop applications for 8 of the 11 coal plants, avoiding 56 million tons of annual carbon emissions. The plan also committed the company to:
• terminate its previous plans to expand coal operations in other states;
• endorse the United States Climate Action Part-

nership platform, including the call for a mandatory federal cap on carbon emissions;
• reduce the company's carbon emissions to 1990 levels by 2020;
• promote demand-side management programs to reduce energy consumption;
• double the company's expenditures on energy efficiency measures;
• double the company's purchases of wind power;
• honor TXU's agreement to reduce criteria pollutants in Texas by 20 percent (the pledge had been contingent upon approval of all 11 plants); and
• establish a Sustainable Energy Advisory Board on which Marston of Environmental Defense will serve.

Making good on its wind pledge, TXU announced in late July 2007 a partnership between its Luminant subsidiary and Shell WindEnergy to develop the world's largest wind farm—a 3,000-megawatt wind project in the Texas Panhandle—as well as other renewable energy projects. In April 2007, however, the *Wall Street Journal* reported that the company is also pursuing plans to build the biggest nuclear plant in the United States to make up for the eight canceled coal plants. Some environmentalists now view nuclear power as a climate solution, while others cite continuing concerns about this energy source.

Source: See endnote 33.

one count, however: money is pouring into clean energy and cleantech.

According to a June 2007 U.N. report, global venture capital and private equity investment in sustainable energy totaled $8.6 billion in 2006, increasing 69 percent over $5.1 billion in 2005, with the number of deals increasing by 12 percent. (See Figure 13–1.) The three most active sectors were biofuels ($2.3 billion), solar ($1.4 billion), and wind ($1.3 billion).[34]

While these investments primarily address the environmental part of the sustainability equation, they sometimes attend to social issues as well. For example, while the majority of the money went into increasing manufacturing capacity (particularly in wind), some went to develop new technologies—such as 20 percent of biofuel investment, some of which supported research for second-generation biofuels, including cellulosic ethanol, that reduce the diversion of cropland

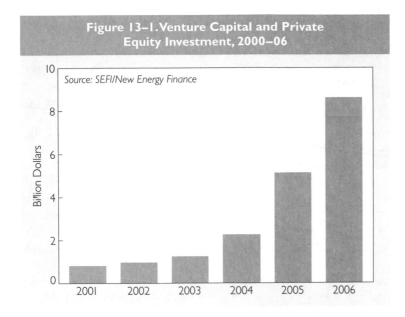

Figure 13–1. Venture Capital and Private Equity Investment, 2000–06

Source: SEFI/New Energy Finance

from food to fuel.[35]

Looking through the lens of cleantech, global venture capital investment increased by 78 percent in 2006 to $2.9 billion, catapulting cleantech into the spotlight as the third largest venture investment category, ahead of telecommunications and medical devices. High demand for global warming solutions such as renewable energy is driving a bull market for clean technology, according to Bob Epstein, co-founder of Environmental Entrepreneurs, who coauthored a study with Cleantech Network on the state of venture capital in cleantech. The report projects that venture capital investments in this sector will exceed $19 billion by 2010—a more than six-fold increase in just four years.[36]

Microfinance Goes Global

Thirty years after Muhammad Yunus lent 43 women from the village of Jobra, Bangladesh, the capital they needed to start small businesses that banks would not lend them—a

mere $27, from his own pocket—he won the Nobel Peace Prize for pioneering microfinance. Yunus, a Chittagong University economics professor when he helped those women, recognized his small loan and the finance institution it led to as both a market opportunity to serve the unserved and an opportunity to alleviate poverty, promote social justice, and foster community. The Nobel Committee made an unprecedented move in linking finance to peace, validating an underlying rationale of sustainability investments.[37]

"The one message that we are trying to promote all the time, is that poverty in the world is an artificial creation," Professor Yunus told the Nobel Committee upon learning he had won the Prize. "It doesn't belong to human civilization, and we can change that, we can make people come out of poverty and have the real state of affairs….The only thing we have to do is to redesign our institutions and policies, and there will be no people who will be suffering from poverty. So I would hope that this award will make this message heard many times, and in a kind of forceful way, so that people start believing that we can create a poverty-free world."[38]

Microfinance broke ground on a number of levels—by empowering women in a patriarchal society, by creating community accountability through lending groups that "collateralized" loans, and by lending such tiny sums. To underwrite the increased technical support necessitated by microfinance while keeping loans as affordable as possible, Grameen Bank (the microfinance institution Yunus founded) split the difference between the lower interest rates of standard commercial loans and the exorbitant rates of local loan sharks.

The success of microfinance opened it up to greater scrutiny and criticism, such as a 2001 *Wall Street Journal* article questioning claims of 95-percent repayment rates. Abraham George of the George Foundation hosts a Web site critical of microfinance, maintaining that it does not reach the poorest of the poor since it primarily focuses on those already running businesses.[39]

To what degree does sustainable investing actually contribute to the achievement of true sustainability?

Nimal Fernando, lead rural finance specialist for the Asian Development Bank, divided attitudes toward microfinance reaching the poorest of the poor into three camps. The first camp simply rejects the notion that microfinance can reach this group on a sustainable basis. The second camp optimistically advocates that such individuals can be reached not only on a sustainable basis but also on a large scale. The third camp recognizes that the potential for reaching this group on a sustainable, large-scale basis is limited but also advocates for the continued search for innovative approaches to expand outreach to the poorest.[40]

Fonkoze, the largest microfinance institution in Haiti, has aspired toward the second solution since recognizing that standard microfinance does not suffice for many of its clients who fall into the poorest of the poor category. It convened a summit on the issue in 2004, including representatives of the Bangladesh Rural Advancement Committee

(BRAC). The summit resulted in Fonkoze adopting the BRAC model for providing microfinance to the extreme poor—the BRAC-Bangladesh program for the Ultra-Poor—by coupling close case supervision with five basic sets of services: enterprise development training, social development, health care, short-term living allowances, and the transfer of assets needed to start businesses.[41]

The success of microfinance has also attracted the richest of the rich. The month before Yunus won the Nobel Prize, Citi and TIAA-CREF (an academic pension giant) each committed $100 million to microfinance. Some people question whether this corrupts the microfinance field, while others heralded the infusion of big money. However, the flood of mainstream investment in microfinance has created a bottleneck straining the capacity of existing microfinance institutions to process the flows.[42]

It also raises the question of whether having industrial countries sink money into microfinance actually acts to siphon money from developing economies, as the interest ultimately ends up in the hands of the already-haves. Is this an acceptable price of making capital available to the poor? Or does it simply create a poverty trap in a world of finite resources and hence finite economics? Microfinance operates on the same principle as the existing capitalist economic structure of profit and debt. Can wealth disparity be solved using the very system that many would argue has created huge wealth disparity?

From a more practical perspective, microfinance seems a better alternative than the current options of entrenched poverty—at least it is a step in the right direction, and the hope is that it can help transform the economy into a more humane system.

Supporting microfinance has even opened up to everyday people. The Web site Kiva.org uses the Internet to connect individual lenders who invest modest sums directly with borrowers, who can receive loans from a number of different lenders. While the loan may be cybernetic, its disbursement still requires infrastructure in the form of local microfinance institutions around the world.[43]

Finally, the social and environmental tenets of sustainability are starting to converge on microfinance, as evidenced by the success of Green Microfinance, whose mission is to promote environmentally sustainable microenterprise and microfinance. In March 2007, for example, Green Microfinance partnered with Fonkoze to study the feasibility of launching a solar energy initiative with Fonkoze clients. The greening of microfinance "represents a competitive advantage at the heart of social enterprise," according to David Satterthwaite, CEO of Prisma MicroFinance and editor of MicroCapital.org, a leading Web site on the subject.[44]

Current Obstacles to Investing in Sustainability

The astonishing maturation of sustainability investments in recent years raises a number of key questions. First, to what degree does sustainable investing actually contribute to the achievement of true sustainability? Take the examples of carbon offsetting and biofuels, which on first blush seem like positive investments for sustainability but which have led to significant debate over whether they actually undermine sustainable development.

Companies and individuals flocked to carbon offsetting, which allocates investment in renewable energy projects or tree planting in proportion to carbon emissions calculations. (See Chapter 7.) Supporters acknowledge the importance of radically reducing emissions first and only then injecting capital into carbon-offsetting projects that would not otherwise receive such infusions—a concept known as additionality. Critics liken offsets to medieval "indulgences," whereby consumer payments assuage people's guilt, thereby reducing their incentive to actually shift from carbon-generating habits. Instead of focusing on additionality, the focus should be on "subtractionality"—in other words, deducting carbon emission from personal, organizational, and broader economic equations.[45]

The biofuel debate injects social considerations into the mix. Biofuel supporters point to the carbon neutrality of the process—renewable biomass absorbs carbon during growth that is then emitted during burning. Opponents point out that the atmosphere does not care where the carbon comes from: a ton of carbon emitted from biofuel warms the planet just as much as a ton of carbon emitted from petroleum. Furthermore, diverting land from food to fuel crops will raise food prices and exacerbate world hunger, opponents argue. Debates such as these push any investments in sustainability to adopt sufficient degrees of sophistication to increase the likelihood of bringing about positive progress instead of fueling regression.[46]

A second key question is raised by the upward trajectory of sustainable investing: What obstacles stand in the way of maximizing the momentum? Unfortunately, significant structural impediments stand in the way. For example, in December 2005 U.K. Chancellor of the Exchequer Gordon Brown suddenly and unexpectedly killed the Operating and Financial Review, a March 2005 regulation requiring companies to disclose environmental, social, and governance information. Brown inexplicably cited "gold-plating" (blindly adopting European Union regulations), confounding members of the U.K. Department of Trade and Industry who had worked for years developing the regulation in-country through transparent consultation with business and the public.[47]

In the United States, the Corporate Sunshine Working Group (consisting of social investors, environmental organizations, unions, and public interest groups) has since 1998 been urging the SEC to enforce regulations requiring companies to disclose data on potentially material financial impacts from environmental and social risks, such as the estimated $10-billion liability Chevron faces if it loses a lawsuit in Ecuadorian courts over its subsidiary Texaco's dumping of toxic wastes into the Amazonian rainforest over two decades. The SEC's response: silence.[48]

Investors, activists, and government watchdogs alike served notice to the SEC that disclosure of environmental and social risks was not optional but mandatory.

Fed up, a coalition of state treasurers, pension funds, institutional investors, and environmental organizations confronted the SEC in September 2007 by filing a petition demanding that companies be required to disclose the financial risks associated with climate change. The coalition cited the scientific consensus and extensive business community action recognizing that the risks and opportunities associated with climate change are material to investment decisions and must be disclosed under existing law. They also noted that Exxon-Mobil, one of the most profitable and largest companies in the world operating in a sector intimately connected to climate change, mentioned the phenomenon only once in its 2006 filings.[49]

This petition followed closely on the heels of New York State Attorney General Andrew Cuomo's issuance of subpoenas to five energy companies to question whether they withheld information on the financial risks associated with plans to build coal-fired power plants. In short, investors, activists, and government watchdogs alike served notice to the SEC and the business community that disclosure of environmental and social risks was not optional but mandatory, as markets thrive only in the presence of complete and accurate information.[50]

Such regulatory and corporate hostility to mere disclosure on sustainability makes it difficult to maintain optimism that regulation will help foster sustainable investing. Those interested in this new approach to investment long ago abandoned hope that regulation would be a primary driver of progress, and instead have created their own mechanisms for fostering corporate disclosure of sustainability information—trusting that transparency will inspire companies to improve sustainability performance.

In late 2006, the Global Reporting Initiative (GRI) released G3, its third generation of sustainability reporting guidelines, which are evolving by default into the generally accepted accounting principles for disclosing environmental, social, and governance information. (See Chapter 2.) Currently, almost 2,500 of the nearly 15,000 sustainability reports logged on CorporateRegister.com comply with GRI guidelines, which were conceived in 1997 by Ceres, a coalition of environmental organizations and activist investors, and drafted with significant input from social investors.[51]

Similarly, more than 300 institutional investors representing over $41 trillion—almost a third of McKinsey's estimated $136 trillion in total global capital markets—have signed onto the fifth iteration of the Carbon Disclosure Project, which asks 2,400 of the world's largest companies to voluntarily report their carbon emissions and management processes. A majority of firms now recognize the financial and reputational benefits of improving their carbon performance—in other words, lowering their carbon emissions. Four fifths of respondents recognize that climate change poses commercial risks or opportunities, and just over three quarters reported implementing greenhouse gas emissions reduction initiatives—compared with 48 percent in 2006.[52]

Of course, actual performance in reducing carbon emission trumps the importance of disclosure, both in sustainability and in financial terms. According to Innovest CEO Matthew Kiernan, leaders in carbon disclosure outperform their same-sector peers financially, but leaders in actual carbon emissions reductions perform even better. However, it is safe to say that the Carbon Disclosure Project plays a significant role in driving both disclosure and emissions reductions—and, presumably, corporate financial performance and hence the performance of sustainability investments.[53]

Complementing the Global Reporting Initiative and the Carbon Disclosure Project are the Principles for Responsible Investment sponsored by the United Nations. Launched in April 2006, some 20 mainstream institutional investors managing $2 trillion in assets announced their commitment to address environmental, social, and governance factors in their investment decisions. By April 2007, membership grew ninefold, to 183 signatories, and the assets under management quadrupled to $8 trillion.[54]

These initiatives demonstrate the significant muscle behind sustainable investing, marching forward in spite of regulatory roadblocks. The sea change in momentum swelling behind this over the past few years gives rise to optimism that the world is approaching a tipping point whereby all investing addresses sustainability factors, as a matter of course. However, the challenge of actually achieving sustainability—of getting the economy to respect ecological limits and human rights—remains well beyond the horizon. Time alone will tell how much sustainable investing contributes to saving the future.

CHAPTER 14

New Approaches to Trade Governance

Mark Halle

At an international conference in Paris in July 2007, former Mexican trade minister Luis Ernesto Derbez remarked that the environment would determine the future of the multilateral trading system. This was a surprising assertion from someone once known as a mainstream supporter of free trade and the international system of rules that govern it. One interpretation of his remark is that humanity is facing a series of grave challenges—including climate change, loss of biological diversity, threats to water sources—that go well beyond the partisan interests of individual states. Addressing these challenges will call on all the institutional ingenuity that society can muster and will require harnessing these institutions to the broader task that these challenges represent. This includes the institutions of international trade—just when, more than ever, they are under scrutiny and attack from many quarters.[1]

This chapter will explore how in the last decade the debate on trade and the trading system has moved from a narrow focus on trade policy and mechanisms to a broader focus on how the system might best contribute to the search for sustainable development. It focuses on the governance of trade and explores what might be done to this governance to bring about the shift that the Mexican minister suggested is needed.

International Trade: Help or Hindrance?

Ever since David Ricardo explained the Law of Comparative Advantage in 1817, it has been an article of faith that international trade is a good thing. Trade contributes to prosperity not only by rewarding the successful trader but by expanding the size of the overall economic pie so that, with good governance, there should be adequate slices for everyone. (See Box 14–1.) Trade contributes

Mark Halle is Director, Trade and Investment, at the Geneva Office of the International Institute for Sustainable Development.

Box 14–1. Good Governance

Governance can be understood as the mechanisms used to ensure that a system or regime advances smoothly and effectively toward the goal it has set for itself and can deal efficiently and justly with the issues that arise along the way. The basic characteristics of good governance include:

- *Transparency:* People affected by decisions have timely access to accurate and up-to-date information on the issue, as well as information on the positions and proposals of the different parties.

- *Participation:* The right to take part in the debate or decisionmaking process links to the extent a stakeholder has interests at play or will be affected by the decisions.

- *Accountability:* Decisionmakers and the regime

itself are answerable for their actions, decisions, and compromises in terms of the stated goals and objectives as well as any statements and declarations they make about their actions and decisions. Accountability includes access to justice for those with a legitimate grievance. In the case of the trading system, accountability seeks an accommodation with the claims of justice made by those who believe the trading system should support sustainable development.

Where the vision for society is well articulated in goals, objectives, and priorities and is broadly known and supported, the exercise of good governance is comparatively easier. Where the goals and objectives are vague, good governance can be near impossible.

Source: See endnote 2.

---

to peace by building both mutual dependence and a better understanding of the trading partner's character, culture, and motivations. Conflict among partners that share commercial interests would disrupt trade and hurt their shared economic interests, so they also share a strong incentive to keep the peace.[2]

Before looking at some of the small print that suggests a more sober view of trade liberalization and its track record, it is appropriate to acknowledge how much of trade theory actually translates into real benefits in practice. International trade has expanded massively since World War II and has accounted for a significant share of the economic expansion that the world has experienced. The gradual lowering of trade barriers in the second half of the last century accelerated both economic growth and the proportion of that growth attributable to trade.

With the expansion of trade, pressure grew to enshrine the rules that would facilitate open trade and prevent backsliding into pro-

tectionism. In a very real sense, it can be argued that the codification of trade rules and the creation of institutions to govern international trade were a response to trade expansion, not the cause of it. The rules and institutions were put in place to ensure that the trading system is as free of conflict as possible. As the perception grows that gross inequalities—or collateral damage to other areas of public policy, such as the environment—can also lead to conflict, the multilateral system is under increasing pressure to address these through the codification of practice and the creation of new ways to prevent such conflict.

Much of the trade expansion since World War II can be attributed to successive rounds of multilateral trade negotiations in the General Agreement on Tariffs and Trade (GATT) and its successor, the World Trade Organization (WTO). These trade negotiations have gradually, round after round, reduced and "locked in" successively lower tariffs and quotas, making them today a small fraction of what they once were. Further, true to trade theory, a good deal of the growth in trade stems from unilateral decisions by countries to eliminate obstacles without seeking concessions from their trade partners in return or from the disappearance of trade barriers through regional integration arrangements.[3]

Trade's contribution to peace is also well documented. Violent conflict is significantly less frequent between countries that enjoy robust trade and operate open economies. In region after region around the world, the removal of trade barriers has been matched by the evaporation of armed conflict.[4]

So why does every successive step in trade liberalization appear to be a long, agonizing process in which microscopic advances are followed by long periods of deadlock, where hopes are continually dashed as endless last chances are missed? Why is it that, after six years of negotiation, the current Doha Round of WTO negotiations is stalled, with an increasingly large proportion of experts and observers wondering if it can be revived and concluded at all in the next few years? Why does the WTO—an institution built on the unimpeachable principles of non-discrimination, transparency of the conditions applying to trade, and peaceful settlement of disputes—face so much hostility?

The remainder of this chapter explores this basic paradox: Why does such a beneficial thing as trade excite such disapproval?

The Goals of the Multilateral Trading System

Ask a WTO delegate what the goal of trade liberalization is and the likely answer will have a good deal to do with stimulating economic growth. If trade stimulates growth, then liberalizing trade increases the volume of trade and therefore stimulates more growth than would occur otherwise. Economic growth, however—like trade liberalization—is a means to an end and not an end in itself. (See Chapter 1.) What goal, then, is the trade regime dedicated to reach, against which it must inevitably be judged?

At its origins in 1947, GATT had a highly utilitarian purpose, based on the need to raise standards of living and to ensure full employment by "developing the full use of the resources of the world" and expanding trade. The WTO, established on 1 January 1995, is an altogether different animal. Its agreements focus less on what happens to manufactured goods at the border than on the trade impacts of domestic policy. Further, the key agreements that make up the WTO package—including a revamped GATT—are part of a "single undertaking." GATT member countries that became the initial WTO members and the countries that joined the organization since then are all bound by these rules (with minor exceptions). Countries are either in or out of the multilateral regime, and it is increasingly impossible to remain out of it. Being part of the system requires accepting the decisions of the WTO's dispute settlement system, which are not only binding but enforceable in the most extreme cases through economic sanctions.[5]

No doubt thanks to the high political profile of the environment at the 1992 Earth Summit in Rio, the Marrakesh Agreements that established the WTO articulated an ambitious and both socially and environmentally responsible goal for the trading system. The governments who signed on agreed in the Preamble "that their relations in the field of trade and economic endeavour should be conducted with a view to raising standards of living, ensuring full employment and a large and steadily growing volume of real income and effective demand, and expanding the production of and trade in goods and services, while allowing for the optimal use of the world's resources in accordance with the objective of sustainable development, seeking both to protect and preserve the environment and to enhance the means for doing so."[6]

They further recognized the particular need for a trading system that boosts the development efforts of the poorer countries by noting "that there is need for positive efforts designed to ensure that developing countries, and especially the least developed among them, secure a share in the growth in international trade commensurate with the needs of their economic development."[7]

So the goal of the multilateral, rules-based trading system managed by the WTO is to harness trade to the task of achieving sustainable development, ensuring that trade openness provides a boost to development in the less-advanced countries, and recognizing the distinct needs of countries at different stages of development.

Unfortunately, while the trade disciplines contained in the WTO texts are binding, enforceable, and set out in precise language, the legal status of the Preamble agreed to in Marrakesh was at first unclear. One leading negotiator of the agreement has remarked that the Preamble was used to "park" notions held to be important by one government or a group of countries but around which no consensus could be built. Most trade lawyers would argue that the Preamble sets tone and context and has exhortatory value but is unenforceable. This view is not shared by the WTO's own dispute settlement system, however. The Appellate Body, for one, has made clear in a few landmark cases that the Preamble is to be regarded as part and parcel of the legal agreements that bind members.[8]

It is important to note here that the environmental community has been among those most suspicious of the multilateral trading system and has often been in the front lines of protests against the North American Free Trade Agreement (NAFTA), the WTO, the Free Trade Area of the Americas, and others. There are several reasons for this.

Extension of free trade reinforces the relative strength of the corporate sector and especially the multinational corporations. This leads to the perception that the trading system is an ally of the corporate sector, which the environmental community continues to distrust.

The trade rules embodied in the WTO appear stronger—and the compliance mechanisms much stronger—than the equivalent environmental rules, whether at the national or international level. When there is overlap and contradiction between the two sets of rules, it is not unreasonable to expect that the trade rules will prevail, especially given that economic policy generally has stronger political support than environmental policy does.

Attempts to extend trade policy to cover services (such as water supply, forestry, protected area management, and so on) smack of an attempt to privatize what the environmental community regards as public goods. As WTO rules on nondiscrimination appear to question domestic policy decisions such as the setting of environmental standards or the adoption of environmental labels, they appear to threaten hard-won environmental progress and to question the ability of the state to act in accordance with the public good.

Finally, early trade dispute cases decided by GATT appeared to attack the ability of states to harness the power of the market to advance environmental goals. One famous case suggested that the trade rules did not allow the United States to distinguish between tuna caught with massive associated dolphin deaths and "dolphin-safe" tuna, because the two were "like" products under the trade rules and no discrimination between them was allowed.[9]

Foundations of the WTO Governance Crisis

Governance crises can arise when the gap between what is declared and what is delivered grows too big. This is the case with the WTO if the text of the Preamble is taken to represent a legitimate articulation of the organization's overriding goal. The results of the Uruguay Round of trade negotiations, which ran from 1986 to 1994 and led to the establishment of the WTO, were sold hard to developing countries. While it was recognized that some countries would benefit more than others, the promoters insisted that all countries would be winners. And in recognition of the adaptation challenges they might face, developing countries were given additional time to implement the new agreements. That, it was felt, should be enough. No one accurately assessed the difficulties developing countries would face.[10]

It soon became evident that not only were many countries having a hard time adapting to the new requirements, some clearly felt they were losing out. It began to emerge that although trade openness could bring benefits, it tended to do so only where certain basic conditions—institutions, capacity, an efficient customs service, an independent judiciary, a solid banking system, and so on—were in place. Developing countries received scant sympathy when they sought to use WTO mechanisms to obtain help in these areas. The gap between rhetoric and reality was proving hard to bridge.

Despite this, many major trading powers felt they were on a roll and should push further. Less than two years after the WTO opened for business, the Singapore ministerial meeting in December 1996 adopted a new agreement on information technology and agreed to "study" four new topics— investment, competition policy, trade facili- tation, and transparency in government pro- curement—with a view to including them in a later round of negotiations. An attempt to launch that new round collapsed in Seattle in late 1999, but two years later and with none of the developing-country concerns addressed adequately, WTO members agreed in Doha, Qatar, in November 2001 to launch a com- prehensive new round of trade negotiations.[11]

Most developing countries went along in large part because the new round was pre- sented as a "Development Round," with the goal of delivering a result genuinely positive for poorer countries and correcting some problems inherited from the Uruguay Round. By implication, at least, this suggested recog- nition of the fact that the promise of the Uruguay Round had proved hollow for many countries. As WTO Director-General Pascal Lamy told the U.N. Economic and Social Council in July 2007: "Trade opening and rule-making are indeed major goals of the WTO. But today a number of the current substantive rules of the WTO do perpetuate some bias against developing countries." He cited the rules on subsidies in agriculture, for example, which tend to favor industrial countries, along with high tariffs that many of those countries apply to agricultural and industrial imports, in particular from devel- oping nations. "A fundamental aspect of the Doha Development Agenda," Lamy noted, "is therefore to redress the remaining imbal- ances in the multilateral trading system and to provide developing countries with improved market opportunities."[12]

More than six years after it was launched, the Doha Round has come to a standstill, and prospects for an early conclusion appear dim. While few participants question either the robust foundation of trade theory or the ben- efits of open, rules-based trade, several prob- lems are increasingly evident.

Trade openness does not, on its own, bring

the benefits that trade theory suggests, as they depend on the right conditions being in place. The trading powers have until recently showed little interest in helping poor countries achieve these conditions.

Concerns for equity, environment, and development are largely incompatible with the hard-ball, mercantilist approach to trade negotiations and the culture that this approach consolidates.

Since trade policy and the trade rules shifted their principal focus from border measures to domestic policy and expanded their reach beyond trade in goods, the relationship between trade policy and public policy interests in these areas can no longer be ignored.

Developing countries are increasingly aware of their power and authority and will no longer accept promises of future benefits. They want tangible results, if not down payments in the form of up-front concessions from richer trading powers as a proof of good faith.

So where does this leave the WTO? And is the present impasse a governance crisis? In terms of transparency and access to information—two of the basic criteria of good governance—the WTO rates well, at least as far as its members are concerned. The creation of the WTO led to a massive increase in public interest in the trading system, and both formal and informal access to accurate, up-to-date information on virtually every aspect of the system's operations is now available to anyone who wishes to receive it.

Participation presents greater challenges. There is widespread agreement that the massive expansion not only of the WTO membership (over 150 countries, twice the size of GATT when the Uruguay Round was launched) but of the number and complexity of the agreements and negotiations has presented poorer countries—especially the smaller ones—with considerable difficulties. In the normal course of events, some 25 for-

mal meetings take place each week at WTO headquarters. But as many as 19 developing countries, for financial reasons, have no representation in Geneva at all; others have just one or two staff covering all U.N.-related events in Geneva.[13]

> There is widespread agreement that the massive expansion of the number and complexity of the agreements and negotiations has presented poorer countries with considerable difficulties.

This is especially difficult for negotiations, since the interests of developing countries do not divide easily along North-South or regional lines or even according to any particular pattern of interests. And yet it is impossible to envisage delicate negotiation of binding and enforceable economic agreements with 150 players in the room. Some form of representational presence must be used, but it is far from clear how that might be organized. The Doha Round has seen considerable experimentation with interest groupings, with some positive impacts on transparency and inclusiveness but so far without appearing to find the magic solution. To some extent, then, the crisis of the WTO is related to the governance challenge of ensuring adequate participation of stakeholders.

This is particularly true beyond the WTO's primary constituency in the trade policy community—in the wider group of stakeholders in civil society, among consumers and other groups whose interests are centrally affected by the shape and nature of the trading system. While some civil society organizations are having a clear impact on the policy debate, the level of participation and the mechanism to make constructive participation possible are far less than optimal for well-governed trade policy.

The real challenge, however, relates to the third pillar of good governance: accountability. At one level, of course, the WTO boasts of its fine record with accountability. It is very much a member-driven organization, and each member is accountable to legislative bodies back home. The crisis relates to the WTO's track record in advancing the goals that the founders established for the system, as set out in the Preamble. There is a very real sense in the WTO community—not to mention the wider trade policy community—that the formal structures available do not guarantee accountability in terms of the objectives set for the system. And it is precisely this failure that has led governments and interested observers to question how the WTO works and how committed its most powerful members are to finding solutions compatible with the overall goal. Indeed, the WTO has no mechanism to assess fidelity to and progress toward its stated goal. (Although the WTO Committees on Environment and Development were invited to monitor the impact of Doha Round proposals on sustainable development, they have not done so.)[14]

An interesting and important exception is the Appellate Body, the WTO's highest "court," which rules on appeals against the findings of Dispute Settlement Panels. As noted earlier, it has invoked the WTO Preamble as evidence that the founders intended the system to support sustainable development, even if the commitment is cast in imprecise terms. It is clear that the Appellate Body has adopted a central position in ruling on the character, purpose, and direction of the system. Beyond that, however, there is little sign that WTO members collectively feel any obligation to correct past decisions that have damaged the prospects for development or the environment.[15]

Civil society has also played an important role in insisting that the WTO be held to account for the impact of its rules and decisions on wider public policy objectives. Although civil society has been notable for criticizing the WTO for its shortcomings and in part for opposing any progress toward further trade liberalization, it is clear that the net impact of civil society input has been to place the multilateral trading system squarely in front of its responsibility to deliver results that support sustainable development.[16]

The Challenge of Respecting WTO Goals

How might the governance challenge best be addressed? It is by now a platitude to decry the negotiated tradeoffs that characterize the WTO culture. It is a culture that saturates the organization, that pervades its operations, and that has done a great deal of damage to the cause of open trade. At its root, the notion is defensible. Whereas lowering trade barriers is by and large favorable over the medium and long term and for most players, there is often a price to be paid by some countries in the short term. This often involves selling particular economic interests short in favor of a solution that is overall better for others (such as consumers) in the short term and for all or most in the longer term. Lowering subsidies for French farmers may cause them adjustment problems, for instance, but it may also lower food prices for the consumer or boost the French service industry. Yet the immediate interests are often politically influential, so the tradeoffs that go on at the WTO serve as a political currency whereby trading partners make concessions in order to provide the political justification for the penalty imposed on the interests that lose out.

If negotiating tradeoffs is an effective way of convincing countries to make politically unpopular but economically necessary concessions, it is not generally a good way to serve wider goals such as equity, poverty alleviation, or environmental responsibility. In any commercial negotiation, commercial power confers negotiating advantage, so the powerful trading countries and blocs have greater negotiating power. This suggests that they will always—or almost always—prevail in a standoff with weaker parties. Further, in any negotiation involving commercial tradeoffs, the result may be more open trade, a larger economic pie, and a greater range of opportunities for traders; it will not automatically do anything to correct the inequities built into the trading system. If both sides make equal concessions, their relative position on the trading totem pole will remain the same. If the European Union is negotiating with the countries of the Southern Africa Customs Union, a successful outcome is unlikely to include a shift in the balance of commercial advantage in favor of the latter.

A second reason that wider goals are ignored relates to how trade policy is developed at the national level. Interest in maintaining a particular tariff or subsidy will be concentrated in a relatively small group of players (truckers, for instance, or dairy farmers) who will usually be well organized to defend an interest they deem crucial to their commercial success. An equally valid interest—for example, closing the gap between rich and poor countries, protecting the environment, or even lowering prices for the consumer—is likely to be far more dispersed and less well organized, at least in terms of affecting trade policy. Thus when national trade representatives set their negotiating priorities and parameters, the weight of immediate commercial interests will always trump less immediate or well organized concerns. So even if rapid, trade-led economic development in Central America is an essential component of any sensible strategy to limit immi-

gration pressure in the United States, for instance, and even if that development might best be served by giving Central America unfettered access to U.S. markets for their goods and services, in reality the partisan interests of U.S. textile workers and fruit producers will tend to prevail.

Finding the right balance among competing interests in formulating trade policy and negotiating positions is hard enough within the confines of trade concerns alone. But ensuring that trade and sustainable development are mutually supportive is considerably more difficult, since it involves the traditionally complex question of policy coherence. It is an inescapable fact that public policy is a hierarchy. Macroeconomic policy, including trade policy, travels first class, whereas the policies that relate to the environment and development travel coach—and often stand-by. The current crisis suggests that there may not be much progress on trade liberalization unless governments begin to demonstrate that they take the environment seriously.

Taking the Environment Seriously in the WTO

It is now abundantly clear that developing countries will not accept an outcome from multilateral trade negotiations that does not confer on them—or at least the more vocal of them—tangible trade benefits and that does not go some way toward correcting existing inequities and imbalances. Although it is hard to imagine an outcome in which all countries will benefit, any acceptable outcome will have to offer clear benefits to developing countries in some form, even if not directly due to trade openness. Development has now become a genuine trade imperative.

If the environment has not achieved this same position, it is nevertheless remarkable how this concern has progressed toward acceptability in the trading system. The early fear that the powerful new WTO would challenge and roll back decades of environmental achievement at the international level has subsided, replaced in both the trade and environmental communities with the far healthier view that each concern relates to and affects the other and that both need to find ways to be mutually supportive. This includes the need to ensure that environmental standards do not become an unwarranted obstacle to market access by developing countries, but also that they are not unnecessarily challenged over their effect on trade. There is growing respect in the trade community for multilateral environmental agreements and even for their need to use trade measures to ensure compliance. The trade community asks only that the distortions to trade be no greater than necessary to achieve the purpose for which they are used.[17]

There remains, however, the problem that the trading system serves an outdated and failed economic paradigm, that it favors the corporate sector at the expense of public policy goals, and that its rules have shifted the balance of benefit further toward the private sector.

Responding to the Crisis at the WTO

Although the WTO agreements have boosted world trade and benefited some countries, they have fallen well short of the promise to reduce the gaps between the rich and poor, between the powerful and the weak, and between those who pursue immediate gain and those who fight for a fairer world. Indeed, the WTO—and trade liberalization more broadly—has come to be regarded as the vanguard of an economic paradigm about which there are increasing doubts. The orga-

nization is perceived by an important and highly vocal segment of society as a central part of the effort to impose the "Washington Consensus" on the rest of the world—an economic system based on a blind belief in the market and predicated on eliminating as many constraints on corporate opportunity as possible. Whereas WTO agreements are by and large unfairly accused of advancing an unpopular economic paradigm, that has not prevented the public perception of the WTO as the vanguard of this paradigm.[18]

The crisis at the WTO reflects both growing doubts about staying on a path that has failed to deliver on its promise and the growing insistence of the developing world that trade liberalization must not aggravate the development problems of poorer countries. The system is responding to this crisis with a broad debate on how to achieve better coherence among different policy areas and active analysis of how the system can deliver genuine development benefits, including the correction of past inequities. There is a clear sense that trade liberalization must not undermine progress toward broadly supported public policy goals such as poverty alleviation, a healthy environment, social justice, or human rights.

Since it has become clear that countries do not automatically benefit from trade openness, a major effort is under way to put in place the conditions that would make such openness a more positive experience. Since 1997 six intergovernmental agencies, including the WTO, have operated the Integrated Framework (IF) for Trade-Related Technical Assistance for Least Developed Countries, demonstrating growing cooperation among international institutions sharing an interest in a common theme. To date, the IF is active in 33 of the world's poorest countries, helping to integrate trade with national development plans and poverty reduction strategies, setting priorities for trade-related technical assistance, and advising on governance reform to enhance participation in the world economy. This approach directly addresses one of the development-oriented goals in the WTO Preamble.[19]

More recently, the WTO has developed a work program on Aid for Trade. Targeting developing countries, particularly the least developed ones, this aims to help governments put in place the [...] tions needed to bene[...] trade. Aid for Trade is [...] oping countries as ver[...] "down payment" they [...] sign up to any package [...] Doha Round.[20]

Efforts are also being [...] negotiations to link a cou[...] respect certain disciplines [...] ity to do so. In the ongoi[...] trade facilitation (the rem[...] tive barriers to trade), c[...] to take on the full set of ob[...] when they have the nec[...] and human capacity in pla[...] not, they will receive tech[...] perhaps through Aid for T[...]

The issue of how trade [...] affect other public policy g[...] in the WTO's Trade Polic[...] nism. This unit undertakes [...] dent studies of member [...] policies and the extent to w[...] the requirements of WTO [...]

This may not be enough [...] need to develop a set of scre[...] sustainable development, alo[...] anism to settle areas of appare[...] patibility. All new trade rule[...] he extent also existing ones, wou[...] ed to these to ensure that their [...] s- tainable development was positive. A forum to seek positive resolution in the case of incompatibility would also be needed, probably sep-

arate from the formal dispute settlement mechanism. The Council for Environmental Cooperation set up under NAFTA was intended to do something like this, although it has never lived up to expectations.

Beyond the interagency level of cooperation on the Integrated Framework, there is a great deal of experimentation going on with forms of collaborative governance that go beyond strict government-to-government interaction. These involve public-private partnerships or public policy partnerships that gather concerned stakeholders in "accountability compacts." The Extractive Industries Transparency Initiative, the World Commission on Dams, and the Forest Stewardship Council are good examples of these.[21]

Despite the encouraging developments and proposals just described, some of the problems that have become evident go well beyond the multilateral trading system itself. The crisis of the WTO also reflects the growing malaise caused by the perception that global change—and particularly economic liberalization—has outrun the world's ability to govern for the general good of humanity. It becomes increasingly clear that the dominant economic paradigm is making poverty, social injustice, and environmental degradation worse, the institutions that serve that paradigm come to be mistrusted.

Thus a cloud of uncertainty hovers over all attempts to push on further down that same road. The multilateral rounds of WTO negotiations and the additional concessions beyond WTO rules that powerful trading powers wrest from their partners through regional and bilateral free trade agreements or sectoral agreements of one kind or another all begin to look like "more of a bad thing." Progress is not progress if the world is heading in the wrong direction.

Yet correcting this, or finding an alternative, is made doubly difficult by the lack of an

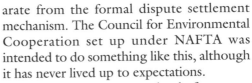

agreement on the paradigm that might offer a broadly preferable alternative. Critics of the current system know that they want a reliable and functioning economy whose quantitative and qualitative growth offers steadily increasing opportunity. They want to correct the inequities that characterize today's world, reducing the gap between rich and poor countries and between rich and poor within countries and building respect for human rights and social justice. And they want to live within the limits imposed by Earth's ecosystems and natural resources. In short, they want to move toward sustainable development and would like the WTO and the other elements of the multilateral trading system to be a force in that direction. They want the WTO to consider the goal set out in its Preamble not as a statement of broad intention but an imperative, a benchmark against which it is judged and against which all proposals to expand its disciplines are evaluated.[22]

In terms of both the collapsing paradigm and the need for the trading system to serve a wider goal, the notion of sustainable development may well mark the way forward. Indeed, it may be the only acceptable way forward. The goal is there in the Preamble. The need to meet it is reinforced in the Doha mandate, and a space has been created in which itineraries toward the goal might be reviewed. All that is missing is the political will to occupy this space and the tools to make the sustainable development paradigm operational.

Accepting That the World Has Changed

One reason for the lack of resolute decisions is that the world is in a state of deep confusion triggered by the deep and fast-paced changes in the balance of power—undoubtedly the most profound power shift since the emergence of a world order based on sovereign nation states almost four centuries ago. Even if the impact on the WTO and other elements of the international system may not yet be fully clear, the rise of China and India has sent out shock waves that have not yet been adequately absorbed. And several other countries are flexing their muscles as well—Argentina, Brazil, Mexico, South Africa, and Viet Nam. In all likelihood the entry of Russia and most of the remaining former Soviet republics into the WTO will trigger further seismic changes, and it is far from clear how these changes can be handled, much less harnessed to sustainable development. The dominant position of the United States and the European Union, which have been substantially able to dictate trade rules, is fading and will never again be recovered.

The apparent redistribution of power among nation-states is happening in parallel with the emergence of a global public domain that demands governance for which organizations based on nation-states are proving inadequate. Indeed, the intergovernmental organizations of the United Nations, the World Bank Group, and others are organized around a postwar order that no longer adequately represents reality. This must give way to a new order focused on optimal stewardship of global public goods. Designing the right institutions for global economic governance will mean rethinking the role and primacy of the nation-state as traditionally understood. It will require reaching a geopolitical settlement no less significant than the order that emerged from the chaos of World War II, but one built on the central recognition of interdependence. And it will involve understanding and finding the right role for a series of new actors in global governance, most prominently corporations and civil society organizations and networks.

The challenge of global economic governance is that of managing multidimensionality. Climate change policy cannot be left to environment ministers, because getting it right involves energy policy, investment policy, foreign policy, and many other sectors. Similarly, trade policy cannot be left solely to trade ministers.

Perhaps the model in this respect is the European Union (EU). For all its faults, the EU has proved adept at advancing a model of governance capable of addressing multidimensional problems—at least those that are of central concern to its member states. It has yet to demonstrate that it can take a multidimensional approach to emerging trading powers or to the challenges of global economic governance. But it also represents a model in another important respect: the acceptance of devolved authority. One problem with the present paradigm is the ambiguity of most states in terms of the authority they have devolved. This is certainly true of the WTO, still stuck in the outdated national sovereignty model that characterized the world of GATT.

This is not only an issue with richer trading countries. The much-vaunted G-20 group of developing countries in the WTO, which has proved a powerful force in countering the traditional dominance of the rich nations, is also torn by issues relating to national sovereignty and domestic politics. And its members have yet to demonstrate that they can lead developing countries to overcome a tendency toward "Third Worldism"—an automatic resistance to change because the proposals come from richer countries. It will be critically important that the emerging powers demonstrate, along with a growing sense of confidence, a positive capacity to take the initiative, to be creative, and to help shape the new order. They have already demonstrated an interest in a system characterized by greater fairness. The question is whether they can take

this further.[23]

Can they contribute to a system designed for citizens, not consumers? Can they help design a system that can mediate effectively among unequal powers or in a situation of enormous complexity and diversity? Can they help craft a system dedicated to the joint goals of promoting political stability and advancing justice? A great deal depends on how the issues are framed. The goal is to move from an economics framed in terms of efficiency to one framed in terms of justice—both procedural justice and outcome justice. Future progress in extending the trading system will depend on the ability to demonstrate that trade liberalization does indeed advance these wider objectives—social justice, human rights, equity, and a healthy environment.

Designing the right institutions for global economic governance will mean rethinking the role and primacy of the nation-state as traditionally understood.

In a very real way, a sustainable future depends not only on dealing with such eminently global issues as climate change (see Box 14–2) or the collapse of biodiversity. It depends on creating a society where nobody is excluded. The challenge is to design a trading system that will harness the power of trade to do good to a system that is characterized by a search for fairness, stability, mediation, the promotion of environmental values, and the imperative of inclusiveness. This requires a trading system that is accountable to the goals set for it and that is genuinely monitored to ensure it is proceeding optimally toward those goals. It requires a system that contributes as solidly as it can to the promotion of the public good, not simply to private interests, and that balances the power of the market with the need for a solid framework

Box 14–2. Multidimensional Problems

There is no magic, single solution to the challenge of controlling greenhouse gases. It is a challenge of energy policy and of managing the transition to sustainable energy sources. This in turn has a great deal to do with the technological transition, access to invention, and intellectual property. It has to do with investment policy and the nature of investment agreements and the settlement of investment disputes. And it has to do with trade policy—the trade rules and how the trading system deals with issues at the frontier between trade policy and related policy areas. In short, the issue cannot be dealt with by treating each of the pieces separately from the

overall picture of which they are but a part.

The same is true of what Paul Collier calls "the bottom billion"—those who are not benefiting from global growth, from trade liberalization, or even from much development assistance and who continue to survive on less than a dollar a day. The present economic approach offers them very little, and the new economic elites in the emerging countries often appear not to pay them much attention either. Yet a sustainable future depends on including them in national economies and societies and on lifting them out of their present misery.

Source: See endnote 24.

of public policy. In short, the world's trading system needs to go back to the goal set out in the Preamble to the WTO Agreements— the optimal use of the world's resources in accordance with the objective of sustainable development. Only this time it needs to be taken seriously.[24]

What Is at Stake?

Today's world is characterized by unfairness, but in any unfair system there are those who benefit. Nothing prevents countries from hunkering down behind their trade barriers and hanging on to what they have. Nothing prevents governments digging in their heels so that the only advances made in trade liberalization are those imposed on weaker countries by the more powerful. Nothing prevents the world from moving back to a period of greater protection, greater conflict, and greater suspicion of other countries. Things need not necessarily get better. They could well grow worse. Indeed, that would normally be the default result in an environment where reaching international agreements is increasingly difficult.

Were it not for the fundamental shift in power, the genuine threats to the future of humanity, and the growing disillusionment of voting publics with their political leaders, this path might well be the one followed. It appears, though, not to be a realistic option beyond the short term, because the world is also moving toward a situation where it is no longer susceptible to domination by one or two powers and must therefore search in earnest for compromise.

A good deal of the efforts of the emerging powers in the trading system are aimed at eliminating trade distortions that benefit rich countries rather than simply protecting their vulnerable economic sectors from foreign competition. Along with global economic rules, there is developing what might be termed the "global public domain," a recognized space in which notions of shared value in protecting global public goods are balanced with the notion of commercial advantage.

This approach is not a statement of "no confidence" in markets. It is simply a recognition that markets function optimally in light of the goals to be reached when they operate within a framework of agreed public policy.

The role of states is no longer to direct the economy but to put in place a favorable policy framework and adequate checks and balances. Within this context, the notion of competition for personal or national advantage is replaced by a "competition for the good," where the rules of the global economy are not allowed to undermine the ability of states to act for the public good

When comparing the WTO and the rest of the multilateral system to this vision, it is clear that they fall short. But the system has increasing difficulty in moving forward precisely because the global community insists on something closer to that vision and has dwindling patience with the WTO's shortcomings.

Who, then, will lead us to the "promised land" hinted at in the WTO's own statement of purpose? Interestingly, it is not in the formal trade policy community that the new movement is evident. It is not the WTO delegates in their representational capacity who are acting in an innovative way. The laboratories for new thinking on trade governance are in spaces created outside traditional institutions, in which new proposals are articulated, reviewed, and debated. Some of the most creative thinking is taking place in organizations like the Evian Group—a forum that gathers a mix of WTO delegates and staff, academics, and civil society representatives. It is found in dialogues organized on these issues by the International Centre for Trade and Sustainable Development in Geneva, which offers senior trade officials a safe space in which to experiment. It is in events organized by the Royal Institute for International Affairs in London or its equivalent in South Africa, Brazil, India, and China, where new ideas are incubated, tested, and refined.[25]

The ideas, approaches, and proposals that emerge in such forums and meetings make their way into the political processes, build a level of trust, and begin to filter into the reform ideas that sooner or later design and install the institutional structures that will allow the world to address new challenges as global change accelerates. It is no different for trade than it is for climate change or biodiversity conservation. In each of these areas, we are building toward what we hope will be a tipping point, a massive collection of political will that will tip the balance in favor of positive action. Each contribution may appear insufficient, but the accumulation can make a big difference. It has done so before in one field after another. There is no reason why it cannot happen when addressing the challenge of governing trade for the good of humanity.

Notes

State of the World:
A Year in Review

October 2006. European Space Agency, "Record Ozone Loss During 2006 Over South Pole" (Paris: 2 October 2006); World Health Organization, "WHO Challenges World to Improve Air Quality," press release (Geneva: 5 October 2006); World Bank, "Natural Disasters on the Rise, 2005 The Zenith Year," press release (Washington, DC: 11 October 2006); U.N. Environment Programme (UNEP), "Further Rise in Number of Marine 'Dead Zones,'" press release (Nairobi: 29 October 2006); "Amazon Deforestation Slows," *Environment News Service*, 27 October 2006; Her Majesty's Treasury, "Publication of the Stern Review on the Economics of Climate Change," press release, 20 October 2006.

November 2006. Boris Worm et al., "Impacts of Biodiversity Loss on Ocean Ecosystem Services," *Science*, 3 November 2006, pp. 787–90; World Wide Fund for Nature, "Climate Change Has Birds Out on a Limb," press release (Gland, Switzerland: 14 November 2006); Commonwealth Scientific and Industrial Research Organisation, "Increase in Carbon Dioxide Emissions Accelerating," press release (Hobart, Tasmania, Australia: 27 November 2006).

December 2006. "Rainforest Gets Protected Status," *BBC News*, 4 December 2006; Baiji.org Foundation, "Yangtze Freshwater Dolphin Expedition 2006," press release (Wuhan, China: 13 December 2006); Tansa Musa, "Two-thirds of Congo Basin Forests Could Disappear," *Reuters*, 15 December 2006; National Oceanic and Atmospheric Administration, "In Record Wildfire Season, NOAA Satellites Aid U.S. Fire Managers," news story (Washington, DC: 4 January 2007).

January 2007. "Board Statement," *The Bulletin of the Atomic Scientists Online*, 17 January 2007; U.S. Climate Action Partnership, "Major Businesses and Environmental Leaders Unite to Call for Swift Action on Global Climate Change," press release (Washington, DC: 22 January 2007).

February 2007. "Summary for Policymakers," in Intergovernmental Panel on Climate Change, *Climate Change 2007: The Physical Basis* (Geneva: February 2007); UNEP, "Globalization & Great Apes: Illegal Logging Destroying Last Strongholds of Orangutans in National Parks," press release (Nairobi: 6 February 2007); Global Wind Energy Council, "Global Wind Energy Markets Continue to Boom—2006 Another Record Year," press release (Brussels: 15 February 2007); University of Missouri-Columbia, "Programmed for Obesity," press release (Columbia, MO: 16 February 2007); The Hon Malcolm Turnbull MP, Minister for the Environment and Water Resources, "World First! Australia Slashes Greenhouse Gases from Inefficient Lighting," press release (Bondi Junction, NSW, Australia: 20 February 2007).

March 2007. Samuel K. Wasser et al., "Using DNA to Track the Origin of the Largest Ivory Seizure Since the 1989 Trade Ban," *Proceedings of the National Academy of Sciences*, 6 March 2007, pp. 4228–33; Council of the European Union, "Brussels European Council, 8/9 March 2007: Presidency Conclusions" (Brussels: 2 May 2007), p. 12; U.S. Department of Energy, "Energy Praises the Nuclear Regulatory Commission Approval of the First United States Nuclear Plant Site in Over 30 Years," press release (Washington, DC: 8 March 2007); Office of the Press Secretary, The White House, "President Bush and President Lula of Brazil Discuss Biofuel Technology," press release (Washington, DC: 9 March 2007); U.S. Food and Drug Administration, "Pet Food Recall/Tainted Animal Feed," at www.fda.gov, updated 31 May 2007; World Wildlife Fund–US, "WWF's Top 10 Rivers at Risk, Rio Grande Makes List," press release (Washington, DC: 19 March 2007).

April 2007. World Bank, "Poverty Drops Below 1 Billion, Says World Bank," press release (Washington, DC: 15 April 2007); Government of China, "Report: Yangtze Water Environment Deteriorating," press release (Beijing: 16 April 2007); United Nations Security Council, "Security Council Holds First-Ever Debate on Impact of Climate Change on Peace, Security, Hearing Over 50 Speakers," press release (New York: 17 April 2007); "Double Hulled Tankers for Heavy Oil Now Law in Europe," *Environment News Service,* 28 April 2007.

May 2007. "S Pacific to Stop Bottom-Trawling," *BBC News Online,* 5 May 2007; Indiana University School of Medicine, "Premature Births May Be Linked to Seasonal Levels of Pesticides and Nitrates in Surface Water," press release (Bloomington, IN: 7 May 2007); Transatlantic21, "sun21 Makes Historic Arrival into New York Harbor," press release (New York: 8 May 2007); The White House, Office of the Press Secretary, "Executive Order: Cooperation Among Agencies in Protecting the Environment with Respect to Greenhouse Gas Emissions from Motor Vehicles, Nonroad Vehicles, and Nonroad Engines," press release (Washington, DC: 14 May 2007).

June 2007. Michael A. Fletcher, "G-8 Leaders Back 'Substantial' Cuts In Gas Emissions," *Washington Post,* 8 June 2007; UNEP, "Investors Flock to Renewable Energy and Efficiency Technologies," press release (Nairobi: 20 June 2007); UNESCO, "Galapagos and Niokolo-Koba National Park Inscribed on UNESCO's List of World Heritage in Danger," press release (Paris: 26 June 2007); U.S. Fish and Wildlife Service, "Bald Eagle Soars Off Endangered Species List," press release (Washington, DC: 28 June 2007).

July 2007. UN Global Compact, "Business Leaders Call for Climate Action," press release (Geneva: 6 July 2007); University of Michigan at Ann Arbor, "Organic Farming Can Feed the World, U-M Study Shows," press release (Ann Arbor: 10 July 2007); Suvendrini Kakuchi, "Japan's Nuclear Plans in Disarray," *Asia Times,* 20 July 2007; University of Colorado at Boulder, "Glaciers and Ice Caps to Dominate Sea-Level Rise Through 21st Century, CU-Boulder Study Says," press release (Boulder: 19 July 2007); "'Once-in-a-Century' Rains Displace Millions in China," *Environment News Service,* 23 July 2007; Flora and Fauna International, "IGCP Responds to Mountain Gorilla Deaths," news release (Cambridge: 24 July 2007).

August 2007. "Spanish Company Chooses Kansas Town for Cellulosic Ethanol Plant," *Associated Press,* 4 August 2007; New York City Department of Health and Mental Hygiene, "Survey Finds Elevated Rates of New Asthma Among WTC Rescue and Recovery Workers," press release (New York: 27 August 2007).

September 2007. Mattel, Inc., "Mattel Announces Recall of 11 Toys as a Result of Extensive Ongoing Investigation and Product Testing," press release (El Segundo, CA: 4 September 2007); The Coca-Cola Company, "Coca-Cola Sets Goal to Recycle or Reuse 100 Percent of Its Plastic Bottles in the U.S.," press release (Atlanta: 5 September 2007); U.S. Geological Survey, "Future Retreat of Arctic Sea Ice Will Lower Polar Bear Populations and Limit Their Distribution," press release (Reston, VA: 7 September 2007); IUCN–World Conservation Union, "Extinction Crisis Escalates: Red List Shows Apes, Corals, Vultures, Dolphins All in Danger," press release (Gland, Switzerland: 12 September 2007); Alfred-Wegener-Institute for Polar and Marine Research, "The Sea-Ice is Getting Thinner—A Closer Look at the Climate and Ecosystem of the Arctic Ocean," press release (Bremerhaven, Germany: 13 September 2007).

Chapter I.
Seeding the Sustainable Economy

1.   Economic growth from Angus Maddison, University of Groningen, "World Population, GDP, and Per Capita GDP, 1–2003 AD" at www.ggdc.net/maddison, viewed 28 September 2007; global output in 2006 from Central Intelligence Agency, *The World Factbook 2007* (Washington, DC: 2007); life expectancy and diseases from "Life Expectancy at Birth, at 65 Years of Age, and at 75 Years of Age, by Race and Sex: United States, Selected Years 1900-2004," in National Center for Health Statistics, *Health, United States, 2006* (Hyattsville, MD: 2006), p. 176.

2.   Quote on temperature from American Association for the Advancement of Science, "AAAS Board Releases New Statement on Climate Change," press release (Washington, DC: 9 December 2006); World Glacier Monitoring Service, "Worldwide Glacier Melting Underlined in Newly Released Data," press release (Zurich: 30 January 2007); National Aeronautics and Space Administration, "Greenland Ice Sheet on a Downward Slide," press release (Greenbelt, MD: 19 October 2006); University of Colorado at Boulder, "Glaciers and Ice Caps to Dominate Sea-Level Rise Through 21st Century, CU-Boulder Study Says," press release (Boulder: 19 July 2007); Julienne Stroeve et al., "Arctic Sea Ice Decline: Faster Than Forecast," *Geophysical Research Letters*, 1 May 2007; European Commission, "Nature Conservation: One in Six European Mammals Threatened with Extinction Shows Assessment by the World Conservation Union (IUCN)," press release (Brussels: 22 May 2007); U.N. Environment Programme (UNEP), "Further Rise in Number of Marine 'Dead Zones,'" press release (Nairobi: 29 October 2006); World Health Organization, "WHO Challenges World to Improve Air Quality," press release (Geneva: 5 October 2006); The National Academies, "Some Pollinator Populations Declining; Improved Monitoring and More Biological Knowledge Needed to Better Assess Their Status," press release (Washington, DC: 18 October 2006); World Energy Council, *2007 Survey of Energy Resources* (London: 2007), p. 44.

3.   Impoverished population from "News & Broadcast: Poverty," World Bank, at web.world bank.org, as of March 2007; Tim Ledwith, "'Progress for Children' Reports Mixed Results on Access to Water and Sanitation Worldwide," UNICEF, 28 September 2006; World Health Organization, "Obesity and Overweight," Fact Sheet No. 311 (Geneva: September 2006).

4.   Global Risk Network, *Global Risks 2007: A Global Risk Network Report* (Davos: World Economic Forum, January 2007).

5.   Maddison, op. cit. note 1; one seventh is a Worldwatch calculation based on U.S. Bureau of the Census, *International Data Base*, electronic database, Suitland, MD.

6.   "Daniel Bernoulli," at Encyclopedia Britannica online, viewed 16 October 2007.

7.   Robert Solow, "Is the End of the World at Hand?" in Andrew Weintraub et al., eds., *The Economic Growth Controversy* (White Plains, NY: International Arts and Science Press, 1973), p. 51.

8.   Population and gross world product from Maddison, op. cit. note 1; Global Footprint Network, "Humanity's Footprint, 1961–2003," at www.footprintnetwork.org, viewed 28 September 2007.

9.   Boris Worm et al., "Impacts of Biodiversity Loss on Ocean Ecosystem Services," *Science*, 3 November 2006, pp. 787-90.

10.   Maddison, op. cit. note 1.

11.   Neva Goodwin, Tufts University, e-mail to authors, 20 September 2007.

12.   UNEP, "IPCC Confirms That Cost-effective Policies and Technologies Could Greatly Reduce Global Warming," press release (Nairobi: 4 May 2007); Nicholas Stern, *The Economics of Climate Change: The Stern Review* (Cambridge, U.K.: Cambridge University Press, 2007); $650 billion is a Worldwatch estimate based on global economy from International Monetary Fund, *World Economic Outlook Database* (Washington, DC: Sep-

tember 2006); Viet Nam from Lori Montgomery, "The Cost of War, Unnoticed," *Washington Post*, 8 May 2007.

13. Stern, op. cit. note 12; low and high estimates from Frank Ackerman, "Debating Climate Economics: The Stern Review vs. Its Critics," report to Friends of the Earth–UK (Medford, MA: Global Development and Environment Institute (GDAE) at Tufts University, July 2007), p. 2.

14. Frank Ackerman and Elizabeth Stanton, *Climate Change: The Costs of Inaction* (Medford, MA: GDAE, October 2006); Frank Ackerman, GDAE, e-mail to Gary Gardner, 21 September 2007; Stern, op. cit. note 12.

15. Millennium Ecosystem Assessment (MA), *Ecosystems and Human Well-Being: Synthesis* (Washington, DC: Island Press, 2005), pp. 2–3.

16. Ibid., p. 55.

17. Robert Costanza, "The Value of the World's Ecosystem Services and Natural Capital," *Nature*, 15 May 1997, p. 253; Andrew Balmford et al., "Economic Reasons for Conserving Wild Nature," *Science*, 9 August 2002, pp. 950–53; Marianne Kettunen and Patrick ten Brink, *Value of Biodiversity: Documenting EU Examples Where Biodiversity Loss Has Led to Loss of Ecosystem Services* (London and Brussels: Institute for European Environmental Policy, June 2006), Annex 6, p. 11.

18. Balmford et al., op. cit. note 17; MA, op. cit. note 15.

19. Maddison, op. cit. note 1; poverty and data on clean water and sanitation from U.N. Development Programme (UNDP), *Human Development Report 2006* (New York: Palgrave Macmillan, 2006), pp. 2, 269; hunger from U.N. Food and Agriculture Organization (FAO), *The State of Food Insecurity in the World, 2006* (Rome: 2006), p. 32.

20. UNDP, op. cit. note 19, p. 269; South America population of 380 million from Census Bureau, op. cit. note 5; income inequality lessening from "Overview," in World Bank, *World Development Report 2006* (Washington, DC: 2006), p. 7.

21. Table 1–1 from James B. Davies et al., *The World Distribution of Household Wealth* (Helsinki: UNU-WIDER, December 2006), p. 3.

22. World Bank, op. cit. note 20, pp. 2–3.

23. Herman E. Daly, *Beyond Growth: The Economics of Sustainable Development* (Boston: Beacon Press, 1996), pp. 33–35.

24. Global Roundtable on Climate Change, "The Path to Climate Sustainability: A Joint Statement by the Global Roundtable on Climate Change," Earth Institute at Columbia University, New York, 20 February 2007; "Kyoto Protocol," U.N. Framework Convention on Climate Change, at unfccc.int, viewed 3 October 2007.

25. Interface, Inc., *Sustainability Report*, at www.interfacesustainability.com, viewed 13 October 2007.

26. Zero Waste New Zealand Trust, at www.zerowaste.co.nz, viewed 11 October 2007; Jo Knight, *Is Zero-waste Conceivable?* (Auckland: Zero Waste New Zealand, October 2007).

27. "Global Military Spending Hits $1.2 Trillion—Study," *Reuters*, 11 June 2007.

28. Millennium Development Goals, at www.un.org/millenniumgoals; Global Call to Action Against Poverty, at www.whiteband.org; The Microcredit Summit Campaign, at www.microcreditsummit.org, viewed 31 July 2007.

29. Daniel Kahneman and Alan B. Krueger, "Developments in the Measurement of Subjective Well-Being," *Journal of Economic Perspectives*, winter 2006, pp. 15–16; "Gallup: Chinese Far Wealthier than a Decade Ago—But Are They Happier?" New Occidental Research, at web.cenet.org.cn/web/Occidental, viewed 30 September 2007.

30. International Association of Public Transport, *Mobility in Cities Database* (Brussels: 2005), p. 3; "Aussie State Commits Big Bucks to

Cycling," *Bicycle Retailer and Industry News*, 1 June 2006, p. 35; "French Create National Cycling Czar Position," *Bicycle Retailer and Industry News*, 15 May 2006, p. 27; "Taiwan Builds Bike Paths, Promotes Cycling," *Bicycle Retailer and Industry News*, 15 July 2006, p. 27; "Brits Take to Bikes, Infrastructure a Big Help," *Bicycle Retailer and Industry News*, 1 July 2006, p. 30; Rachel Gordon, "Cycling Supporters on a Roll," *San Francisco Chronicle*, 21 August 2006; Amsterdam and United States from John Pucher and Lewis Dijkstra, "Promoting Safe Walking and Cycling to Improve Public Health: Lessons from the Netherlands and Germany," *American Journal of Public Health*, September 2003, p. 1509.

31. Kate Zernike, "Fight Against Fat Shifts to the Workplace," *New York Times*, 12 October 2003.

32. Andrew Revkin, "A New Measure of Well-being from a Happy Little Kingdom," *New York Times*, 4 October 2005.

33. "More Information on Environmentally Related Taxes, Fees, and Charges," at www2.oecd.org, viewed 11 October 2007; Markus Nigge and Benjamin Gorlach, *Effects of Germany's Ecological Tax Reforms on the Environment, Employment and Technological Innovation* (Summary) (Berlin: Ecologic, August 2005), p. 14; nitrogen oxide from International Institute for Sustainable Development, "The Nitrogen Oxide Charge on Energy Production in Sweden," at www.iisd.org, viewed 11 October 2007; 34 percent from Gary Wolff, *When Will Business Want Environmental Taxes?* (San Francisco: Redefining Progress, 2000), p. 5.

34. Congestion Charge Secretariat, *Facts and Results from the Stockholm Trials* (Stockholm: December 2006).

35. Gretchen C. Daily et al., "Ecosystem Services: Benefits Supplied to Human Societies by Natural Ecosystems," *Issues in Ecology*, spring 1997, p. 2.

36. Renée Johnson, *Recent Honey Bee Colony Declines* (Washington, DC: U.S. Congressional Research Service, 20 June 2007), p. 2; Dr. David Pimentel, Cornell University, discussion with Thomas Prugh, 27 July 2007.

37. Cameron Walker, "Taking Stock: Assessing Ecosystem Services Conservation in Costa Rica," *Ecosystem Marketplace*, 21 May 2007; Ricardo Bayon, "Case Study: The Mexico Forest Fund" *Ecosystem Marketplace*, 2004; Jessica Wilkinson, Ecosystem Marketplace, discussions with Ricardo Bayon, 2007.

38. Jared Blumenfeld, "New Approaches to Safeguarding the Earth," *San Francisco Chronicle*, 4 August 2003.

39. Ibid.

40. Maastricht from European Environmental Agency, *Late Lessons from Early Warnings: The Precautionary Principle, 1896–2000*, Environmental Issue Report No. 22 (Copenhagen: January 2002), p. 14; Danish Environmental Protection Agency, "The Precautionary Principle: Extracts and Summary from the Danish Environmental Protection Agency's Conference on the Precautionary Principle," *Environment News No. 35* (Copenhagen: 1998); Los Angeles from "Preferring the Least Harmful Way," *Rachel's Environment and Health News*, 26 January 2000; "San Francisco Adopts the Precautionary Principle, March 20, 2003," *Rachel's Democracy and Health News*, 18 June 2003.

41. Robert Costanza et al., *Introduction to Ecological Economics* (Boca Raton, FL: St. Lucie Press, 1997), p. 211.

42. Elinor Ostrom et al., "Revisiting the Commons: Local Lessons, Global Challenges," *Science*, 9 April 1999, p. 278.

43. Ibid.

44. Elinor Ostrom, *Governing the Commons: The Evolution of Institutions for Collective Action* (New York: Cambridge University Press, 1990), pp. 61 ff.

45. Peter Barnes, *Capitalism 3.0* (San Francisco: Berrett Koehler, 2006).

46. Tomales Bay Institute, *The Commons Rising: A Report to Owners* (Minneapolis, MN: 2006), pp. 6, 15.

47. African Centre for Women, "Report of the Ad Hoc Expert Group Meeting to Consider Modalities of Setting Up an African Bank for Women," at www.uneca.org.

48. U.N. Statistics Division, "Women's Wages Relative to Men's," in "Statistics and Indicators on Men and Women," database at unstats.un .org/unsd, viewed 29 July 2007; Equal Pay Act from Equal Employment Opportunity Commission, www.eeoc.gov/policy/epa.html, viewed 1 August 2007; 77¢ from Representative Mike Honda, "Statement on Equal Pay Day," Washington, DC, 24 April 2007.

49. Food production from FAO, "Gender and Food Security: Agriculture," at www.fao.org/GEn der/en/agri-e.htm; UNDP, *Human Development Reports 2001* and *2002* (New York: Oxford University Press, 2002, 2002); Aditi Thorat, "Grameen and the Question of Replicability," *Global Envision*, 28 October 2005.

50. Evelyn Dresher, "Valuing Unpaid Work," presented at Counting Women's Work Symposium, UN Platform for Action Committee Manitoba, Brandon, MB, May 1999; Erna Hooghiemstra, Ans Oudejans, and Saskia Keuzenkamp, *On the Trail of Unpaid Work: A Method of Integrating Information about Unpaid Work into Socioeconomic Policy* (The Hague: Social and Cultural Planning Office of the Netherlands, January 2002).

51. Paul Hawken, Amory Lovins, and L. Hunter Lovins, *Natural Capitalism: Creating the Next Industrial Revolution* (New York: Little, Brown and Company, 1999).

52. "Toyota Worldwide Hybrid Sales Top 1 Million," *Associated Press*, 7 June 2007; CFL sales and share of total from Charles Fishman, "How Many Lightbulbs Does it Take to Change the World? One. And You're Looking at It," *Fast Company*, September 2006, p. 74; organic sales and area from Helga Willer and Minou Yuseffi, *The World*

of Organic Agriculture: Statistics and Emerging Trends 2007* (Bonn: International Federation of Organic Agriculture Movements, 2007), pp. 9, 11; consumption share from Bureau of Economic Analysis, U.S. Department of Commerce, "National Income and Product Accounts Table, Gross Domestic Product," at www.bea.gov, viewed 2 October 2007.

53. Wal-Mart from Fishman, op. cit. note 52; BP Alternative Energy investment from Vivienne Cox, chief executive, Gas, Power & Renewables BP, plc, "The Business Case for Low-Carbon Power: An International Perspective," speech to the Indian Institute of Energy, 19 March 2007; 5 percent is a Worldwatch calculation based on $8 billion over a decade, or an average of $800 million per year, compared with an average $16 billion in annual capital investments for the years 2004, 2005, and 2006, from British Petroleum, *Annual Report 2006* (London: 2006), p. 27.

54. James Stack et al., *Cleantech Venture Capital: How Public Policy Has Stimulated Private Investment* (CleanTech Venture Network and Environmental Entrepreneurs, May 2007), pp. 8, 10; Cleantech Group, LLC, *China Cleantech Venture Capital Investment Report* (Cleantech Venture Network, 2007), p. v.

55. Commission on Oil Independence, *Making Sweden an Oil-Free Society* (Stockholm: June 2006).

56. Walter Hook, "Bus Rapid Transit: The Unfolding Story," in Worldwatch Institute, *State of the World 2007* (New York: W. W. Norton & Company, 2007), pp. 80–81.

Chapter 2.
A New Bottom Line for Progress

1. Ronald Wright, *A Short History of Progress* (New York: Carroll and Graff, 2005), p. 5.

2. Rondo Cameron and Larry Neal, *A Concise Economic History of the World from Paleolithic Times to the Present* (Oxford: Oxford University Press, 2003), p. 387.

3. In Figure 2–1, gross world product data from International Monetary Fund, *World Economic Outlook Database,* electronic database, Washington, DC, updated September 2005; human development index from U.N. Development Programme, *Human Development Report 2006* (New York: Palgrave Macmillan, 2006), p. 288; all other figures from World Bank Group, *World Indicators Online,* electronic database, updated May 2007.

4. Fischer cited in Philip Lawn, "Sustainable Development: Concepts and Indicators," in Philip Lawn, ed., *Sustainable Development Indicators in Ecological Economics* (Cheltenham, U.K.: Edward Elgar, 2006), p. 18.

5. Box 2–1 from the following: Sudan from United Nations, Under-Secretary for Humanitarian Affairs, "600,000 at Immediate Risk of Starvation," press release (Geneva: 23 February 2001), and from Alfred de Montesquiou, "African Union Force Ineffective, Complain Refugees in Darfur," *Washington Post,* 16 October 2006; Sri Lanka from T. J. Helgest, "Tsunami Disaster in Sri Lanka," at academic.evergreen.edu/g/gross manz/HelgestJ, viewed 20 June 2007, from Amantha Perera, "Sri Lanka: War Refugees Stressed by Mass Resettlement," *IPS News,* 28 May 2007, and from Amantha Perera, "Sri Lanka Civilians – Real Losers in the Civil War," *IPS News,* 22 March 2007; U.S. war spending from Bureau of Economic Analysis, *National Economic Accounts, Table 1.1.5,* electronic database, Washington, D.C., updated 28 June 2007; U.S. income inequality from David Clay Johnston, "U.S. Income Gap is Widening Significantly, Data Shows," *New York Times,* 29 March 2007.

6. Johnston, op. cit. note 5.

7. Daniel Kahneman, Ed Diener, and Norbert Schwartz, eds., *Well-being: The Foundation of Hedonic Psychology* (New York: Russell Sage Foundation Publications, 2003), cited in Bill McKibben, *Deep Economy* (New York: New York Times Books, 2007), pp. 32–33; Ed Diener and Martin Seligman, "Beyond Money: Toward an Economy of Well-Being," *Psychological Science in the Public Interest,* July 2004, p. 5.

8. World Bank, *World Development Indicators 2007* (Washington, DC: 2007), p. 185.

9. World Commission on Environment and Development, *Our Common Future* (New York: Oxford University Press, 1987), p. 43; Andres Edwards, *The Sustainability Revolution: Portrait of a Paradigm Shift* (Gabriola Island, BC: New Society Publishers, 2005), pp. 128–30.

10. Characterization of GPI from Philip Lawn, "Introduction," in Lawn, op. cit. note 4, p. 11.

11. Table 2–2 data from John Talberth, Clifford Cobb, and Noah Slattery, *Sustainable Development and the Genuine Progress Indicator: An Updated Methodology and Application in Policy Settings* (Oakland, CA: Redefining Progress, 2007).

12. Threshold effect from Manford Max-Neef, "Economic Growth and Quality of Life: A Threshold Hypothesis," *Ecological Economics,* November 1995, pp. 115–18.

13. Joseph Kahn and Jim Yardley, "As China Roars, Pollution Reaches Deadly Extremes," *New York Times,* 26 August 2007.

14. U.N. Statistical Division, *Global Assessment of Environment Statistics and Environmental-Economic Accounting* (New York: 2007), p. 2; for Pembina Institute's economic, environmental, and social policy series, see www.fiscallygreen.ca/gpi/indicators.php.

15. Nic Marks et al., *The Happy Planet Index: An Index of Human Well-Being and Environmental Impact* (London: New Economics Foundation and Friends of the Earth, 2006).

16. Ibid.

17. Details of Bhutan program and quote from Gopilal Acharya, "Literature on Gross National Happiness," at travelbhutan.tripod.com/druk.html, viewed 23 June 2007.

18. Emissions reduction scenario summarized by Bill Chameides, chief scientist, Environmental

Defense, "Action Needed to Stop Global Warming: Worldwide Emissions," at environmental defenseblogs.org/climate411/2007/03/14/world wide_emissions, posted 14 March 2007; gross world product data from "Chapter 2: An Overview of the Scenario Literature," in Nebojsa Nakicenovic and Robert Swart, eds., *Special Report on Emissions Scenarios* (New York: Cambridge University Press, for Intergovernmental Panel on Climate Change, 2000).

19. Index of representational equity from Redefining Progress, "Scenarios for Sustainability," fact sheet (Oakland, CA: 2007); GINI coefficient from World Bank, op. cit. note 8, p. 69.

20. Wright, op. cit. note 1, p. 129; Millennium Ecosystem Assessment, *Ecosystems and Human Well-being* (Washington, DC: Island Press, 2003).

21. World Wide Fund for Nature (WWF), *Living Planet Report 2006* (Gland, Switzerland: WWF, Global Footprint Network, and the Zoological Society of London, 2006), p. 1; Convention on Biological Diversity, *Indicators for Assessing Progress Towards the 2010 Target: Ecological Footprint and Related Concepts* (Nairobi: U.N. Environment Programme, 2004), p. 5.

22. Localization definition from Redefining Progress et al., *Building a Resilient and Equitable Bay Area: Towards a Coordinated Strategy for Economic Localization* (Oakland, CA: 2006), p. 2; World Bank, "World Bank Sees 'Localization' As Major New Trend in 21st Century," press release (Washington, DC: 15 September 1999).

23. Associated Press, "Are Consumer Concerns over Food Miles Driving Natural Food Supermarkets to Begin Buying Local?" 30 April 2007.

24. Andrew Savitz and Karl Weber, *The Triple Bottom Line* (San Francisco: John Wiley and Sons, 2006), p. 209.

25. Marine Stewardship Council Web site, at www.msc.org.

26. Global Reporting Initiative, *GRI Performance Indicators*, at www.globalreporting.org/ ReportingFramework/G3Online/Performance Indicators.

27. 3M information from Daniel C. Esty and Andrew S. Winston, *Green to Gold* (New Haven, CT: Yale University Press, 2006), p. 107.

28. Green Mountain Coffee Roasters, Inc., *Social Responsibility Report* (Waterbury, VT: 2007), pp. 89–90, 116–19.

29. Green Electronics Council, "Electronic Product Environmental Assessment Tool: The Criteria," at www.epeat.net/Criteria.aspx.

30. ST Microelectronics from Savitz and Weber, op. cit. note 24, p. 35; DuPont from Esty and Winston, op. cit. note 27, p. 105; Advanced Micro Devices, Inc., *Global Climate Protection Plan 2006* (Sunnyvale, CA: AMD, Inc., 2006), p. 17.

31. WHO Collaborating Centres in Occupational Health, "Global Strategy on Occupational Health for All: Recommendation of the Second Meeting of the WHO Collaborating Centres in Occupational Health, 11–14 October 1994, Beijing, China," at www.ccohs.ca/who/contents.htm; Turk Polytechnic, *Corporate Sustainability Report* (Turku, Finland: 2005), p. 31.

32. Mountain Equipment Co-op, *Making Our Route: 2005 Corporate Sustainability Report* (Vancouver, BC: 2005), pp. 31–34.

33. Overseas Development Institute, *Tips and Tools for South African Tourism Companies on Local Procurement, Products and Partnerships* (London: 2005).

34. Novartis, Inc., *Implementing a Living Wage Globally, The Novartis Approach* (Basel, Switzerland: 2006).

35. European Commission, "Beyond GDP: Measuring Progress, True Wealth, and the Well Being of Nations," conference announcement, at www.beyond-gdp.eu, viewed 22 June 2007.

36. World Bank Institute, *Overview of Use of Benefit-Cost and Cost Effectiveness Analysis for*

Environmental Management (Washington, DC: 2002), p. 5.

37. Esty and Winston, op. cit. note 27, pp. 24–27.

38. Savitz and Weber, op. cit. note 24, p. 210.

Chapter 3. Rethinking Production

1. Reduced energy use from Marc Gunther, "The Green Machine." *Fortune Magazine*, 27 July 2006; Cynthia Henry, "A Model of Corporate Action," *Philadelphia Inquirer*, 15 February 2007.

2. Paul Hawken, Amory Lovins, and L. Hunter Lovins, *Natural Capitalism: Creating the Next Industrial Revolution* (New York: Little, Brown and Company, 1999), p. 52; Annan quoted in "The State of the World? It Is on the Brink of Disaster?" *The Independent* (London), 30 March 2005.

3. Hawken, Lovins, and Lovins, op. cit. note 2, p. 111.

4. For more information on Natural Capitalism and how to implement these principles, see www.natcapsolutions.org. The entire text of the book *Natural Capitalism* and many other reference works can be downloaded for free from this site.

5. William McDonough and Michael Braungart, *Cradle to Cradle: Remaking the Way We Make Things* (New York: North Point Press, 2002).

6. Ernst von Weizsäcker, Amory B. Lovins, and L. Hunter Lovins. *Factor Four: Doubling Wealth, Halving Resource Use* (London: Earthscan, 1997); adoption of Factor Four philosophy in European Union environmental policy also described in Ester van der Voet et al., *Policy Review on Decoupling*, Commissioned by European Commission (Leiden, Netherlands: Institute of Environmental Sciences, 2005); Australian Ministry of the Environment and Heritage, *Visions, Management Tools and Emerging Issues Towards an Eco-Efficient and*

Sustainable Enterprise, Second Environmental Economics Round Table Proceedings (Canberra: 2000); Factor Ten Club members available at www.factor10-institute.org; Friedrich Schmidt-Bleck, *The Factor 10/MIPS-Concept: Bridging Ecological, Economic, and Social Dimensions with Sustainability Indicators* (Tokyo: Zero Emissions Forum, United Nations University, 1999), p. 6.

7. Stephan Schmidheiny with the Business Council for Sustainable Development, *Changing Course* (Cambridge, MA: The MIT Press, 1992); definition from World Business Council for Sustainable Development Web site, at www.wbcsd.org.

8. Programs and executive committee from "About the WBCSD," at www.wbcsd.org.

9. National Business Initiative, "Case Study—Anglo American/Mondi: Improved Energy & Efficiency," 3 January 2007, at www.wbcsd.org.

10. STMicroelectronics, *Sustainable Development Report* (Geneva: 2003). Perfluorocarbon is a powerful greenhouse gas emitted during the production of aluminum (a fluorocarbon is a halocarbon in which some hydrogen atoms have been replaced by fluorine); it is used in refrigerators and aerosols. Sulfur hexafluoride is another potent greenhouse gas. It one of the most popular insulating gases.

11. STMicroelectronics, *Environmental Report* (Geneva: 2001); correlation of year's payback to real after tax rate of return from Hawken, Lovins, and Lovins, op. cit. note 2, p. 267.

12. STMicroelectronics, op. cit. note 10; Murray Duffin, Center for Energy and Climate Solutions, discussion with author.

13. "Sustainability 360: Doing Good, Better, Together," Remarks of H. Lee Scott, Jr., CEO and President of Wal-Mart Stores, Inc., Lecture to the Prince of Wales's Business & the Environment Programme, 1 February 2007.

14. Ibid.

15. Gunther, op. cit. note 1.

16. "Sustainability 360," op. cit. note 13.

17. Gunther, op. cit. note 1.

18. Lee Scott, discussion with author, Business Milestone meeting, March 2007.

19. James P. Womack and Daniel T. Jones, *Lean Thinking* (New York: Simon & Schuster, 1996); "The History of Six Sigma," at www.isix sigma.com.

20. Box 3–1 from Norihiko Shirouzu, "How Does Toyota Maintain Quality? Mr. Oba's Hair Dryer Offers a Clue," *Wall Street Journal*, 15 March 2001.

21. Chicago Manufacturing Center (CMC), "Green Plants Sustainable Leadership Program," at www.cmcusa.org.

22. For more information, see PortionPac, at www.portionpaccorp.com.

23. Marvin Kline, founder, PortionPac, discussion with author.

24. Walters cited in CMC, "PortionPac: At a Glance," at www.cmcusa.org.

25. Walter Stahel with G. Reday, *Jobs for Tomorrow: The Potential for Substituting Manpower for Energy* (New York: Vantage Press, 1981).

26. Walter Stahel, "Pillars of Sustainability," Product-Life Institute, Geneva.

27. Ibid.

28. Ibid.

29. Hawken, Lovins, and Lovins, op. cit. note 2, pp. 157–58, 170.

30. Ibid., Chapter 3.

31. William Lazonick, "Corporate Restructuring," in Stephen Ackroyd et al., eds., *The Oxford Handbook of Work & Organization* (Oxford: Oxford University Press, 2005), pp. 577–601.

32. Stahel, op. cit. note 26.

33. Interface Dream Team meeting, Netherlands, discussion with author, 2001.

34. Janine Benyus, *Biomimicry* (New York: William Morrow, 1997); Fuller quote from coolquotes.wordpress.com/2006/09/26/r-buck minster-fuller-quote-on-beauty.

35. Biomimicry Institute, "Biomimicry in a Nutshell," at www.biomimicry.net/biomimicryintro duction.htm. Box 3–2 from Ray Anderson, at Wingspread Conference, discussion with author, 1 October 2007.

36. Biomimicry Institute, "Biomimicry Design Process," at www.biomimicry.net/designmeth odologyA.htm.

37. "EcoCover: Redesigning Waste for a Tangible Benefit,"at www.ecocover.com.

38. Ibid.

39. Biomimicry Institute, "Mother-of-Pearl Inspires Lightweight Building Materials," at www.biomimicry.net/casestudyabalone.htm.

40. Ibid.

41. "Toyota Announces 'Sustainable Plant' Activities," *Industry Week*, 27 July 2007.

42. Ibid.

43. Biomimicry Institute, op. cit. note 35.

44. Ibid.

45. This concept was first presented in "Catch the Wave," *The Economist*, 18 February 1999; Figure courtesy of The Natural Edge Project, Australia, 30 October 2006.

46. For a detailed synthesis of this thesis, see K. Hargroves and M. Smith, *The Natural Advantage of Nations: Business Opportunities, Innovation and Governance in the 21st Century* (London: Earthscan, 2005), developed by The Natural Edge Pro-

ject, at www.naturaledgeproject.net, 30 October 2006.

47. General Electric, at www.ge.com/ecomagination; Gunther, op. cit. note 1.

48. Kevin Voigt, "Business Sees Green in Going Green," *CNN Report*, 21 December 2006.

49. David Reilly, "Profit as We Know It Could Be Lost With New Accounting Statements," *Wall Street Journal*, 12 May 2007.

50. John Elkinton, *Cannibals With Forks: The Triple Bottom Line of 21st Century Business* (Oxford: Capstone Publishing Ltd., 1997).

51. Margo Alderton, "Green Is Gold, According to Goldman Sachs Study," The CRO (Corporate Responsibility Officer), at www.thecro.com, 11 July 2007.

Chapter 4.
The Challenge of Sustainable Lifestyles

1. "Ethical Man," *BBC Newsnight*, 22 May 2007.

2. Data on income, household structure and size, and energy consumption supplied by BBC team.

3. Historical data and forecasts from J. Ablett et al., *The "Bird of Gold": The Rise of India's Consumer Market* (London: McKinsey Global Institute, 2007); population projections from U.S. Bureau of the Census, *International Data Base*, Suitland, MD, updated 16 July 2007.

4. HSBC Holdings plc, *HSBC Climate Confidence Index 2007* (London: 2007).

5. U.N. Population Division, *World Population Prospects: The 2004 Revision* (New York: 2006).

6. See Gary Gardner, Erik Assadourian, and Radhika Sarin, "The State of Consumption Today," in Worldwatch Institute, *State of the World*

2004 (New York: W. W. Norton & Company, 2004).

7. Carbon footprints based on data supplied by the BBC Newsnight team and only include the carbon dioxide (CO_2) emissions from the burning of fossil fuels; they include the direct household emissions from electricity, cooking, and transport and an estimate of indirect emissions based on the household income. Table 4–1 based on data in International Energy Agency (IEA) *CO_2 Emissions from Fuel Combustion 1971–2004* (Paris: Organisation for Economic Co-operation and Development (OECD), 2006).

8. Cumulative CO_2 emissions in different countries from World Resources Institute, *EarthTrends: Environmental Information*, online database, Washington, DC, 2007.

9. Figure 4–1 from IEA, op. cit. note 7; Netherlands Environmental Assessment Agency, "China Now No. 1 in CO2 Emissions: USA in Second Position," *Climate Change Dossier*, 19 June 2007; "Summary for Policymakers," in Intergovernmental Panel on Climate Change (IPCC), *Climate Change 2007: Mitigation of Climate Change* (New York: Cambridge University Press, 2007).

10. IPCC, *Climate Change 2001: Third Assessment Report* (New York: Cambridge University Press, 2001).

11. D. Farrell et al., *From 'Made in China' to 'Sold in China': The Rise of the Chinese Urban Consumer* (London: McKinsey Global Institute, 2006).

12. For examples of utilitarian model, see Andreu Mas-Colell, Michael D. Whinston, and Jerry R. Green, *Microeconomic Theory* (Oxford: Oxford University Press, 1995), and David Fischer, Stanley Dornbusch, and Rudiger Begg, *Economics*, 7th ed. (Maidenhead, U.K.: McGraw-Hill, 2003); for the theory of "revealed preference," see Paul Samuelson, "A Note on the Pure Theory of Consumers' Behaviour," *Economica*, February 1938, pp. 61–71.

13. "Science of desire" from Ernest Dichter, *A*

Handbook of Consumer Motivations (New York: McGraw Hill, 1964).

14. For the social role of goods, see Mary Douglas and Baron Isherwood, *The World of Goods* (New York: Basic Books, 1996); quote from Yiannis Gabriel and Tim Lang, *The Unmanageable Consumer* (London: Sage Publications Ltd., 2006), p. 81.

15. For symbolic role of consumer goods, see Helga Dittmar, *The Social Psychology of Material Possessions—To Have Is to Be* (New York: St Martin's Press, 1992); for "evocative power," see Grant McCracken, *Culture and Consumption* (Bloomington and Indianapolis: Indiana University Press, 1990); Mihály Csíkszentmihályi and Eugene Rochberg-Halton, *The Meaning of Things—Domestic Symbols and the Self* (New York: Cambridge University Press, 1981).

16. On self-esteem striving, see Jamie Arndt et al., "The Urge to Splurge: A Terror Management Account of Materialism and Consumer Behavior," *Journal of Consumer Psychology*, vol. 14, no. 3 (2004), pp. 198–212.

17. Opinion Leader Research, 2006 *Shifting Opinions and Changing Behaviour*, Commissioned by Sustainable Consumption Roundtable (London: 2006).

18. "Ethical Man," op. cit. note 1.

19. "Islands of prosperity" from Madhav Gadjil and Ramachandra Guha, *Ecology and Equity— The Use and Abuse of Nature in Contemporary India* (New York: Routledge, 1995), p. 34.

20. On the correlates of subjective well-being (or reported life-satisfaction), see, for example, John F. Helliwell, "How's Life? Combining Individual and National Variables to Explain Subjective Wellbeing," *Economic Modelling*, March 2003, pp. 331–60.

21. Figure 4–2 from Ronald Inglehart and Hans-Dieter Klingemann, "Genes, Culture, Democracy, and Happiness," in Ed Diener and Eunkook Suh, *Culture and Subjective Well-being* (Cambridge, MA: The MIT Press, 2000). Income figures are World Bank purchasing power parity estimates in 1995 dollars.

22. Ruut Veenhoven, *World Database of Happiness*, Erasmus University, Rotterdam, Netherlands.

23. Richard Layard, *Happiness—Lessons from a New Science* (London: Penguin, 2005); The WHO World Mental Health Survey Consortium, "Prevalence, Severity and Unmet Need for Treatment of Mental Disorders in the World Health Organization World Mental Health Surveys," *Journal of the American Medical Association*, 2 June 2004, pp. 2581–89.

24. Alain de Boton, *Status Anxiety* (London: Penguin Books, 2005); Tim Kasser, *The High Price of Materialism* (Cambridge, Mass: The MIT Press, 2002); Tim Jackson, Wander Jager, and Sigrid Stagl, "Beyond Insatiability—Needs Theory and Sustainable Consumption," in Lucia A. Reisch and Inge Røpke, eds., *The Ecological Economics of Consumption* (Cheltenham, U.K.: Edward Elgar Publishing, 2004).

25. Data on "moral lives" and happiness from Layard, op. cit. note 23, pp. 29, 81; see also Robert D. Putnam, *Bowling Alone* (New York: Simon and Schuster, 2000); family breakdown data from *Population Trends* (London, Office for National Statistics, various years), cited in Tim Jackson, *Chasing Progress? Beyond Measuring Economic Growth* (London: New Economics Foundation, 2004), p. 3.

26. Layard, op. cit. note 23, p. 34.

27. Richard Gregg (Gandhi's student) originally published his paper on voluntary simplicity in the Indian Journal *Visva Bharati Quarterly*; Duane Elgin, *Voluntary Simplicity* (New York: William Morrow, reprinted 1993); Mihály Csíkszentmihályi, "The Costs and Benefits of Consuming," *Journal of Consumer Research*, September 2000, pp. 262–72.

28. Amitai Etzioni, "Voluntary Simplicity: Characterisation, Select Psychological Implications and Societal Consequences," *Journal of Economic Psy-*

chology, October 1998, pp. 619–43.

29. Findhorn Foundation, *Annual Report 2005/6* (Forres, Scotland: 2006); Plum Village, at www.plumvillage.org/.

30. Simplicity Forum, at www.simplicityforum.org/index.html; Downshifting Downunder, at downshifting.naturalinnovation.org/index.html.

31. Clive Hamilton and Elizabeth Mail, *Downshifting in Australia: A Sea-change in the Pursuit of Happiness*, Discussion Paper No. 50 (Canberra: The Australia Institute, January 2003); U.S. data from Merck Family Fund, *Yearning for Balance: Views of Americans on Consumption, Materialism, and the Environment* (Takoma Park, MD: 1995).

32. Kasser, op. cit. note 24; Kirk Warren Brown and Tim Kasser, "Are Psychological and Ecological Well-being Compatible? The Role of Values, Mindfulness, and Lifestyle," *Social Indicators Research*, November 2005, pp. 349–68.

33. Buy Nothing Day, at adbusters.org/metas/eco/bnd/index.php.

34. Transition Towns, at transitiontowns.org; "U.S. Mayors Climate Protection Agreement," endorsed by the U.S. Conference of Mayors Meeting, Chicago, June 2005.

35. Limits of voluntary simplicity from Etzioni, op. cit. note 28, and from Seonaidh McDonald et al., 2006, "Toward Sustainable Consumption: Researching Voluntary Simplifiers," *Psychology and Marketing*, June 2006, pp. 515–35; involuntary downshifting from Inglehart and Klingeman, op. cit. note 21.

36. Robert Wright, *The Moral Animal—Why We Are the Way We Are: The New Science of Evolutionary Psychology* (London: Abacus, 1994).

37. The quotation is from a review of Matt Ridley, *The Red Queen: Sex and the Evolution of Human Nature* (London: Penguin Books, 1994), cited on book cover.

38. Ridley, op. cit. note 37; Leigh van Valen, "A New Evolutionary Law," *Evolutionary Theory*, vol. 1 (1973), pp. 1–30.

39. Russell W. Belk, Güliz Ger, and Søren Askegaard, "The Fire of Desire: A Multisited Inquiry into Consumer Passion," *Journal of Consumer Research* 30, December 2003, pp. 325–51.

40. S. Venkatesan, "Pathology of Power: Caste and Capabilities," OneWorld South Asia, 24 October 2006; life expectancy in India from Registrar General of India, "SRS Based Abridged Life Tables," SRS Analytical Studies, Report No. 3 (New Delhi: 2003).

41. Richard G. Wilkinson, *The Impact of Inequality: How to Make Sick Societies Healthier* (London: Routledge, 2005). Figure 4–3 from Office for National Statistics, *Sustainable Development Indicators in Your Pocket 2007* (London: Department for Environment, Food and Rural Affairs (Defra), 2007).

42. Distress in unequal societies from Oliver James, *Affluenza* (London: Vermillion, 2007), Appendix 1 and 2.

43. See, for example, W. Hamilton, "The Evolution of Altruistic Behavior," *American Naturalist*, vol. 97 (1963), pp. 354–56; a more accessible description can be found in Wright, op. cit. note 36; quote from Richard Dawkins, "Sustainability Does Not Come Naturally: A Darwinian Perspective on Values," The Values Platform for Sustainability Inaugural Lecture at the Royal Institution, 14 November 2001 (Fishguard, U.K.: The Environment Foundation).

44. Robert M. Axelrod, *The Evolution of Cooperation* (New York: Basic Books, 1984).

45. For infrastructure of consumption, see OECD, *Towards Sustainable Consumption: An Economic Conceptual Framework* (Paris: 2002), p. 41.

46. Wage disparities from Stephen Bradley, *In Greed We Trust: Capitalism Gone Astray* (Victoria, BC: Trafford Publishing, 2006); discounted long-term costs from Nicholas Stern, *The Economics of Climate Change: The Stern Review* (Cambridge: Cambridge University Press, 2007); materials signaling status from Juliet B. Schor, *The Overspent American* (New York: Basic Books, 1998); National Consumer Council, *Shopping Generation* (London: 2006).

47. Avner Offer, *The Challenge of Affluence* (Oxford: Oxford University Press, 2006).

48. Parenthood from ibid., Chapter 14; savings rates from Norman Loayza et al., *Saving in the World: The Stylized Facts* (Washington DC: World Bank, 1998); consumer debt from Ben Woolsey, "Credit Card Industry Facts and Personal Debt Statistics (2006–2007)," at Creditcards.com, and from William Branigin, "Consumer Debt Grows at Alarming Pace, at msnbc.msn.com, 12 January 2004.

49. Quote from Rio Rivas and David H. Gobeli, "Accelerating the Rate of Innovation at Hewlett Packard," Industrial Research Institute, undated.

50. "Iron cage" was first applied to capitalism by Max Weber, *The Protestant Ethic and the Spirit of Capitalism*, tr. Talcott Parsons (New York: Charles Scribner's Sons, 1958); application to consumerism in George Ritzer, *The McDonaldization of Society* (New York: Pine Forge Press, 2004).

51. U.N. Population Division, op. cit. note 5.

52. Sustainable Consumption Roundtable, *I Will If You Will: Towards Sustainable Consumption* (London: Sustainable Development Commission, 2006).

53. Role of policy from ibid.; Tim Jackson, "Challenges for Sustainable Consumption Policy," in Tim Jackson, *Earthscan Reader in Sustainable Consumption* (London: Earthscan/James and James, 2006); sustainable consumption policy from Defra, *Securing the Future: Implementing UK Sustainable Development Strategy* (London: Her Majesty's Stationery Office, 2005), Chapters 2 and 3.

54. Stern, op. cit. note 46.

55. Darren Murph, "Australia to Phase Out Incandescent Bulbs by 2010," Engadget.com, 20 February 2007; Conrad Quilty-Harper, "All of EU to Switch Off Energy Inefficient Lights Within Three Years," Engadget.com, 10 March 2007; Sustainable Development Commission, *Looking Back, Looking Forward* (London: 2006).

56. Defra, "Wellbeing and Sustainable Development," at www.sustainable-development.gov.uk , updated 6 June 2007; Canada from Andrew C. Revkin, "A New Measure of Wellbeing from a Happy Little Kingdom," *New York Times*, 4 October 2005; State Environmental Protection Agency, *China Green National Accounting Study Report 2004* (Beijing: 2006).

57. "Global Ad Spending Expected to Grow 6%," *Brandweek*, 6 December 2005; "Internet Advertising Nears £1 Billion for First Six Months of 2006," Internet Advertising Bureau, 4 October 2006.

58. Proceedings and publications from the WHO conference available at www.euro.who.int/obesity/conference2006; Ministry of Children and Equality, "The Norwegian Action Plan to Reduce Commercial Pressure on Children and Young People," at www.regjeringen.no/en; ban on advertising green cars reported in *Edmonton Journal*, 7 September 2007; David Evan Harris, "São Paulo: A City Without Ads," *Adbusters*, September-October 2007.

59. Local Development Institute, *A Model of Local Economy in 200 Districts Based on Sufficiency Economy: An Action Research Project* (Bangkok, Office of Village Fund National Committee, 2002–03); Yuwanan Santitaweeroek, "Thailand's Silk Microenterprises and the Sufficiency Economy," PhD Dissertation (Guildford, U.K.: University of Surrey, forthcoming); Bhutan from Revkin, op. cit. note 56.

Chapter 5. Meat and Seafood:
The Global Diet's Most Costly Ingredients

1. Meat and seafood production, Figure 5–1, and Table 5–1 from U.N. Food and Agriculture

Organization (FAO), *FAOSTAT Statistical Database*, at faostat.fao.org, updated 30 June 2007, and from FAO, *Yearbook of Fishery Statistics* (Rome: 2006). The United Nations recently revised the way it totals seafood, so data in this chapter do not match earlier Worldwatch publications. Since seafood is generally consumed fresh or within a few months of being caught, statistics on consumption and production are nearly identical.

2.   Nanna Roos et al., "Fish and Health," in Corinna Hawkes and Marie T. Ruel, eds., *Understanding the Links Between Agriculture and Health for Food, Agriculture, and the Environment*, 2020 Focus No. 13 (Washington, DC: International Food Policy Research Institute (IFPRI), May 2006); seafood data from FAO, *FAOSTAT*, op. cit. note 1; supply of protein from Meryl Williams, "The Transition in the Contribution of Living Aquatic Resources to Food Security," Food, Agriculture, and the Environment Discussion Paper 13 (Washington, DC: IFPRI, 1996).

3.   For more on factory farming, see Danielle Nierenberg, *Happier Meals: Rethinking the Global Meat Industry* (Washington, DC: Worldwatch Institute, September 2005), and Michael Pollan, *The Omnivore's Dilemma: A Natural History of Four Meals* (New York: Penquin Press, 2006).

4.   Humane Society of the United States, "An HSUS Report: Welfare Issues with Selective Breeding for Rapid Growth in Broiler Chickens and Turkeys," Washington, DC, February 2006.

5.   For the history of fishing technology, see Dietrich Sahrhage and Johannes Lundbeck, *A History of Fishing* (Berlin: Springer-Verlag, 1992); 70 million tons from FAO, *FAOSTAT*, op. cit. note 1; 90 percent from Ransom A. Myers and Boris Worm, "Rapid Worldwide Depletion of Predatory Fish Communities," *Nature*, 15 May 2003, pp. 280–83.

6.   National Science and Technology Council, Committee on Environment and Natural Resources, *Integrated Assessment of Hypoxia in the Northern Gulf of Mexico* (Washington, DC: National Oceanic and Atmospheric Administration (NOAA), May 2000); Amy Wold, "'Dead Zone' Threatens Fisheries," *The Advocate*, 10 September 2007; National Marine Fisheries Service, NOAA, *Fisheries of the United States 2006* (Silver Spring, MD: July 2007).

7.   Symbiotic role of fish farms from B. A. Costa-Pierce, ed., *Ecological Aquaculture: The Evolution of the Blue Revolution* (Oxford, U.K.: Blackwell, 2002); symbiotic role of livestock from Pollan, op. cit. note 3, p. 210.

8.   Danielle Nierenberg, "Factory Farming in the Developing World," *World Watch*, May/June 2003; "Meet Niman Ranch Family Farmer Tim Roseland," Niman Ranch Web site, at www.niman-ranch.com, viewed August 2007.

9.   FAO, *Mixed Crop-Livestock Farming: A Review of Traditional Technologies Based on Literature and Field Experience* (Rome: 2001); Michael Greger, *Bird Flu: A Virus of Our Own Hatching* (New York: Lantern Books, 2006).

10.   Iowa State University, "Alternatives to Gestation Stalls Reviewed at Iowa State," press release (Ames, IA: 19 April 2007).

11.   Dr. William Weida, Executive Director of the GRACE Factory Farm Project, discussion with Danielle Nierenberg, July 2007.

12.   Henning Steinfeld et al., *Livestock's Long Shadow: Environmental Issues and Options* (Rome: FAO, 2006); Daniele Finelli, "Meat is Murder on the Environment," *New Scientist*, 18 July 2007; C. Cederberg and M. Stadig, "System Expansion and Allocation in Life Cycle Assessment of Milk and Beef Production," *International Journal of Life Cycle Assessment*, vol. 8, no. 6 (2003), pp. 350–56.

13.   Farmed fish from FAO, *FAOSTAT*, op. cit. note 1; growth from Christopher L. Delgado et al., *Outlook for Fish to 2020: Meeting Global Demand* (Washington, DC, and Penang, Malaysia: IFPRI and WorldFish Center, October 2003).

14.   Rosamond Naylor and Marshall Burke, "Aquaculture and Ocean Resources: Raising Tigers of the Sea," *Annual Reviews in Environmental*

Resources, vol. 30 (2005), pp. 185–218; Jackie Alder and Daniel Pauly, *On the Multiple Uses of Forage Fish: From Ecosystems to Markets*, Fisheries Centre Research Report (Vancouver, BC: Sea Around Us Project, Fisheries Centre, University of British Columbia, 2006), pp. vii, 3.

15. Naylor and Burke, op. cit. note 14.

16. Ibid.

17. Campaign from Don Staniford, Pure Salmon Campaign, discussion with Brian Halweil, 16 July 2007; world's largest salmon farming company from Marine Harvest, "Pan Fish Aquires Marine Harvest to Form the World's Largest Fish Farming Company," press release (Oslo, Norway: 6 March 2006).

18. Costa-Pierce, op. cit. note 7; Maeve Kelly et al., "Nutrient Re-cycling or Utilising 'Waste' in Open Water Aquaculture," Scottish Association for Marine Science, presentation at Soil Association conference, Stirling, U.K., March 2006; synergies and 50 percent from Shawn Robinson, research scientist, Fisheries and Oceans Canada, Aquaculture Division, St Andrews Biological Station, St Andrews, NB, discussion with Brian Halweil, 19 September 2007.

19. Cleaner fish from Per Gunnar Kvenseth, Villa Salmon, Vikebukt, Norway, discussion with Brian Halweil, 31 August 2007; "Lice from Fish Farms Called Threat," *Associated Press*, 20 September 2007; benefits of integrated system from Costa-Pierce, op. cit. note 7.

20. Cost of removing nitrogen from the water from Bob Rheault, Moonstone Oysters and East Coast Shellfish Growers Association, discussion with Brian Halweil; Rowan Jacobsen, *A Geography of Oysters* (New York: Bloomsbury USA, 2007); M. A. Rice, "Environmental Impacts of Shellfish Aquaculture: Filter Feeding to Control Eutrophication," in M. Tlusty et al., eds., *Marine Aquaculture and the Environment: A Meeting for Stakeholders in the Northeast* (Falmouth, MA: Cape Cod Press), pp. 77–84.

21. Rowan Jacobsen, "Restoration on the Half Shell," *New York Times*, 9 April 2007; dead zones from J. Michael Beman, Kevin R. Arrigo, and Pamela A. Matson, "Agricultural Runoff Fuels Large Phytoplankton Blooms in Vulnerable Areas of the Ocean," *Nature*, 10 March 2005, pp. 211–14.

22. WorldFish Center, "Rice-Fish Culture: A Recipe for Higher Production," at www.world fishcenter.org, viewed 4 September 2006; projections are Worldwatch estimates based on ibid.

23. Randall E. Brummett et al., "Targeting Aquaculture Development in Africa: A Case Study from Cameroon," Humid Forest Ecoregional Center, Yaoundé, Cameroon, unpublished report; Randall E. Brummett, WorldFish, Humid Forest Ecoregional Center, Yaoundé, Cameroon, e-mail to Brian Halweil, 17 September 2007.

24. Environmental Working Group (EWG), *Corn Subsidies in the United States 1995–2005* and *Soybean Subsidies in the United States 1995–2005*, Farm Subsidy Database, at farm.ewg.org/farm, 12 June 2007; Organisation for Economic Co-operation and Development (OECD), *Agricultural Policies in OECD, Monitoring and Evaluation 2006* (Paris: 2006).

25. EWG, op. cit. note 24; EWG, *Livestock Subsidies in the United States 1995–2005*, Farm Subsidy Database, at farm.ewg.org/farm, 12 June 2007.

26. Ussif Rashid Sumaila and Daniel Pauly, *Catching More Bait: A Bottom-up Re-estimation of Global Fisheries Subsidies*, Fisheries Centre Research Report (Vancouver, BC: Sea Around Us Project, Fisheries Centre, University of British Columbia, 2006).

27. Daniel Pauly and Jay Maclean, *In a Perfect Ocean* (Washington, DC: Island Press, 2006), p. 68; OECD, op. cit. note 24.

28. Fleet fuel use from Cornelia Dean, "Fishing Industry's Fuel Efficiency Gets Worse as Ocean Stocks Get Thinner," *New York Times*, 20 December 2005; energy provided by fish from Peter H. Tyedmers et al., "Fueling Global Fishing Fleets,"

Ambio, December 2005, pp. 635–38.

29. Ussif Rashid Sumaila, "Running on Empty," from "10 Solutions to Save the Ocean," *Conservation*, July-September 2007; University of British Columbia, "Gov't Subsidies Make Ocean 'Stripmining' Economically Viable: UBC Researchers," press release (Vancouver, BC: 17 November 2006).

30. FAO, "Loss of Biodiversity in Livestock—Policy Options," at virtualcentre.org.

31. Pauly and Maclean, op. cit. note 27, p. 72.

32. Wayne Arnold, "Surviving Without Subsidies," *New York Times*, 2 August 2007.

33. Ibid.

34. Tundi Agardy, "A Separate Peace," from "10 Solutions to Save the Ocean," *Conservation*, July-September 2007.

35. James A. Bohnsack, Southeast Fisheries Science Center, University of Miami, FL, discussion with Brian Halweil, 15 May 2006; James A. Bohnsack, "Marine Reserves: They Enhance Fisheries, Reduce Conflicts, and Protect Resources," *Oceanus*, vol. 36, no. 3 (1993).

36. Andrew Balmford et al., "The Worldwide Costs of Marine Protected Areas," *Proceedings of the National Academy of Sciences*, 29 June 2004, pp. 9694–97; D. Zeller, "From *Mare Liberum* to *Mare Reservarum*: Canada's Opportunity for Global Leadership in Ocean Resource Governance," in A. Chircop and M. McConnell, eds., *Ocean Yearbook* (Chicago: University of Chicago Press, 2005), pp. 1–18.

37. Marine Stewardship Council (MSC), "History of MSC" and "About MSC," at www.msc.org, updated 14 September 2006.

38. MSC membership from www.msc.org and from Jessica Wenban-Smith, communications manager, MSC, London, e-mail to Brian Halweil, 12 January 2005.

39. Kate Moser, "Sustainable Seafood Casts a Wider Net," *Christian Science Monitor*, 3 April 2006; Henry Lovejoy, president and founder, EcoFish, Dover, NH, discussion with Brian Halweil, 21 August 2006; Tim O'Shea, chairman and CEO, CleanFish, San Francisco, discussion with Brian Halweil, 4 September 2006.

40. Lovejoy, op. cit. note 39.

41. Jerry Hirsch, "Animal Welfare Issue Boiling," *Los Angeles Times*, 2 July 2007.

42. "Buyers Navigate Sustainable Seafood," *SeaFood Business*, October 2004, pp. 22–23; Moser, op. cit. note 39; Wal-Mart Stores, Inc., "Wal-Mart Stores, Inc. Introduces New Label to Distinguish Sustainable Seafood," press release (Bentonville, AR: 31 August 2006); Carol Ness, "Wal-Mart to Push Sustainable Shrimp," *San Francisco Chronicle*, 23 May 2007.

43. Hirsch, op. cit. note 41; Whole Foods, "Farm Animal and Meat Quality Standard," at www.wholefoodsmarket.com, viewed August 2007.

44. Eat Wild, *Directory of Pasture-raised Farmers*, at www.eatwild.com, viewed August 2007.

45. Cape Code Commercial Hook Fishermen's Association, at www.ccchfa.org; Eric Hesse, Cape Bluefin and Cape Code Commercial Hook Fishermen's Association, discussion with Brian Halweil, 30 January 2006.

46. Doug Woodby et al., *Commercial Fisheries of Alaska*, Special Publication No. 05–09 (Anchorage, AK: Alaska Department of Fish and Game, June 2005); Nick Joy, managing director, Loch Duart Ltd., Scotland, presentation at Seafood Summit 2006: Sustainability and the Future of Seafood, Seattle, WA, 29–31 January 2006; shift in fishers' mindset from Rod Fujita, scientist, Environmental Defense, Oakland, CA, discussion with Brian Halweil, 24 July 2006; Hesse, op. cit. note 45.

47. Harry Aiking, Joop de Boer, and Johan Vereijken, eds., *Sustainable Protein Production and Consumption: Pigs or Peas?* (Berlin: Springer,

2006); C. T. Hoogland et al., "Spoiling the Appetite? Changing Patterns of Meat and Fish Consumption and the Role of Knowledge about Production—A Qualitative Investigation," presentation at the 6th Biennial Conference on Environmental Psychology, Bochum, 19–21 September 2005; Carolien T. Hoogland, Joop de Boer, and Jan J. Boersema, "Transparency of the Meat Chain in the Light of Food Culture and History," *Appetite*, August 2005, pp. 15–23.

48. Slow Food International, at www.slow food.com; Slow Fish, "The Return of Slow Fish: Sustainable Seafood Salone Back in Genoa," press release (Bra, Italy: Slow Food International, 2005); see also Slow Fish Web site, at www.slowfish.it.

49. Sarah Weiner, "Slow Food and Fishing," in *The Slow Food Companion* (Bra, Italy: 2005), p. 33.

50. Daniel Pauly, "Babette's Feast in Lima," *Sea Around Us Project Newsletter*, November/December 2006; Patricia Majluf, Center for Environmental Sustainability, Cayetano Heredia University, Lima, Peru, e-mail to Brian Halweil, 20 August 2007.

51. Pauly, op. cit. note 50; Majluf, op. cit. note 50.

52. Martin Hall, "Eat More Anchovies," from "10 Solutions to Save the Ocean," *Conservation*, July-September 2007.

53. Martin Fackler, "Waiter, There's Deer in My Sushi," *New York Times*, 25 June 2007.

54. Marion Burros, "The Hunt for a Truly Grand Turkey, One that Nature Built," *New York Times*, 21 November 2001; "Poultry," Heritage Foods USA, at www.heritagefoodsusa.com, viewed August 2007; Heritage Foods customer service representative, discussion with Danielle Nierenberg.

55. Patrick Mulvany and Susanne Gura, "Reclaiming Livestock Keepers' Rights," *Seedling*, January 2007.

56. Increased demand from Hank Pellissier,

"Shark Fin Soup: An Eco-Catastrophe?" *San Francisco Chronicle*, 20 January 2003; $200 a bowl, $700 per kilogram, and Ecuador from Juan Forero and Alyssa Lau, "Hidden Cost of Shark Fin Soup: Its Source May Vanish," *New York Times*, 5 January 2006; roughly 100 million shark deaths from IUCN–World Conservation Union, "Threatened Shark Species Receive International Focus," press release (Queensland, Australia: 6 March 2003).

57. Active Conservation Awareness Program, WildAid, at wildaid.org; Thai Airways International Public Company Limited, "THAI Cancels Shark Fin Soup Service on Board," press release (Bangkok: 2000); Maria Cheng, "More Than We Can Chew: Environment Groups Are Trying to Change Hong Kong's Destructive Eating Habits. Can They Pull It Off?" *Asiaweek*, 27 October 2000; The Walt Disney Company, *Enviroport 2005* (Burbank, CA: 2005); Doug Crets and Mimi Lau, "HKU Bans Shark Fin Dishes," *The Standard* (Hong Kong), 3 November 2005.

58. Ayrshire Farm Veal Flyer, at www.ayrshire farm.com, viewed August 2007.

Chapter 6.
Building a Low-Carbon Economy

1. "Summary for Policymakers," in Intergovernmental Panel on Climate Change (IPCC), *Climate Change 2007: The Physical Science Basis* (New York: Cambridge University Press, 2007), p. 2.

2. Figure 6–1 from the following: K. W. Thoning et al., *Atmospheric Carbon Dioxide Dry Air Mole Fractions from quasi-continuous measurements at Barrow, Alaska; Mauna Loa, Hawaii; American Samoa; and South Pole, 1973–2006* (Boulder, CO: Earth System Research Laboratory, National Oceanic and Atmospheric Administration, October 2007); C. D. Keeling and T. P. Whorf, "Atmospheric CO_2 Records from Sites in the SIO Air Sampling Network," and A. Neftel et al., "Historical CO2 Record from the Siple Station Ice Core," both in Carbon Dioxide Information Analysis Center (CDIAC), *Trends: A Compendium of Data on Global Change* (Oak Ridge, TN: Oak

Ridge National Laboratory, U.S. Department of Energy, 2007).

3. E. Jansen et al., "Palaeoclimate," in IPCC, op. cit. note 1, p. 449.

4. IPCC, op. cit. note 1, pp. 342, 350, 537, 543; M. Serreze et al., "Perspectives on the Arctic's Shrinking Sea-Ice Cover," *Science*, 16 March 2007, pp. 1533–36.

5. Alan Greenspan, *The Age of Turbulence: Adventures in a New World* (New York: Penguin Press, 2007); Nicholas Stern, *The Economics of Climate Change: The Stern Review* (Cambridge, U.K.: Cambridge University Press, 2007).

6. "Summary for Policymakers," op. cit. note 1; International Energy Agency, *Key World Energy Statistics*, (Paris: 2007), p. 6; recent carbon emissions by Worldwatch based on G. Marland et al., "Global, Regional, and National Fossil Fuel CO_2 Emissions," in CDIAC, op. cit. note 2; BP, *Statistical Review of World Energy* (London: 2007).

7. J. Hansen et al., "Dangerous Human-made Interference with Climate: A GISS ModelE Study," *Atmospheric Chemistry and Physics*, vol. 7, no. 9 (2007), pp. 2287–312; 0.8 degrees Celsius is the midpoint of estimates of warming, as reported in IPCC, op. cit. note 1, p. 5.

8. T. Barker et al., "Technical Summary," in IPCC, *Climate Change 2007: Mitigation* (New York: Cambridge University Press, 2007), p. 39.

9. In Table 6–1, business-as-usual case described in International Energy Agency, *Energy Technology Perspectives—Scenarios and Strategies to 2050* (Paris: 2006), pp. 44–46, 451–52, and "stabilization" scenario based on Category II emission mitigation scenarios described in Barker et al., op. cit. note 8, on G. A. Meehl, "Global Climate Projections," in IPCC, op. cit. note 1, and on annual energy growth of 0.7 percent for 2006 to 2030, described in F. Bressand et al., *Curbing Global Energy Demand Growth: The Energy Productivity Opportunity* (McKinsey Global Institute, May 2007), p. 13, declining in proportion to gross domestic product growth to 0.6 percent for 2030 to 2050; U.S. Department of Energy, *International Energy Outlook 2007* (Washington, DC: 2007), pp. 5, 73; Barker et al., op. cit. note 8, pp. 39, 42.

10. Recent and historical carbon emissions derived from BP, op. cit. note 6, and from Marland et al., op. cit. note 6; Table 6–2 calculated by Worldwatch with data from BP, op. cit. note 6, from Marland et al., op. cit. note 6, from Population Reference Bureau, *2006 World Population Data Sheet* (Washington, DC: 2006), from U.S. Bureau of the Census, "Population, Population Change and Estimated Components of Population Change: April 1, 2000 to July 1, 2006," Washington, DC, December 2006, and from International Monetary Fund (IMF), *World Economic Outlook* (Washington, DC: April 2007); energy demand growth estimated in Bressand et al., op. cit. note 9, p. 11.

11. "Growth and Responsibility in the World Economy," G–8 Summit Declaration, Heiligendamm, Germany, June 2007, p. 15; approximate share of emissions by source provided in Barker et al., op. cit. note 8, p. 28.

12. Worldwatch Institute estimate of required industrial-country emissions reductions.

13. S. Pacala and R. Socolow, "Stabilization Wedges: Solving the Climate Problem for the Next 50 Years with Current Technologies," *Science*, 13 August 2004, pp. 968–72.

14. National Petroleum Council, *Hard Truths: Facing the Hard Truths about Energy* (Washington DC: July 2007), pp. 127, 135.

15. IPCC Working Group III, *IPCC Special Report on Carbon Dioxide Capture and Storage* (New York: Cambridge University Press, 2005), pp. 201–04; MIT Energy Initiative, *The Future of Coal: Options for a Carbon-Constrained World* (Cambridge, MA: Massachusetts Institute of Technology, 2007), p. 52.

16. MIT Energy Initiative, op. cit. note 15, pp.

xi–xii; International Energy Agency, op. cit. note 9, p. 24.

17. Remarks by U.S. Vice President Cheney at the Annual Meeting of the Associated Press, Toronto, Canada, April 2001; World Energy Council, *Energy and Climate Change Executive Summary* (London: May 2007), p. 5.

18. U.S. Department of Energy, *Monthly Energy Review* (Washington, DC: September 2007), p. 16; energy productivity based on data from IMF, op. cit. note 10; International Energy Agency, op. cit. note 9, pp. 48–57; U.S. Department of Energy, *International Energy Annual 2004* (Washington, DC.: 2006), Table E.1; BP, op. cit. note 6; estimate of useful energy from G. Kaiper, *US Energy Flow Trends—2002* (Livermore, CA: Lawrence Livermore National Laboratory, 2004).

19. Bressand et al., op. cit. note 9, p. 9.

20. B. Griffith et al., *Assessment of the Technical Potential for Achieving Zero-Energy Commercial Buildings* (Golden, CO: National Renewable Energy Laboratory, 2006); Bressand et al., op. cit. note 9, p. 13.

21. S. Mufson, "U.S. Nuclear Power Revival Grows," *Washington Post,* September 2007. Box 6–1 from the following: Worldwatch Institute nuclear energy database compiled from statistics from the International Atomic Energy Agency, press reports, and Web sites; "Nuclear Dawn," *The Economist,* 6 September 2007; "Atomic Renaissance," *The Economist,* 6 September 2007; Satu Hassi, European Parliament member, e-mail to Christopher Flavin, 19 February 2007; The Keystone Center, *Nuclear Power Joint Fact-Finding* (Keystone, CO: 2007), p. 30; MIT Energy Initiative, *The Future of Nuclear Power* (Cambridge, MA: Massachusetts Institute of Technology, 2003), p. 25.

22. Figure 6–2 based on data from United Nations Development Programme, *World Energy Assessment: Energy and the Challenge of Sustainability* (New York: 2000), and from T. B. Johansson et al., "The Potentials of Renewable Energy; Thematic Background Paper," International Conference for Renewable Energies, Bonn, Germany, January 2004. Table 6–3 from Mark S. Mehos and Brandon Owens, *An Analysis of Siting Opportunities for Concentrating Solar Power Plants in the Southwestern United States* (Golden, CO, and Boulder, CO: National Renewable Energy Laboratory and Platts Research and Consulting, 2004); International Energy Agency, Photovoltaic Power Systems Programme, *Potential for Building Integrated Photovoltaics, 2002 Summary* (Paris: 2002), p. 8; Richard Perez, Atmospheric Sciences Research Center, State University of New York at Albany, e-mail to Janet Sawin, Worldwatch Institute, 11 July 2006; Battelle/Pacific Northwest Laboratory, *An Assessment of Available Windy Land Area and Wind Energy Potential in the Contiguous United States* (Richland, WA: August 1991), based on 2004 U.S. end-use demand from U.S. Energy Information Administration, "Annual Electric Power Industry Report," Table 7.2, in *Electric Power Annual 2005* (Washington, DC: 2005); Robert Perlack et al., *Biomass as Feedstock for a Bioenergy and Bioproducts Industry: The Technical Feasibility of a Billion Ton Annual Supply* (Oak Ridge, TN: Oak Ridge National Laboratory, April 2005); Massachusetts Institute of Technology, *The Future of Geothermal Energy* (Cambridge, MA: 2006), p. 1-1; John D. Isaacs and Walter R. Schmitt, "Ocean Energy: Forms and Prospects," *Science,* 18 January 1980, pp. 265–73.

23. B. Parsons et al., *Grid Impacts of Wind Power Variability: Recent Assessments from a Variety of Utilities in the United States* (Golden, CO: National Renewable Energy Laboratory, 2006); P. B. Eriksen et al., "System Operation with High Wind Penetration," *IEEE Power & Energy Magazine,* November/December 2005, pp. 65–74; C. Archer and M. Jacobson, "Supplying Baseload Power and Reducing Transmission Requirements by Interconnecting Wind Farms," Stanford University, February 2007.

24. K. Yeager, "Facilitating the Transition to a Smart Electric Grid," testimony to the Subcommittee on Energy and Air Quality, Committee on Energy and Commerce, Washington, DC, May 2007.

25. D. Marcus, "Moving Wind to the Main-

stream: Leveraging Compressed Air Energy Storage," *Renewable Energy Access,* October 2007; TXU, "TXU Halts Efforts to Obtain Permits for Eight Coal-Fueled Units," press release (Dallas, TX: 1 March 2007); TXU, "Luminant and Shell Join Forces to Develop a Texas-Sized Wind Farm," press release (Dallas, TX: 27 July 2007).

26. Willett Kempton and Jasna Tomiç "Vehicle-to-Grid Power Implementation: From Stabilizing the Grid to Supporting Large-scale Renewable Energy," *Journal of Power Sources,* 1 June 2005, pp. 280–94.

27. U.S. Department of Energy, "Brazil," in *Country Analysis Briefs* (Washington, DC: September 2007); Martin Bensmann, "Green Gas on Tap," *New Energy,* April 2007, pp. 66–69; International Energy Agency, *IEA—PVPS Annual Report 2005* (Paris: 2005), p. 66.

28. Environmental and Energy Study Institute (EESI), "FY 08 Appropriations for Renewable Energy and Energy Efficiency: Full House and Senate Committee Vote for Increase in EE/RE Funding," *Issue Update* (Washington, DC, 18 July 2007).

29. Worldwatch Institute calculation of 2004–06 renewable energy growth rates based on data from American Wind Energy Association, "Wind Power Capacity in U.S Increased 27% in 2006 and Is Expected to Grow an Additional 26% in 2007," press release (Washington DC: 23 January 2007), from Birger Madsen, BTM Consult, e-mail to Janet Sawin, 8 March 2007, from European Wind Energy Association, "European Market for Wind Turbines Grows 23% in 2006," press release, (Brussels: 1 February 2007), from Christoph Berg, F.O. Licht, e-mails to Rodrigo G. Pinto, Worldwatch Institute, 20–22 March 2007, from Global Wind Energy Council, "Global Wind Energy Markets Continue to Boom—2006 Another Record Year," press release (Brussels: 2 February 2007), and from Prometheus Institute, *PV News,* April 2007, p. 8. Figure 6–3 from REN21, *Renewables Global Status Report 2007* (draft) (Paris: May 2007).

30. New Energy Finance, *Global Trends in Sustainable Energy Investment* (London: 2007); Vestas WindSystems, AS, *Vestas Annual Report 2006* (Randers, Denmark: 2007); EESI, op. cit. note 28.

31. Sasha Rentzing, "Sun Aplenty," *New Energy,* June 2007.

32. Boston Consulting Group, *The Experience Curve Reviewed* (Boston: reprint, 1972).

33. European Climate Exchange, "Historical Data—ECX CFI Futures Contract," at www.europeanclimateexchange.com, viewed 11 October 2007; photovoltaic cost forecast based on Travis Bradford, Prometheus Institute, e-mails to Janet Sawin, 5–8 April 2007.

34. Equivalent carbon price calculated using crude oil price for September 2007 and September 2002 from U.S. Department of Energy, "World Crude Oil Prices," Washington DC, updated 11 October 2007, and approximate crude oil carbon content from U.S. Department of Energy, *Emissions of Greenhouse Gases in the United States 1998* (Washington DC: November 1999), Table B4; Senator Jeff Bingaman, "Low Carbon Economy Act of 2007," proposed legislation, Washington DC, July 2007.

35. Douglass C. North, *Institutions, Institutional Change, and Economic Performance* (Cambridge, U.K.: Cambridge University Press, 1990).

36. Feng An et al., *Passenger Vehicle Greenhouse Gas and Fuel Economy Standards: A Global Update* (Washington, DC: International Council for Clean Transportation, 2007), pp.18, 24, 32; Assembly Member L. Levine, Assembly Bill 722, Sacramento, California, introduced February 2007; "World First! Australia Slashes Greenhouse Gases from Inefficient Lighting," press release (Canberra, Australia: Department of the Environment and Water Resources, 20 February 2007). "Chinese Agree to Nix Incandescents," Greenbiz.com, 3 October 2007.

37. North Carolina Solar Center and the Interstate Renewable Energy Council, Database of State Incentives for Renewables & Efficiency, at www.dsireusa.org, 14 October 2007; Environmental Technologies Action Plan, *Spain's New Building Energy Standards Place the Country Among the Leaders in Solar Energy in Europe* (Brussels: European Commission, September 2006); "First Heating Law for Renewable Energy in Germany," *Energy Server* (Newsletter for Renewable Energy and Energy Efficiency), 2 August 2007.

38. Figure 6–4 is a Worldwatch calculation based on California Energy Commission, *California Electricity Consumption by Sector* (Sacramento: California Energy Commission, 2006), on U.S. Department of Energy, *State Energy Consumption, Price, and Expenditure Estimates (SEDS)* (Washington, DC: 2007), on U.S. Department of Energy, *Annual Energy Review 2006* (Washington, DC: 2007), on A. Gough, California Energy Commission, e-mail to James Russell, Worldwatch Institute, 31 August 2007, and on Census Bureau estimates.

39. John S. Hoffman, "Limiting Global Warming: Making it Easy by Creating Social Infrastructure that Supports Demand Reductions Through More-Effective Markets," unpublished paper, 2007.

40. J. Sawin, "The Role of Government in the Development and Diffusion of Renewable Energy Technologies: Wind Power in the United States, California, Denmark and Germany, 1970–2000," Doctoral Thesis, The Fletcher School of Law and Diplomacy, September 2001.

41. M. Ragwitz and C. Huber, *Feed-In Systems in Germany and Spain and a Comparison* (Karlsruhe, Germany: Fraunhofer Institut fr Systemtechnik und Innovationsforschung, 2005); ranking based on Bradford, op. cit. note 33.

42. Stern, op. cit. note 5, pp. 233–34.

43. E. Shuster, *Tracking New Coal-Fired Power Plants* (Washington, DC: National Energy Technology Laboratory, U.S. Department of Energy, October 2007).

44. "Germany to Close its Coal Mines," *Spiegel Online*, 30 January 2007; United States Climate Action Partnership, "U.S. Climate Action Partnership Announces its Fourth Membership Expansion," press release (Washington, DC: September 2007); European Council, "The Spring European Council: Integrated Climate Protection and Energy Policy, Progress on the Lisbon Strategy," press release (Brussels: 12 March 2007); National Development and Reform Commission, *China's National Climate Change Programme* (Beijing: June 2007); Pew Center on Global Climate Change, "Climate Change Initiatives and Programs in the States," press release (Arlington, VA: 11 September 2006); "Statement of H. E. Luiz Incio Lula da Silva, President of the Federative Republic of Brazil, at the general debate of the 62nd Session of the United Nations General," press release (New York: Ministry of External Relations, 25 September 2007).

Chapter 7. Improving Carbon Markets

1. The Kyoto Protocol covers six greenhouse gases that affect the climate with differing strengths: carbon dioxide, methane, nitrous oxide, hydrofluorocarbons, perfluorocarbons, and sulfur hexafluoride.

2. Carbon to become the world's biggest commodity market from James Kanter, "In London's Financial World, Carbon Trading Is the New Big Thing," *New York Times*, 6 July 2007.

3. U.N. Framework Convention on Climate Change (UNFCCC), "Kyoto Protocol," at unfccc.int; UNFCCC, "Status of Ratification," at unfccc.int, viewed 1 October 2007.

4. Emissions scenarios linked with warming projections from "Summary for Policymakers," in Intergovernmental Panel on Climate Change, *Climate Change 2007: Mitigation of Climate Change* (New York: Cambridge University Press, 2007), p. 15.

5. Chad Damro and Pilar Luaces-Méndez, "The Kyoto Protocol's Emissions Trading System: An EU-US Environmental Flip-Flop," Working Paper No. 5 (Pittsburgh, PA: University of Pittsburgh European Union Center and Center for West European Studies, August 2003).

6. UNFCCC, at unfccc.int, viewed 1 October 2007.

7. UNFCCC Secretariat, "Kyoto Protocol Parties Move Closer to Trading Emission Allowances," press release (Vienna: 30 August 2007).

8. Table 7–1 from World Bank, *State and Trends of the Carbon Market 2007* (Washington, DC: May 2007), p. 3, and from Katherine Hamilton et al., *State of the Voluntary Carbon Markets 2007: Picking Up Steam* (San Francisco: Ecosystem Marketplace, July 2007), p. 5.

9. World Bank, op. cit. note 8, p. 3.

10. European Communities, "EU Action Against Climate Change," brochure, September 2005; European Union reduction target from UNFCCC, cited in International Financial Services London (IFSL) Research, *Carbon Markets & Emissions Trading* (London: June 2007), p. 1.

11. World Bank, op. cit. note 8, p. 3; IFSL Research, op. cit. note 10, p. 3; European Communities, op. cit. note 10, pp. 5–6; numbers and registry from European Union, "ETS: Community Independent Transaction Log," at ec.europa.eu, viewed 9 August 2007.

12. European Communities, op. cit. note 10, p. 7; European Commission, "Climate Change: Commission Proposes Bringing Air Transport into EU Emissions Trading Scheme," press release (Brussels: 20 December 2006).

13. Ricardo Bayon, Amanda Hawn, and Katherine Hamilton, *Voluntary Carbon Markets* (London: Earthscan, 2007), pp. 9–10; Hamilton et al., op. cit. note 8, p. 14; World Bank, op. cit. note 8, pp. 3, 17.

14. Chicago Climate Exchange, "Auditing and Compliance," at www.chicagoclimatex.com, viewed 20 July 2007; Chicago Climate Exchange, "Chicago Climate Exchange Surpasses 2006 Volume in First Half of 2007," press release (Chicago: 2 July 2007).

15. Chicago Climate Exchange, "Emissions Reduction Commitment," at www.chicagoclimatex.com, viewed 20 July 2007. All CCX members must commit to reduce greenhouse gas emissions to 6 percent below their baseline—the average of their annual emissions between 1998 and 2001; Chicago Climate Exchange, "Membership Categories," at www.chicagoclimatex.com, viewed 1 October 2007.

16. United States Climate Action Partnership (USCAP), "Major Businesses and Environmental Leaders United to Call for Swift Action on Global Climate Change," press release (Washington, DC: 22 January 2007); USCAP, "About Our Members," at www.us-cap.org, viewed 19 September 2007; Alex Dewar et al., Natural Resources Defense Council (NRDC), *Cap and Trade Policy in the United States* (draft) (Washington, DC: August 2007), p. 3.

17. Steven Mufson, "Europe's Problems Color U.S. Plans to Curb Carbon Gases," *Washington Post*, 9 April 2007; "Australia PM Pledges Climate Plan," *BBC News*, 3 June 2007. Box 7–1 based on the following: Regional Greenhouse Gas Initiative, "About RGGI," viewed 20 July 2007, at www.rggi.org; 10 states from Hannah Fairfield, "When Carbon is Currency," *New York Times*, 6 May 2007; Dewar et al., op. cit. note 16, pp. 4, 6; Felicity Barringer, "Officials Reach California Deal to Cut Emissions," *New York Times*, 31 August 2006; Point Carbon, "Carbon Market North America," 1 August 2007, at www.pointcarbon.com; Ricardo Bayon, "A Green Thumb for the Invisible Hand," *Milken Institute Review*, February 2007, p. 24; Ontario Ministry of the Environment, "Ontario to Explore Joining Forces with U.S. States on Climate Change Initiative, March 30," press release (Ottawa: 30 March 2007).

18. Dewar et al., op. cit. note 16, p. 12. Figure 7–1 from European Climate Exchange, at euro peanclimateexchange.com, viewed 11 October 2007, converted to dollars using historical exhange rates at oanda.com.

19. IFSL Research, op. cit. note 10, p. 3; Dewar et al., op. cit. note 16, pp. 11–12; British and German windfall profits from Jörg Haas and Peter

Barnes, "Who Gets the Windfall from Carbon Trading?" unpublished, at www.boell.de/down loads/oeko/EU_Sky_trust_final.pdf, p. 1. Dollar amount converted from euros using exchange rate on 1 October 2007. Box 7–2 from Cameron Hepburn et al., "Auctioning of EU ETS Phase II Allowances: How and Why?" *Climate Policy*, no. 6 (2006), pp. 137–60; Lehman Brothers, *The Business of Climate Change II* (London: September 2007), pp. 50–54.

20. Haas and Barnes, op. cit. note 19, p. 3.

21. World Wide Fund for Nature–UK (WWF–UK), *Emission Impossible: Access to JI/CDM Credits in Phase II of the EU Emissions Trading Scheme* (Godalming, Surrey, U.K.: June 2007), pp. 3–4; Philippe Ambrosi, World Bank, e-mail to Zoë Chafe, 3 October 2007.

22. IFSL Research, op. cit. note 10, p. 3; December 2008 carbon price from Point Carbon, updated 28 September 2007.

23. Dewar et al., op. cit. note 16, p. 11; 100 percent auctions from Melanie Nakagawa, NRDC, and Tomas Wyns, Climate Action Network Europe, e-mail to Zoë Chafe.

24. Fairfield, op. cit. note 17; Point Carbon, "Maine Governor Signs RGGI Legislation," *Carbon Market North America* (Washington, DC: 20 June 2007), p. 2; Dewar et al., op. cit. note 16, p. 3; Haas and Barnes, op. cit. note 19, p. 1; Peter Barnes, *Who Owns the Sky?* (Washington, DC: Island Press, 2001); "The Lieberman-Warner America's Climate Security Act of 2007: Annotated Table of Contents," 2 August 2007.

25. UNFCCC Secretariat, "Annual Green Investment Flow of Some 100 Billion Dollars Possible as Part of Fight against Global Warming," press release (Vienna: 19 September 2006); development aid from Organisation for Economic Co-operation and Development (OECD), at www.oecd.org.

26. Katia Karousakis, *Joint Implementation Current Issues and Emerging Challenges* (Paris: OECD, October 2006), pp. 7–8; World Bank, op. cit. note 8, pp. 3–4.

27. CDM statistics and Figure 7–2 from Jørgen Fenhann, "CDM Pipeline," U.N. Environment Programme (UNEP) Risø Centre, database, updated 1 October 2007.

28. Ibid.

29. IFSL Research, op. cit. note 10, p. 5; "The Nairobi Framework—Catalyzing the CDM in Africa," at cdm.unfccc.int/Nairobi_Frame work/index.html, viewed 3 August 2007.

30. IFSL Research, op. cit. note 10, p. 5; 50 percent of credits is a Worldwatch calculation based on Fenhann, op. cit. note 27.

31. Perverse incentive problem from "Kudos for a Working Eco-treaty," *Christian Science Monitor*, 17 September 2007; Michael Wara, "Is the Global Carbon Market Working?" *Nature*, February 2007, pp. 595–96. Euros converted to dollars using exchange rate of 1 October 2007.

32. IFSL Research, op. cit. note 10, p. 5. Worldwatch analysis of HFC-23 project trends based on Fenhann, op. cit. note 27. Figure 7–3 from ibid. Table 7–2 includes only registered CDM project activities and is based on cdm.unfccc.int/Projects and on ji.unfccc.int/JI_Projects unless otherwise noted: Pearl River Basin from *Unasylva*, "World of Forestry," vol 57, no 225 (2006); BRT Bogotá from "TransMilenio Integrates Kyoto Protocol Clean Development Mechanism," *Transport Innovator*, September-October 2006; Lawley fuel switch from "Statkraft Signs CDM Deal in South Africa," Statkraft, press release (Oslo: 21 April 2005); Osorio from Elecnor, "Elecnor Group Records Consolidated Net Profits of 32.8 Million Euros for the First 9 Months of 2006," press release (Madrid: 13 November 2006); Donetsk District Heating from Foundation Joint Implementation Network, "District Heating System Rehabilitation in Donetsk, Ukraine," at www.jiqweb.org/rehabilitation.htm; Podilsky Cement from TÜV SÜV Group, "First Joint Implementation Project Worldwide Registered," press release (Ukraine: Kamyanets-Podilsky, May 2007).

33. UNFCCC, "Land Use, Land Use Change,

and Forestry: Background," at unfccc.int; UNFCCC, "LULUCF—Developments at Past COP and SB Sessions: Marrakesh Accords and COP 7," at unfccc.int.

34. U.S. Environmental Protection Agency, *Greenhouse Gas Mitigation Potential in US Forestry and Agriculture* (Washington, DC: November 2005); Robert T. Watson et al., *Land Use, Land Use Change, and Forestry: Special Report of the Intergovernmental Panel on Climate Change* (Cambridge, U.K.: Cambridge University Press, 2000); World Bank, op. cit. note 8, p. 30; Biocarbon Fund and Forest Carbon Partnership Facility from World Bank, "Carbon Finance at the World Bank: List of Funds," at www.carbonfinance.org.

35. Climate, Community, and Biodiversity Alliance, at www.climate-standards.org.

36. World Bank, op. cit. note 8, pp. 24, 29.

37. Ibid., p. 4.

38. Michael Wara, *Measuring the Clean Development Mechanism's Performance and Potential*, Working Paper No. 56 (Stanford, CA: Program on Energy and Sustainable Development, Stanford University, July 2006); Mark Trexler, EcoSecurities Global Consulting Services, e-mail to Zoë Chafe, August 2007.

39. Bayon, Hawn, and Hamilton, op. cit. note 13, p. 12; small projects from UNFCCC, "Way Cleared for Kyoto Mechanisms to Boost Green Investment in Developing Countries–CDM Executive Board," press release (Vienna: 27 June 2007), and from Sebastian Mallaby, "Carbon Policy That Works," *Washington Post*, 23 July 2007; bundling from "Greenhouse Gas Emission Reduction and Industry," World Bank, powerpoint, February 2007.

40. WWF–UK, op. cit. note 21, pp. 7–9; "U.N. Rejects Big Kyoto Project in Equatorial Guinea," *Reuters*, 31 July 2007.

41. IFSL Research, op. cit. note 10; Hamilton et al., op. cit. note 8, p. 5.

42. Adam Stein, "Terrapass Launches Partnership with Expedia to Bring Carbon Balanced Flight to All Travelers," 28 August 2006, at www.terrapass.com; Terrapass, "Projects," at www.terrapass.com, viewed 2 August 2007; "Carbon Offsetting," Jiva Dental, at www.jivadental.co.uk, viewed 2 August 2007. Box 7–3 based on the following: "Carbon Neutral: Oxford Word of the Year," Oxford University Press, at blog.oup.com/2006/11/carbon_neutral_; Kevin Smith, *The Carbon Neutral Myth* (Amsterdam: Transnational Institute, February 2007); GHG Protocol Initiative, at www.ghgprotocol.org.

43. Michael Gillenwater, *Redefining RECs: Untangling Attributes and Offsets*, Discussion Paper (Princeton, NJ: Woodrow Wilson School of Public and International Affairs, Princeton University, August 2007).

44. Smith, op. cit. note 42.

45. Ibid.

46. See Clean Air–Cool Planet, *A Consumers' Guide to Retail Carbon Offset Providers* (Portsmouth, NH: 2006).

47. Dan Milmo, "EasyJet Slams 'Snake Oil Sellers' in Offset Market and Goes it Alone," *Guardian* (London), 30 April 2007.

48. Hamilton et al., op. cit. note 8, p. 39; Trexler, op. cit. note 38.

49. Hamilton et al., op. cit. note 8, p. 43.

50. Ibid., pp. 40–41; 40 organizations from "Gold Standard: Rationale" and "Gold Standard: How Does it Work?" at www.cdmgoldstandard.org. viewed 3 August 2007.

51. World Business Council on Sustainable Development, "Completion of the Voluntary Carbon Standard Framework," press release (Geneva: 31 July 2007).

52. "UN Climate Debate Tries to Kick-Start New Treaty," *Reuters*, 6 August 2007; Nicholas Stern, *The Economics of Climate Change: The Stern*

Review (Cambridge, U.K.: Cambridge University Press, 2007), p. 325.

53. UNFCCC Secretariat, "Vienna UN Conference Shows Consensus on Key Building Blocks for Effective International Response to Climate Change," press release (Vienna: 31 August 2007); U.S. carbon dioxide emissions from fossil fuel burning is a Worldwatch estimate based on British Petroleum, *BP Statistical Review of World Energy* (London: 2007), and on G. Marland et al., "Global, Regional, and National Fossil Fuel CO_2 Emissions," *Trends: A Compendium of Data on Global Change* (Oak Ridge, TN: Oak Ridge National Laboratory, 2007); "UN Climate Debate Tries to Kick-Start New Treaty," op. cit. note 52.

54. Environmental Defense, *CDM and the Post-2012 Framework*, Discussion Paper (New York: August 2007), p. 2; Joanna Lewis and Elliot Diringer, *Policy-based Commitments in a Post-2012 Climate Framework*, Working Paper (Arlington, VA: Pew Center on Global Climate Change, May 2007), pp. 13–14; UNFCCC, op. cit. note 39; Trexler, op. cit. note 38.

55. WWF-UK, op. cit. note 21, p. 10; Environmental Defense, op. cit. note 54, p. 3; Stern, op. cit. note 52, p. ix; Paul Kelly, "Carbon the Currency of a New World Order," *The Australian*, 21 March 2007.

56. Daniel Bodansky, *International Sectoral Agreements in a Post-2012 Climate Framework*, Working Paper (Arlington, VA: Pew Center on Global Climate Change, May 2007).

57. Bayon, op. cit. note 17.

Chapter 8.
Water in a Sustainable Economy

1. L. Emerton et al., *The Present Economic Value of Nakivubo Urban Wetland, Uganda* (Nairobi: Eastern Africa Regional Office, IUCN–The World Conservation Union, September 1999); J. Turpie et al., *Economic Valuation of the Zambezi Basin Wetlands* (Harare: Regional Office for Southern Africa, IUCN, 1999); Randall A. Kramer et al., "Ecological and Economic Analysis of Watershed Protection in Eastern Madagascar," *Journal of Environmental Management*, March 1997, pp. 277–95.

2. World Water Assessment Programme, *The United Nations World Water Development Report 2: Water, A Shared Responsibility* (Paris: UNESCO, 2006); forecast from International Water Management Institute (IWMI), *World Water Supply and Demand 1995–2025* (Colombo, Sri Lanka: 2000); current status and river systems from David Molden, ed., *Water for Food, Water for Life: A Comprehensive Assessment of Water Management in Agriculture* (London and Colombo, Sri Lanka: Earthscan and IWMI, 2007), chapter 2 and p. 551; implications of scarcity in the value of water from W. M. Hanemann, "The Economic Conception of Water" in Peter P. Rogers, M. Ramon Llamas, and Luis Martinez-Cortina, eds., *Water Crisis: Myth or Reality* (London; New York: Taylor & Francis, 2006), pp. 61–92.

3. Figure 8–1 from Molden, op. cit. note 2, p. 11.

4. Table 8–1 from World Resources Institute (WRI), *EarthTrends: Environmental Information*, online database, 2007; reliance of the poor on agriculture from Molden, op. cit. note 2, p. 551.

5. With regard to beef production, it is important to note that in some contexts livestock can be fed crop residues or graze in rangeland unsuitable for more profitable uses, making them efficient users of otherwise uneconomic water. See Molden, op. cit. note 2, p. 487; comprehensive assessment results in Molden, op. cit. note 2.

6. See Molden, op. cit. note 2, Chapter 2.

7. Sector water use data from WRI, op. cit. note 4.

8. Water access data from U.N. Development Programme (UNDP), *Human Development Report 2006* (New York: Palgrave Macmillan, 2006), p. 7; Annette Prüss-Üstün et al., "Unsafe Water, Sanitation and Hygiene," in M. Ezzati et al., eds., *Comparative Quantification of Health*

Risks: Global and Regional Burden of Disease Attributable to Selected Major Risk Factors (Geneva: World Health Organization, 2004), pp. 1321–51.

9. Millennium Development Goals, at www.un .org/millenniumgoals; costs of meeting goals from James Winpenny, *Financing Water for All: Report of the World Panel on Financing Water Infrastructure*, Third World Water Forum, World Water Council and Global Water Partnership, 2003; U.N. Population Division, *World Population Prospects: The 2004 Revision* (New York: 2006); United Nations, *MDG Goals Report 2006* (New York: Department of Economic and Social Affairs, 2006); cost of infrastructure maintenance from the World Business Council on Sustainable Development, *Water Facts and Trends*, at www.wbcsd.org, August 2005.

10. Millennium Ecosystem Assessment (MA), *Ecosystems and Human Well-being: Synthesis* (Washington, DC: Island Press, 2005); Megan Dyson, Ger Bergkamp, and John Scanlon, eds., *FLOW— The Essentials of Environmental Flows* (Gland, Switzerland: IUCN, 2003).

11. Technical Advisory Committee, *Integrated Water Resources Management*, TAC Paper 4 (Stockholm: Global Water Partnership, 2000).

12. Meredith A. Giordano and Aaron T. Wolf, "The World's Freshwater Agreements: Historical Developments and Future Opportunities," in U.N. Environment Programme, *International Freshwater Treaties Atlas* (Nairobi: 2002); Claudia W. Sadoff and David Grey, "Beyond the River: the Benefits of Cooperation on International Rivers," *Water Policy*, vol. 4, no. 5 (2002), pp. 389–403; Jerome Delli Priscoli and Aaron T. Wolf, *Managing and Transforming Water Conflicts* (New York: Cambridge University Press and UNESCO, forthcoming).

13. J. A. Allan, "Virtual Water—The Water, Food, and Trade Nexus: Useful Concept or Misleading Metaphor?" *Water International*, March 2003, pp. 4–11.

14. UNDP, op. cit. note 8.

15. Important examples of work on reforming economic decisionmaking include David W. Pearce, *Blueprint 3: Measuring Sustainable Development* (London: Earthscan, 1993); Herman Daly and J. B. Cobb, *For the Common Good* (Boston: Beacon Press, 1989); John Dixon and M. M. Hufschmidt, eds. *Economic Valuation Techniques for the Environment* (Baltimore, MD: Johns Hopkins University Press, 1986); and Kirk Hamilton, *Where Is the Wealth of Nations?* (Washington, DC: World Bank 2006). Groundwater abstractions from Molden, op. cit. note 2, p. 395.

16. Box 8–2 from Mark Smith, Dolf de Groot, and Ger Bergkamp, eds., *PAY—Establishing Payments for Watershed Services* (Gland, Switzerland: IUCN, 2006).

17. Box 8–3 from Dublin Statement on Water and Sustainable Development, adopted at the International Conference on Water and the Environment: Development Issues for the 21st Century, Dublin, Ireland, 26–31 January 1992.

18. To follow the rapid innovations in industry, see Water Environment Federation Web site, at www.wef.org; potential in rainfed agriculture from Molden, op. cit. note 2, pp. 315–17.

19. See PUB Singapore, at www.pub.gov.sg/ home/index.aspx.

20. See Lucy Emerton and Elroy Bos, *VALUE— Counting Ecosystems as Water Infrastructure* (Gland, Switzerland: IUCN, 2004); Lucy Emerton, *Counting Coastal Ecosystems as an Economic Part of Development Infrastructure* (Colombo, Sri Lanka: IUCN, 2006); Jenny Jarvie, "Coastal Buyout Talk Roils Lives in Mississippi Striving for a Comeback," *Los Angeles Times*, 2 October 2007.

21. For current developments see the Newsletter of the Global Environmental Flows Network, at www.iucn.org/themes/wani.

22. World Commission on Dams, *Dams and Development: A New Framework for Decision-Making* (London: Earthscan, 2000); Robin Gregory, Tim McDaniels, and Daryl Fields, "Decision Aiding, Not Dispute Resolution: Creating Insights

Through Structured Environmental Decisions," *Journal of Policy Analysis and Management*, summer 2001, pp. 415–32.

23. Sustainable Agriculture Initiative, at www .saiplatform.org.

24. For better-targeted pricing schemes, see, for example, John J. Boland and Dale Whittington, "The Political Economy of Water Tariff Design in Developing Countries: Increasing Block Tariffs Versus Uniform Price with Rebate," in Ariel Dinar, ed., *The Political Economy of Water Pricing Reforms* (New York: Oxford University Press, 2000), pp. 215–35. For Box 8–4, for a thorough exposition on water subsidies see Kristin Komives et al., *Water, Electricity, and the Poor: Who Benefits from Utility Subsidies?* (Washington, DC: World Bank, 2005).

25. United Nations, *Handbook of National Accounting: Integrated Environmental and Economic Accounting 2003* (New York: 2003); U.N. Statistics Division, "Handbook on Integrated Environmental and Economic Accounting for Water Resources," draft (New York: United Nations, May 2006).

26. See Hamilton, op. cit. note 15, and Kirk Hamilton and Michael Clemens, "Genuine Savings Rates in Developing Countries," *World Bank Economic Review*, vol. 13, no. 2 (1999), pp. 333–56.

27. A. K. Chapagain, A. Y. Hoekstra, and H. H. G. Savenije, "Water Saving Through International Trade of Agricultural Products," *Hydrology and Earth System Sciences*, vol. 10, no. 3 (2006), pp. 455–68.

28. Table 8–2 and payment for environmental services categorization from Smith, de Groot, and Bergkamp, op. cit. note 16.

29. Molden, op. cit. note 2; MA, op. cit. note 10; Organisation for Economic Co-operation and Development, *Water Management: Performance and Challenges in OECD Countries* (Paris: 1998).

30. Molden, op. cit. note 2; MA, op. cit. note 10.

Chapter 9.
Banking on Biodiversity

1. Box 9–1 from the following: data and Figure from Millennium Ecosystem Assessment, *Ecosystems and Human Well-being: Biodiversity Synthesis* (Washington, DC: World Resources Institute, 2005), pp. 2–4, 47; E. O. Wilson, "TED Prize Wish: Help Build the Encyclopedia of Life," TED Conference, March 2007; population forecast from U.N. Population Division, *World Population Prospects: The 2004 Revision* (New York: 2006).

2. Eileen Campbell, "The Case of the $150,000 Fly," *Ecosystem Marketplace*, 26 April 2006.

3. Ibid.

4. Edward O. Wilson, *The Diversity of Life* (New York: W. W. Norton & Company, 1992); Campbell, op. cit. note 2.

5. Jessica Wilkinson, Ecosystem Marketplace, discussions with author, 2007.

6. Clean Water Act, 33 U.S.C. § 1251.

7. K. ten Kate, J. Bishop, and R. Bayon, *Biodiversity Offsets: Views, Experience, and the Business Case* (Gland, Switzerland, and London: IUCN–World Conservation Union and Insight Investment, 2004).

8. For more on the CWA and its Section 404, see www.epa.gov/watertrain/cwa.

9. Box 9–2 from Alice Kenny, "Parthenon Capital Fuels Wildlands, Inc. Rapid Growth," *Ecosystem Marketplace*, 23 April 2007.

10. Wilkinson, op. cit. note 5.

11. Deborah Fleischer, "Wetland Mitigation Banking: Environmentalists Express Concerns," *Ecosystem Marketplace*, 25 April 2005.

12. Alice Kenny, "Ohio Study Shows Mitigation Banks Not Living Up to Potential," *Ecosystem Marketplace*, 24 August 2006.

13. Ibid.

14. Deborah L. Mead, "History and Theory—The Origin and Evolution of Conservation Banking," in Ricardo Bayon, Jessica Fox, and Nathaniel Caroll, eds., *Conservation & Biodiversity Banking* (London: Earthscan, in press).

15. Various government officials, discussions with author.

16. Box 9–3 from Ronald Bailey, "Who Pays for the Delhi Sands Fly?" *Reasononline*, 27 July 2005.

17. Ricardo Bayon, "A Bull Market in Woodpeckers," *Milken Institute Review*, 2005.

18. Ecosystem Marketplace figures provided by Wilkinson, op. cit. note 5. A comprehensive database of species banks will soon be available from the Ecosystem Marketplace. See also J. Fox et al., "Conservation Banking," in J. M. Scott, D. D. Goble, and F. W. Davis, eds., *The Endangered Species Act at Thirty: Conserving Biodiversity in Human-dominated Landscapes* (Washington, DC: Island Press, forthcoming).

19. Campbell, op. cit. note 2.

20 Ibid.

21. Ibid.

22. Jessica Fox, "Conservation Banking: Moving Beyond California," *Ecosystem Marketplace*, 2004; Robert Bonnie, "Guest Feature: Bankng on Endangered Specieds Conservation," *Ecosystem Marketplace*, 16 November 2004; Wilkinson, op. cit. note 5.

23. Table 9–1 from K. ten Kate and M. Inbar, in Bayon, Fox, and Caroll, op. cit. note 14, from ten Kate, Bishop, and Bayon, op. cit. note 7, and from Bruce McKenney, "Environmental Offset Policies, Principles, and Methods: A Review of Selected Legislative Frameworks" Biodiversity Neutral Initiative, 30 March 2005. Australia examples from Louisa Mamouney, discussion with author, from Jane Scanlon, "Australians Revving Up to Bank on the Bush," *Ecosystem Marketplace*, 13 September 2006, from Gary Stoneham, discussion with author, and from Department of Sustainability and Environment, State of Victoria, "Bush Broker: Native Vegetation Credit Registration and Trading, An Information Paper," 2006.

24. Wilkinson, op. cit. note 5.

25. Erik Ness, "The Big Red Barn in the Great Green Field: Green Payments and American Agriculture," *Ecosystem Marketplace*, 21 March 2006.

26. Ten Kate, Bishop, and Bayon, op. cit. note 7; Joshua Bishop et al., *Building Biodiversity Business: Report of a Scoping Study* (Gland, Switzerland, and London: IUCN and Shell International Limited, October 2006).

27. Careesa Gee, "Grain for Green," *Ecosystem Marketplace*, 24 February 2006.

28. Ricardo Bayon, "Case Study: The Mexico Forest Fund," *Ecosystem Marketplace*, 2004.

29. Ibid.

30. Cameron Walker, "Taking Stock: Assessing Ecosystem Services Conservation in Costa Rica," *Ecosystem Marketplace*, 21 May 2007.

31. Mark Eigenraam, "EcoTender: Paying for Ecosystem Services, not Lemons," *Ecosystem Marketplace*, 12 October 2005.

32. Ibid.

33. For information on the Business and Biodiversity Offset Program, see www.forest-trends .org/biodiversityoffsetprogram. Note that Forest Trends is the parent organization of Ecosystem Marketplace.

34. Ten Kate, Bishop, and Bayon, op. cit. note 7; list of benefits to companies adapted from ten Kate and Inbar, op. cit. note 23.

35. BBOP, op. cit. note 33.

Chapter 10.
The Parallel Economy of the Commons

1. J. Stephen Lansing, *Perfect Order: Recognizing Complexity in Bali* (Princeton, NJ: Princeton University Press, 2006).

2. Ibid.

3. Ibid.

4. Ibid.

5. "Knowledge to the People" (interview with Jimmy Wales), *New Scientist*, 3 February 2007, pp. 44–45; Yochai Benkler, *The Wealth of Networks* (New Haven, CT: Yale University Press, 2006), pp. 70–74; "About Wikipedia," at en.wikipedia.org/wiki/Wikipedia:About.

6. Quote from Benkler, op. cit. note 5, p. 71.

7. "Knowledge to the People," op. cit. note 5.

8. "About Wikipedia," op. cit. note 5; *Nature* cited in Benkler, op. cit. note 5, p. 73.

9. Elinor Ostrom, *Governing the Commons* (New York: Cambridge University Press, 1990).

10. Herbert Gintis et al., eds., *Moral Sentiments and Material Interests* (Cambridge, MA: The MIT Press, 2005).

11. Box 10–1 from the following: E. P. Thompson, *Customs in Common* (New York: The New Press, 1993); Eric Kerridge, *The Common Fields of England* (New York: Manchester University Press, 1992); Liam Clare, *Enclosing the Commons* (Dublin: Four Courts Press, 2004); William B. Weeden, *Economic and Social History of New England, 1620–1789* (Williamstown, MA: Corner House Publishers, 1978; orig published 1890); Steven Hahn, *The Roots of Southern Populism* (New York: Oxford University Press, 1983), pp. 239–68; Mark Dowie, "The Fate of the Commons: Privatization v. the Public Trust," *Orion*, July/August 2003.

12. Garrett Hardin, "The Tragedy of the Commons," *Science*, 13 December 1968, pp. 1243–48.

13. Thompson, op. cit. note 11, p. 107.

14. Ostrom, op. cit. note 9, pp. 69–82.

15. Ibid., pp. 82–88; James Kho and Eunice Agsaoay-Saño, *Country Study on Customary Water Laws and Practices: Philippines* (Rome: U.N. Food and Agriculture Organization, undated), pp. 7–9.

16. Ostrom, op. cit. note 9.

17. Ibid., pp. 61–65.

18. Ibid.

19. Robert Higgs, "How the Western Cattlemen Created Property Rights," *The Freeman*, March 2005, pp. 36–37.

20. Garrett Hardin, "The Tragedy of the Commons," in David R. Henderson, ed., *The Concise Encyclopedia of Economics* (Indianapolis, IN: Liberty Fund, Inc., 2002); Joanna Berger, "The Tragedy of the Commons," *Environment*, December 1998.

21. Hardin, op. cit. note 20; compare Lawrence R. Heaney, *The Causes and Effects of Deforestation* (Chicago: The Field Museum, 2007).

22. M. Scott Taylor, *Buffalo Hunt: International Trade and the Virtual Extinction of the North American Bison*, Working Paper No. 12969 (Washington, DC: National Bureau of Economic Research, March 2007); Rebecca Clarren and William deBuys, articles in "Taking on Goliath," *Orion*, November/December 2006; "Coalbed Methane BOOM," *High Country News*, Special Report, undated; Charlie Leduff, "Last Days of the Baymen," *New York Times*, 29 April 1997.

23. Adam Smith, *Theory of Moral Sentiments* (Indianapolis, IN: Liberty Fund Press, 1982), pp. 116–17.

24. Geoffrey Gray, "Mogul Dick Parsons Likes Cigars, Believes in Terror," *New York Magazine*, 17 September 2007, p. 12.

25. David Harris interview, *Living on Earth*, National Public Radio, 29 March 1996.

26. Ibid.

27. Ibid.

28. Adam Smith, *The Wealth of Nations* (New York: Bantam Classic Edition, 2003), p. 941.

29. Bureau of Labor Statistics, "Union Members Summary," 26 January 2007.

30. See, for example, Thomas D. Peacock and Donald R. Day, "Nations Within a Nation: The Dakota and Ojibwe of Minnesota," *Daedalus*, June 2000, p. 137; David A. Kaplan, "Born Free, Sold Dear," *Newsweek*, 6 May 1991, p. 52; Chris Clarke, "The Battered Border: Immigration Policy Sacrifices Arizona's Wilderness," *Earth Island Journal*, autumn 2006, p. 21.

31. Marian Burros, "Plan Would Expand Ocean Fish Farming," *New York Times*, 6 June 2005; "Congressman Proposes Ads on NASA Assets," *Wall Street Journal*, 11 April 2007.

32. Sarah Alexander, American Community Gardening Association, discussion with author, 22 June 2007; Rhoda Amon, "A Stop-and-Grow Lifestyle: Older Residents Plant the Seeds of Friendship by Tending a Community Garden," *Newsday*, 16 September 2007; Lauren E. Baker, "Tending Cultural Landscapes and Food Citizenship in Toronto's Community Gardens," *The Geographical Review*, July 2004; Diane Wang, *A Study of Community Gardens as Catalysts for Positive Social Change* (Chicago: Environmental Studies Program, University of Chicago, 19 May 2006); Bill Lohman, "Community Gardens Grow More Than Plants: Improvements Include Economic and Social Issues," *Richmond Times-Dispatch*, 12 August 2001.

33. Project for Public Spaces Web site, at www.pps.org.

34. Ibid.

35. Agricultural Marketing Service, U.S. Department of Agriculture, "USDA Releases New Farmers Market Statistics," press release (Washington, DC: 5 December 2006).

36. Mark Lakeman, cofounder, City Repair Project, discussion with author, 5 April 2007; Community Greens Web site, at www.community greens.org/ExistingGreens/existinggreens.htm.

37. Colin Woodard, *The Lobster Coast* (New York: Penguin Books, 2004), p. 269. See also James M. Acheson, *The Lobster Gangs of Maine* (Hanover, NH: University of New England Press, 1988).

38. Woodard, op. cit. note 36, pp. 240–41.

39. For pressures at local level, see, for example, Gary Washburn, "If Price Is Right City Sights Will Carry New Name Tags," *Chicago Tribune*, 29 April 2006, and Stuart Elliot, "Town Square as Billboard: Short on Cash, Municipalities Are Renting Out Public Spaces to Marketers," *New York Times*, 23 June 2003.

40. See generally Peter Barnes, *Who Owns the Sky?* (Washington, DC: Island Press, 2001), and Peter Barnes, *Capitalism 3.0* (San Francisco, Berrett-Koehler, 2006). Box 10–2 from the following: Pacific Forest Trust Web site, at www.paci ficforest.org; Marin Agricultural Land Trust Web site, at www.malt.org; "Cooperative Solutions, Healthy Streams," Oregon Water Trust, at owt.org; Robin Finn, "A Serious Obsession with Playgrounds," *New York Times*, 27 July 2007; Robert Fox Elder, "Protecting New York City's Community Gardens," *New York University Environmental Law Journal*, vol. 13, issue 3 (2006), pp. 769–800.

41. Barnes, *Who Owns the Sky?*, op. cit. note 39.

42. Ibid., pp. 50–53.

43. Stephen Castle with James Kanter, "Europe Moves to Make Big Polluters Pay for Emissions," *New York Times*, 5 June 2007; Testimony of Dallas Burtraw, senior fellow, Resources For the Future, before the Subcommittee on Global Climate Change, House Committee on Energy and Commerce, 29 March 2007; "Tories Plan to Fight

Climate Change with Taxes and Green Tape," *Guardian* (London), 14 September 2007; Hannah Fairfield, "When Carbon Is Currency," *New York Times*, 6 May 2007; Scott Allen and Beth Daley, "Patrick to OK Fees for Power Plants," *Boston Globe*, 18 January 2007.

44. Churchill quote from Willis Mason West, *The Story of World Progress* (Boston: Allyn and Bacon, 1922), p. 530.

45. Robert V. Andelson, ed., *Land Value Taxation Around the World* (Malden, MA: Blackwell Publishing, 2001); Tom Condon, "Filling in the Blanks to Aid Comeback," *Hartford Courant*, 3 September 2006; Walter Rybeck, "Transit-Induced Land Values: Development and Revenue Implications," *Commentary* (Council on Urban Economic Development}, 24 October 1981.

46. Alan Thein Durning and Yoram Bauman, *Tax Shift: How to Help the Economy, Improve the Environment, and Get the Tax Man off Our Backs* (Seattle, WA: Northwest Environment Watch, 1998), pp. 62–63.

Chapter 11. Engaging Communities for a Sustainable World

1. Visit to Los Angeles Ecovillage, 16–18 May 2007; Lois Arkin, co-founder of Los Angeles Ecovillage, discussion with author, 17 May 2007; *Los Angeles Eco-Village Overview* (Los Angeles: CRSP Institute for Urban Ecovillages, 2003).

2. Arkin, op. cit. note 1; *Los Angeles Eco-Village Overview*, op. cit. note 1.

3. Visit to Los Angeles Ecovillage, op. cit. note 1; Arkin, op. cit. note 1; *Los Angeles Eco-Village Overview*, op. cit. note 1.

4. Box 11–1 from Graham Meltzer, *Sustainable Communities: Learning from the Cohousing Model* (Victoria, BC: Trafford, 2005), pp.1–3.

5. Community Renewables Initiative, *Lydney Local Power: A Market Town Energy Project Generating Benefits for the Whole Community* (Glouces-

tershire, U.K.: Severn Wye Energy Agency (SWEA): June 2006); Kierson Wise, project manager, SWEA, e-mail to Joy Chen, Worldwatch Institute, 12 September 2007; nine tons from Department for Environment, Food, and Rural Affairs, *Experimental Statistics on Carbon Dioxide Emissions at Local Authority and Regional Level* (London: October 2005).

6. "The Findhorn Ecovillage: Renewable Energy Systems," at www.ecovillagefindhorn.com, viewed 3 October 2007; 40 percent from Jonathan Dawson, president of the Global Ecovillage Network and resident of Findhorn Ecovillage, e-mail to author, 27 September 2007.

7. Table 11–1 from the following: Inverie from Angela Williams, Development Manager, Knoydart Foundation, e-mail to Joy Chen, Worldwatch Institute, 6 August 2007, and from "Knoydart Renewables," at www.knoydart-foundation.com, viewed 3 October 2007; ZEGG (Center for Experimental Culture Design) at www.zegg.de, viewed 3 October 2007; Hammarby Sjöstad from Timothy Beatley, "Circular Urban Metabolism in Stockholm," in Worldwatch Institute, *State of the World 2007* (New York: W. W. Norton & Company, 2007), p. 19; Kibbutz Lotan from www.kibbutzlotan.com, viewed 3 October 2007; Christie Walk from Douglas Farr, *Sustainable Urbanism: Urban Design With Nature* (Hoboken, NJ: John Wiley & Sons, in press); Berea College Ecovillage from visit, 29 January 2007, from Richard Olson, director of Berea College Sustainable and Environmental Studies, discussion with author, 29 January 2007, and from Meghan Bihn, "Berea College's Ecovillage Provides Educational Opportunities and Green Housing for Students," *Spire*, February 2006; Ecoovila from Jonathan Dawson, *Ecovillages: New Frontiers for Sustainability* (Bristol, U.K.: The Schumacher Society, 2006), pp. 32–33; The Solaire from Edward A. Clerico, "The Solaire—A Case Study in Urban Water Reuse," in *Business Sustainability: Planning for a Responsible Future*, Conference Proceedings (Philadelphia, PA: Temple University, February 2007), p. 6; BedZED from Jonathan Dawson, "BedZED and Findhorn: How Do They Compare?" *Permaculture Magazine*, No. 49, pp. 48–52; Farr, op. cit. this note.

8. Quote from Robert and Diane Gilman, *Ecovillages and Sustainable Communities* (Holte, Denmark: Gaia Trust, 1990); Stephen Tinsley and Heather George, *Ecological Footprint of the Findhorn Foundation and Community* (Forres, U.K.: Sustainable Development Research Centre, August 2006); Dawson, *Ecovillages*, op. cit. note 7, p. 29.

9. Meltzer, op. cit. note 4.

10. Number of ecovillages from Global Ecovillage Network, at gen.ecovillage.org/index.html, viewed 11 October 2007; number of co-housing communities from The Cohousing Association of the United States, "US Cohousing Communities," at directory.cohousing.org, viewed 4 April 2007, from Canadian Cohousing Network, "Community Summary," at cohousing.ca/summary.htm, viewed 4 April 2007, from Greg Bamford, "'Living Together on One's Own': Cohousing for Older People, A New Housing Type in Denmark and the Netherlands," conference paper, 2004, from UK Co-housing Network, at www.cohousing.org.uk, viewed 4 April 2007, and from Dick Urban Vestbro, Chair of National Association of Collective Housing Units, Kollektivhus NU, Sweden, e-mail to author, 9 March 2007 (note: the number of co-housing communities includes those that are still under construction or being planned).

11. Phinney Ecovillage from Alex Fryer, "Neighborhoods Battle Global Warming on a Small Scale," *Seattle Times*, 15 May 2007, and from Web site, at www.phinneyecovillage.net, viewed 3 October 2007.

12. Robert D. Putnam, *Bowling Alone: The Collapse and Revival of American Community* (New York: Simon & Schuster, 2000), p. 19.

13. Ibid.; Miller McPherson, Lynn Smith-Lovin, and Matthew E. Brashears, "Social Isolation in America: Changes in Core Discussion Networks over Two Decades," *American Sociological Review*, June 2006, pp. 353–75.

14. Putnam, op. cit. note 12, pp. 327–32.

15. Meltzer, op. cit. note 4, pp. 137–45.

16. Kenneth Mulder, Robert Costanza, and Jon Erickson, "The Contribution of Built, Human, Social and Natural Capital to Quality of Life in Intentional and Unintentional Communities," *Ecological Economics*, August 2006, pp. 13–23.

17. Olson, op. cit. note 7; "Green Steps: Berea College's Movement Toward Sustainability," informational flyer (Berea, KY: Berea College, 21 October 2004).

18. Ray Oldenburg, *The Great Good Place* (New York: Marlowe & Company, 1999), pp. xvii–xix.

19. Judy Wicks, "In Business For Life," *Yes!* winter 2007, pp. 46–49; Justin Martin, "Judy Wicks, Owner: White Dog Cafe, Philadelphia," *Fortune Small Business*, June 2003, p. 87; Ann Karlen, White Dog Community Enterprises, discussion with author, 8 February 2007; White Dog Community Enterprises, at www.whitedogcafefoundation.org, viewed 4 October 2007.

20. History from William H. Ukers, *All about Coffee* (New York: The Tea and Coffee Trade Journal Company, 1922), pp. 18, 102, 110–11; millions from National Coffee Association of U.S.A. Inc., *National Coffee Drinking Trends 2007* (New York: 2007), p. 33, and "Coffee: The Standard Breakfast Drink Grows Up," *Nation's Restaurant News*, 19 August 2002; Green Café Network, at www.greencafenetwork.org, viewed 3 October 2007; Kirstin Henninger, founding director, Green Café Network, discussion with author, 7 September 2007.

21. Edie Farwell, resident at Cobb Hill, discussion with author, 1 October 2007; Cobb Hill Cheese Web site, at cobbhill.org/cheese, viewed 1 October 2007; visit to Lakabe, 17–18 September 2007; Mabel Cañada, co-founder of Lakabe, discussion with author, 17 September 2007; visit to Earthaven Ecovillage, March 2007; Diana Leafe Christian, Earthaven Ecovillage, discussion with author, 15 March 2007; Earthaven Web site, at www.earthaven.org/agriculture/Red_Moon_Herbs.php, viewed 1 October 2007; localization benefits from Michael H. Shuman, *The Small-Mart Revolution: How Local Businesses Are Beating the Global Competition* (San Francisco: Berrett-Koehler

Publishers, Inc., 2006).

22. Matthew Hora and Judy Tick, *From Farm to Table: Making the Connection in the Mid-Atlantic Food System* (Washington, DC: Capital Area Food Bank, 2001); Rich Pirog et al., *Food, Fuel and Freeways: An Iowa Perspective on How Far Food Travels, Fuel Usage, and Greenhouse Gas Emissions* (Ames, IA: Leopold Center for Sustainable Agriculture, June 2001); David S. Reay, "Costing Climate Change," *Philosophical Transactions: Mathematical, Physical and Engineering Sciences*, 15 December 2002, pp. 2947–61.

23. Dorothy Blair, Carol C. Giesecke, and Sandra Sherman, "A Dietary, Social and Economic Evaluation of the Philadelphia Urban Gardening Project," *Journal of Nutrition Education*, vol. 23, no. 4 (1991), pp. 161–67; Donna Armstrong, "A Survey of Community Gardens in Upstate New York: Implications for Health Promotion and Community Development," *Health and Place*, December 2000, pp. 319–27.

24. Farmers' markets from Agricultural Marketing Service, "USDA Releases New Farmers Market Statistics," press release (Washington, DC: U.S. Department of Agriculture, 5 December 2006); community-supported agriculture from Robyn Van En Center, online database, at www.wilson.edu/wilson/asp/content.asp?id=1645, viewed 4 October 2007; Brian Halweil and Danielle Nierenberg, "Farming the Cities," in Worldwatch Institute, op. cit. note 7, p. 53.

25. Growing Power, at www.growingpower.org, viewed 5 October 2007; Erika Allen (Growing Power) and Anthony Flaccavento, "Funding Your Community Food Projects with Social Enterprises," presented at Southern Sustainable Agriculture Working Group: Practical Tools and Solutions for Sustaining Family Farms Conference, 27 January 2007.

26. Rooted in Community, at www.rootedincommunity.org, viewed 5 October 2007.

27. Peter Rosset and Medea Benjamin, *Two Steps Backward, One Step Forward: Cuba's Nationwide Experiment with Organic Agriculture* (San Francisco: Global Exchange, 1993); The Community Solution, *The Power of Community: How Cuba Survived Peak Oil* (Yellow Springs, OH: 2006); Mario Gonzalez Novo and Catherine Murphy, "Urban Agriculture in the City of Havana: A Popular Response to a Crisis," *Growing Cities Growing Food: Urban Agriculture on the Policy Agenda: A Reader on Urban Agriculture* (Resource Centres on Urban Agriculture & Food Security, 2001) pp. 329–47.

28. Erik Assadourian, "Cultivating the Butterfly Effect," *World Watch Magazine*, January/February 2003, pp. 28–35. Box 11–2 from the following: visit to Can Masdeu, 15 September 2007; Luke Cordingley, "Can Masdeu: Rise of the Rurbano Revolution," in Brett Bloom and Ava Bromberg, eds., *Making Their Own Plan* (Chicago, IL: White Walls, Inc. 2004); James Howard Kunstler, *The Long Emergency: Surviving the Converging Catastrophes of the Twenty-First Century* (New York: Atlantic Monthly Press, 2005).

29. Relocalization Network, *2006 Relocalization Network Report* (Sebastopol, CA: Post Carbon Institute, 2007); Relocalization Network, "Alphabetical List of Groups," at www.relocalize.net, viewed 5 October 2007.

30. Business Alliance for Living Local Economies, at www.livingeconomies.org, viewed 9 October 2007.

31. Willits Economic LocaLization, "WELL Overview," at www.willitseconomiclocalization.org, viewed 9 October 2007; Transition Towns wiki, at transitiontowns.org, viewed 9 October 2007.

32. Stuart Gillespie, "Scaling Up Community Driven Development: A Synthesis of Experience," *Food Consumption and Nutrition Division Discussion Paper No. 181* (Washington, DC: International Food Policy Research Institute, June 2004); The Goldman Environmental Prize, "Hammerskjoeld Simwinga: Transforming Communities through Sustainable Development," at www.goldmanprize.org, viewed 9 October 2007.

33. Hilary French, "Sacred Mountain," *World*

Watch Magazine, May/June 2004, pp. 18–25; Nancy Chege, Kenyan National Coordinator of COMPACT, discussion with author, March 2006.

34. Social Investment Forum (SIF), *2005 Report on Socially Responsible Investing Trends in the United States* (Washington, DC: January 2006); p. 28; CDP Publication Committee, *Providing Capital, Building Communities, Creating Impact* (San Francisco: National Community Capital Association, undated), p. 4.

35. SIF, op. cit. note 34; Dawson, *Ecovillages*, op. cit. note 7, p. 48.

36. ShoreBank Pacific, at www.eco-bank.com/services/commercial/lending.html, viewed 9 October 2007; David C. E. Williams, CEO of ShoreBank Pacific, Letter to Stakeholders of Shore-Bank Pacific, 30 June 2006.

37. Scott Malone, "New Age Town in U.S. Embraces Dollar Alternative," *Reuters*, 19 June 2007; 4,000 from Ravi Dykema, "Complementary Currencies for $ocial Change: An Interview with Bernard Lietaer," *Nexus*, July/August 2003.

38. Colin C. Williams et al., "Local Exchange and Trading Schemes (LETS): A Tool for Community Renewal?" *Community, Work & Family*, December 2001, pp. 355–61; *fureai kippu* from Dykema, op. cit. note 37.

39. "Greyston Bakery: Let 'Em Eat Cake," *60 Minutes*, CBS, broadcast 11 January 2004; Greyston Bakery, at www.greystonbakery.com, viewed 9 October 2007; Population and Community Development Association, www.pda.or.th/eng, viewed 9 October 2007; Birds & Bees Resort, at www.cabbagesandcondoms.co.th, viewed 9 October 2007; Kit Snedaker, "A Restaurant with a Mission: Cabbages and Condoms, Bangkok," GoNOMAD.com, 2007, at www.gonomad.com/features/0011/snedaker_cabbages.html, viewed 9 October 2007.

40. Visit to Los Angeles Ecovillage, op. cit. note 1; Arkin, op. cit. note 1.

41. Richard E. White and Gloria Eugenia González Mariño, "Las Gaviotas: Sustainability in the Tropics," *World Watch Magazine*, May/June 2007, pp. 18–23.

42. The Ecovillage Training Center, at www.the farm.org, viewed 5 October 2007; Gaia University at www.gaiauniversity.org, viewed 5 October 2007.

43. Homeowners associations from Caitlin Carpenter, "As an Energy-saver, the Clothesline Makes a Comeback," *Christian Science Monitor*, 24 August 2007; carbon dioxide (CO_2) emissions are a Worldwatch calculation based on Energy Information Administration, *End-Use Consumption of Electricity, 2001* (Washington, DC: U.S. Department of Energy, May 2005) (assuming 500-megawatt coal-fired power plants running at 90 percent capacity and 0.703 kilograms of CO_2 emissions per kilowatt-hour generated); Right to Dry Campaign from Project Laundry List, at www.laundrylist.org, viewed 5 October 2007.

44. Box 11–3 from the following: price of original purchase from Chris Ling, Katherine Thomas, and Jim Hamilton, "Triple Bottom Line in Practice: From Dockside to Dockside Green," Community Research Connections, undated; contamination history from Hans Tammemagi, "Victoria Project Goes from Brown to Green," *Seattle Daily Journal of Commerce*, 26 October 2006; timeline for completion from Thomasina Barnes, "Green Credentials Take Center Stage," (Toronto) *Globe and Mail*, 13 July 2007; number of units, excess energy, and green technology summary from Dockside Green, *Annual Sustainable Report 2006* (Vancouver, BC: 2006), pp. 4, 7, 30–31; penalty pledge and harbor industry heritage from Dockside Green, at www.docksidegreen.com, viewed 2 August 2007; sewage treatment savings from Chris Wood, "Global Warming's Threat to BC: Seeking Solutions," *The Tyee*, 31 August 2006.

45. LEED for Neighborhood Development, at www.usgbc.org, viewed 5 October 2007; Jennifer Henry, program manager, LEED for Neighborhood Development, U. S.Green Building Council, discussion with author, 21 June 2007.

46. Database of LEED projects available at www.usgbc.org, viewed 5 October 2007; LEED for Neighborhood Development, op. cit. note 45; Henry, op. cit. note 45.

47. Sarah James and Torbjorn Lahti, *The Natural Step for Communities: How Cities and Towns Can Change to Sustainable Practices* (Gabriola Island, BC: New Society Publishers, 2004); Sustain Dane, "Eco-municipalities," at www.sustain dane.org, viewed 5 October 2007.

48. Local Works, "Campaign for the Sustainable Communities Bill," at www.localworks.org, viewed 9 October 2007; "The Sustainable Communities Bill," at www.neweconomics.org/gen, viewed 9 October 2007.

49. Bill McKibben, *Deep Economy: The Wealth of Communities and the Durable Future* (New York: Times Books, 2007), p. 149; Bernhard Poetter, "People Power, Danish-style," *OnEarth*, summer 2007, p. 20.

50. "Million Solar Roofs Bill (SB 1) Signed into Law," press release (Los Angeles: Environment California, 21 August 2006).

Chapter 12. Mobilizing Human Energy

1. U.S. Agency for International Development and Comité Inter-Etate pour la Lutte contre la Sécheresse au Sahel, *Investing in Tomorrow's Forests: Toward an Action Agenda for Revitalizing Forests in West Africa* (Washington, DC: 2002); Lydia Polgreen, "In Niger, Trees and Crops Turn Back the Desert," *New York Times*, 11 February 2007.

2. Figure 12–1 from Institut Géographique National du Niger (1975) and Center for EROS, U.S. Geological Survey (2003); Mike McGahuey, Chris Reij, Tony Rinaudo, George Taylor, and Bob Winterbottom, e-mails to author, 9 September to 1 October 2007.

3. Polgreen, op. cit. note 1; McGahuey et al., op. cit. note 2; data on estimated tree coverage from G. Gray Tappan, geographer, SAIC, Center

for EROS, U.S. Geological Survey, e-mail to author, 11 October 2007.

4. McGahuey et al., op. cit. note 2.

5. Yamba Boubacar et al., *Sahel Study: Niger Pilot Study Report* (Washington, DC: International Resource Group, 2005); Chris Reij, "More Success Stories in Africa's Drylands Than Often Assumed," in *Forum sur la Souveraineté Alimentaire* (Niamey, Niger: Resau des Organisations Paysannes et de Producteurs Agricoles de L'Afrique de L'Ouest, 2006).

6. Deepa Narayan et al., eds., *Voices of the Poor: Crying Out for Change* (New York: Oxford University Press, 2000).

7. Polarized positions from Jeffrey D. Sachs, *The End of Poverty: Economic Possibilities for Our Time* (New York: Penguin Press, 2005), and from William Easterly, *White Man's Burden: Why the West's Efforts to Aid the Rest Have Done So Much Ill and So Little Good* (London: Penguin Books, 2006).

8. Poor record of western-inspired development plans from William Easterly, *The Elusive Quest for Growth* (Cambridge, MA: The MIT Press, 2002); quote from World Bank, *Economic Growth in the 1990s: Learning from a Decade of Reform* (Washington, DC: 2005). Box 12–1 from the following: donors becoming selective from Dollar and Levin (2004), as cited in Carol Lancaster, *Foreign Aid: Diplomacy, Development, Domestic Politics* (Chicago: University of Chicago Press, 2007), p. 53; on reform of development assistance, see, for example, The Carter Center, *Development Cooperation Forum: Achieving More Equitable Globalization* (Atlanta, GA: 2007), David Gouldsbrough, *Does the IMF Constrain Health Spending in Poor Countries?* (Washington, DC: Center for Global Development, 2007), and Oxfam International, *Oxfam International Submission to the World Bank/IMF 2005 PRS Review* (Oxford, U.K.: June 2005); data on decline in absolute poverty from World Bank, *World Development Indicators 2004* (Washington, DC: 2004); varying progress of nations from Dani Rodrik, ed., *In Search of Prosperity: Analytic Narratives on*

Economic Growth (Princeton, NJ: Princeton University Press, 2003).

9. Dani Rodrik, "Goodbye Washington Consensus, Hello Washington Confusion? A Review of the World Bank's *Economic Growth in the 1990s: Learning from a Decade of Reform*," *Journal of Economic Literature*, December 2006, pp. 973–87.

10. Amartya Sen, *Development as Freedom* (New York: Alfred A. Knopf, 2000); Michael Woolcock and Deepa Narayan, "Social Capital: Implications for Development Theory, Research, and Policy," *World Bank Research Observer*, August 2000, pp. 225–49; World Bank, *World Development Report 2000/2001* (New York: Oxford University Press, 2001).

11. Paolo Freire, *Pedagogy of the Oppressed* (New York: Seabury Press, 1970); Ghazala Mansuri and Vijayendra Rao, *Community-Based and -Driven Development: A Critical Review*, Working Paper 3209 (Washington, DC: World Bank, 2004); Robert Chambers, *Whose Reality Counts: Putting the First Last* (Warwickshire, U.K.: ITDG Publishing, 1997).

12. Limited impact of community-based approaches from Jason Clay, *Borrowed from the Future: Challenges and Guidelines for Community-Based Natural Resource Management* (New York: Ford Foundation, 2004). Box 12–2 from the following: lessons of integrated rural development programs from John Farrington et al., *Do Area Development Projects Have a Future*, Natural Resource Perspectives No. 82 (London: Overseas Development Institute, December 2002); structural change from Bill Cooke and Uma Kothari, eds., *Participation: The New Tyranny?* (New York: Zed Books, 2001).

13. Cooke and Kothari, op. cit. note 12.

14. For complexity of communities, see, for example, Irene Gujit and Meera Kaul Shah, *The Myth of Community: Gender Issues in Participatory Development* (London: Intermediate Technology Publications, 1998).

15. Narayan et al., op. cit. note 6.

16. Deepa Narayan, *Empowerment and Poverty Reduction: A Sourcebook*, 1st ed. (Washington, DC: World Bank, 2002), pp. 13–29.

17. Jobless growth in India from Bhattacharya and Sakthivel (2004), as cited in Deepa Narayan and Elena Glinskaya, eds., *Ending Poverty in South Asia: Ideas That Work* (Washington, DC: World Bank, 2007).

18. John Blaxall, "Collective Action by Women Workers," in Narayan and Glinskaya, op. cit. note 17, p. 68–103.

19. Ibid.

20. Bhatt quoted in ibid., p. 70.

21. Daniel Taylor-Ide and Carl Taylor, *Just and Lasting Change: When Communities Own Their Futures* (Baltimore, MD: Johns Hopkins University Press, 2002); Daniel Taylor, Carl Taylor, and Jessie Oak Taylor-Ide, *A Future of Hope: From Seeds of Human Energy to the Scale of Social Change* (New York: Columbia University, in press).

22. Taylor-Ide and Taylor, op. cit. note 21; Box 12–3 from ibid.

23. Arjun Appadurai, "The Capacity to Aspire: Culture and the Terms of Recognition," in Vijayendra Rao and Michael Walton, eds., *Culture and Public Action* (Stanford, CA: Stanford University Press, 2004), pp. 59–84.

24. "Beginning Social Change: The Principles of Seed-Scale as Shown in Arunachal Pradesh, India," in Taylor, Taylor, and Taylor-Ide, op. cit. note 21.

25. Ibid.

26. Ibid.

27. Daniel Taylor, president, Future Generations, discussion with author, 1 August 2007; Tage Kanno, program director, Future Generations Arunachal, e-mail to author, 12 October 2007.

28. Box 12–4 is adapted from Taylor-Ide and

Taylor, op. cit. note 21, pp. 47–61.

29. Negative impacts of explosion approach from Laurie Garrett, "Do No Harm: The Global Health Challenge," *Foreign Affairs,* January/February 2007, and from Celia W. Dugger, "CARE Turns Down Federal Funds for Food Aid," *New York Times,* 16 August 2007; Taylor-Ide and Taylor, op. cit. note 21; Hassan Zaman, "Microfinance in Bangladesh: Growth, Achievements, Lessons," in Narayan and Glinskaya, op. cit. note 17; Lídia Cabral, John Farrington, and Eva Ludi, *The Millennium Village Project—A New Approach to Ending Rural Poverty in Africa?* Natural Resource Perspectives 101 (London: Overseas Development Institute, August 2006).

30. Scott Guggenheim, World Bank, "Crises and Contradictions: Understanding the Origins of a Community Development Project in Indonesia," 2003, at siteresources.worldbank.org/INTINDONESIA.

31. Patrick Barron, Rachael Diprose, and Michael Woolcock, *Local Conflict and Community Development in Indonesia: Assessing the Impact of the Kecamatan Development Program* (Jakarta: World Bank, 2006).

32. World Bank, "Afghanistan's National Solidarity Program: Overview & Challenges," 2007, at web.worldbank.org, viewed 31 July 2007.

33. Samiullah Naseri, former National Solidarity Program community facilitator, discussion with author, 11 June 2007.

34. "Going to Scale: Nature Conservation in Tibet—Empowerment, Not Enforcement," in Taylor, Taylor, and Taylor-Ide, op. cit. note 21.

35. Ibid.; recovery of fauna populations in Robert J. Fleming, Dorji Tsering, and Liu Wulin, *Across the Tibetan Plateau: Ecosystems, Wildlife, and Conservation* (New York: W. W. Norton & Company, 2007)

36. For more on the global development architecture, see The Carter Center, *Development Cooperation Forum: Human Security and the Future of*

Development Cooperation (Atlanta, GA: 2002); for trade policy, see Joseph E. Stiglitz, *Globalization and Its Discontents* (New York: W. W. Norton & Company, 2002); Kevin Watkins and Penny Fowler, *Rigged Rules and Double Standards: Trade, Globalization, and the Fight Against Poverty* (London: Oxfam International, 2002); Paul Collier, *The Bottom Billion* (New York: Oxford University Press, 2007),

37. For U.S. tied aid percentage, see data in the Center for Global Development, *2007 Commitment to Development Index* (Washington, DC: 2007); for reduction in value of tied aid, see Department for International Development, *Background Briefing: Untying Aid* (London: September 2001).

38. Deepa Narayan, *Measuring Empowerment: Cross Disciplinary Perspectives* (Washington, DC: World Bank, 2005).

39. Easterly, op. cit. note 7.

40. Collier, op. cit. note 36.

Chapter 13. Investing for Sustainability

1. Anthony Ling et al., *Introducing GS SUSTAIN* (New York: Goldman Sachs Global Investment Research, 22 June 2007); Anthony Ling et al., *Introducing the Goldman Sachs Energy Environmental and Social Index* (New York: Goldman Sachs Global Investment Research, 24 February 2004); Goldman Sachs, *Environmental Policy* (New York: November 2005); Goldman Sachs, *Goldman Sachs Environmental Policy: 2006 Year-End Report* (New York).

2. Ling et al., *Introducing GS SUSTAIN*, op. cit. note 1; Marjorie Kelly, "Holy Grail Found," *Business Ethics*, winter 2004.

3. Intergovernmental Panel on Climate Change, *Climate Change 2007: Mitigation of Climate Change* (New York: Cambridge University Press, 2007).

4. Thanks to David Myers of Lehigh University

for the definition of investing as delayed consumption; discussion with author, Green Mountain Summit on Investor Responsibility, Newport, RI, 19 July 2007.

5. Stacy A. Teicher, "A Quick History of Values-based Investing," *Christian Science Monitor,* 9 February 2004.

6. Peter Kinder, *"Socially Responsible Investing": An Evolving Concept in a Changing World* (Boston: KLD Research & Analytics, September 2005).

7. "Pax History," Pax World Web site, at pax world.com, viewed 24 September 2007; "Our Story—History," Shorebank Web site, at www.shorebankcorp.com, viewed 24 September 2007; Calvert Social Investment Foundation, *Calvert Community Investment Note Prospectus* (Bethesda, MD: 30 April 2007).

8. Social Investment Forum, *2005 Report on Socially Responsible Investing Trends in the United States* (Washington, DC: January 2006); Nelson Information, *Directory of Investment Managers* (Port Chester, NY: 2005).

9. Corporatemonitor, *Sustainable Responsible Investment in Australia–2006* (Evans Head, Australia: September 2006), p. 1; Social Investment Forum, *2005 Report on Socially Responsible Investing Trends in the United States: 10-Year Review* (Washington, DC: January 2006), p. v; Social Investment Organization, *Canadian Social Investment Review 2007* (Toronto, ON: March 2007), p. 5; Eurosif, *European SRI Study 2006* (Paris: 2006), p. 11.

10. McKinsey Global Institute, *Mapping the Global Capital Market 2006: Second Annual Report,* January 2006. Table 13–2 drawn from Web sites and annual reports of Social Investment Forum, Eurosif, Social Investment Organization, Corporatemonitor, and Cangen Biotechnologies.

11. Joe Keefe, "From Socially Responsible Investing to Sustainable Investing," *Green Money Journal,* summer 2007.

12. Ibid.

13. U.N. Environment Programme (UNEP) Finance Initiative, *The Materiality of Social, Environmental and Corporate Governance Issues to Equity Pricing: 11 Sector Studies by Brokerage House Analysts at the Request of the UNEP Finance Initiative Asset Management Working Group* (Geneva: June 2004).

14. William Baue, "Enhanced Analytics Initiative Offers Sell-Side Analysts Cash to Cover Intangibles," *SocialFunds.com,* 23 November 2004.

15. Bill Baue, "Citigroup, Lehman Brothers, and UBS Report on Climate Risks and Opportunities for Investing," *SocialFunds.com,* 27 February 2007; "Climate Change Investment Research," JPMorgan Web site, at www.jpmorgan.com/pages/jpmorgan; Ling et al., *Introducing GS SUSTAIN,* op. cit. note 1.

16. Michael Kramer, Natural Investment Services, e-mails to author, 12 and 13 July 2007.

17. Natural Investment Services, *Natural Investment News,* spring 2004; Michael Kramer, Natural Investment Services, e-mail to author, 14 July 2007.

18. Stephen Davis, Jon Lukomnik, and David Pitt-Watson, *The New Capitalists: How Citizen Investors are Reshaping the Corporate Agenda* (Boston: Harvard Business School Publishing, 2006), pp. 3, 175.

19. Stacy A. Teicher, "A Quick History of Values-based Investing," *Christian Science Monitor,* 9 February 2004.

20. Martine Costello, "One Stockholder's Mission," *CNN/Money,* 19 December 1997.

21. Anne Moore Odell, "Executives and the Environment: Looking Back at Proxy Season 2007," *SocialFunds.com,* 27 July 2007.

22. Edward Iwata, "Boardrooms Open Up to Investors' Input; More Companies Listening to

Their Concerns, Taking Action," *USA Today*, 7 September 2007.

23. Discussion with author.

24. Social Investment Forum, "SaveShareholderRights.org Reveals Investor Backlash Against Potential Curbing of Shareholder Rights," 19 September 2007, at www.socialinvest.org; Social Investment Forum, "Record 22,500 Investors Speak Out Against Potential SEC Curbs on Shareholder Resolutions, Role in Board Nominations," press release (Washington, DC: 10 October 2007).

25. Rainforest Action Network, *Dirty Money: Citi*, at ran.org; *Collevecchio Declaration on Financial Institutions and Sustainability*, January 2003, available at www.foe.org.

26. "FAQ," The Equator Principles, at www.equator-principles.com, viewed 24 September 2007.

27. William Baue, "The Equator Principles: Can They Deliver Social and Environmental Responsibility from Banks?" *Green@Work*, July/August 2003; Arvind Ganesan, *Is 2007 the End for Voluntary Standards?* (New York: Human Rights Watch and Business for Social Responsibility, December 2006); Cary Coglianese and Jennifer Nash, *Beyond Compliance: Business Decision Making and the US EPA's Performance Track Program* (Cambridge, MA: Regulatory Policy Program, Mossavar-Rhamani Center for Business and Government, Kennedy School of Government, Harvard University, 2006). Box 13–2 from the following: Bill Baue, "Bank of China International Investment Managers Launches First SRI Fund in China," *SocialFunds.com*, 6 June 2006; Michelle Chan-Fishel, *Time to Go Green: Environmental Responsibility in the Chinese Banking Sector* (Washington, DC: BankTrack and Friends of the Earth–US, May 2007); Michelle Chan-Fishel, discussion with author; Andrew Newton, "How the Other Half Lends," Special Report on Financial Sector Responsibility, *Ethical Corporation*, November 2006; Bill Baue, "Fidelity Divests Large Chunk of Sudan-Related Holdings," *SocialFunds.com*, 22 May 2007; Charles Piller, "Buffett Rebuffs Efforts to Rate Corporate Conduct," *Los Angeles Times*, 7 May 2007; Berkshire Hathaway, "Shareholder Proposal Regarding Berkshire's Investment in PetroChina," May 2007; Investors Against Genocide, "Berkshire Hathaway Sells Over $1 Billion of PetroChina Since July 11; Steady Series of Sales a Clear Indicator that Buffett is on Divestment Path," 20 September 2007.

28. Flaherty cited in Toby Webb and John Russell, "A Point of Principle," Special Report on Financial Sector Responsibility, *Ethical Corporation*, November 2006.

29. Andrew Newton, "A Convenient Truce," Special Report on Financial Sector Responsibility, *Ethical Corporation*, November 2006.

30. Number of banks from Equator Principles Web site, at www.equator-principles.com, viewed 24 September 2007; share of finance capacity from International Finance Corporation, "IFC Welcomes Adoption of Equator Principles by Banco Galicia," press release (Washington, DC: 29 March 2007); Bill Baue, "Revised Equator Principles Fall Short of International Best Practice for Project Finance," *SocialFunds.com*, 12 July 2006.

31. World Bank, *Striking a Better Balance—The World Bank Group and Extractive Industries: The Final Report of the Extractive Industries Review. World Bank Group Management Response* (Washington, DC: September 2004); Bill Baue, "Communities, Corporations, and the Difference Between Consent and Consult," *The CRO*, July 2007.

32. Box 13–3 from the following: Jim Kharouf, "Commentary," *Environmental Markets Newsletter*, 13 June 2007; Thomas Kostigen, "The Green in Hedge Funds Isn't All about Money," *MarketWatch*, 29 June 2007; William Hutchings, "Man Group Raises Green Hedge Fund, *eFinancialNews.com*, 3 September 2007.

33. John Hill and Graham Wark, *Coal: Missing the Window* (Citigroup Global Markets, 18 July 2007); Francesca Rheannon, "Jitters About Regulatory Outlook Rile Confidence in Coal Mining Stocks," *SocialFunds.com*, 12 August 2007. Box 13–4 from the following: Bill Baue, "TXU Share-

owners File Three Resolutions Questioning Wisdom of Pulverized Coal Plants," *SocialFunds.com*, 19 December 2006; Felicity Barringer and Andrew Ross Sorkin with Matthew L. Wald, "In Big Buyout, Utility to Limit New Coal Plants," *New York Times*, 25 February 2007; Jim Marston, "TXU Buyout Tied to Environmental Agreement," *Climate 411*, 27 February 2007; "TXU to Set New Direction As Private Company; Public Benefits Include Price Cuts, Price Protection, Investments in Alternative Energy and Stronger Environmental Policies," press release (Dallas: TXU, 26 February 2007); "TXU Plans to Build Biggest Nuclear Plants in US-WSJ," *Reuters*, 9 April 2007.

34. Data and Figure 13–1 from Chris Greenwood et al., *Global Trends in Sustainable Energy Investment 2007* (Nairobi: UNEP Sustainable Energy Finance Initiative and New Energy Finance, June 2007); Bill Baue and Sanford Lewis, "Will Nuclear Power Save Us from Global Warming?" *Corporate Watchdog Radio*, 6 September 2006; William Baue, "Nuclear Power: Still an Environmental Scourge or Now a Climate Change Mitigator?" *SocialFunds.com*, 9 June 2005.

35. Greenwood et al., op. cit. note 34.

36. James Stack et al., *Cleantech Venture Capital: How Public Policy Has Stimulated Private Investment* (San Francisco: CleanTech Venture Network and Environmental Entrepreneurs, May 2007).

37. Bill Baue, "Nobel Prize Links Microfinance to Peace," *SocialFunds.com*, 17 October 2006.

38. Adam Smith, Nobelprize.org, "Poverty in the World is an Artificial Creation," interview with Professor Muhammad Yunus, 13 October 2006.

39. Daniel Pearl and Michael M. Phillips, "Grameen Bank, Which Pioneered Loans for the Poor, Has Hit a Repayment Snag," *Wall Street Journal*, 27 November 2001; Vivek George, "Uncovering the Truth Behind Poverty—Is Micofinance the Answer to Poverty?" at www.abrahamgeorge.blogspot.com.

40. Nimal Fernando, "Microfinance Outreach to the Poorest: A Realistic Objective?" *Focal Point for Microfinance* (Asian Development Bank), March 2004.

41. William Baue, "Fonkoze Helps Transform Microfinance to Reach the Poorest of the Poor in Haiti," *SocialFunds.com*, 18 November 2005.

42. Bill Baue, "Microfinance Crosses Continental Divide with $100 Million Commitment from TIAA-CREF," 9 October 2006.

43. Nicholas Kristof, "You, Too, Can Be a Banker to the Poor," *New York Times*, 27 March 2007.

44. Satterthwaite quoted in "Quotes from the Field," Green Microfinance Web site, at www.greenmicrofinance.org, viewed 25 September 2007.

45. George Monbiot, "Selling Indulgences," *The Guardian* (London), 19 October 2006; Bill Baue, "Carbon Offsets: Modern-Day Indulgences to Assuage Carbon Guilt or Market Mechanism for Supporting Clean Energy," *Socialfunds.com*, 4 April 2007.

46. Bill Baue and Francesca Rheannon, "Biofuels—Pros and Cons," *Corporate Watchdog Radio*, 5 July 2007; Lester Brown, "Distillery Demand for Grain to Fuel Cars Vastly Understated; World May Be Facing Highest Grain Prices in History" (Washington, DC: Earth Policy Institute, January 2007); George Monbiot, "A Lethal Solution," *The Guardian* (London), 27 March 2007.

47. Cynthia A. Williams and John M. Conley, "Triumph or Tragedy? The Curious Path of Corporate Disclosure Reform in the U.K.," *William and Mary Environmental Law and Policy Review*, winter 2007, pp. 317–62.

48. William Baue, "Film Depicts Environmental and Social Reporting Disappearing in SEC Black Hole," *SocialFunds.com*, 7 January 2004; Frente de Defensa de la Amazonia, "Chevron Using Unethical Tactics to Avoid Judgment in $10 Billion Rainforest Trial; Series of Legal Setbacks in Ecuador Haunt Company; Charges of Fabricating Evidence," 8 August 2007; "FAQ," Corporate

Sunshine Working Group Web site, at www.cor
poratesunshine.org/faq.html, viewed 25 September 2007.

49. Ceres, "Major Investors, State Officials, Environmental Groups Petition SEC to Require Full Corporate Climate Risk Disclosure," press release (Washington, DC: 18 September 2007).

50. Felicity Barringer and Danny Hakim, "New York Subpoenas 5 Energy Companies," *New York Times*, 16 September 2007.

51. William Baue, "Lighthouse G3: Third Generation GRI Guidelines Shine a Beacon for Sustainability Reporters," *SocialFunds.com*, 30 September 2005; "2500 Comply with GRI Search of 15,008 CSR Reports for 'GRI Adherence' Yields 2,492 Reports," *CorporateRegister.com*, viewed 25 September 2007; Halina Szejnwald Brown, Martin de Jong, and Teodorina Lessidrenska, *The Rise of the Global Reporting Initiative (GRI) as a Case of Institutional Entrepreneurship*, Working Paper No. 36 (Cambridge, MA: Corporate Social Responsibility Initiative, Kennedy School of Government, Harvard University, May 2007).

52. "Carbon Disclosure Project and Wal-Mart Launch Climate Change Partnership; President Clinton to Speak at CDP Fifth Global Annual Forum Today; Latest Findings on Corporate Climate Data to be Announced," Carbon Disclosure Project, 24 September 2007; McKinsey Global Institute, op. cit. note 10.

53. Matthew Kiernan, Innovest, discussion with author, 30 August 2007.

54. Anne Moore Odell, "Principles for Responsible Investment Quadruples Assets in First Year," *SocialFunds.com*, 1 June 2007.

Chapter 14.
New Approaches to Trade Governance

1. Luis Eduardo Derbez, Keynote Address, Emerging Powers in Global Governance Conference, Institut du Développement Durable et des Relations Internationales and International Institute for Sustainable Development (IISD), Paris, 5 July 2007.

2. Jagdish Bhagwati, Arvind Panagariya, and T. N. Srinivasan, *Lectures on International Trade*, 2nd ed. (Cambridge, MA: The MIT Press, 1998); Edward D. Mansfield and Brian M. Pollins, eds., *Economic Interdependence and International Conflict: New Perspectives on an Enduring Debate* (Ann Arbor: University of Michigan Press, 2003); Oli Brown et al., eds., *Trade, Aid, and Security: An Agenda for Peace and Development* (Sterling, VA: Earthscan, 2007); Robert O. Keohane and Joseph S. Nye, *Power and Interdependence*, 2nd ed. (Glenview, IL: Scott Foresman and Company, 1989). Box 14–1 draws on U.N. Economic and Social Commission for Asia and the Pacific, "What Is Good Governance?" at www.unescap.org, undated; see also Philippe Sands, *Lawless World* (London: Penguin Books, 2006), Chapter 1.

3. Sylvia Ostry, *The Post–Cold War Trading System: Who's on First?* A Century Foundation Book (Chicago: University of Chicago Press, 1997); Jagdish Bhagwati, *Free Trade Today* (Princeton, NJ: Princeton University Press, 2002).

4. Bhagwati, Panagariya, and Srinivasan, op. cit. note 2; Mansfield and Pollins, op. cit. note 2; Brown et al., op. cit. note 2; Keohane and Nye, op. cit. note 2.

5. Preamble to the General Agreement on Tariffs and Trade 1947 agreement, at www.wto.org/english; Gary P. Sampson, *The WTO and Sustainable Development* (Tokyo: United Nations University Press, 2005).

6. Quote cited in World Trade Organization (WTO), "Relevant WTO Provisions: Text of 1994 Decision," at www.wto.org.

7. WTO, *The Legal Texts: The Results of the Uruguay Round of Multilateral Trade Negotiations* (Cambridge, U.K.: Cambridge University Press, 1994).

8. Ambassador Nobutoshi Akao, Japanese negotiator in the Uruguay Round, discussion with author; see also Howard Mann and Stephen Porter, *The State of Trade and Environment Law: Implications for Doha and Beyond* (Winnipeg, MB: IISD, 2003), and Sands, op. cit. 2.

9. Mann and Porter, op. cit. note 8.

10. See Sylvia Ostry, "The Uruguay Round North-South Grand Bargain: Implications for Future Negotiations," in Daniel L. M. Kennedy and James D. Southwick, eds., *The Political Economy of International Trade Law* (Cambridge, U.K.: Cambridge University Press, 2002), pp. 285–300.

11. Robert Wolfe, "Crossing the River by Feeling the Stones: Where the WTO is Going after Seattle, Doha and Cancun," *Review of International Political Economy*, August 2004, pp. 574–96.

12. Statement by Pascal Lamy, Director General of the WTO to the High-level Segment, Substantive Session of U.N. Economic and Social Council, Geneva, Switzerland, 5 July 2007; see also Faizel Ismail, "A Development Perspective on the WTO July 2004 General Council Decision," *Journal of International Economic Law*, June 2005, pp. 377–404.

13. For membership information, see www.wto.org.

14. For invitation to committees, see WTO Ministerial Declaration, WT/MIN(01)/DEC/1, 20 November 2001, WTO, paragraph 51.

15. See Mark Halle, "The WTO and Sustainable Development," in Yasuhei Taniguchi, Alan Yanovich, and Jan Bohanes, eds., *The WTO in the Twenty-first Century—Dispute Settlement, Negotiations, and Regionalism in Asia* (Cambridge, U.K.: Cambridge University Press, 2007).

16. See Susan Ariel Aaronson, *Taking Trade to the Streets: The Lost History of Public Efforts to Shape Globalization* (Ann Arbor: University of Michigan Press, 2001)

17. Sampson, op. cit. note 5; Halle, op. cit. note 15.

18. Dani Rodrik, Harvard University, "Goodbye Washington Consensus, Hello Washington Confusion?" prepared for *Journal of Economic Literature*, January 2006; William Finnegan, "The Economics of Empire—Notes on the Washington Consensus," *Harper's Magazine*, May 2003.

19. For details of the Integrated Framework, see www.integratedframework.org.

20. World Trade Organization, Recommendations of the Task Force on Aid for Trade, Geneva, 27 July 2006.

21. For information on these partnerships, see www.eitransparency.org, www.dams.org, and www.fsc.org/en.

22. See Robert Wolfe, "Decision-Making and Transparency in the 'Medieval' WTO: Does the Sutherland Report Have the Right Prescription?" *Journal of International Economic Law*, September 2005, pp. 631–45, and Robert Wolfe, *Can the Trading System Be Governed? Institutional Implications of the WTO's Suspended Animation*, Working Paper No. 30 (Waterloo, ON: Centre for International Governance Innovation, September 2007); Oxfam, "WTO: Open Letter on Institutional Reforms in the World Trade Organization," Oxford, U.K., October 2005; Dani Rodrik, Harvard University, "The Global Governance of Trade As If Development Really Mattered," prepared for the U.N. Development Programme, October 2001; Philip I. Levy, "Do We Need an Undertaker for the Single Undertaking? Considering the Angles of Variable Geometry," October 2004.

23. See Robert Wolfe, "Comment: Adventures in WTO Clubland," *Bridges*, June-July 2007, pp. 21–22.

24. In Box 14–2, "bottom billion" from Paul Collier, *The Bottom Billion* (New York: Oxford University Press, 2007).

25. For information on these organizations, see www.eviangroup.org, www.ictsd.org, and www.chathamhouse.org.uk/research/eedp.

Index

Abalone, biomimicry of, 42
accountability in good trade governance, 197, 202
Adbusters, 59
additive approach to development, 175
Advanced Micro Devices, 29
advertising to children, 59
Afghanistan, 176
agriculture. *See also* commons management;
    meat and seafood industries
    community gardens, 145, 148, 151, 157–59
    development programs, 166–67, 177
    farmers' markets, 145–46, 158
    global trade in, 119
    pollution from animal feed production
      runoff, 63
    trust model for farmland, 148
    water use in, 109–10, 116, 117, 119
Aid for Trade, 205
AIDS, 162
air pollution, 147–49
Alaska
    Native Claims Settlement Act, 144
    public oil royalties (Alaska Permanent Fund),
      98, 149
    wild salmon fishery, 71
Algeria, 79
allowance-based carbon trading, 92–98
American Indians, 142, 144
anchovy industry, Peru, 73
Anderson, Ray, 41
AngloAmerican, 34, 136
Annan, Kofi, 32
antibiotics used in meat industry, 70, 71
Appadurai, Arjun, 172
architecture, energy efficiency of, 29, 37–38,
    80, 163, 164
Army Corps of Engineers, U.S., 127, 128, 129
Arunachal Pradesh, India, 173–74

Australia
    biodiversity offsets in, 132, 135
    carbon credit markets in, 94, 95
    eco-efficiency in, 34
    energy efficiency in, 58, 88
    natural resources, accounting for, 13
    property tax, commons-based approach to,
      150
    simplicity movement in, 52
    socially responsible investing in, 183
automobiles, 16, 82, 84, 88

Balinese water temples, Indonesia, 138–39
Bangladesh, 67, 175, 191, 192
Bangladesh Rural Advancement Committee,
    192
Bank of America, 188
banking environmental credits
    biodiversity. *See* biodiversity, economic
      value of
    carbon. *See* carbon credits and carbon markets
    commons-based vs. market-based approach
      to air pollution, 147–49
    as investment for sustainability, 193
banking for sustainability. *See* investment for
    sustainability
BankTrack, 187, 188
Barnes, Peter, 14–15, 96, 98, 147
batteries, long-life, 84
beef industry. *See* meat and seafood industries
behavioral economics, 140
benefit-cost analysis, 30
Benyus, Janine, 40, 42
Berea College Ecovillage, KY, 156
BerkShares, 161
Berkshire Hathaway, 189
Bernoulli, Daniel, 5
Bhatt, Ela, 172

Bhutan, 12, 25, 60
BioBanking (New South Wales, Australia), 132
BioCarbon Fund, 99
biodiversity, economic value of, 123–37
    cap-and-trade schemes, 124, 132
    endangered species and habitats, protecting,
        125–27, 130–32
    government determination of, 124
    government-mandated programs, benefits
        and drawbacks of, 132–35
    loss of biodiversity, problem of, 125
    voluntary offsets, 135–36
    voluntary transactions determining, 124
    wetlands development, 116
    wetlands mitigation banking, 127–30
biofuels, 17, 84, 85, 88, 110, 188, 190, 193
biogas (methane), 29, 65, 75–77, 84, 99, 142,
    189
biological approach to development, 174, 175,
    176–77
biomass power, 81–83
biomimicry, 40–42
"bird of gold" in India, 44, 48
blueprint approach to development, 175–76
Boesky, Ivan, 143
Boton, Alain de, 50
bottom trawling, 68
Bourbon Red turkeys, 73
Brazil, 17, 59, 84, 88, 90, 133
Brinker, Jeffrey, 42
British Petroleum, 16, 85
Brown, Gordon, 193
Buddhist model for sustainable lifestyles, 52, 60
Buffett, Warren, 189
buildings, energy efficiency of, 29, 37–38, 80,
    163, 164
Bulgaria, 100
Burger King, 71
Burlington, VT, 155
bus rapid transit, 17
Bush Administration, 145
BushBroker (Victoria, Australia), 132
BushTender (Victoria, Australia), 135
Business Alliance for Living Local Economies,
    160
Business and Biodiversity Offsets Program, 136
Business for Social Responsibility, 30
Buy Nothing Day, 53

Cabbages and Condoms, Thailand, 162
cafes as "third places," 156–57

California
    carbon emissions trading in, 95, 97
    endangered species and habitats, protecting,
        125–27, 131–32
    Marin Agricultural Land Trust, 148
    Million Solar Roofs initiative, 165
    regulation of energy market in, 88
    wetlands mitigation banking in, 128
Calvert Social Investment Fund, 182
Cameron, Rondo, 18
Cameroon, 67
campaign or explosion approach to
    development, 174, 175
Can Masdeu, Spain, 159
Canada
    carbon capture and storage in, 79
    carbon credits and carbon market in, 95
    community gardens in, 145
    green accounting systems in, 24
    socially responsible investing in, 183
    sustainable communities in, 163
    women's unpaid work, value of, 15
    workplace well-being in, 29–30
cap-and-trade schemes
    biodiversity, valuing, 124, 132
    carbon credits and carbon markets, 93–98
    water, 121
Cape Cod Commercial Hook Fishermen's
    Association, 71
capital, natural resources as, 113
carbon capture and storage, 78–79
carbon credits and carbon markets, 87, 91–106
    allowance-based, 92–98
    California Climate Action Registry, 95, 97
    cap-and-trade schemes, 93–98
    certification and verification schemes,
        104–05
    Chicago Climate Exchange, 94–95, 102
    Clean Development Mechanism, 92, 93, 96,
        98–102, 106
    commons-based vs. market-based approach
        to, 149
    Ecosystem Marketplace, 102
    emissions trading, 92
    EU emissions trading scheme, 10, 14, 87,
        92–94, 95–97, 106, 149
    fugitive emissions, 98–99
    future of, 104–06
    as investment for sustainability, 193
    Joint Implementation, 92, 93, 96, 98,
        100–02

Kyoto Protocol, 90, 91, 92, 97, 98–101, 105–06
land use, land use change, and forestry projects, 99–100, 101, 103–04
New South Wales market (Australia), 94
origins and current mechanisms, 92–93
permission to emit, 96–98
project-based transactions, 93, 98–101
public distribution of emissions permit income, 98
Regional Greenhouse Gas Initiative, 95, 97
renewable energy credit, 103
voluntary markets, 100–04, 105
Western Climate Initiative, 95
Carbon Disclosure Project, 194–95
carbon emissions, reducing. See low-carbon economy
carbon footprint, 23, 25, 47–48, 58
carbon neutrality, 28, 29, 103
carbon offsets. See carbon credits and carbon markets
carbon taxes, 31, 87, 106
Carroll, Lewis, 54
cars, 16, 82, 84, 88
cattle industry. See meat and seafood industries
cellulosic ethanol, 190
cement manufacturing, 76
Ceres, 194
certification of sustainability
carbon credits and carbon markets, 104–05
meat and seafood industries, 69–71
progress, redefining, 27–28
water transactions, 121
Chambers, Robert, 170
Chan-Fishel, Michelle, 188
Chen Shui-bian, 74
Cheney, Dick, 79
Chevron, 194
Chicago, IL, local sustainable food system in, 157
Chicago Climate Exchange, 94–95, 102
Chicago Manufacturing Center, 36–37
child marriage in India, 174
children, advertising to, 59
China
biodiversity requirements in, 134, 135
carbon credits and carbon markets activity, 98, 99
development programs in, 169, 177
happiness and wealth levels, 11
investment for sustainability in, 186–87, 187, 188–89

low-carbon economics in, 77, 79, 81, 90
seafood diet in, 61, 74
sustainable economics in, 8, 16–17, 22–24
sustainable lifestyles and consumer economics in, 47, 48, 49
China Methane Recovery Fund, 189
China National Petroleum Corporation, 189
Churchill, Winston, 149
Citi, 184, 186–90, 192
civil society
development, role in, 178
investment for sustainability and, 185
progress, redefining, 21, 30
sustainable economics and, 17
trade governance and, 201–02, 206, 209
Clean Development Mechanism, 92, 93, 96, 98–102, 106
Clean Water Act, U.S., 127, 128
CleanFish, 70
cleantech, investment in, 16–17, 190–91
climate change
carbon emissions and, 75–77, 89 90
economic effects of, 6–7
political will to address, 89–90
sustainable communities and, 159
sustainable lifestyles and, 46
Climate, Community and Biodiversity Alliance, 99–100, 105
Climate Group, 105
co-housing communities, 154. See also sustainable communities
coal, 78–79, 83, 84, 89, 189, 190, 194
Cobb Hill Cohousing community, Hartland, VT, 157
Collevecchio Declaration on Financial Institutions and Sustainability, 186–87
Collier, Paul, 178, 179, 208
Colombia, 134, 162
Colton, CA, 125–27, 131–32
commons management, 138–50
community-based, 146–47
corporatization/privatization, adverse effects of, 142–45
enclosure, reversing, 144–46
government ownership, 147
market-based approaches, 147–49
open access regimes, 142
population control and, 142
property, commons as form of, 140
property tax and land use, 149–50
scaling up, 146–50

commons managment (*continued*)
  social behavior leading to, 138–42, 146–47
  sustainable economics aiming at
    revitalization of, 14–15
  "tragedy of the commons," concept of,
    14–15, 140–42
  trust model, 147–49
communities. *See also* sustainable communities
  defined, 152
  vitality as indicator of economic progress,
    28, 30
community banks, 161
community-based commons management,
  146–47
community-based development, 168, 170–71
community currencies, 161–62
community development financial institutions,
  161
community-driven development, 160–61, 168,
  170–71, 172. *See also* development
community gardens, 145, 148, 151, 157–59
community-supported agriculture, 158
compact fluorescent lightbulbs, 16
COMPACT program, 160–61
Compuware Corporation, 145
Cone, Ben, 131
Conservation International, 136
consumer economics, 48–50. *See also* sustainable
  lifestyles
Cornell University, 37–38
corporate microeconomics indicators, 20,
  43–44
Corporate Sunshine Working Group, 194
CorporateRegister.com, 194
corporatization/privatization of commons,
  142–45
Costa Rica, 13, 15, 116, 134–35
"cradle to cradle" concept, 38–40
credits and banking
  biodiversity. *See* biodiversity, economic
    value of
  carbon. *See* carbon credits and carbon
    markets
  commons-based vs. market-based approach
    to air pollution, 147–49
  as investment for sustainability, 193
Csíkszentmihályi, Mihály, 52
Cuba, 158, 159
Cuomo, Andrew, 194
Curitiba, Brazil, 17
currencies, local or community, 161–62

Dalits of India, 54
Damanhur, Italy, 161
Darden Restaurants, 70–71
Davis, Stephen, 185
Dawes Act (U.S.), 144
Dawkins, Richard, 55
Delhi Sands Flower-loving Fly (U S), 125–27,
  131–32
Denmark, 13–14, 88–89, 165
Derbez, Luis Ernesto, 196
Detroit, MI, 145
Deutsche Bank, 149, 184
development, 166–79
  additive approach to, 175
  biological approach to, 174, 175, 176–77
  blueprint approach to, 175–76
  changes in programs for, 168–71
  community-driven vs. community-based,
    168, 170–71, 172
  explosion or campaign approach, 174, 175
  freedom of choice and action, programs
    increasing, 171–74
  globalization and, 178
  growth vs., 5–6, 10, 11–12. *See also* progress,
    redefining
  international donor assistance issues, 178–79
  participatory techniques, problems with,
    170–71
  progress, sustainable development as key to
    redefining, 21–22
  scaling up, 174–78
  social aspect of, 168
  top-down, expert-driven approaches, 170,
    174–75
  trade and trade governance, sustainable
    development paradigm for, 178, 200–09
diet. *See* meat and seafood industries
digital electrical grids, 83–84
Dockside Green Victoria, BC, Canada, 163
Doha Round, WTO, 119, 198, 200, 202, 205,
  206
Dow Chemical, 89, 185
downshifting, 52, 53
Downshifting Downunder, 53
drinking water, 110
Dublin Principles, 113–15
Dunlap, Al, 39
DuPont, 32, 34, 39, 40, 85

Earth Institute, 175
Earth Summit (1992), 198

Easterly, Bill, 179
EasyJet, 104
Eatwild.com, 71
eco-efficiency, 28, 29, 33–38
Eco-magination (GE), 35, 43
eco-municipality, 164
EcoCover Limited, 41
EcoFish, 70
ecological concerns regarding trade governance
    and WTO, 199, 203–04, 207, 208
ecological footprint analysis, 23, 26
economic localization, 23, 26–27, 157–61
economics. See also prices; sustainable economics
    behavioral economics, 140
    conventional economic theory, problems of,
        4–6, 39–40, 87, 113
    indicators of progress. See progress, redefining
    of sustainable communities, 161–62
ecosystem degradation
    biodiversity loss, 125
    economic systems and, 7–8
    sustainable communities reversing, 151, 162
    water, 112
Ecosystem Marketplace, 102, 105
ecotaxes. See taxation
EcoTender (Victoria, Australia), 135
ecovillages. See sustainable communities
Ecuador, 74, 188, 194
Edison, Thomas, 89
Edwards, Andres, 21
Ehrlich, Paul, 46
ejido system of land tenure in Mexico, 144
electric power industry, 87
electricity grid, 82–84
Electronic Product Environmental Assessment
    Tool framework, 29
eminent domain, 128
emissions trading, 92. See also carbon credits
    and carbon markets
enclosure of commons, reversing, 144–46
End Poverty Now, 11
Endangered Species Act, U.S., 126, 127, 130
endangered species and habitats, protecting,
    125–27, 130–32
energy and energy industry
    biofuels, 17, 84, 85, 88, 110, 188, 190, 193
    biogas (methane), 29, 65, 75–77, 84, 99,
        142, 189
    biomass power, 81–83
    buildings, energy efficiency of, 29, 37–38,
        80, 163, 164

carbon capture and storage, 78–79
climate change and carbon emissions, 75–77
coal, 78–79, 83, 84, 89, 189, 190, 194
electric power industry, 87
electricity grid, 82–84
ethanol, 84, 190–91
geothermal power, 81, 82, 83
global energy needs, increase in, 77–78
government mandates on, 88
hydropower, 81, 82, 83, 110
markets for new energy technologies, 86–89
nuclear power, 81, 190
oil, gas, and petroleum, 78, 85, 87, 98, 149
photovoltaics, 86
progress redefined by renewable energy
    metrics, 23, 25
solar power, 81–82, 83, 84, 165
storage of power, 82, 84
sustainable communities, energy efficiencies
    practiced by, 152, 165
sustainable lifestyles and, 58
wind power, 81–82, 82, 84, 86
Energy, U.S. Department of, 77, 79
Engineers, U.S. Army Corps of, 127, 128, 129
Enhanced Analytics Initiative, 185
Environmental Defense, 190
Environmental Entrepreneurs, 191
Environmental Protection Agency, U.S., 36,
    127–29
Environmental Working Group, 67
Epstein, Bob, 191
Equator Principles, 16, 187
equity. See poverty and wealth inequality
Esty, Daniel C., 31
ethanol, 84, 190–91
Etzioni, Amitai, 52
European Union
    biodiversity requirements in, 134
    eco-efficiency in production processes, 34
    emissions trading scheme, 10, 14, 87,
        92–94, 95–97, 106, 149
    energy efficiency mandates, 58, 88
    as governance model, 207
    investment for sustainability in, 183, 193
    low-carbon economics in, 79, 81, 88, 90
    meat and seafood production in, 67
    sustainable lifestyles in, 58
Evian Group, 209
evolutionary psychology of consumerism, 53–55
exotic (nonlocal) breeds, discouraging use of, 68
Expedia, 102

explosion or campaign approach to
development, 174, 175
Extractive Industries Transparency Initiative, 205
Exxon-Mobil, 194

Farmers' markets, 145–46, 158
farming. *See* agriculture
feebates, 12
Fernando, Nimal, 192
Fidelity Investments, 189
Financial Accounting Standards Board, 44
financial incentives in meat and seafood
industries, 67–69
Findhorn Ecovillage, UK, 52, 152, 154
Finland, 29, 81
Fischer, Irving, 19
Fish and Wildlife Service, U.S., 131
fishing and fish farming. *See* marine ecosystems;
meat and seafood industries
Fonkoze (Haiti), 192, 193
food miles, 27
Ford, Henry, 89
Forest Carbon Partnership Facility, 99
Forest Stewardship Council, 205
Forest Trends, 136
forestry
carbon credits, projects involving, 99–100,
101, 103–04
Niger forest code changes, 166–67, 177
Qomolangma National Nature Preserve,
Tibet, 177–78
fossil fuel emissions. *See* climate change; energy
industry; low-carbon economy
free trade. *See* trade and trade governance
Free Trade Area of the Americas, 199
Freire, Paolo, 170
Friends of the Earth-US, 188
Frijns, Johann, 188
fugitive emissions, 98–99
Fuller, Buckminster, 40
fureai kippu (caring relationship tickets) in
Japan, 161–62
Fusaro, Peter, 189
Future Generations, 172, 173

G-8 Economic Summit (2007), 77–78
G-20 Group, 207
Gabriel, Yiannis, 49
Gadjil, Madhav, 49
Gaia University, 163
Galvin Electricity Initiative, 84

Gandhi, Mahatma, 52
gas and oil, 78, 85, 87, 98, 149
gene pool, privatization/corporatization of,
144–45
General Agreement on Tariffs and Trade, 197,
198, 199, 201, 207
General Electric, 10, 35–36, 39, 40, 43, 85
General Motors, 84, 90, 145, 185
Generation Investment Management, 184
genuine progress indicator, 22–24
George, Abraham, and George Foundation, 192
geothermal power, 81, 82, 83
Germany
ecotaxes, 12
low-carbon economics in, 80, 84, 88, 89
sustainable communities in, 153, 154
Gilbert, John and Lewis, 185
GINI coefficient of social equity, 23, 25–26
Giuliani, Rudolph, 148
Global Development and Environment
Institute, 7
global diet. *See* meat and seafood industries
Global Environment Facility, 134, 160–61
Global Exchange Associates, 189
Global Footprint Network, 5, 26
Global Reporting Initiative, 27, 28, 31, 194
global warming. *See* climate change
globalization, 18–19, 178. *See also* trade and
trade governance
Goldman Sachs, 44, 85, 180, 184, 188, 190
Gore, Al, 184
governance of trade. *See* trade and trade
governance
government mandates
on biodiversity, 132–35
on energy, 88
phase-out of incandescent bulbs, 58, 88
governments
biodiversity value, determining, 124
climate change, political will to address,
89–90
commons management by, 147
as development aid recipients, 169
sustainable economics, role in, 12, 17
sustainable lifestyles, encouraging or
discouraging, 55–60
GRAIN, 73–74
Grain for Green (China), 134, 135
Grameen Bank, 15, 192
Great Barrington, MA, 161
green accounting systems, 22–24

Green Building Rating System, 29
Green Café Network, 157
Green Microfinance, 193
Green Mountain Coffee Roasters, 29
Green Revolution, 138
green taxes. *See* ecotaxes or green taxes; taxation
greenhouse gases, 28–29, 32, 34–35, 43. *See also* carbon credits and carbon markets
Greenland ice sheet, 76
GreenPlants Sustainable Leadership Program, 36
Greenspan, Alan, 76
Greystone Bakery, New York City, 162
gross domestic product
    consumer economics and, 48
    inadequacy as measure of progress, 18, 19, 20, 22, 30, 59
    water, value of, 112, 118
gross national happiness in Bhutan, 12, 25
gross world product, 25
groundwater abstraction and overuse, 112
Growing Power, 157
growth vs. development, 5–6, 10, 11–12. *See also* progress, redefining

Haas, Jörg, 96
Haiti, 192
Hall, Martin, 73
Hansen, James, 77
happiness and wealth levels, 11, 50–52
happy planet index, 23, 24–25
Hardin, Garrett, 140–42, 146
Harris, David, 143
Harrisburg, Pennsylvania, 150
HCFCs, 98–99
health and well-being
    fureai kippu (caring relationship tickets) in Japan, 161–62
    happiness and wealth levels, 11, 50–52
    as progress indicator, 23, 24–25, 28, 29–30, 59
    social status, relationship to, 54–55
    in sustainable communities, 155
    sustainable economy, creating, 11–12
    workplace well-being, 28, 29–30
hedge funds, 187–91
hedonics, 21
Heinrich Böll Foundation, 96
Henry, Jennifer, 164
heritage breeds, encouraging use of, 64, 69, 73
Heritage Foods U.S.A., 69, 73
HFC-23, 98–99

Hill, John, 189
Hoffman, John, 88
home-owner associations, 163
Honda, 40
Hong Kong, 74, 150, 189
HSBC Bank, 46, 58, 184, 188
huerta system in Spain, 141
Hurricane Katrina, 116
Hurwitz, Charles, 143
hybrid motor vehicles, 16, 82, 84
hydropower, 81, 82, 83, 110

Ilocos Norte, Philippines, 141
Immelt, Jeffrey, 43
index of representational equity, 23, 25–26
India
    "bird of gold," 44, 48
    carbon credits and carbon markets activity, 98, 99
    climate change, attitudes toward, 46
    Dalits, 54
    development programs in, 169, 171–74
    energy needs, increasing, 77
    sustainable lifestyles in, 45–47, 52, 53, 54
Indians, American, 142, 144
individualism and sustainable lifestyles, 56
Indonesia, 138–39, 176
Industrial Research Institute, 57
Industrial Revolution, 5, 7, 15–16, 39, 42–43, 80
inequity. *See* poverty and wealth inequality
Inglehart, Ronald, 50
innovation and novelty driving consumerism, 57
Innovest, 195
Institutional Shareholder Services, 186
Integrated Framework for Trade-Related Technical Assistance for Least Developed Countries, 204–05
Inter-American Tropical Tuna Commission, 73
Interface Carpets, 10, 40, 41
Interfaith Center on Corporate Responsibility, 185, 186
Intergovernmental Panel on Climate Change, 6, 47–48, 77
intermittency of alternative electricity sources, 82–83
International Centre for Trade and Sustainable Development, 209
International Conference on Financing for Development (Monterrey, Mexico, 2000), 169

International Conference on Water and the
    Environment (Dublin, 1992), 113
International Emissions Trading Association, 105
International Finance Corporation, 187
international initiatives
    development aid, 178–79
    sustainable economy, creating, 9–10
International Labour Organization, 187
International Organization for Standardization,
    104–05
international trade, governance of. *See* trade and
    trade governance
investment for sustainability, 180–95
    defined, 181
    Equator Principles, 187
    microfinance, 181, 191–93
    obstacles and opportunities, 193–95
    project finance, 181, 186–87
    shareowner activism, 182, 185–86
    socially responsible investing, 181, 182–85
    venture capital, private equity, and hedge
        funds, 181, 187–91
Investors Against Genocide, 189
"invisible hand" economic theory, 6
Iowa, pig farming in, 64
Islam, sustainable lifestyles under, 60
Italy, 161
Ithaca Hours, 161

Jacobsen, Rowan, 66
Japan
    eco-efficiency in, 34
    fureai kippu (caring relationship tickets),
        161–62
    happiness and wealth levels, 11, 50
    low-carbon economics in, 79, 80, 84, 88
    meat and seafood production in, 67, 73
    women's wages in, 15
Jiva Dental, 102–03
Jobra, Bangladesh, 191
Joint Implementation, 92, 93, 96, 98, 100–02
Jones, Dan, 36
JPMorgan, 184

Kasser, Tim, 50
Kecamatan Development Program, Indonesia, 176
Keefe, Joe, 183
Kenmar Global ECO Fund, 189
Keystone Center, 81
Kierman, Matthew, 195
Kiva.org, 192–93

Klemm, Kevin, 132
Klingemann, Hans-Dieter, 50
Kohlberg Kravis Roberts & Co., 190
Kramer, Michael, 184–85
Kyoto Protocol
    carbon credits and carbon markets, 90, 91,
        92, 97, 98–101, 105–06
    post-2012 target, 105–06
    sustainable economy and, 10
    sustainable lifestyles and, 53

Labor productivity, 39–40
labor unions, 144
Lafarge, 34
Lakabe, Spain, 157
Lamy, Pascal, 200
land use
    carbon credits and, 99–100, 101, 103–04
    property tax, commons-based approach to,
        149–50
Lang, Tim, 49
Las Gaviotas, Colombia, 162
laundry lines, outdoor bans on, 163
Law of the Sea Treaty, 149
Layard, Richard, 52
Le Maire, Isaac, 185
Leadership in Energy and Environmental
    Design, 29, 37–38, 163, 164
League for Pastoral Peoples, 73
lean manufacturing, 36, 37
LED lighting systems, 35–36
Lee, Ang, 74
Lehman Brothers, 184, 190
liberalization of trade. *See* trade and trade
    governance; World Trade Organization
lifestyle. *See* sustainable lifestyles
lighting, eco-efficient, 16, 35–36, 58, 80, 88
livestock. *See* meat and seafood industries
living wages, promoting, 30
Loblaws, 70
lobster fisheries in Maine, 146
localization, economic, 23, 26–27, 157–61
Los Angeles, CA, 14, 151–52, 162, 164
Los Angeles Ecovillage, 151–52, 162, 164
low-carbon economy, 75–90
    climate change and, 75–77, 89–90
    electricity grid, 82–84
    energy markets, 86–89
    global energy needs and, 77–78
    integration of new technologies into existing
        energy system, 82–84

investment in, 84–86
storage of power in, 82, 84
strategies leading to, 78–79
tax or regulatory cap on carbon emissions, 87
viability of alternative technologies, 79–82
Lukomnik, Jon, 185
Lydney, UK, 152

Maastricht Treaty, 13
Mack, John, 129
Madagascar, 107
Maine lobster fisheries, 146
Man Group, 189
Marin Agricultural Land Trust, 148
marine ecosystems. *See also* meat and seafood
    industries
    bottom trawling, 68
    certifications of sustainable practices, 27
    commons-based approach to seabed mining,
        149
    economic effects of resource scarcity, 5
    Law of the Sea Treaty, 149
    Maine lobster fisheries, 146
    reserves, establishment of, 69, 72
    "tragedy of the commons" and, 142, 145
Marine Harvest, 66
Marine Stewardship Council, 27, 70
markets
    carbon markets. *See* carbon credits and
        carbon markets
    commons-based vs. market-based approach
        to air pollution, 147–49
    economic concept of market efficiency, 6, 12
    energy markets, 86–89
    water management, market-based tools for,
        117–21
Marrakesh Agreements, 198–99
Marston, Jim, 190
Massachusetts, 71, 145, 146, 161
materialism, 21
McDonough, William, 33
McKibben, Bill, 21
McKinsey Global Institute, 80, 194
meat and seafood industries, 61–74
    antibiotics, use of, 70, 71
    certification and labeling programs, 69–71
    changes in production methods increasing,
        62–63
    ethical practices, consumer and business
        demand for, 69–71
    exotic (nonlocal) breeds, 68

    financial incentives and subsidies, 67–69
    food chain, moving down, 71–74
    heritage breeds, 64, 69, 73
    marine reserves, establishing, 69, 72
    pollution from animal feed production
        runoff, 63
    price of product, 62, 63, 71–72
    rates of consumption, 61, 62, 63
    shellfish farming, ecological advantages of,
        66–67
    sustainable production methods for, 63–67
Merrill Lynch, 184
methane (biogas), 29, 65, 75–77, 84, 99, 142,
    189
Mexico, 13, 134, 135, 144
micro-generators, 84
MicroCapital.org, 193
microcredit and microfinance, 11, 16, 175, 181,
    191–93
Microcredit Summit Campaign, 11
"miles to market" indicator of economic local-
    ization, 23, 26–27
Milken, Michael, 143
Millennium Development Goals, 11, 110, 168,
    169, 174
Millennium Ecosystem Assessment, 7–8, 125
Millennium Village Project, 175
Million Solar Roofs initiative (California), 165
Milwaukee, WI, 157
Mondi South Africa, 34
Monterrey International Conference on
    Financing for Development, 169
Morgan Stanley, 190
Morgan, Steve, 128
motor vehicles, 16, 82, 84, 88
Motorola, 36
Mountain Equipment Co-op, 29
Murphy, A. S., 143
Myanmar, 15

Nairobi Framework, 98
Narayan, Deepa, 179
National Environmental Trust, 65–66
National Forestry Trust Fund, 134
National Renewable Energy Laboratory, 82
National Solidarity Program, Afghanistan, 176
Native Americans, 142, 144
Natural Capitalism, 33, 36
natural resources. *See also* commons
    management, and specific resources
    as capital, 113

natural resources (*continued*)
    economic accounting for, 5, 12–13
    progress redefined as protection and
       restoration of, 23, 26
Natural Resources Defense Council, 190
Neal, Larry, 18
Nelson Information, 182
neoclassical economic theory, problems of, 4–6,
    39–40, 87, 113
Nestlé, 117
Netflix, 10
Netherlands, 72
New South Wales carbon credit market
    (Australia), 94
New Urbanism, 146
New York City, 145, 147, 148, 162
New York State, 145, 157
New Zealand, 10–11, 68–69
NGOs. *See* nongovernmental organizations
Niger, 166–68, 177
Nochol, Toby, 104
nongovernmental organizations
    development programs. *See* development
    investment for sustainability and, 185,
       186–87, 190
    progress, redefining, 24, 27, 30
    sustainable communities and, 158–60, 162,
       164
    trade governance and global power shifts,
       206
North American Free Trade Agreement, 144,
    199, 205
North, Douglass, 87
North Luangwa Wildlife Conservation and
    Community Development Programme,
    Zambia, 160
Norway, 59, 65, 66, 68, 79
Novartis, 30
novelty and innovation driving consumerism, 57
nuclear power, 81, 190

Oakey, David, 41
Offer, Avner, 56–57
offsets
    biodiversity. *See* biodiversity, economic
       value of
    carbon. *See* carbon credits and carbon
       markets
    commons-based vs. market-based approach
       to air pollution, 147–49
    as investment for sustainability, 193

Ogive Index, 23, 26
Ohio, 129
oil and gas, 78, 85, 87, 98, 149
Oldenburg, Ray, 156
Operating and Financial Review (UK), 193
Oregon, 145, 146, 148
Oregon Water Trust, 148
organic foods, 16
Organisation for Economic Co-operation and
    Development, 12, 30, 34, 59

Pacala, Stephen, 78
Pacific Forest Trust, 148
Pacific Lumber, 143–44
Pacific Northwest Laboratory, 82
Pack, Jules, 188
Pago por Servicios Ambientales Hidrológicos,
    Mexico, 134, 135
Pago por Servicios Ambientales, Costa Rica,
    134–35
Parsons, Richard, 143
participation and good trade governance, 197
participatory development techniques, critiques
    of, 170–71. *See also* development
Pauly, Daniel, 67
Pax World Balanced Fund, 182, 183
peace, contribution of trade to, 197, 198
Pembina Institute, 24
Pennsylvania, 150
per capita income as measure of progress, 19–20
Peru, 73
PetroChina, 188–89
petroleum industry, 78, 85, 87, 98, 149
Philadelphia, PA, 156, 157
Philippines, 64, 139, 141, 142, 145
Phinney Ridge Ecovillage, Seattle, WA, 154
photovoltaics, 86
phthalates, 13–14, 36
Pitt-Watson, David, 185
Plum Village, France, 52
pollution, 63, 121, 147–49
Population and Community Development
    Association, 162
population growth, 46, 142, 166, 177
pork industry. *See* meat and seafood industries
PortionPac Chemical Corporation, 36–38
Portland, OR, 145, 146
poultry industry. *See* meat and seafood
    industries
poverty and wealth inequality
    commons management, social equity in, 147

community vitality as indicator of economic
progress, 30
development to aid poor. *See* development
economic systems and, 6, 8–9, 10–11, 15
natural capital, protecting and restoring,
23, 26
per capita income as measure of progress, 20
progress defined by social equity, 23, 25–26
social enterprises, 162
water management, 111–12
women, valuing work of, 15
power industry. *See* energy and energy industry
precautionary principle, 10, 13–14
prices
inclusion of ecological costs in, 10, 12
in meat and seafood industries, 62, 63,
71–72
of water, 112, 117–18
private equity investing for sustainability, 181,
187–91
privatization/corporatization of commons,
142–45
production processes, rethinking, 32–44. *See
also* meat and seafood industries
biomimicry, 40–42
corporate microeconomics indicators, 43–44
eco-efficiency, 33–38
Industrial Revolution processes, 39, 42–43
labor productivity, 39–40
as new wave in industrial innovation, 42–44
product longevity, 28, 29, 38–40
progress, redefining, 18–31
certification of sustainability, 27–28
community vitality, 28, 30
corporate microeconomics indicators, 20,
43–44
eco-efficiency, 28, 29
economic localization, 23, 26–27
encouraging use of new indicators, 30–31
genuine progress indicator and other green
GDPs, 22–24
globalization, 18–19
gross domestic product, 18, 19, 20, 22, 30, 59
growth vs. development concepts, 5–6, 10,
11–12
health and well-being indicators, 23, 24–25,
28, 29–30, 59
new macroeconomic indicators, 22–27
new microeconomic indicators, 27–30
renewable energy/carbon footprint, 23, 25
reporting and disclosure, role of, 31

social equity, 23, 25–26
sustainable development as key to, 21–22
traditional indicators, inadequacy of, 19–21
zero waste, 27–29
project-based carbon trading, 93, 98–101
project finance as investment for sustainability,
181, 186–87
Project Laundry List, 163
property, commons as form of, 140
property tax and land use, 149–50
Pure Salmon Campaign, 66
Putnam, Robert, 154

Qomolangma National Nature Preserve,
Tibet, 177–78

Rainforest Action Network, 186–87
red cockaded woodpeckers, 131
Red Lobster, 70–71
Redefining Progress, 22
Regional Greenhouse Gas Initiative, 95, 97
religion and sustainability, 52, 59–60, 185
Relocalization Network, 159–60
renewable energy. *See* energy industry
renewable energy credit, 103
Ricardo, David, 4, 196
Riverside Land Conservancy, 131
Rodrik, Dani, 168
Rooted in Community, 157
Royal Dutch Shell, 34, 40, 85
Royal Institute for International Affairs (UK),
209
Russia, 78, 100, 206

Salmon farming and fishing, 65–66, 71, 73.
See also meat and seafood industries
San Francisco, CA, 14, 157
Sandia Labs, 42
sanitation, use of water for, 110
São Paulo, Brazil, 59
Satterthwaite, David, 193
Save Darfur Coalition, 189
Savitz, Andrew, 27, 31
scale
commons management, scaling up, 146–50
development programs, scaling up, 174–78
of global economy, 9–11
Scott, Lee, 36
Scott Paper, 39
the Sea Around Us Project, 67
seabed mining, commons-based approach to, 149

seafood industry. *See* meat and seafood industry
Seattle, WA, 154
Securities and Exchange Commission, 185, 186, 194
Seed-Scale, 172–74, 177
Self-Employed Women's Association, 171–72
sexuality and consumerism, 54
shareowner activism, 182, 185–86
shark finning, 74
Shedge, Vidya, 46, 47, 49
shellfish farming, ecological advantages of, 66–67
ShoreBank (Chicago, IL), 182
Shorebank Pacific (Washington State), 161
Sieben Linden Ecovillage, Germany, 154
Simplicity Forum, 52–53
simplicity movement, 52–53
Singapore, 116, 150
site value taxation, 149–50
Six Sigma System, 36
Sky Trust, 147–49
Sloping Lands Conversion Program, China, 134, 135
Slow Food International, 72
smart growth, 163–64
Smith, Adam, 4, 6, 143, 144
Smithfield Foods, 65, 69, 71
social behavior
    commons management resulting from, 138–42, 146–47
    corporations not exhibiting, 143
    sustainable lifestyles and, 55–60
social capital, 152, 154–55, 168
Social Carbon, 105
social construct, property as, 140
social enterprise, 162
social equity and inequity. *See* poverty and wealth inequality
Social Investment Forum, 186
social status, relationship of health and well-being to, 54–55
socially responsible investing, 181, 182–85
Socolow, Robert, 78
solar power, 81–82, 83, 84, 165
South Africa, 134, 185
Spain, 88, 89, 141, 157, 159
Sprint Corporation, 12
Stahel, Walter, 38–40
Stern, Nicholas, and Stern Report, 6–7, 58, 76, 89
STMicroelectronics, 34–35

storage of power, 82, 84
subsidies in meat and seafood industries, 67–69
Sudan, 189
Sudan Divestment Task Force, 189
Summertown, TN, 162
Summit Polymers Inc., 37
sustainability
    of carbon use. *See* carbon credits and carbon markets
    certification programs. *See* certification of sustainability
    in development. *See* development
    investment in. *See* investment for sustainability
    of meat and seafood consumption. *See* meat and seafood industries
    Natural Capitalism framework, 33
    of production process. *See* production processes, rethinking
    progress, as redefinition of, 21–22. *See also* progress, redefining
    religion and, 52, 59–60, 185
    social enterprises, 162
    Stahel's five pillars of, 38–40
    trade governance and WTO, sustainable development paradigm for, 205–09
Sustainable Agriculture Initiative, 117
sustainable communities, 151–65
    co-housing, 154
    definition of community, 152
    economic localization in, 157–61
    energy efficiencies practiced by, 152, 165
    examples of, 153
    financing, 161–62
    health and well-being in, 155
    mobilizing wider society via, 162–65
    physical design of, 152–54
    shared resources, 155–56
    social capital, 152, 154–55
    "third place" concept, 156–57
Sustainable Communities Act (UK), 164
Sustainable Consumption Roundtable, 49, 57–58
sustainable economics, 3–17
    adjusting economic scale, 9–11
    biodiversity and. *See* biodiversity, economic value of
    commons management, revitalizing, 14–15
    conceptual reform leading to, 9–15
    consumer economics, 48–50
    consumer power in, 16

conventional economic theory, problems of,
4–6, 39–40, 87, 113
development vs. growth, 5–6, 10, 11–12
government role in, 12, 17
low-carbon. *See* low-carbon economy
market efficiency, concept of, 6, 12
microcredit and microfinance, 11, 16, 175,
181, 191–93
natural resources, accounting for, 5, 12–13
nature and economic activity, interaction of, 5
as new wave in industrial innovation, 15–17
precautionary principle, 10, 13–14
prices, inclusion of ecological costs in, 10, 12
risks to conventional economies, 3–4, 6–9
of water. *See* water
women, valuing work of, 10, 15
sustainable lifestyles, 45–60
carbon footprint, 47
consumer economics and, 48–50
evolutionary psychology and, 53–55
happiness and wealth levels, 50–52
individualism and, 56
mathematics of, 46–48
means of supporting development of, 57–60
religion and, 52, 59–60
simplicity movement, 52–53
social and political institutions encouraging
or discouraging, 55–60
Sweden, 12, 15, 17, 34, 59, 65
Switzerland, 139, 141–42, 146
System of Environmental and Economic
Accounting, 118

Taxation
carbon taxes, 31, 87, 106
concept of ecotaxes or green taxes, 12
property tax and land use, 149–50
tax shifting, 40
water use, 121
Taylor, Daniel, 172
technological efficiency and carbon footprint,
47–48
TerraPass, 102
Texas Pacific Group, 190
Thailand, 52, 60, 162
The Farm, Summertown, TN, 162
Thich Nhat Hahn, 52
"third place" concept, 156–57
Thompson, E. P., 141
Three Gorges Dam, China, 187
3M, 28–29, 40

TIAA-CREF, 192
Tibet, 177–78
Tomales Bay Institute, 14–15, 96, 147
Törbel, Switzerland, 142
Toronto, Canada, 145
total economic value, 113, 114
Toyota, 16, 34, 36, 37, 42, 84
trade and trade governance, 196–209. *See also*
World Trade Organization
accountability, 197, 202
benefits of trade, 196–98
characteristics of good trade governance, 197
developing nations and, 178, 200–09
ecological concerns regarding, 199, 203–04,
207, 208
environmental concerns and, 199
General Agreement on Tariffs and Trade,
197, 198, 199, 201, 207
global change, accepting, 206–08
goals of, 198–99, 202–03, 208
hostility toward, 198, 199, 207
participation, 197
progress, trade volume as measure of, 19–20
sustainable development paradigm for, 205–09
transparency, 197
"tragedy of the commons," concept of, 14–15,
140–42. *See also* commons management
Transition Towns, 53, 160
Transnational Institute, 103
transparency in good trade governance, 197
triple bottom line, 27, 31, 44
Trust for Public Land, New York City, 148
trust model of commons management, 147–49
tuna farming and fishing, 65, 68, 71, 72, 73,
199. *See also* meat and seafood industries
TXU, 84, 190
Tyson Foods, 70

UBS, 184
Uganda, 103, 107
Ukraine, 100
Unilever, 27, 34, 70
unions, 144
United Kingdom
cattle production in, 65
climate change, attitudes toward, 46
commons management and enclosure,
140, 144
happiness and wealth levels, 50, 51
investment for sustainability in, 193
sustainable communities in, 152–54, 160, 164

United Kingdom (*continued*)
  sustainable lifestyles and consumer
    economics in, 46, 49–51, 53, 54, 57–58
United Nations
  Convention on Biological Diversity, 26
  corporate responsibility summit, 184
  development conferences, 169
  Development Programme, 8, 112, 160–61,
    168
  Environment Programme, 34, 184
  Food and Agriculture Organization, 68
  Principles for Responsible Investment, 195
  structure and global power shifts, 206
  System of Environmental-Economic
    Accounting for Water, 118
United States Climate Action Partnership,
    94–95, 190
United States. *See also* specific cities and states
  Army Corps of Engineers, 127, 128, 129
  biodiversity, valuing. *See* biodiversity,
    economic value of
  carbon credits and carbon market in, 92,
    94–95, 97–98, 102–03
  climate change, attitudes toward, 46
  commons management and enclosure in,
    140, 142, 144, 145, 147
  Department of Energy, 77, 79
  development assistance provided by, 178
  Environmental Protection Agency, 36,
    127–29
  Fish and Wildlife Service, 131
  GPI and GDP in, 22, 24
  happiness and wealth levels, 50, 51
  investment for sustainability in, 183, 194
  low-carbon economics in, 79, 81, 88, 89, 90
  Mayors Climate Protection Agreement, 53
  meat and seafood production in, 64, 65, 67
  per capita income as measure of progress, 20
  precautionary principle at work in, 14
  Superfund legislation, 31
  sustainable communities in. *See* sustainable
    communities
  sustainable lifestyles and consumer
    economics in, 46, 47, 52, 57
  women's wages in, 15
Universities Superannuation Scheme (U.K.), 184
Uruguay Round, WTO, 200, 201
U.S. Green Building Council, 164

Value-enhancing SRI, 182
Varkey, George, 45–47, 49

venture capital
  as investment for sustainability, 181, 187–91
  low-carbon economy, technological
    investment in, 86
  sustainable economy, creating, 16–17
Vermont, 155, 157
Vestas Wind Systems, 85
Victoria, Australia, 132, 135
Victoria, BC, Canada, 163
Viet Nam, 52, 71
voluntary biodiversity offsets, 135–36
voluntary carbon markets, 100–04, 105
Voluntary Carbon Standard Framework, 105
voluntary simplicity, 52
Vulcan Materials Corporation, 131–32

Wal-Mart, 16, 35–36, 71
Wales, Jimmy, 138–39
Walters, Dale, 37–38
Washington Consensus, 168, 204
Washington, D.C., metropolitan area, 150
Washington state, 15, 37, 150, 154, 161
waste minimization and zero waste, 10, 27–29,
    34–35
water, 107–22
  aligning economic and water policies,
    121–22
  as capital, 113
  commons management of, 138–39, 141
  Dublin Principles, 113–15
  environmental flow requirements, 110–11
  equitable access, 111–12
  groundwater abstraction and overuse, 112
  health and safety standards for, 119
  hydropower, 81, 82, 83, 110
  innovations regarding, 115–21
  management of, 111–12, 116–21
  markets, 117
  payment schemes, 119–21
  pollution credits, 121
  pollution from animal feed production
    runoff, 63
  prices, 112, 117–18
  scarcity of, 107–09
  uses of, 109–11
  valuation of, 112–15
Waveriders, 31
wealth inequality. *See* poverty and wealth
    inequality
Weber, Karl, 27, 31
Weida, William, 64

Welch, Jack, 39
well-being. *See* health and well-being
WELL (Willits Economic LocaLization)
      initiative, 160
Western Climate Initiative, 95
wetlands, 116, 127–30
White Dog Cafe, Philadelphia, PA, 156
Whole Foods, 69, 71
Wicks, Judy, 156
Wikipedia, 138–39
WildAid, 74
Wildlands Inc., 128
Willits, CA, 160
Wilson, E. O., 125, 126
wind power, 81–82, 82, 84, 86
Winston, Andrew, 31
Womack, James, 36
women
      development programs involving, 171–72,
            173–74
      economic opportunity for, 10, 15
      investment for sustainability and, 182
      microfinance programs for, 191
      in Niger, 166, 167
      unpaid work, valuing, 15
Woodard, Colin, 146
World Bank
      benefit-cost analysis, use of, 30
      development, involvement in, 168, 169,
            175–76
      on economic indicators, 21
      on economic localization, 26
      on ecosystem degradation, 7
      forestry and land use projects funded by, 99
      global power shifts and structure of, 206
      International Finance Corporation, 187
      on poverty and wealth inequality, 8–9
World Business Council for Sustainable
      Development, 34, 36, 103, 104, 105

World Commission on Dams, 117, 205
World Commission on Environment and
      Development, 21
World Economic Forum, 4, 105
World Energy Council, 3, 79
World Health Organization, 29, 59
World Parks Congress (2003), 69
World Summit on Sustainable Development
      (2002), 69
World Trade Organization, 197–98
      developing nations and, 200–09
      Doha Round, 119, 198, 200, 202, 205, 206
      ecological concerns regarding, 199, 203–04,
            207, 208
      global change, accepting, 206–08
      goals of, 198–99, 202–03, 208
      governance crisis of, 200–02
      hostility toward, 198, 199, 207
      Marrakesh Agreements establishing, 198–99
      overexpansion of, 200
      responding to crisis at, 204–06
      sustainable development paradigm for,
            205–09
      Uruguay Round, 200, 201
      on water, 119
World Values Survey, 50
World Wide Fund for Nature-UK, 96–97, 188
World Wildlife Fund, 70, 105
Wright, Ronald, 26

Yamagata, Tadashi, 73
Yeager, Kurt, 84
Yunus, Muhammad, 191–92

Zambia, 160
zanjera system in Philippines, 141
zero-net-energy buildings, 80
zero waste, 10, 27–29, 34–35
Zero Waste New Zealand, 10

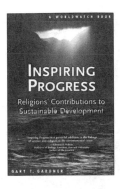

Worldwatch's Newest Research Reports

**No. 173 Beyond Disasters:
Creating Opportunities for Peace**

CONTENTS:

- Natural Disasters on the Rise
- Designing Aid to Benefit All
- Storm Clouds and Silver Linings
- Case Studies: Aceh, Sri Lanka, Kashmir
- Creating Future Opportunities for Peace

**No. 174 Oceans in Peril:
Protecting Marine Biodiversity**

CONTENTS:

- The Diversity of the Oceans
- Dangers of Fishery Depletions
- Changing Climate, Changing Seas
- Polluting the Marine Environment
- Freedom for the Seas

**No. 175 Powering China's Development:
The Role of Renewable Energy**

CONTENTS:

- China's Energy Crossroads
- The Promise of Renewables
- Wind Power
- Solar Energy
- Solar Hot Water and Heating
- Bioenergy
- China's Renewable Energy Future

*Each of above Reports and earlier
Worldwatch research Papers
(see facing page):
$12.95 plus shipping and handling.*

Worldwatch Papers

Note: Starting with No. 173, our research Papers are now called Worldwatch Reports and the format was changed to 8½ x 11 paper size with 4-color to maximize ease of reading.

On Climate Change, Energy, and Materials

169: Mainstreaming Renewable Energy in the 21st Century, 2004
160: Reading the Weathervane: Climate Policy From Rio to Johannesburg, 2002
157: Hydrogen Futures: Toward a Sustainable Energy System, 2001
151: Micropower: The Next Electrical Era, 2000
149: Paper Cuts: Recovering the Paper Landscape, 1999

On Ecological and Human Health

165: Winged Messengers: The Decline of Birds, 2003
153: Why Poison Ourselves: A Precautionary Approach to Synthetic Chemicals, 2000
148: Nature's Cornucopia: Our Stakes in Plant Diversity, 1999
145: Safeguarding the Health of Oceans, 1999
142: Rocking the Boat: Conserving Fisheries and Protecting Jobs, 1998
141: Losing Strands in the Web of Life: Vertebrate Declines and the Conservation of Biological Diversity, 1998
140: Taking a Stand: Cultivating a New Relationship With the World's Forests, 1998

On Economics, Institutions, and Security

168: Venture Capitalism for a Tropical Forest: Cocoa in the Mata Atlântica, 2003
167: Sustainable Development for the Second World: Ukraine and the Nations in Transition, 2003
166: Purchasing Power: Harnessing Institutional Procurement for People and the Planet, 2003
164: Invoking the Spirit: Religion and Spirituality in the Quest for a Sustainable World, 2002
162: The Anatomy of Resource Wars, 2002
159: Traveling Light: New Paths for International Tourism, 2001
158: Unnatural Disasters, 2001

On Food, Water, Population, and Urbanization

172: Catch of the Day: Choosing Seafood for Healthier Oceans, 2006
171: Happier Meals: Rethinking the Global Meat Industry, 2005
170: Liquid Assets: The Critical Need to Safeguard Freshwater Ecosytems, 2005
163: Home Grown: The Case for Local Food in a Global Market, 2002
161: Correcting Gender Myopia: Gender Equity, Women's Welfare, and the Environment, 2002
156: City Limits: Putting the Brakes on Sprawl, 2001
154: Deep Trouble: The Hidden Threat of Groundwater Pollution, 2000
150: Underfed and Overfed: The Global Epidemic of Malnutrition, 2000

Price of each Paper: $12.95 plus shipping & handling.
To see our complete list of Papers, visit www.worldwatch.org/taxonomy/term/40